Liberalism, Imperialism, and the Historical Imagin

This book examines the ways in which imperial agendas informed the writing of history in nineteenth-century Britain and how historical writing transformed imperial agendas. Using the published writings and personal papers of Walter Scott, J. A. Froude, James Mill, Rammohun Roy, T. B. Macaulay, E. A. Freeman, W. E. Gladstone, and J. R. Seeley among others, Theodore Koditschek sheds new light on the role of the historical imagination in the establishment and legitimation of liberal imperialism. He shows how both imperialists and the imperialized were drawn to reflect back on Empire's past as a result of the need to construct a modern, multi-national British imperial identity for a more economically expansive and enlightened present. By tracing the imperial lives and historical works of these pivotal figures, Theodore Koditschek illuminates the ways in which discourse altered practice, and *vice versa*, as well as how the history of Empire was continuously written and re-written.

THEODORE KODITSCHEK is Associate Professor of History at the University of Missouri, Columbia.

Liberalism, Imperialism, and the Historical Imagination

Nineteenth-Century Visions of a Greater Britain

Theodore Koditschek

CAMBRIDGE
UNIVERSITY PRESS

CAMBRIDGE
UNIVERSITY PRESS

University Printing House, Cambridge CB2 8BS, United Kingdom

Published in the United States of America by Cambridge University Press, New York

Cambridge University Press is part of the University of Cambridge.

It furthers the University's mission by disseminating knowledge in the pursuit of education, learning and research at the highest international levels of excellence.

www.cambridge.org
Information on this title: www.cambridge.org/9781107638273

© Theodore Koditschek 2011

First published 2011
First paperback edition 2013

A catalogue record for this publication is available from the British Library

ISBN 978-0-521-76791-0 Hardback
ISBN 978-1-107-63827-3 Paperback

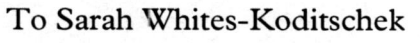

To Sarah Whites-Koditschek

Contents

Acknowledgements   x
List of abbreviations   xii

Introduction   1
   1 Historiography and methodology   4
   2 Plan of the chapters   9

1 Imagining Great Britain: Union, Empire, and the burden
   of history, 1800–1830   17
   1 Maria Edgeworth's romance of Anglo-Irish Union   22
   2 Edgeworth, Owenson, and the burdens of history   26
   3 The border crossings of Walter Scott   31
   4 The Waverley romances of Anglo-Scottish Union   37
   5 The reception of Scott's British Unionist romance   48
   6 Conclusion: from British to imperial Union   52

2 Imagining a British India: history and the reconstruction
   of Empire   56
   1 Orientalism, old and new   59
   2 Scottish orientalism and the romance of British India   66
   3 John Malcolm and the romance of British India   71
   4 Mountstuart Elphinstone and the project of Indian modernization   77
   5 James Mill and the British assault on Indian history 82
   6 Rammohun Roy's Union of Anglo-Indian history   90
   7 Conclusion   97

3 Imagining a Greater Britain: the Macaulays
   and the liberal romance of Empire   99
   1 The first Macaulay and the second British Empire   101
   2 The second Macaulay and the historian's Empire   106
   3 Frustrations in Whig politics   113
   4 Encounter with colonial India   118
   5 Progressive (English) history as liberal (imperial)
      politics by other means   123
   6 The historical romance of the British center   129
   7 Peripheral nightmares: the Indian and Irish centers do not hold   136

    8 The reception of Macaulay's *History*   143
    9 Conclusion   149

4 Re-imagining a Greater Britain: J. A. Froude:
   counter-romance and controversy   151
    1 Froudian whips   152
    2 Henrician flips   160
    3 Victorian anxieties and Elizabethan adventures   164
    4 Protestantism and the British Union   169
    5 Froude's Greater British Victorian vision   174
    6 Froude revises Anglo-Irish history   178
    7 W. E. H. Lecky's Anglo-Irish counter-history   183
    8 Ethnic evolution and Froude's imperial scheme   189
    9 Racial exclusion and Froude's oceanic dream   193
   10 The race against *Froudacity*   200
   11 Conclusion   202

5 Greater Britain and the "lesser breeds":
   liberalism, race, and evolutionary history   206
    1 The advent of evolution and *longue durée* history   210
    2 John Lubbock and the evolution of "savagery"   215
    3 Empire and the classification of racial and evolutionary others 218
    4 The evolution of Aryanism: Henry Maine
       and imperial racial divergence   226
    5 R. C. Dutt: evolution and the liberal middle-class other   233
    6 E. A. Freeman: the rise of the Anglo-Saxon in racial and
       evolutionary history   240
    7 E. A. Freeman: the triumph of Anglo-Saxonism
       in the nineteenth century   245
    8 The failure of hybrid evolutionism: a tale of two Greens   250
    9 William Stubbs and the evolution of the English Constitution 254
   10 The English Constitution and Anglo-Indian history   258

6 Indian liberals and Greater Britain: the search
   for union through history   263
    1 The Calcutta bhadralok and British racial ideology   264
    2 Keshub Chandra Sen and the quest for spiritual history   269
    3 Brahmo Samaj and the evolution of spirituality   271
    4 Bankimchandra Chattopadhyay and the contradictions
       of imperial history   279
    5 Surendranath Banerjea and the Indianization
       of Macaulay's constitutional romance   286
    6 Dadabhai Naoroji: imperial mis-government and
       the history of the "drain"   293
    7 R. C. Dutt and the riches of ancient Hindu civilization   297
    8 R. C. Dutt and the history of modern Indian poverty   304
    9 Conclusion: liberal imperialism's reappearance on the periphery 311

Epilogue: From liberal imperialism to Conservative
Unionism: losing the thread of progress in history   314
  1 Gladstone's progress: from youthful reactionary to aging radical   315
  2 Midlothianizing India: evolutionary objects or historical agents?   318
  3 Midlothianizing Ireland: conquered colony or Celtic "Home Rule"?   325
  4 Chamberlain and Seeley: Unionism, history, and progress
    in the high imperial age   334
  5 The strange death of liberal imperialism   341

Index   346

Acknowledgements

Several individuals and institutions have facilitated my work on this book. In 1999, Terry Brotherstone invited me to participate in the Mackie Conference at the University of Aberdeen, where I presented a paper on T. B. Macaulay and Empire, which gradually evolved into what is now Chapter 3. Both Terry and Anna Clark gave me valuable feedback on this evolving chapter over the next few years. In addition, Anna helped me to narrow the larger project, giving it a clearer focus and a more manageable length. In 2002–3, a grant from the University of Missouri Research Council relieved me of teaching duties, giving me a year to devote largely to research. My friends in the University of Missouri English Department, notably Nancy West, Devoney Looser, and Noah Heringman, gave me much-valued advice and encouragement, especially Noah, who read and carefully commented on versions of Chapters 1, 2, 4, and 5. In the History Department, LeeAnn Whites and Linda Reeder helped me in formulating my initial book proposal, and Kerby Miller assisted me in all matters pertaining to Ireland and the Irish. In addition, he has given me important feedback on several versions of Chapters 1 and 4.

An invitation to the Nicholson Conference on British Studies at the University of Chicago in 2005 gave me a much-needed boost of intellectual stimulation, and connected me up with Andrew Sartori, who commented helpfully on an earlier version of Chapter 2. I am particularly grateful to Catherine Hall for her invitation to participate in the 2008 Neale Conference at University College, London, which was the perfect environment for helping me tie together the various strands of my book. I also greatly benefited from the specific comments and encouragement of Geof Eley, Christopher Bayly, Mrinalini Sinha, and Catherine herself on my paper, which became the core for Chapter 5. At Cambridge University Press, Michael Watson has shepherded the manuscript through the review process with efficiency and tact. I also benefited from the work of three anonymous reviewers, whose comments have led me to tighten the argument and rethink a few points. In preparing the final manuscript, I have been greatly assisted by Karen Laird and especially Angela Rehbein, while

Michael Bednar cleared up a few points about Rajputs and the history of ancient India. Fiona Little's expert copyediting saved me from several infelicities and errors. All remaining mistakes are my own. Finally I wish to thank my wife, Sara Gable, for reading the introduction, and telling me that it worked. She has made the last six years, when this book was written, into a very happy time. I dedicate the book to my daughter in the hope that she will live to see the day when liberalism trumps imperialism, rather than the other way around.

Abbreviations

BKCS	Meredith Borthwick, *Keshub Chunder Sen: A Search for Cultural Synthesis* (Calcutta, 1977)
BME	Marilyn Butler, *Maria Edgeworth: A Literary Biography* (Oxford, 1972)
CLR	Sophia Dobson Collet, *The Life and Letters of Raja Rammohun Roy* [1900], ed. D. K. Biswas and P. K. Ganguli (Calcutta, 1962)
CM	John Clive, *Macaulay: The Shaping of an Historian* (New York, 1974)
DEHI	Romesh Chunder Dutt, *The Economic History of India*, I, *Under Early British Rule* (London, 1903); II, *The Victorian Age* (London, 1906)
DF	Waldo Hilary Dunn, *James Anthony Froude, A Biography*, I, *1818–56* (Oxford, 1961); II, *1857–94* (Oxford, 1963)
DHAI	Romesh Chunder Dutt, *The History of Ancient India*, 2 vols. [1889–90] (New Delhi, 2000)
DNB	*Dictionary of National Biography*, 22 vols. (London and New York, 1908–9)
ECRE	Maria Edgeworth, *Castle Rackrent and Ennui*, ed. Marilyn Butler (New York, 1992)
EIC	East India Company
FEI	J. A. Froude, *The English in Ireland in the Eighteenth Century*, 3 vols. [1872–4] (New York, 1888)
FHE	J. A. Froude, *History of England from the Fall of Wolsey to the Death of Elizabeth*, 12 vols. (London, 1862–70, New York, 1969)
FNC	E. A. Freeman, *The History of the Norman Conquest of England*, 5 vols. (Oxford, 1867–78); I, II, 3rd edn. (Oxford, 1877); III, IV, 2nd edn. (Oxford, 1875, 1876)
GLD	J. N. Gupta, *Life and Work of Romesh Chunder Dutt, CIE* (London, 1911)
ICS	Indian Civil Service

JWS   Edgar Johnson, *Sir Walter Scott: The Great Unknown*, 2 vols. (New York, 1970)

LHI   W. E. H. Lecky, *A History of Ireland in the Eighteenth Century*, 5 vols. (London, 1892)

MEL   T. B. Macaulay, *Essays and Lays of Ancient Rome* (London, 1899)

MHE   T. B. Macaulay, *The History of England from the Accession of James II*, 5 vols. [1848–61] (New York, n.d.)

MJAF   Julia Markus, *James Anthony Froude: The Last Undiscovered Great Victorian* (New York, 2005)

MLS   P. C. Mazoomdar, *The Life and Teachings of Keshub Chunder Sen* (Calcutta, 1931)

MMW   T. B. Macaulay, *Miscellaneous Writings and Speeches* [1860] (London, 1897)

NUBR   Dadabhai Naoroji, *Poverty and Un-British Rule in India* (London, 1901)

ODNB   *Oxford Dictionary of National Biography*, 60 vols. (Oxford, 2004)

PLM   *The Letters of Thomas Babington Macaulay*, ed. Thomas Pinney, 6 vols. (Cambridge, 1974, 1974, 1976, 1977, 1981, 1981)

SCH   William Stubbs, *The Constitutional History of England*, 3 vols. [1874, 1875, 1878], I, II, 3rd edn. (Oxford, 1880); III, 2nd edn. (Oxford, 1878)

SEE   John Seeley, *The Expansion of England* [1883] (London, 1885)

SHML   Walter Scott, *The Heart of Mid-Lothian* [1818] (London, 1994)

SRR   Walter Scott, *Rob Roy* [1817] (London, 1995)

SW   Walter Scott, *Waverley* [1814] (London, 1972)

TBM   Thomas Babington Macaulay

TLL   George O. Trevelyan, *The Life and Letters of Lord Macaulay*, 2 vols. [1876] (Oxford, n.d.)

Dates of original publication are shown in square brackets.

Note to readers: Due to space limitations, the footnotes provide only the most directly relevant supporting materials, and the most essential historiographical discussions. Further elaboration on some points can be found online at https://mospace.umsystem.edu/xmlui/handle/10355/7818. Interested readers will see that these files are organized to correspond to the chapters and footnotes in the book. However, Cambridge University Press has not reviewed this material, and disclaims all responsibility for its content, which is entirely the author's.

Introduction

Four months after Adam Smith published his *Wealth of Nations*, the American Declaration of Independence put it to the test. The British Empire, which had risen with the mercantilist system of privilege and protectionism, now seemed to have joined that system in a spiral of mutual collapse: free trade, Smith had argued, would bring economic growth, social advancement, and political autonomy for colonies.[1] So it transpired, over the next few generations, that Britain found a far better trading partner in the United States than she had ever possessed with her thirteen colonies.[2] Like individuals, nations seemed to be learning that their enlightened self-interest was to respect the rights of others. On both levels, this required equality before the law, which, in turn, seemed to precipitate a further installment of benefits and liberties. If "liberalism" is thus defined as a loose constellation, encompassing free trade, free labor, free association, free press, and formal equality, then it is safe to say that by the middle of the nineteenth century, Britain had gone quite far toward becoming a liberal society.[3] And yet these liberties were not always what they seemed. Free trade might mean freedom to starve. Free labor could be the freedom to be exploited. Equality appeared to be for propertied white men alone. Freedom of press and association were too often honored in the breach. And yet of all these contradictions, the most glaringly obvious was that the British Empire

---

[1] Adam Smith, *An Inquiry into the Nature and Causes of the Wealth of Nations* [1776] (New York, 1937), 1–143, 397–465, 523–626. Smith points out that "parting good friends" would bring benefits both to Britain and to her American colonies. He also entertains a more radical scenario in which the Empire could be preserved if it were reorganized in a more egalitarian and decentralized way (583–93). See also Oliver M. Dickerson, *The Navigation Acts and the American Revolution* (New York, 1963).

[2] Between 1774 and 1800 British exports to the (incipient) United States tripled. Calculated from Ralph Davis, *The Industrial Revolution and British Overseas Trade* (Leicester, 1976), 88–109; Patrick Colquhoun, *A Treatise on the Wealth, Power and Resources of the British Empire* [1815] (New York, 1965), 29–47; B. R. Mitchell, *Abstract of British Historical Statistics* (Cambridge, 1962), 310–11.

[3] Harold Perkin, *The Origins of Modern English Society* (London, 1969).

had not disappeared. On the contrary, during this period a "second" British Empire had arisen that was more extensive, farther-flung, and in many ways more coercive than the one that it replaced. Indeed, by 1860, the new Empire of free trade encompassed at least 175 million people, on 2.7 million square miles, spread over every continent on the globe.[4]

This Empire may not have been created in a fit of absence of mind, but it did suffer from an absence of obvious legitimation. The disparity between the ideal of freedom and a reality of coercive imperial expansion posed serious moral, cultural, and political problems for Britons throughout the nineteenth century. Under the old mercantilist Empire such problems could scarcely have arisen, since coercion had been assumed as the norm. Freedom (like every other good) had been held as a privileged possession under this order, to be monopolized on the basis of birth, law, or power. It was only with the collapse of this system of monopoly and privilege that the problem of explaining coercion and inequality became acute.[5] How could political inequality be justified? How was imperial expansion to be rationalized in liberal terms? Why should the Empire be extended to some places, but not to others? How far should the benefits of freedom that were supposed to operate in the metropolis be extended to the periphery, and to which peripheral groups? How far, and how fast, should free labor replace slavery in the surviving plantation colonies? When was coercion justified, and when should it be removed?[6]

While there were no hard and fast answers to any of these questions, this book argues that they could be managed, and sometimes provisionally

---

[4] The best study of the consolidation of the second British Empire is Christopher Bayly, *Imperial Meridian: The British Empire and the World, 1780–1830* (London, 1989). See also Ronald Hyam, *Britain's Imperial Century* (London, 1976); P. J. Marshall, *The Making and Unmaking of Empires* (Oxford, 2005); P. J. Cain and A. G. Hopkins, *British Imperialism: Innovation and Expansion: 1688–1914* (London, 1993); and the relevant chapters in Andrew Porter (ed.), *The Oxford History of the British Empire*, III, *The Nineteenth Century* (Oxford, 1999). Figures calculated from Henry Morris, *The History of Colonization*, II (New York, 1908), 85, and Mitchell, *Abstract of British Historical Statistics*, 6–7.

[5] For example, Christopher Brown's recent *Moral Capital* (Chapel Hill, 2006) shows that the American Revolution weakened metropolitan political support for slavery by diminishing the power of this nastiest part of the old coercive mercantilist Empire. The result was a new political climate in which liberal abolitionism could thrive.

[6] The last few years have occasioned a vigorous debate on the question of just how far consciousness of the Empire pervaded domestic culture within Britain. Bernard Porter, *The Absent-Minded Imperialists* (Oxford, 2004), argues that the Empire's domestic impact has been greatly exaggerated by recent practitioners of the "new imperial (cultural) history." C. Hall and S. Rose (eds.), *At Home with the Empire: Metropolitan Culture and the Imperial World* (Cambridge, 2006), make the contrary case, with Richard Price, "One Big Thing: Britain, its Empire, and their Imperial Culture," *Journal of British Studies*, 45 (2006), 602–27, offering a *via media*. My own view is that Porter defines "Empire" too narrowly, but that his questions need to be asked, since the only way to understand something is to recognize its limits. For example, my focus on "liberal imperialism" in this book was motivated by a desire to understand how liberalism

resolved, by discourses about history. The central discourse here was derived from the enlightenment idea of progress. By the end of the eighteenth century this had been refined in the form of a four-stage model of social, economic, cultural, and political development (also first formulated by Adam Smith) in which societies were ranged from "savage" (those based on hunting and gathering) to "barbarian" (generally applied to pastoralists and part-time horticulturalists) and "agricultural" (traditional feudal or absolutist states), and to commercial (modernizing capitalist societies). Under conditions of uneven development, it was widely believed that more advanced societies would dominate those at lower stages of development, and that a liberal, commercial capitalist society like Britain had a right (perhaps even a duty) to exercise formal or informal control over various far-flung primitives, either for their own benefit, to spread market freedom, or to save them from being exploited by some other powerful, autocratic state.[7]

Stated so emphatically, however, this hardly made a plausible case. Radical Liberals like Richard Cobden, for example, argued that socioeconomic advancement provided no warrant for empire building, and he attributed Britain's massive Empire to less honorable motives.[8] So far from betokening the triumph of liberal capitalism, it reflected the enduring power of a landed aristocracy that still dominated the British political system, and which played the game of geo-politics in an essentially mercantilist way. While there was much to be said for this explanation, the aristocracy alone could not have sustained the new Empire. Much of it had been acquired during or after the Great War against Napoleon and the French Revolution (1791–1815), which was played out not just in Europe, but on a global stage. Thus forged in the crucible of war, amid a great wave of patriotism that permeated parts of every social

played out in an imperial context, and how imperialism was transformed by those who wanted to turn it into a liberal project. Purist liberals and ardent imperialists might insist that these were two quite separate things. I think that history proves them wrong.

[7] J. B. Bury, *The Idea of Progress* (New York, 1932); Frank Manuel, *The Prophets of Paris* (Cambridge, Mass., 1962); Karen O'Brien, *Narratives of Enlightenment* (Cambridge, 1997); Adam Smith, *Lectures on Jurisprudence* (Oxford, 1978); Adam Ferguson, *An Essay on the History of Civil Society* [1768] (Cambridge, 1995); John Millar, *The Origin of the Distinction of Ranks* [1771] (Bristol, 1990); Ronald Meek, *Social Science and the Ignoble Savage* (Cambridge, 1976).

[8] John Morley, *The Life of Richard Cobden* (London, 1881); Bernard Semmel, *The Liberal Ideal and the Demons of Empire: Theories of Imperialism from Adam Smith to Lenin* (Baltimore, 1993), 1–56; G. R. Searle, *Entrepreneurial Politics in Mid-Victorian Britain* (Oxford, 1993), 51–201; A. J. P. Taylor, *The Troublemakers: Dissent over Foreign Policy, 1792–1939* (London, 1957), 11–94. Throughout this book I observe a distinction between "Liberals" (upper case), who were in some sense members of the Liberal Party, and "liberals" (lower case), who conformed to the broad definition that I offer in the first paragraph of this introduction.

class, the new Empire became a national project, although there were always dissenters, and support wavered over time and was often lacking in depth.[9] Though aristocrats benefited disproportionately as soldiers and colonial administrators, many motives drew in sectors of the middle class: the desire to spread Christianity, to redeem the suffering slaves, to save aborigines (or to settle their lands), to protect existing possessions, and to cure the evils that the first Empire had left behind all inspired the second Empire in different ways. In each case the call to action was built on a particular reading of history that drew out the progress narrative in a particular way.[10] This book then is a history of the progress narrative, as it was deployed over the course of the nineteenth century to explain and justify Britain's imperial activity within a liberal framework.

1   Historiography and methodology

Until quite recently the phenomenon of liberal imperialism has been relatively neglected. With a few exceptions, liberalism was generally assumed to be a British phenomenon, while imperialism was something that happened on the periphery.[11] However, in the last decade, scholars have begun to bring the two together, following the salutary injunction that metropole and colony must be understood in a common frame. Here, the breakthrough book has been Uday Singh Mehta's *Liberalism and Empire*, published in 1999.[12] As a political theorist, Mehta writes at a high level

[9] Bayly, *Imperial Meridian*; Linda Colley, *Britons: Forging the Nation, 1707–1837* (New Haven, 1992).

[10] David Brion Davis, *The Problem of Slavery in the Age of Revolution, 1770–1823* (Ithaca, New York, 1975); Robin Blackburn, *The Overthrow of Colonial Slavery, 1776–1848* (London, 1988), 1–160; Susan Thorne, *Congregational Missions and the Making of an Imperial Culture in Nineteenth-Century England* (Stanford, 1999); Alan Lester, *Imperial Networks: Creating Identities in Nineteenth Century South Africa and Britain* (London, 2001); Brown, *Moral Capital*. On aristocracy and empire see David Cannadine, *Ornamentalism: How the British Saw their Empire* (Oxford, 2001). For a recent analysis of the way in which imperial "progress" played out spatially in the metropolitan imagination see John Marriott, *The Other Empire: Metropolis, India and Progress in the Colonial Imagination* (Manchester, 2003).

[11] The major exception was John Gallagher and Ronald Robinson's path-breaking "Imperialism of Free Trade" [1953], which elicited a few rebuttals and elaborations; all these essays reprinted in A. G. L. Shaw (ed.), *Great Britain and the Colonies* (London, 1970). See also the authors' *Africa and the Victorians: The Climax of Imperialism* (Garden City, 1961). Even today, the full implications of the Robinson–Gallagher thesis have not been worked out. Other early classics are W. K. Hancock, *Empire in the Changing World* (New York, 1943); Eric Stokes, *The English Utilitarians and India* (Cambridge, 1959); and Thomas Metcalfe, *Ideologies of the Raj* (Cambridge, 1994).

[12] Uday Singh Mehta, *Liberalism and Empire* (Chicago, 1999). For seminal formulations of the injunction that metropole and colony need to be treated in a unified frame see Frederick Cooper and Ann Laura Stoler (eds.), *Tensions of Empire: Colonial Cultures in a Bourgeois World*

of abstraction, focusing on a handful of canonic liberal thinkers (most notably James Mill and John Stuart Mill and John Locke) who engaged with the phenomenon of Empire in a significant way. His core argument is that when liberalism encounters the "strangeness" of Empire, all of its fundamental propositions are reversed. The presumptive universalism of abstract liberal principles is compromised when these principles encounter the actuality of the colonial other. Because this other appears strange to the "universal" western philosopher, (s)he is deemed deficient in normative rationality, and thus unworthy of the political rights and civic inclusions which liberalism in theory offers up. By looking at liberalism from a peripheral perspective, Mehta has identified fresh paradoxes in a series of classic texts that were previously regarded as well understood. In the nineteenth century, he reminds us, whole classes of the community were excluded from political participation even in the imperial center: women and workers, as well as children, criminals, and "idiots." On the periphery, entire societies were blanketed and rejected in a comparable manner, because they were built upon customs, institutions, and cultures that western liberals deemed to be irrational, effeminate, infantile, criminal, or idiotic.

Mehta's powerful critique of the exclusionary potential in liberal theory is a major breakthrough, and it stands as a necessary corrective to those who assume the opposite – that some emancipatory potential is inherent in liberalism from the start. Yet his abstract, categorical reversal is also limiting in ways that are not acknowledged in his book. Indeed his argument does not hold equally well for other canonic liberals, most notably Jeremy Bentham and Adam Smith himself, as Jennifer Pitts has shown.[13] More fundamentally, Mehta's account of liberal imperialism neglects the question of how the ideas of great thinkers played out on the ground.

In 2002, this problem was taken up by Catherine Hall's *Civilising Subjects: Colony and Metropole in the English Imagination, 1830–1867*. This magisterial social history provides an important counterweight to Mehta, moving discussion from the rarefied heights of theory to the more messy, contested terrain of liberalism as it played out on two imperial grounds. Although Hall never explicitly uses the term, hers is, in fact, the first real study of liberal imperialism as a hegemonic project. She builds her analysis around the insight that the Baptist missionaries who traveled to the Caribbean during the last decade of slavery were among

---

(Berkeley, 1997), 1–40; and Antoinette Burton, "Who Needs the Nation? Interrogating 'British' History," in Catherine Hall (ed.), *Cultures of Empire: A Reader* (New York, 2000), 137–53.

[13] *A Turn to Empire: The Rise of Imperial Liberalism in Britain and France* (Princeton, 2005), 23–58, 103–22. For a further critique of Mehta see Andrew Sartori, "The British Empire and its Liberal Mission," *Journal of Modern History*, 78/3 (2006), 623–42.

the most important shock-troops of liberal imperialism, translating the
ideas of the great secular and religious liberal thinkers into a pragmatic
reforming program for Britain's colonial order. Arriving at a critical
moment, when slavery was being de-legitimized, they successfully distinguished themselves from the planters in the eyes of the black population,
many of whose members they converted not just to Christianity, but also
to a new emancipatory conception of the Empire.[14]

As Hall shows, this liberal imperial alliance remained strong through
the 1830s and early 1840s. From the late 1840s, however, it began to
unravel as the Jamaican freedmen developed their own ideas about
the meaning of "British" freedom, and the various metropolitan actors
became gradually disillusioned with the results of liberal colonial reform.
Casting a wide net through both Birmingham and Jamaica, Hall shows
just how variegated were the patterns of differing responses to this crisis of
liberal imperialism. Many of the freedmen were exercised about betrayed
promises, whereas many white Britons in both locations were alarmed
by this spirit of black independence, disturbed by black violations of
separate-spheres domesticity, or panicked at rumors of impending revolt.
Still others were troubled by the collapse of the plantation economy, or
by challenges to Britain's export industries. Some were convinced by new
exclusionary theories of race, while yet others clung proudly to the old
liberal imperial ideals.[15]

One way to find patterns in this diversity might be seek a level midway
between the sweeping macro-theory of Mehta and the meticulous micro-
history of Hall. It is on this middle ground that I have tried to situate my
"narratives of progress," which are all variants of Mehta's grand liberal
theory, but which have assumed the form of concrete discourses, articulated
by actual people, with specific motives, operating in circumscribed historical contexts. To this end, I have focused each of my chapters on the work of
a small group of related individuals, each of whom contributed *both* to
historical writing *and* to the project of reconstructing the nineteenth-century
British Empire along liberal lines. Using published writings, personal

---

[14] Catherine Hall, *Civilising Subjects: Colony and Metropole in the English Imagination,
1830–1867* (Chicago, 2002), 1–139.

[15] Hall, *Civilising Subjects*, 140–441. Some of the most innovative recent scholarship emphasizes decentralized imperial networks and inter-colonial linkages; see Durba Ghosh and
Dane Kennedy (eds.), *Decentering Empire: Britain, India and the Transcolonial World* (New
Delhi, 2005). Nevertheless, Hall's work demonstrates the enduring significance of the
metropole–periphery polarity in what was, almost by definition, a power asymmetry
between the two. Perhaps it is worth noting that the most idealistic advocates of what I
call "liberal imperialism," from Grattan to Gokhale, wanted to de-center the Empire into
a federation of self-governing states. So long as the Empire lasted, this effort failed. When
it succeeded, the Empire was transformed into something else.

correspondence, and other biographical materials, I triangulate between the lives these men and women led, the history they were writing, and the new imperial initiatives that they either rationalized or directly made. Texts are closely interrogated, but always in the context of their authors' agendas and imperial roles. The variants of the progress narrative that my subjects applied in colonial settings are thus aligned with the sagas they believed about themselves. The family lives that they personally experienced are juxtaposed against the family metaphors employed in their works. These individuals were neither the greatest minds, nor the grandest proconsuls of their era, but they either commanded large readerships, participated in policy-making, or attempted some combination of the two.[16]

It is no accident that most of the writers and actors treated in this volume began their lives as British outsiders. From their personal anxieties about (and aspirations toward) British inclusion, they constructed their larger visions of what trans-imperial liberalism should mean. For this reason, the narratives of progress they constructed could always be divided into two distinct parts: (1) the progress already achieved, which had opened the way for *their* inclusion; and (2) the progress not yet achieved, but impending in the future, that would enable excluded others to join the advance. In the first half of the nineteenth century, when liberal imperialism was expanding, Progress 1 was often quite limited – and tended to be circumscribed by metaphors of "union," as we shall soon see. The great optimism about the prospects for Progress 2 rested on confidence (a) that economic growth would be rapid and relatively seamless, (b) that cultural differences could be easily transcended, and (c) that the remnants of traditional society could be disposed of without the perils of a rotting corpse. When these three conditions appeared fulfilled, it was relatively easy to turn the progress narrative into a romance. But romances are easily punctured simply by looking at their components from a more skeptical or jaundiced point of view.

Here, I think, lies the great value of my focus on history as a medium for liberal imperial ideals. For history can be told in multiple ways. It thus provided a pliable vehicle for different people to interpret a common set of facts in differing terms. This is particularly important in approaching the second half of the nineteenth century, when it became clear that

---

[16] A biographical approach to imperial history, long out of fashion, is now re-emerging in post-modern dress, as a way of reintroducing human experience, agency, and contingency into processes that are too easily depicted in impersonal, structural terms. In addition to Hall's *Civilising Subjects*, see Antoinette Burton, *At the Heart of Empire: India and the Colonial Encounter in Late Victorian Britain* (Berkeley, 1998); and David Lambert and Alan Lester (eds.), *Colonial Lives across the British Empire: Imperial Careering in the Long Nineteenth Century* (Cambridge, 2006).

(a) economic growth was no longer automatic, (b) large cultural differences were not easily bridged between distant peoples of differing languages, religions, and races, and (c) metropolitan elites were coming to believe that traditional society should be kept on life-support on the colonial periphery. As we shall see, different people responded to this situation in different ways, and wrote different histories of progress that would either keep it *to* themselves, demand it *for* themselves, or establish more stringent conditions on which it might be slowly granted to colonial others who differed from the metropolitan self.

A further challenge lies in the inherently dynamic character of this British Empire, especially for those who conceived it in "progressive" terms. National and imperial identities were intertwined with one another in ways that we are only now just beginning to understand.[17] The political Union(s) that formed (and transformed) the British state were closely connected to corresponding bouts of imperial expansion through which domestic Union was secured and sustained. Conversely, developments on multiple proliferating peripheries had implications for identities of Britishness in the center. Although the phrase "Greater Britain" was coined only in the Victorian era, it had been evident from the start that Britain had no choice but to become greater, if she wished to remain great.[18] The original Union of England and Wales with Scotland (1707) already exhibited some imperial overtones, inasmuch as it entailed the integration of Scottish Highlanders, who were deemed to be barbarians in need of improvement by metropolitan elites. These overtones were further amplified by the Union with Ireland (1800), when the dictates of "progress" entailed integrating an entire nation – different in religion,

---

[17] Colley, *Britons* is the classic work, especially pp. 101–48, which link the reconstruction of Britishness with late eighteenth-century crises of Empire. Yet Colley conspicuously leaves Ireland out of her story, thereby neglecting the ways in which it would complicate her central dichotomy between the Protestant British self and a Catholic French other. For more explicit treatments of the relationship between Britishness and imperial expansion see Tom Nairn, *The Break-Up of Britain* (London, 1977); Keith Robbins, *Great Britain: Identities, Institutions and the Idea of Britishness* (London, 1998), especially 206–33; Kathleen Wilson, *The Island Race: Englishness, Empire and Gender in the Eighteenth Century* (London, 2003); T. M. Devine, *Scotland's Empire, 1600–1815* (London, 2004); and Allan Macinnes, *Union and Empire: The Making of the United Kingdom in 1707* (Cambridge, 2007), to mention only a few of the most important recent works.

[18] As we shall see (Chapter 5), the phrase was coined, in 1868, by Charles Dilke. Yet as early as 1828, William Huskisson, the Colonial Secretary, observed that "England cannot afford to be little. She must be what she is, or nothing" (quoted in John S. Galbraith, "Myths of the 'Little England' Era," in Shaw (ed.), *Great Britain and the Colonies*, 29; see also page 30 for similar quotes from Cobden). To avoid the danger of anachronism, I introduce the phrase in connection with Rammohun Roy and the Macaulays, who clearly exhibited that enlarged, ultimately universalistic, sense of global Britishness which Dilke articulated a few decades later in comparable terms.

culture, language, and socio-economic structure – that now had to be made one with the metropolitan polity. By incorporating Ireland directly into the British state, under a more or less common set of institutions and laws, the government of William Pitt sought to reincarnate one critical part of the old Empire in a presumptively liberal structure. This Act of Union therefore constitutes the starting point for my book.

2   Plan of the chapters

The analysis begins, in Chapter 1, "Imagining Great Britain," by focusing on the novels of Maria Edgeworth. Written just before and after the Act of Union, these influential works applied the progress narrative to the case of Ireland in elemental form: through the British connection, Irish landlords, like Edgeworth's father, would bring enlightenment to a backward, benighted peasantry, promoting economic prosperity through education, thus training the people to become citizens of a modern capitalist polity. These didactic, optimistic tales of improvement were haunted, however, by an unacknowledged history of colonial violence, which belied the happy ending that Edgeworth (usually) supplied. By contrast, Sydney Owenson (Lady Morgan) wrote a very different set of novels, on the premise that the consummation of the Anglo-Irish Union (both literal and figurative) required a painful reckoning with the oppressions and expropriations of Irish history. As former agents of foreign domination, who were now re-making themselves into authentic national leaders, Anglo-Irish landlords had to take responsibility for the crimes of their ancestors, and embrace (symbolically betroth) the Gaelic traditions of the Irish masses, before they could hope to lead Ireland into the British modernizing age.

Neither Edgeworth's nor Owenson's novels provided satisfactory romances of Union, since neither could plausibly resolve the contradictions of dominance through an effective reckoning with history. Such a resolution was provided a decade later, however, by the historical novels of Walter Scott. In Scott's tales, the contradictions of Anglo-Scotland were successfully projected back to a bygone age of conflict, division, and imperial arrogance, which the forces of progress had now successfully transcended. Because these historical struggles could be depicted as having been overcome, they could be recounted in celebratory romances of reconciliation and reunion, in which victors and vanquished alike could turn the lost cause into an object of pleasing nostalgia, which would enable both to move on together to the more prosaic (but inescapable) future of modernity.

Although imperial themes are not directly at the center of the Waverley novels, Scott's romance foreshadowed and influenced future discourse on the subject in four significant ways. (1) The novels themselves were enormously popular, and remained so throughout the nineteenth century, not only in Britain but also elsewhere, including all the British colonies. Although Scott was not a conventional historian, there is a good deal of evidence to indicate that he had a greater impact on the historical imagination of the public than any historian during his lifetime. Indeed, among Scott's most attentive fans were historians of the next generation (for example, Macaulay) who drew on the novelist in emplotting their multi-volume national and constitutional narratives. (2) Although Scott's romances are "liberal" in the sense that they acknowledge the advantages of market capitalism, Scott himself was a political Tory who sought to redeem tradition by de-fanging its threatening aspects, thus rendering it compatible with modernity. From this point onward even conservatives would discover that they had to accept key elements of the progress narrative if they wished to be taken seriously. (3) By exploring the history of Union through the medium of fiction, Scott (like Edgeworth and Owenson before him) was able to capture the resonances of "union" in all its marital, familial, class, and gender manifestations. In this manner Scott (and those who followed him) could play with the idea of "union," imagining possible variants that could not (yet) solidify into realistic political form. Normative notions of British masculinity and femininity could be set up as standards by which colonial others would be judged. Their union(s) with the metropole might be depicted as happy, dysfunctional, barren, or deranged. Colonial children could be figured as obedient, obstreperous, incorrigible, dying out, or even disowned. Through such metaphors, colonial strangeness could be domesticated, cultural difference could be naturalized, and history could be revised in a variety of ways.[19] (4) Scott showed how two different and asymmetric cultures could be melded into a single imagined community. Here, however, we will see the atypicality of the Anglo-Scottish case. England and Scotland were physically contiguous, being connected by a common Protestantism, strong linguistic and ethnic ties, and a long record of political collaboration. In

---

[19] Some of the most interesting work here is being done by literary scholars and feminist historians, e.g. Mary Jean Corbett, *Allegories of Union* (Cambridge, 2000), Philippa Levine (ed.), *Gender and Empire* (Oxford, 2004), and other references in Chapter 1. Throughout this book, I have observed the (somewhat awkward) convention of reserving upper-case "Union" to refer to specific political amalgamations that produced actual or projected multi-national states, e.g. the Anglo-Scottish Union of 1707, the British-Irish Union of 1800, or the abortive proposals for imperial federation in the later nineteenth century. Lower-case "union" has been employed for other, more metaphorical uses of the term.

the imagined imperial unions of the nineteenth century, almost none of these conditions would apply.[20]

Chapter 2, "Imagining a British India," examines what was surely the gravest ideological challenge for early nineteenth-century imperialists. How could they devise a progress narrative to justify dictatorial rule over peoples half a world away, with completely different languages, religions, cultures, and ethnicities? That the governing body, the East India Company, was a mercantilist holdover and that India itself was essentially an empire in its own right seemed to make the task even harder. It was to address these formidable challenges that a powerful historical genre, "orientalism," had been devised toward the end of the eighteenth century, when it was famously forged by the great classicist Sir William Jones. I examine the vicissitudes of orientalism during the first quarter of the nineteenth century, when it was taken up by a new generation of Scottish historian-imperialists who were involved both in spreading British rule to south, central, and northern India and in adapting this hitherto elitist neo-classical genre of scholarship to address the needs of a modernizing age. For James Tod and John Malcolm, this meant a Scott-inspired quest to co-opt Rajput nobles and Maratha warlords to the aims of British policy. To this end, they produced *Waverley*-like romantic histories which were more satisfactory (Tod) or less so (Malcolm), and which tried to introduce these characters with strange names to the British public.

Mountstuart Elphinstone, who began as a romantic, ended up, while Governor of Bombay, recognizing the value of Benthamite utilitarianism as a guide to policy in modernizing Indian society. Yet Elphinstone's hopes that orientalism and utilitarianism might be juxtaposed and reconciled were undermined by the categorical triumph of a militantly anglocentric version of the latter, which was purveyed in James Mill's extremely influential *History of British India* – an anti-orientalist counter-romance that sounded the death knell for imagining the Anglo-Indian union in trans-cultural terms. By refiguring India from a storied civilization to a cesspool of barbarism, Mill devised a new progress narrative that opened the door to the racism of the late Victorian Raj. And yet his book was intended as a radical document, offering the hope that if only Indians would give up their retrograde culture (under British utilitarian tutelage) they too would become modern, independent, successful players in the global capitalist game. The chapter concludes with a look at Rammohun Roy, the Indian Brahman who was also a utilitarian reformer, who ransacked the history of all three major world religions to find a synthesis in which cultural romance and rational improvement could be combined.

---

[20] Benedict Anderson, *Imagined Communities* (London, 1983).

Chapter 3, "Imagining a Greater Britain," examines the high tide of liberal imperialism, when the progress narrative was reconnected with a distinctively anglocentric romance that nevertheless proclaimed its universality. We begin, at the turn of the nineteenth century, with Zachary Macaulay, an anti-slavery activist who posited Christian conversion as a universal panacea, bringing freedom and progress to benighted primitives and victims of the old imperial cruelty everywhere around the globe. Needless to say, this vision of universal progress through conversion proved to be a non-starter in places like Ireland and India, which had deeply entrenched religions of their own. It did, however, pave the way for a secularization and historicization of the same hegemonic vision by T. B. Macaulay, the Evangelical's son.

The bulk of the chapter explores the links between the younger Macaulay's evolving vision of history and his career of upward mobility, first as a Whig wordsmith and politician and then as an Indian proconsul, legal codifier, and architect of an anglocentric system of higher education. I make the case that it was during Macaulay's time in India that he made the decision to write a great epic of late seventeenth-century British history, as a means of pursuing liberal imperial politics by other means. In Macaulay's rendering, the history of Britain was no mere national story, but a transcendent episode, when the prospects for universal progress were irreversibly realized. To his hundreds of thousands of readers everywhere around the globe he offered this story as an alternative to multi-ethnic union – an opportunity for *parvenus* everywhere to prove their liberal bona fides by buying into the anglocentric progress narrative through which he had made himself.

A close reading of Macaulay's *History* and associated essays reveal their multiple levels: domestic, imperial, and progressive. I show how his selective adaptation of the Waverley formula enabled him to turn an insular political narrative into an expansive secular version of the manly, centrist Greater British liberalism that his father had cast in a narrower religious frame. At the same time, I show how this rhetorical achievement came at a considerable intellectual price – leaving the epic a mere fragment of what its author originally intended, while also transforming it into a sometimes heavy-handed didactic primer. Instructing Indians, Irishmen, and English workers (in the manner of his father and James Mill), Macaulay made it clear that if they wanted political rights, they had to abandon their retrograde dysfunctional cultures and buy into his English middle-class romance. Indeed, it was in his handling of Irish and Indian history that Macaulay's analysis fell apart. Suddenly his tone became defensive, as he wrestled with the contradiction that the history which middle-class Englishmen experienced as progress and freedom, others experienced as coercion, exploitation, and constraint. The chapter concludes by examining Macaulay's reception, especially in the colonies, where readers tried to separate their attraction to the romance, with its paeans to freedom, from their resistance to its arrogance and ethnocentric contempt.

Chapter 4, "Re-imagining a Greater Britain," examines how the liberal imperial romance was contested during the later Victorian period, by focusing on the life, writings, and controversies of J. A. Froude, the leading historian of the post-Macaulay generation. Between 1856 and 1870, Froude produced a twelve-volume *History of England* that focused on the Tudor period and countered Macaulay's approach at every turn. Overtly pro-Protestant and intensely nationalistic, Froude was less concerned with the liberty of the subject than with the security of the state. In his account the progress narrative assumes an anglocentric form that is explicitly exclusionary, being achieved through the conquest of feckless inferior peoples whose historical role is to serve and submit. Perceiving Albion's Protestant isle as surrounded by dangerous European rivals and by disorderly Catholic and colored others, Froude refigured British manliness into a harder authoritarian frame. His personal attraction to this hard-edged masculinity was conditioned by his experience of a harsh, motherless childhood. However, his counter-romance also struck a chord with the metropolitan reading public that had its own reasons for imperial and geo-political panic in the Crimean War, the Indian and Jamaica Revolts, and other colonial challenges. At the same time, Froude's devaluation of civil liberties, and praise of providential autocrats, precipitated a series of incisive liberal counterattacks. In particular, Froude's publication of an inflammatory anti-Catholic *History of Ireland* led to several nationalist rebuttals, including W. E. H. Lecky's powerful neo-liberal Anglo-Irish *History*.

In his later years, Froude became increasingly preoccupied with the Empire and its role in protecting Britain from foreign competition. In the writings that followed his extensive travels the progress narrative is effectively stopped. Here Froude transposed onto a global Victorian landscape the categories that he had devised for his Tudor *History*. The Tudor yeoman became a slum-blighted proletarian, but emigration to the open skies of Australasia might renew the hereditary vigor of his breed. The Irish Home Ruler was still causing trouble, but he had now been joined across the Atlantic by Jamaican freedmen, who had the temerity to seek alternatives to plantation work. Once again, Froude's voice did not go unanswered, eliciting responses from liberal critics, both white and black. The chapter concludes with an assessment of Froude as a polarizing figure – helping to shatter the liberal consensus but offering only contentious solutions in their place. Froude's specific crochets probably resonated with only a minority of readers, but his glorification of Anglo-Saxon pioneers and his evisceration of insubordinate racial others reflected a much broader sea-change in metropolitan public opinion that was given credence by new evolutionary theories and new timescales of chronology. These developments are examined in Chapter 5, "Greater Britain and the 'lesser breeds.'"

The appearance of Darwin's *Origin of Species* in 1859 was accompanied by overwhelming evidence of human antiquity. Taken together these two developments had a profound effect, not only on ideologies of race and empire management, but also on the writing of history. Most existing studies focus on the work of a few notorious "scientific racists" such as Robert Knox and James Hunt, who tried to argue that Blacks and Whites were separate species.[21] These individuals, however, were never very influential, and much more attention needs to be given to the large body of less dogmatic ethnologists, pre-historians, and classifiers of racial difference, many of whom were imperial officials and most of whom saw race as a graded hierarchy of superiority and descent. By supplementing Darwinism with a vague neo-Lamarckism, the option was kept open that – very slowly, over centuries – races could deteriorate or improve. The key point here is that the new scientific ideologies of evolution and race remained broadly *historical* in their thrust. They simply drew the progress narrative out over a much longer timescale and cast severe doubt on the assumption of earlier liberals like James Mill or the Macaulays that "backward" races could be rapidly improved. Racial improvement could happen only over the *longue durée*. For the short term, imperial policy should be devoted to managing primitive peoples, giving them the (paternal, but authoritarian) government that they needed and resisting those who would cause trouble by trying to force-march the pace of progress. Since such policies were being adopted for other reasons, evolutionary theory came to the rescue, giving them an air of scientific objectivity.

The dramatic slackening of the progress narrative that evolution seemed to impose also had a significant impact on the writing of history. With history now stretched over a multi-millennial *longue durée*, humanity could be divided along a continuum of racial quality. The superior races (i.e. Anglo-Saxons and, to a lesser degree, other Aryans) were deemed to be fast-evolving, and therefore capable of acting purposefully and progressively in history. By contrast, the more or less inferior races were

---

[21] Most notably Christine Bolt, *Victorian Attitudes to Race* (London, 1971), Nancy Stepan, *The Idea of Race in Science: Great Britain, 1800–1960* (London, 1982), and other references in Chapter 5.

relegated to the *longue durée* timescale of evolution. Where the former were historical subjects, the makers of history, the latter were conceived as the objects of evolution, to be classified, managed, and restrained. In the later parts of the chapter, I examine the impact of this new evolutionary approach on the writing of history between the 1860s and the 1880s. While the old-style narrative histories continued to be written, they were no longer on the lavishly conjunctural scale of a Froude or Macaulay, and they were more attentive to the deep structures and evolutionary processes that were operating underneath. I focus first on the evolutionary histories of H. S. Maine, which were profoundly connected to his work as an Indian administrator in the 1860s, and *vice versa*. I also devote considerable attention to three influential historians of medieval England, E. A. Freeman, J. R. Green, and William Stubbs. All three were guardedly influenced by the new evolutionism, although they each maintained a studied ambiguity as to whether it was the Anglo-Saxon race or the English Constitution that was the fast-evolving entity. Freeman generally opted for the first, and Green and Stubbs for the second of these alternatives. At the end of the chapter I touch on the work of an Indian scholar-imperialist, R. C. Dutt, who reacted to the anglocentric evolutionism of Maine *et al.* and who drew on the work of H. T. Buckle to sketch an unfinished evolutionary analysis of his own.

In Chapter 6, "Indian liberals and Greater Britain," we return to the subcontinent. In the University of Calcutta and in minor government offices, a rising generation of middle-class intellectuals was creating its own variant of the liberal imperial romance, at the very moment when its metropolitan counterpart was giving its up. The first task for the Indians was to devise their own versions of the progress narrative – to escape from the status of racialized objects, in which they were being placed by metropolitan evolutionary science, and to re-position themselves as consequential actors in history-worthy events. For Keshub Chandra Sen and his followers in Brahmo Samaj this meant taking up the mantle of Rammohun Roy, in his claim of a special Indian vocation for spirituality. This position was ratcheted one step higher by the historical novelist Bankimchandra Chattopadhyay, who acquiesced reluctantly in British rule for the present, seeing it as a prelude to a re-spiritualized India in some future age.

A third response, exemplified in my account by Surendranth Banerjea and Dadabhai Naoroji, was to embrace Macaulay's progress narrative, arguing that the time had come for the British to redeem their promise of modernization by granting India institutions of self-government. Finally, I close with R. C. Dutt, who was driven by British recalcitrance to shift from celebrating the riches of ancient Indian civilization to exploring the sources of modern Indian poverty. Notwithstanding their sharp criticism of existing British policy, these men all strongly believed in the value of the British Empire and ardently hoped for India to take her rightful place as an equal partner in some future imperial federation. By this time, however, most metropolitan Britons were reading the progress narrative in a very different way.[22]

In the Epilogue I return to the problem of Union as it appeared during the Home Rule crisis of the last two decades of the nineteenth century. I suggest that Gladstone's failure to achieve his policy of devolution was in part the consequence of an historical rhetoric that had lost its resonance. The call for Protestant Britons to redress the crimes of their ancestors, which Sydney Owenson had issued so hopefully at the beginning of the century, no longer sat well with mainstream middle-class and upper-middle-class English opinion. Additionally, Gladstone's own limitations – haunted as he was by ghosts from his own family's slave-owning past – impeded him in applying his Irish Home Rule vision to India and other "colored" colonies. Meanwhile Liberal Unionists, under the leadership of the former radical Chamberlain, migrated to an alternative progress narrative of Sir John Seeley, which focused on the expansion of England (becoming Britain) and her rise, via imperialism, to the status of a great power. Self-professedly realist and unromantic, and focused on the quest for Britain's geo-political security, Seeley ignored Irish and Indian aspirations for self-government, advocating instead a closer Union with the Anglo-Saxon colonies. Rarely has a historian so misread the future in imagining the past.

---

[22] For imperial federation see Duncan Bell, *The Idea of Greater Britain* (Princeton, 2007), and other references in Chapter 5. For recent work on Unionism and imperial citizenship see Iain McLean and Alistair McMillan, *State of the Union: Unionism and the Alternative in the United Kingdom since 1707* (Oxford, 2005), and Daniel Gorman, *Imperial Citizenship: Empire and the Question of Belonging* (Manchester, 2006).

1   Imagining Great Britain: Union, Empire, and the burden of history, 1800–1830

There is no European nation which, within the course of half a century or little more, has undergone so complete a change as this kingdom of Scotland. The effects of the insurrection of 1745 – the destruction of the patriarchal power of the Highland chiefs, the abolition of heritable juris-dictions of the lowland nobility and barons, the total eradication of the Jacobite party ... commenced this innovation. The gradual influx of wealth and extension of commerce have since united to render the present people of Scotland a class of beings as different from their grand-fathers as the existing English are from those of Queen Elizabeth's time.
>   Walter Scott, *Waverley* [1814] (London, 1972), "Postscript," 492

The history of colonies has in it some points of peculiar interest as illustrating human nature. On such occasions the extremes of civilized and savage life are suddenly and strongly brought into contact with each other, and the results are as interesting to the moral observer as those which take place on the mixture of chemical substances are to physical investigation.
>   Walter Scott to Robert Southey, March 23, 1818, in Scott, *The Letters of Sir Walter Scott*, ed. J. C. Grierson (London, 1933), V: 115

On September 7, 1798, an Anglo-Irish gentleman, Richard Edgeworth, gathered his wife, eldest daughter Maria, and six other children. Abandoning their ancestral home in fear for their lives, the family has-tened to the relative safety of the Protestant enclave of Longford Town with a train of mixed Protestant and Catholic yeomanry in tow. Since May, when a republican rebellion in Dublin had sparked an agrarian uprising in the south, the Edgeworths had been on tenterhooks. The landing of a French force at Killala, County Mayo, on August 22, put their estate directly in the line of rebel advance. Lacking adequate arms and uncertain of his non-sectarian militia, Edgeworth believed he had no choice but to abandon his property.[1] Like many other Anglo-Irish

---

[1] BME, 137–8, and *The Memoir of Richard Lovell Edgeworth, Begun by Himself, and Concluded by his Daughter, Maria Edgeworth*, 2 vols. [1820] (Shannon, 1969), II: 205–38. On the uprisings of 1798 see Marianne Elliott, *Partners in Revolution: The United Irishmen and France* (New Haven, 1982), 165–240, and Nancy J. Curtin, *The United Irishmen: Popular Politics in Ulster and Dublin, 1791–1798* (Oxford, 1994).

Ascendancy landlords, he was deeply relieved by the British victory at Ballinamuck on September 8, when the insurgents were defeated. And yet no sooner had the danger of invasion receded than Edgeworth and his company found themselves facing a more perilous threat. Distrusted as a liberal by his fellow Protestants, he was now targeted as a crypto-rebel. Frenzied Orange revelers surrounded him in Longford Town and nearly lynched him when he was denounced as a "spy." After this frightening episode, the family returned to the eerie silence of their abandoned estate. "Within the house, everything was as we had left it," Maria later recalled. "A map that we had been consulting was still open on the library table, with pencils and slips of paper containing the first lessons in arithmetic in which some of the young had been engaged." Why, the Protestant neighbors whispered, had Edgeworthstown House been spared by the marauders, who had plundered every other estate?[2]

Why, asked the Prime Minister at about the same time, was Ireland such a recurrent disaster? Consulting his own global maps from London, William Pitt reflected on the alarming sequence of recent English events: poor harvests, rising prices, bread riots, budget deficits, banking crises, radical conspiracies, and a barely averted invasion by 100,000 soldiers of the army of France. Had the Irish Rebellion been better co-ordinated with these near catastrophes, the British state would likely have collapsed.[3] If the British Empire were to survive its war against the mobilized energies of revolutionary France, something would have to be done about Ireland, the weakest link in the imperial chain. By the end of the year Prime Minister Pitt had made his decision: Ireland had to be incorporated directly into the Union, much as Scotland had been a century before.[4] Yet this was easier said than done, for Ireland was plagued by deep

---

[2] BME, 139; *Memoir of Richard Lovell Edgeworth*, II: 205–38, 232; Frances Anne Edgeworth, *A Memoir of Maria Edgeworth with Selections from her Letters*, 3 vols. (London, 1867), I: 83–93. For additional letters see Augustus J. C. Hare, *The Life and Letters of Maria Edgeworth*, 2 vols. (Boston, 1894).

[3] "This country," Pitt told the House of Commons on January 22, "is at this time engaged in the most momentous conflict that ever occurred in the history of the world. A conflict in which Great Britain is distinguished for having made the only manly and successful stand against the common enemy of civil society" (*Cobbett's Parliamentary History of England* (London, 1819), XXXIV: 267; see also 242–9, 258). On Pitt's response to the crisis of 1797–1800, see J. Holland Rose, *William Pitt and the Great War* (Westport, 1971), 299–320, 339–64, and John Ehrman, *The Younger Pitt: The Consuming Struggle*, III (London, 1996), 1–157, 258–64. On social conditions, see E. P. Thompson, *The Making of the English Working Class* (New York, 1963), 472–97, and Asa Briggs, *The Making of Modern England: Age of Improvement, 1783–1867* (New York, 1959), 129–83.

[4] For accounts of British government thinking about Ireland during this period, see Patrick Geoghegan, *The Irish Act of Union: A Study in High Politics* (New York, 1999), and G. C. Bolton, *The Passing of the Irish Act of Union: A Study in Parliamentary Politics* (Oxford, 1966).

divisions and hatreds, which left moderate propertied men like Edgeworth very thin on the ground. For two and a half centuries, a series of inter-locking dysfunctions – military conquest, political despotism, mass pov-erty, religious conflict, and ethnic strife – had left an atmosphere of chronic cynicism and disorder. Sullen antagonism was punctuated by periodic insurrection, and was finally resolved by sharp repression and the return of martial law.[5]

To be sure, in the context of the old imperial order, the internal divisions precipitated by these dysfunctional cycles possessed a certain mercantilist functionality. By distributing privilege and wealth in uneven channels, they had kept all groups subordinated to the English metropol-itan center, while articulating a distinctively colonial Irish socio-political hierarchy. At the top were the post-conquest Protestant landlords, sepa-rated by religion from middling-class dissenters and dispossessed Catholic gentlemen. This prevented the formation of *any* independent national elite. Far below lay the mass of poor, mostly Catholic tenants and cottiers, who lived in misery at the bottom of the heap. By the beginning of the nineteenth century, however, these status distinctions were becoming less acceptable. Rising capitalist wealth generated demands for economic liberalization and political equality, which now combined with the exigencies of total war. Under these circumstances, it was necessary to mobilize *all* sectors of the imperial polity. By incorporat-ing Ireland directly into the Union, Pitt hoped to turn Irish weakness into a source of British strength. Once Ireland's government was folded into the institutions of the United Kingdom, and its people were incorporated into Britain's economy, the way would be opened for socio-economic modernization. Efficient central administration and the redress of legit-imate Catholic grievances could then be effected in a manner that would not endanger overall Anglo-Protestant archipelagic supremacy.[6]

As Prime Minister Pitt would soon discover, the Edgeworths were exactly the new local leaders who had to be enlisted in his Unionist scheme. As an improving Protestant landlord, eager to transcend sec-tarian divisions, Richard Edgeworth was the very model of a modern Irish gentleman. Descended from an old English family that had come to Ireland with the Elizabethan conquest, Richard had begun as a typical absentee landlord. Yet his English upbringing had exposed him to the enlightenment, which turned him into a self-taught mechanical genius who invented streamlined carriages as well as transport braking, signal-ing, and traction equipment that presaged the railroad, the telegraph,

[5] R. F. Foster, *Modern Ireland, 1600–1972* (London, 1988), 3–286.
[6] Ehrman, *Younger Pitt*, III: 158–94.

and the tank. A perusal of Smith's *Wealth of Nations* convinced Edgeworth that human societies, no less than mechanical devices, could be studied, engineered, and reformed by scientific means. Thus in 1782, Edgeworth returned to Ireland, immersed himself in the Patriot movement, got elected to Grattan's Parliament, and became a leading figure in Dublin affairs. On his own estates, in Edgeworthstown, County Longford, he became an advocate of agrarian improvement. "Education" was the central concept tying together all aspects of Edgeworth's reforming schemes: political education for Ireland's male property-holders, education in industrious habits for his tenants, and useful knowledge for his children at home. Following the associational psychology of Locke and Hartley, Edgeworth believed that it was the landlord's duty to provide the optimal environment for each to learn, according to his or her needs.[7]

As the energies of Irish reformers began to dissipate, however, Edgeworth came to see that only political Union with Britain could provide an effective environment for educating Ireland and bringing the nation into the modern epoch. However, in 1799, when the government began to press this objective, Edgeworth realized that the moment was inopportune, for there were few genuine Unionists like himself anywhere in the country. The mass of the Catholic population, repressed and demoralized, remained scarcely reconciled to the permanence of British rule. Pitt's failure to obtain Catholic Emancipation as *quid pro quo* for political fusion would leave them even more embittered and disenfranchised during the coming decades. Most fatally, the Unionist cause had precious little support among his own ruling Protestant provincial elite. The close-run revolt of 1798 had concentrated their minds for a moment, but as soon as the immediate danger had passed, they sought a quick return to business as usual. Direct rule from London was unappealing, since it might curb their own privileges as a ruling oligarchy. To get the Irish Parliament to abolish itself, Pitt had to indulge in the very practices of bribery and intimidation that had long made that body a watchword for corruption and venality.[8]

---

[7] BME, 1–96; Jenny Uglow, *The Lunar Men: Five Friends whose Curiosity Changed the World* (New York, 2002); *Memoir of Richard Lovell Edgeworth*, I: 1–330; Tom Dunne, "A Gentleman's Estate should be a Moral School: Edgeworthstown in Fact and Fiction, 1760–1840," in Raymond Gillespie and Gerard Moran (eds.), *Longford: Essays in County History* (Dublin, 1991), 95–122.

[8] Geoghegan, *Irish Act of Union*; Bolton, *Passing*; Oliver MacDonagh, *Ireland* (Englewood Cliffs, 1968), 1–42; Edgeworth, *A Memoir*, I: 101. See essays in Daire Keogh and Kevin Whelan (eds.), *Acts of Union: The Causes, Contexts and Consequences of the Act of Union* (Dublin, 2001), as well as those in Michael Brown, Patrick Geoghegan, and James Kelly

As Richard Edgeworth and his daughter watched this sickening spectacle they saw that Union could not be left to the politicians, and that the benefits of making Ireland British would have to be explained. If "consensual" Union was obtainable only through the usual corrupt methods, it would arrive stillborn, forestalling the very benefits that its advocates sought. To force political Union on a resistant population would render it tantamount to another re-conquest, tainting the ideal of consensual "Britishness" and littering the path of modernization with yet more obstacles of coercion and disdain. The achievement of a truly liberal constitutional Union would require education in the broadest, Edgeworthian sense: without an imaginative union that brought Britons and Irish together in mutual understanding, statutory Union would remain illegitimate in the popular mind. Breathing life into inert forms required a spirit of confraternity – an imagined community, in the terms of Benedict Anderson – around which a new and enlarged sense of British national identity could be forged.[9]

All the differences – political, economic, social, religious, and ethnic – which divided Irishmen from other Britons, and also fractured the Irish from within, would have to be bridged by new narratives of Irishness. Such narratives might then succeed in convincing the populations of *both* countries that British Union was natural and inevitable – a coalescence that was in the interest of both nations and was a fulfillment of some foreordained historical inevitability. Richard Edgeworth, the enlightenment rationalist, mechanical inventor, and practical reformer, was not himself well suited to the creation of such a persuasive, bi-national romance. However, as Pitt's Union wended its ugly way through the debauched Irish Parliament, he learned that his daughter, Maria, had written a novella along these lines. She had proven a worthy coadjutor in all his formal educational ventures. Now, through the genre of fiction, she was ready to strike out on a pedagogical project uniquely her own. So, in 1800, under the title *Castle Rackrent*, the Edgeworths answered the Act of Union by publishing a book.[10]

(eds.), *The Irish Act of Union, 1800: Bicentennial Essays* (Dublin, 2003), and those in Terry Brotherstone, Anna Clark, and Kevin Whelan (eds.), *These Fissured Isles* (Edinburgh, 2005).

[9] BME, 180–5. On March 31, 1800, Richard Edgeworth wrote to his friend Erasmus Darwin that "such a union would identify [unify] the nations so that Ireland should be as Yorkshire to Great Britain, would be an excellent thing" (quoted in Marilyn Butler, "Introduction," in ECRE, 35). Yet two months earlier Maria had written that though "the Union would be advantageous to all the parties concerned, England has not any right to do to Ireland, good against its will" (Edgeworth, *A Memoir*, I: 101).

[10] See Butler, "Introduction," in ECRE; Willa Murphy, "A Queen of Hearts or an Old Maid? Maria Edgeworth's Fictions of Union," in Keogh and Whelan (eds.), *Acts of Union*, 187–201.

1   Maria Edgeworth's romance of Anglo-Irish Union

If Maria Edgeworth's first goal was to teach other Anglo-Irish landlords to act like her father, *Castle Rackrent* was an audacious and witty reminder that the Edgeworths themselves had not always been so well behaved. Drawing on early lore of her own distant ancestors, the author alters the family chronicle on only one crucial point: where the Edgeworths came to Ireland with the Elizabethan conquerors, the Rackrents are depicted as an aboriginal family (formerly the O Shaughlins) who changed their name (and presumably their religion) at the time of the Reformation. By thus participating indirectly in the original sin of colonial takeover, the Rackrents are condemned to the vicious cycle signified by their name.[11] First came Sir Tallyhoo, followed by Sir Patrick, who died beloved in three counties while leaving his estate hopelessly in debt. He was succeeded by Sir Murtagh – a tightfisted penny-pincher, who married a Skinflint and refilled the family coffers, but departed unloved. His heir, Sir Kit, was a dashing army officer and a profligate spender, who put the estate in the hands of avaricious middlemen, while fleecing a Jewish heiress whom he kept under house arrest. Sir Kit has finally been succeeded by the last Rackrent, Sir Condy – a man whose openhanded benevolence has made him beloved by his neighbors and tenants, but whose habitual drunkenness and profligate spending have eventually lost him the family estate.[12]

Both the comedy and the intellectual force in this story lie in the fact that it is told not by a member of the Rackrent family, but through the voice of Thady Quirk, an aged peasant and loyal family retainer, who has served through thick and thin as the steward of the estate. Blindly loyal to a social order that is collapsing, Thady appears to the sophisticated, anglicized reader as a figure of fun. Yet his very obstinacy and oblivious fatalism endow him with a kind of independence that enables him to articulate the values of a corrupted establishment, which is no longer capable of explaining or even understanding itself. Here is a local dynasty whose roots can be traced back through several centuries, and yet it remains in many ways still a foreign imposition, ill aclimatized to the Irish soil on which it stands. In the closed, self-contradictory world of the Rackrents, traditional

[11] Maria Edgeworth, *Castle Rackrent* [1800] (New York, 1965). For the parallels between the Rackrents and earlier generations of Edgeworths see *The Black Book of Edgeworthstown and other Edgeworth Memories, 1585–1817*, ed. Harriet Jessie Butler and Harold Edgeworth Butler (London, 1927), 73–121.
[12] Edgeworth, *Castle Rackrent*, 1–23. See also analyses in W. J. McCormack, *Ascendancy and Tradition in Anglo-Irish Literary History from 1789 to 1939* (Oxford, 1985), 97–122; and Thomas Flanagan, *The Irish Novelists, 1600–1850* (New York, 1959), 53–79.

paternalism entails indebtedness, while indebtedness destroys paternalism, so that every true value gets inverted, and every virtue becomes a vice.[13]

Anglo-Ireland, Maria seems to be saying, is no longer capable of modernizing (or even educating) itself. In the end the Rackrents lose their lands to Thady's son, Jason Quirk, an avaricious Catholic, the exact opposite of Condy Rackrent, except for their common inability to play the pedagogical landlord's role. The solution, Maria concludes, can come only from England. "Nations as well as individuals," she tells her readers, "gradually lose their attachment to their identity, and the present generation is amused, rather than offended, by the ridicule that is thrown upon its ancestors ... When Ireland loses her identity, by an union with Great Britain, she will look back, with a smile of good-humored complacency, on the Sir Kits and Sir Condys of her former existence."[14] This bow to the past is ironic in that *Castle Rackrent*, with all its comic touches, aggressively evades the bitter lessons of Anglo-Irish history. Even taken at face value, as "a tale of other times," the novella echoes with many silences. The explanatory notes, which the author adds for the comprehension of the modern British reader, only serve to deepen the mystery. The English conquest (in which the Edgeworths had participated) is never mentioned, yet it inescapably haunts the ghostly scene. We glimpse it in the enigma of Thady. Disturbingly aggressive in his very obsequiousness, he remains a largely mysterious character.[15] Does his deferential facade mask some sanguinary cut-throat, the man of 1798, who momentarily erupted and then just as quickly disappeared back underground? Of course, none of this is ever discussed by the hidden author (posing as a mere editor). If we will let her, she allows us to take Thady as a buffoon and enjoy his stage-Irish dialect and minstrelsy.

Although *Castle Rackrent* was no immediate bestseller, it gradually worked its way into circulation, selling several thousand copies over the next twenty-five years. Widely acknowledged as a new departure in its genre, it was arguably also the first truly British novel, with a bi-national cast of characters, which brought English and Irish readers literally together on the same page. In later years, however, Maria expressed some dissatisfaction that *Rackrent* had remained her most popular book. The enigmatic quality of its message, and the fact that Rackrentism

[13] Edgeworth, *Castle Rackrent*, 25–85.   [14] ECRE, 63.
[15] Terry Eagleton, *Heathcliffe and the Great Hunger: Studies in Irish Culture* (London, 1995), 161–7; Edgeworth, *Castle Rackrent*, ix, x. For an analysis of the relationship between text and critical apparatus, see Brian Hollingsworth, *Maria Edgeworth's Irish Writing: Language, History, Politics* (New York, 1997), 71–107.

remained alive and well in nineteenth-century Ireland, diminished its value in her estimation.[16] The task of the Unionist writer, serving as educator and reformer, was to teach the traditional Irishman to become a British utility maximizer, rather than to romanticize him as a figure of fun. Progress in Ireland required a progress narrative, a story of how improvement could be brought to a backward country: who should bring it, and what form it should take. So, with this in mind, Maria Edgeworth returned to the library-cum-schoolroom in Edgeworthstown House. During 1804–5, she began a second "Irish" novel, which she revised and published in 1809 under the title *Ennui*.

Unlike *Castle Rackrent*, *Ennui* makes no claim to being "a tale of other times." It is an overtly didactic story, focused explicitly on the social problems of the present and on the search for means by which they might be resolved. The Anglo-Irish landlord, who had appeared as a comic subject in *Castle Rackrent*, is now reintroduced as an educative agent, returning to Ireland, after a protracted English sojourn, with the gift of enlightenment. The plot turns on the story of the Earl of Glenthorn, a wealthy Irish landlord who suffers from a case of terminal boredom. Neither the Grand Tour nor a life of gambling and entertainment has provided this restless aristocrat with fulfillment. Only a serious accident has prevented him from blowing out his brains. Laid up for some weeks, however, Glenthorn's taste for life is reawakened by an old Irish nurse. This nurse, who was also his wet-nurse in infancy, persuades him to seek a new life of interest and activity by returning to his ancestral homeland.[17]

As he comes within sight of the battlements of Glenthorn Castle, "a number of men, who appeared to be dwarfs when compared with the height of the building, came out with torches in their hands."

These people seemed "born for my use"; the officious precipitation with which they ran to and fro; the style in which they addressed me; some crying "Long life to the Earl of Glenthorn!" some blessing me for coming to reign over them; all together gave more the idea of vassals than of tenants, and carried my imagination centuries back to feudal times.[18]

Maria regards Glenthorn's desire to play the paternalist as broadly sound. The trick is to avoid falling into feudal dysfunction, and to combine paternalism with an improving agenda of popular education and agrarian reform. Indeed, the rest of the novel is an extended exploration of the way these two apparently contradictory imperatives might be fused.

[16] Butler, "Introduction," in ECRE, 32–56; Ina Ferris, *The Achievement of Literary Authority: Gender, History and the Waverley Novels* (Ithaca, 1991), 19–78, 105–36.
[17] ECRE, 143–69.   [18] ECRE, 177–8.

The lesson in modernity is initially laid out by Glenthorn's Scottish agent, McLeod, and – more obliquely – by a Dublin lawyer, Mr. Devereux. Yet neither is capable of effectual teaching, since McLeod's plans depend on the authority of the landlord, and Devereux is dispatched away from Ireland to the colonies. Glenthorn himself has the best of intentions, but encounters great difficulty in expunging his own ennui. The need to foil an insurrection momentarily rouses his energies, but the adrenaline burst is not sustained. Redemption comes only when a case of switched infants strips him of his hereditary estates. Paradoxically, this legal disestablishment turns out to be an emancipatory release, compelling him to learn self-reliance. Unshackled from his inherited fortune, the ex-Glenthorn is obliged to earn it back on his own.[19]

The pedagogical aspirations of *Ennui* have been widely noted, yet they lead in the end to the novel's self-subversion, since the real story is what most characters have failed to learn.[20] The indigenous peasantry remains hopelessly savage, as exemplified in the sad demise of Christy O'Donaghoe, whose precipitous elevation to the Glenthorn earldom only provides the occasion for his wife's extended kin to eat him out of house and home. The development of industrious habits and rational calculation in this child-like population must be the work of many decades of subjugation to the benevolent paternalist landlord. Yet so long as the Anglo-Irish elites remain trapped in their Rackrent-like quagmire, they too cannot become effective educators, since they themselves have not learned how to combine the capitalist's initiative with their more habitual gentlemanly roles. Since the novel offers no truly plausible pedagogue, it has to convey its lessons through the author's bag of magic tricks: exchanged places, romantic entanglements, and the ex-Glenthorn's ultimate marriage to the residuary legatee of his own (former) estate. In reality, Maria concludes that the gentleman-capitalist admixture must be imported from Britain, where Union has long permitted a healthy hybridization of economic classes and social roles. Yet, once again, the historical silences and evasions of Maria's novel undercut the plausibility of her account. She does not seem to have realized that Ireland's inability to turn gentlemen into capitalists derives less from the incompleteness of the modern liberal Union than from the legacy of violence and "primitive accumulation" left by the original English conquests of earlier centuries. Finding this subject too painful and explosive, Maria Edgeworth left it for another Anglo-Irish female writer, Sydney Owenson (Lady Morgan),

---

[19] ECRE, 70–361.
[20] Sharon Murphy, *Maria Edgeworth and Romance* (Dublin, 2004), 151–65; Hollingsworth, *Edgeworth's Irish Writing*, 122–47.

whose *Wild Irish Girl* (1806) cast the educative allegory of Union in a very different conceptual frame.

2   Edgeworth, Owenson, and the burdens of history

Superficially, *The Wild Irish Girl* is similar in plot to *Ennui*. Like Glenthorn, the protagonist, Mortimer, is first encountered in England, where he is sunk in listlessness and over-refinement. Having wasted his time and money in dissipation, he is banished by his father to the wilds of the west of Ireland, where no distractions will interfere with his preparation for the Bar. Yet no sooner does Mortimer arrive in this picturesque country than he becomes utterly captivated by Irish scenery, Irish wit, and Irish hospitality. At the end of his journey, deep in the heart of Old Ireland, he finds Inismore, the ruined castle of a dispossessed Irish "prince," whose family was deposed by his own ancestors during the Cromwellian wars. Here he discovers the antidote to his own self-loathing and gains a new meaning and purpose in life. In the company of Glorvina, the Prince's beautiful, harp-playing daughter, and an erudite, enlightened French-educated priest, Mortimer turns his attention to the problem of Anglo-Ireland. Unlike Edgeworth, with her imported English schemes for Irish improvement, Owenson leaves Mortimer to listen and learn from his native interlocutors. With their encouragement, and through their tutelage, he immerses himself in Gaelic culture, language, music, and poetry.[21]

Although much of Owenson's novel is overwritten, and her harp-plucking princess is a foretaste of today's Celtic kitsch, her historical consciousness enables her to penetrate dimensions of the Anglo-Irish encounter to which the more intellectually sophisticated Edgeworth had no access. This is because Owenson (in contrast to Edgeworth) is willing to acknowledge the unpleasant truth that conquest is the central fact of Anglo-Irish history. Mortimer (and later, it transpires, his father, as well) has been drawn to Ireland out of a recognition of English injustice and a personal desire to make amends for his own ancestors' brutality. That unredeemed past, which remains a skeleton in the Edgeworth closet, is, in Owenson's novel, revealed for all to see. In the sixteenth and seventeenth centuries, the English had come to Ireland as conquerors and oppressors.

---

[21] Sydney Owenson, Lady Morgan, *The Wild Irish Girl* [1806] (Oxford, 1999); Butler, "Introduction," in ECRE, 24. Since *Ennui* was published after *The Wild Irish Girl*, we cannot rule out the possibility that it was Edgeworth who was influenced by Owenson, rather than *vice versa*. Nevertheless, *Ennui* was likely drafted before *The Wild Irish Girl* was published. Perhaps both writers were traveling in parallel tracks, unbeknownst to one another.

Now, in the age of liberalism and voluntary union, they can return as
friends and protectors, but only after they have acknowledged the damage
of their ancestors' rapacity. When they have gained the trust of their
injured Irish neighbors and tenants, the possibilities for Irish improvement and self-reform will open up. The novel ends, predictably enough,
with the marriage of Mortimer and Glorvina, which effects the union of
Ireland's old Celtic and new British elites.[22]

In this the dearest, most sacred, and most lasting of all human ties, let the names of
Inismore and Mortimer be inseparably blended, and the distinctions of English
and Irish, of Protestant and Catholic, for ever buried. And, while you look forward
with hope to this family alliance being prophetically typical of a national unity . . .
lend your own individual efforts towards the consummation of an event so
devoutedly to be wished by every liberal mind, by every benevolent heart.[23]

While dismissing Owenson's novels as "vulgar . . . trash," Maria
Edgeworth published a reply of sorts with her third Irish novel, *The
Absentee*. Even more than her previous efforts, this book is addressed to
her readers in England, particularly the Anglo-Irish landlords who have
abandoned their estates for the lure of London high society. Unlike
Owenson, Edgeworth does not think that they need to embrace Celtic
culture or feel contrition for their ancestors' misdeeds. The landlord's
error is simply his absenteeism, and his mere return to Ireland is presented
as the solution to Ireland's woes.[24] Lord Colambre, the hero, achieves this
realization early in the novel, but he is stymied by his mother's addiction to
London's *beau monde*. At great expense to the family (and their rack-
rented tenants), she has tried to climb into London's best aristocratic
circles, only to be despised for her Irish accent and *parvenu* pretensions.
Salvation comes from renouncing this debased and effeminizing agenda,
and from restoring dynastic power to the male patriarchs of the family,
who understand that their place in the world hinges on their return from
the metropolis to the periphery and on the active paternalist management

---

[22] Owenson, *Wild Irish Girl*, 170–252. Owenson put her own view of Irish reform into the
mouth of her priest: "A brave, though misguided people, is not to be dragooned out of a
train of ancient prejudices, nurtured by fancied interest and real ambition, and confirmed
by ignorance, which those who deride, have made no effort to dispel. It is not by physical
force, but moral influence, the illusion is to be dissolved" (190). See also Joep Leerson,
*Remembrance and Imagination: Patterns in the History and Literary Representation of Ireland
in the Nineteenth Century* (Dublin, 1997), 33–67.

[23] Owenson, *Wild Irish Girl*, 250. For an insightful comparison of Owenson's and
Edgeworth's "Unionist" marriage plots, see Mary Jean Corbett, *Allegories of Union in
Irish and English Writing, 1790–1870* (Cambridge, 2000), 51–81. For an account that
compares Owenson with Scott, see Ian Dennis, *Nationalism and Desire: Early Historical
Fiction* (London, 1997), 45–86.

[24] Quoted in BME, 448.

of their Irish estates. If Owenson's union was allegorized as a loving marriage between unequal partners, Edgeworth's is a wholly hierarchical relation between a benevolent father and his dependent wards, which leaves him with all the power and consigns them to a near-permanent minority status.[25]

By 1817, when Edgeworth published her final Irish novel, *Ormond*, the memories of 1798 had faded, but her father's dreams of agrarian reform had also become a distant memory. That Ireland will be British is now taken for granted, but the plot turns on what kind of Britishness it can achieve. Writing as her beloved father was dying, Maria makes the reformer, Sir Herbert Annaly, into a remote figure who succumbs to a wasting disease. The prevailing Anglo-Irish norm is exemplified by Sir Ulick O'Shane, a charming, devious, high-living landlord, well connected with the powerful in Dublin, who draws on heavy speculation and political jobbing to augment his income, which he needs to mask the lax management of his estates. Traditional Ireland is represented by King Corny, Ulick's cousin, an open-hearted but utterly ineffectual anachronism who has been marginalized to the backwater of the "Black Islands," where he holds his archaic court with despotic authority. His daughter is no harp-plucking princess à la Glorvina, but a flighty and uneducated girl who is swept off her feet by the superficial gallantry of a Franco-Irish adventurer. Though she is taken off to the aristocratic intrigues of Paris, this French dalliance is no longer dangerous to Britain. It is merely enervating and degrading to the Irish, as the hero, Ormond, discovers toward the end. Fortunately, he is able to foil Sir Ulick's desperate attempt to retrieve his bankrupt estate by borrowing against Ormond's paternal legacy. After Ulick dies from shame at these proceedings, Ormond is left free to marry the daughter of the English reformer, Annaly, and inherit the properties of most of the book's leading characters.[26]

This hasty, absurdly happy ending suggests that Maria was growing tired of her fables of union and of trying to reconcile herself to a Britain in which a genuine Anglo-Irish partnership might never be achieved. When asked why she never wrote another Irish novel, she lamented that "it is impossible to draw Ireland as she now is in a book of fiction – realities are too strong, party passions too violent to bear to see, or care to look at their faces in the looking-glass. The people would only break the glass, and

---

[25] Maria Edgeworth, *The Absentee* [1812] (London, 1999); Corbett, *Allegories of Union*, 1–50. For an exhaustive reinterpretation of Morgan and Edgeworth that reads their historical messages through their spacial journeys see Ina Ferris, *The Romantic National Tale and the Question of Ireland* (Cambridge, 2002).

[26] Maria Edgeworth, *Ormond* [1817] (London, 1999); Hollingsworth, *Edgeworth's Irish Writing*, 148–220.

curse the fool who held the mirror up to nature – distorted nature, in a fever."[27] The "party passions" that Edgeworth had in mind when she wrote these words in 1834 were those raised by the Catholic Association of Daniel O'Connell, which had the temerity to organize the tenants on her estate and persuade them to vote against the instructions of the Edgeworth family. She testily wrote to a friend:

We hope that this country will not come to an explosion, and that O'Connell who has no real regard for anything but the hurrahs of the mob, will not succeed in effecting a dissolution of the union between England and Ireland, which would dissolve all remains of law in Ireland and would leave most of property at the mercy of those who want it.[28]

Edgeworth's equation of O'Connellism with an assault on property betrays just how far she had lost touch with reality, since no one could have been clearer than O'Connell in his renunciation of violence or in his defense of the sanctity of property. Even his demand for repeal of the Union was actually an appeal for re-negotiating it on terms of greater equality. "The people of Ireland," he proclaimed, "are ready to become a portion of the Empire . . . They are ready to become West Britons, if made so in benefits and justice; but if not, we are Irishmen again."[29] Richard Edgeworth could not have said it better. One can only conclude either that the aging Maria had forgotten the youthful ideals of her father or (more likely) that she was disconcerted by the realization that her family's class was incapable of bringing them to fruition. No doubt it was depressing to acknowledge that, after a full generation, Pitt's Union had changed nothing: the Anglo-Irish landlords remained an alien element, with only a tenuous and insecure hold on the country. Several centuries after their conquest and confiscations they had been unable to transmute their colonial domination into consensual hegemony.[30]

Did this mean that Sydney Owenson had been correct? Did the failure of the landlords lie in their inability to confront the dark deeds of their ancestors? Could Maria Edgeworth have crafted a more compelling romance of nineteenth-century Anglo-Ireland if she had faced up to the grim truths of Anglo-Irish history? There is no reason to think that

[27] Quoted in BME, 452; Michael Hurst, *Maria Edgeworth and the Public Scene* (Coral Gables, 1969), 56.
[28] Maria Edgeworth to Rachel Lazarus, November 7–8, 1832, *The Education of the Heart: The Correspondence of Rachel Mordecai Lazarus and Maria Edgeworth*, ed. Edgar E. MacDonald (Chapel Hill, 1977), 241; Hurst, *Public Scene*, 29–140.
[29] Oliver MacDonagh, *The Emancipist: Daniel O'Connell* (London, 1989), 1–144, quote on 136; Feargus O'Ferrall, *Daniel O'Connell* (Dublin, 1981).
[30] For Maria Edgeworth's later life in Edgeworthstown, see BME, 401–99; Hurst, *Public Scene, passim.*

Edgeworth would have accepted this conclusion. Since the landlord-educator was the proper bearer of the progress narrative, it would be an exercise in self-subversion to dwell morbidly on the historical sins of his or her dynasty. But it may not be entirely accidental that Edgeworth ended her own experiments in Anglo-Irish fiction at the very moment when her reading table was inundated with progress narratives of a very different kind: a flood of bi-national romances, which happily embraced the role of historical recitation in Union creation, even as it relocated the ensuing fusion to a different part of the British Isles. As Edgeworth read Walter Scott's string of Anglo-Scottish romances that appeared in the years after 1814, she praised his "moral enthusiasm." With perhaps a touch of envy, she marveled at the drive of his narrative and the optimism of his plots, which always seemed to resolve into happy endings, without any visible didactic effort on the author's part.[31] Here indeed were romances of union, in which the history of division and conflict could be happily included, since their effect was merely to dramatize the transcendent unity with which they closed. For his part, when Scott later reflected on his career as a novelist, he gave credit to the inspiration of Maria Edgeworth's work. "I felt that something might be done for my own country, along the lines that she had undertaken with her Irish novels," he recalled. By making the English familiar with the more positive attributes of their Irish neighbors, she had "done more to complete the Union than perhaps all the legislative enactments by which it had been followed up."[32]

Like so many of Scott's commentaries on his own literary *opus*, these somewhat coy remarks were penned in the knowledge that all his readers, of every nationality, would agree in viewing the Anglo-Scottish Union as a success. His praise of Edgeworth (qualified by "perhaps") was thus a backhanded form of self-congratulation, implicitly contrasting her uncertain efforts with his own manifest triumphs.[33] Why did Walter Scott

---

[31] For Edgeworth's reaction to *Waverley*, see her letter to the author (whom she strongly suspected to be Scott), in Edgeworth, *A Memoir*, I: 303–9. Her reaction to visiting Scotland and staying with Scott in 1823 is detailed in Edgeworth, *A Memoir*, II: 211–41. Her reaction to Scott's visit to Edgeworthstown two years later is recorded in Edgeworth, *A Memoir*, II: 259–64.

[32] SW, 523.

[33] The official life of Scott was written by his son-in-law, J. G. Lockhart, *Memoir of the Life of Sir Walter Scott*, 9 vols. [1836–8] (Boston, 1887), hereafter cited as *Memoir of Scott*, and abridged in *The Life of Sir Walter Scott*, 2 vols. (New York, n.d.), hereafter cited as *Life of Scott*. The standard modern biography is JWS, usefully supplemented by John Sutherland, *The Life of Sir Walter Scott: A Critical Biography* (Oxford, 1995), which takes a more skeptical view. For details of the relationship between Scott and Edgeworth, see JWS, 810–15, 839–44, 851–7, 899–915, and Dennis, *Nationalism and Desire*, 61–129.

succeed where Maria Edgeworth had failed? Some would say it was because he was a better writer. Much more to the point, the same historical circumstances that vitiated her efforts tended to favor his project. On every level, these two authors were differently situated in relation to the Union that they sought to celebrate. The Anglo-Scottish Union long predated Scott's appearance and had already endured for over a century when he began to glorify it in print. By contrast, the Anglo-Irish Union was coterminous with Edgeworth's novels and bore the weight of a disunited history that had yet to be overcome. The Battle of the Boyne – ever remembered and yet unmentioned – ate away like an acid at Edgeworth's vision of Britain. The Battle of Culloden – largely transcended, but still unsung – became the platform from which Scott's vision of Britain triumphantly annunciated its case. Her genius was to defy the oppositions of history and (at least in fiction) to imagine a more progressive, multinational future. His genius was to take the disparate materials that history had bequeathed him and to craft a romance of multi-national inclusion – to use the new and rapidly evolving genre of the novel to show how ancient oppositions had been progressively overcome.[34] Where Edgeworth was a teacher trying to purvey her lessons in an increasingly uncongenial place, Scott was a borderer, making repeated raids on both sides of multiple frontiers. By spinning his tales of cross-country adventure, he turned himself (and his readers) into vicarious adventurers who attempted bi-national borderings all their own. Union, which had eluded the original borderers, could finally be forged and triumphantly celebrated by the author, who bordered on the margins between the ink and the page.

3   The border crossings of Walter Scott

Walter Scott's borderings were so overdetermined that he may have regarded them less as a choice than as a fate. Born the scion of an ancient border family, Scott had the Anglo-Scottish interface in his blood. Amid the ruins of rural Roxburghshire, at his grandmother's knee, he listened to

[34] The critical literature on Scott is now voluminous. I have found the following particularly useful: Georg Lukacs, *The Historical Novel* (London, 1962); David Daiches, "Scott's Achievement as a Novelist," in D. D. Devlin (ed.), *Modern Judgments: Walter Scott* (London, 1968), 33–62; David Brown, *Walter Scott and the Historical Imagination* (London, 1979); Ferris, *Literary Authority*; Ian Duncan, *Modern Romance and Transformations of the Novel: The Gothic, Scott, and Dickens* (Cambridge, 1992); Jane Millgate, *Walter Scott: The Making of a Novelist* (Toronto, 1984); Graham McMaster, *Scott and Society* (Cambridge, 1981); Caroline McCracken-Flesher, *Possible Scotlands: Walter Scott and the Story of Tomorrow* (Oxford, 2005); and Christopher Harvie, "Scott and the Image of Scotland," in Raphael Samuel (ed.), *Patriotism: The Making and Unmaking of British National Identity*. II, *Minorities and Outsiders* (London, 1989), 173–92.

hair-raising tales of distant ancestors – Jacobite rebels, border smugglers, and cattle thieves.[35] When school forced a return to his father's house in Edinburgh, he accepted that his living would be earned as a lawyer, but vowed that his leisure hours would be informed by romantic dreams. Cooped up indoors, forced to master Greek and Latin, he found that his youthful mind was always wandering along spine-tingling tales of the border or some chivalric adventure of '45. Indeed, Walter might have bolted from his father's close discipline, had not a mild case of infantile paralysis left him permanently lame in one leg. Mercilessly teased by thoughtless servants and schoolfellows, the lad came to realize that his masculine mettle would have to be demonstrated on a cognitive plane. His adventures would be lived vicariously, in stories. Denied the full heroism of sinew and of muscle, he would seek a higher heroism of the mind and of the pen.[36]

During his twenties, Scott worked his way up through Scotland's legal profession, cultivating literary aspirations on the side. Traipsing through his circuits as a border county sheriff, he collected local lore and transcribed old ballads after his depositions had been taken and his judgments had been filed. The result was three volumes of *Minstrelsy of the Scottish Border* (1800–2), which fixed into print the surviving fragments of a dying oral culture. It was in the course of compiling this relatively conventional collection that Scott began to conceive of authorship in a more boundless, transcendent way. The new approach seems to have been precipitated by the same imperial crisis of 1797–8 that had motivated Maria Edgeworth to take up her pen. Being a man, and a Scot, Scott initially responded to the threat of invasion viscerally, by abandoning the study and joining the Edinburgh Volunteers. Mock cavalry charges in defense of the homeland pumped much-needed testosterone into the guardsman's listless frame. After hours of trumpet rolls and strenuous horsemanship, the half-cripple would limp back home, exhausted, bedecked in his splendid uniform, and face aglow with patriotic British pride.[37]

Yet, at a certain point, Scott inevitably realized that the bookshop, not the battleground, would be his field of conquest. His antiquarian labors had shown that traditional culture was fragmenting at the very moment when the exigencies of war and Empire necessitated that national

---

[35] Walter Scott, "Memoir of his Early Years," appended as the first chapter to Lockhart's *Life of Scott*, I: 1–16; JWS, I: 3–17. For more on Scott's family background, see Lockhart, *Memoir of Scott*, I: 87–107; Sutherland, *Scott: A Critical Biography*, 1–25.

[36] Scott, "Memoir of his Early Years," 17–43; JWS, I: 18–49; Lockhart, *Memoir of Scott*, I: 107–61; Sutherland, *Scott: A Critical Biography*, 26–44.

[37] Lockhart, *Memoir of Scott*, I: 72–4, 162–218; Lockhart, *Life of Scott*, I: 44–68; JWS, I: 53–124, 131–4; Sutherland, *Scott: A Critical Biography*, 45–68, 88–108.

solidarity be reconstructed in altered terms. If the ancient bard had finally disappeared, who would catalyze community values in his place? Was modern society inherently splintered and anomic? The outpouring of patriotism that was unleashed during the 1790s showed that this was not necessarily the case. But these cultural energies had to be concentrated and channeled by some modern paladin of print literature who would re-create bardship in modern form. The old epics had expressed clan values of heroism and loyalty, but these were now weakened by capitalism and individuality. Yet heroism and loyalty could be rediscovered on a national level, by celebrating the leadership that combines material improvement with trans-local unity. Where the old epic had taken cohesion and identity for granted, a new (multi)-national epic was required to re-create them, by showing how cohesion had been wrested from historical conflicts and how a (multi)-national identity could be forged through a common history. Finally, these epics provide a dress rehearsal for liberal Empire, in which peripheral nations acquiesce in a necessary submission, while metropolitans learn to welcome them with respect and dignity.[38]

As Scott felt the boundary-bursting summons of this new bardic agenda, *The Lay of the Last Minstrel* swiftly flowed from his pen. The scene is set in Branksome Castle, on the Anglo-Scottish frontier, two generations before the Union of the British crowns. Scotland faces the prospect of an English invasion, while it is internally divided into warring clans. Through Cranstoun's remorseful courage and Lady Margaret's defiant magic, the clans are reunited and Scotland is saved. As he ventriloquized in the antiquated accents of "the last minstrel," Scott discovered his own modern authorial voice. In the beginning, the aged bard seems broken down and faint-hearted. But as his *Lay* wins the acclaim of an audience of noblewomen, he steadily gains in confidence and vigor. By the end of his poem, the bard has entered his own epic, emerging as a hero of national consciousness in his own right.[39]

When Scott's poem was published in 1805, it became an instant best-seller, going through three editions in the first year and selling 27,000 copies over the course of a decade. Three years later, *The Lay* was followed up by a successor, *Marmion*, which proved even more popular, selling 27,000 copies in three years. In 1810, *The Lady of the Lake* appeared,

---

[38] Katie Trumpener, *Bardic Nationalism: The Romantic Novel and the British Empire* (Princeton, 1997), offers a paradigm for understanding this process. The role of Scott within it is treated most illuminatingly by Duncan, *Modern Romance*.

[39] Walter Scott, *The Lay of the Last Minstrel* (Edinburgh, 1806). In *Walter Scott*, Millgate perceptively analyzes Scott's early poetry and considers its role in making him the romantic novelist he became. See also JWS, I: 211–44, especially 223; Lockhart, *Memoir of Scott*, II: 105–77; Lockhart, *Life of Scott*, I: 75–128.

exhausting several editions of 25,000 in a mere three months.[40] Nothing like this had ever been seen before. The literary marketplace had been expanding for a full generation, but Scott was the first writer to become so successful commercially as to earn a fortune from literature alone. Like that of most entrepreneurs, however, Scott's originality lay in bringing together elements that others had pioneered. As a number of literary scholars have recently demonstrated, the multiple genres which Scott interconnected – realism, tragedy, comedy, the gothic, the romantic, the epic, and the national – had all been greatly refined over the previous generation by writers ranging from Ann Radcliffe to Charlotte Smith and from Horace Walpole to J. W. Goethe. Scott's genius was to meld all these materials together in his own unique fashion, and to propel them into the dynamic, transformative medium of real-world history.[41]

Moreover, the product was released only after it had been extensively "test-marketed." All of Scott's early works were circulated in draft to a series of auditors and readers, whose reactions led to many alterations and revisions in the final text. In an environment where literature was becoming increasingly feminized as women writers rose to prominence in the literary scene, Scott was determined to re-appropriate their characteristic themes. Through his readings of Elizabeth Hamilton and Jane Porter, and his friendships with Anna Seward and Joanna Baillie, Scott absorbed their perspectives and concerns. Under their influence he learned the romance of renunciation, the sovereignty of sentiment, and the pathos of defeat. In his hands, however, these themes were threaded through a hard core of manly adventure, turning nostalgia from a compensatory consolation to a stage in the consummation of bourgeois masculinity.[42]

The significance of these border raids into the realm of the feminine can be seen in Scott's handling of the union theme. For all his early epics were set in late medieval or early modern North Britain and dramatized critical episodes in the forging of a Scottish national consciousness, in which the challenge of confronting an alien English other compels previously antagonistic Scottish factions to unite. While these rhapsodies were attractive to Scottish readers for obvious reasons, their extraordinary commercial success was a function of their popularity on the other side of the border, where English audiences lapped them up. Here we cannot but contrast

---

[40] JWS, I: 225, 279, 334–5.

[41] Trumpener, *Bardic Nationalism*; Ferris, *Literary Authority*, 1–59.

[42] The question of gender as a trope in Scott's writing is examined in Ferris, *Literary Authority*, 79–226, Duncan, *Modern Romance*, 62–93, and JWS, I: 159–66, 225–372. For the impact of German romanticism see Lockhart, *Memoir of Scott*, I: 234–8; JWS, I: 96, 129, 135, 159, 165, 170–1. William Macintosh, *Scott and Goethe: German Influence on the Writings of Sir Walter Scott* (Port Washington, 1970).

Edgeworth's and Owenson's laborious didactic efforts to enlist English readers in the sad state of modern Ireland with Scott's driving, swash-buckling adventures, in which Britons – whatever their national domicile – are invited to don the imaginary tartan plaid. The lesson was clear: historical romances of superseded conflicts could appeal equally well to descendants on both sides of the battle if the pathos was attractively presented and the combat was sufficiently remote. At a time when Britain was locked in death-struggle with Napoleonic France, it was inspiring to look back on Scott's sublime scenes and heroic virtues, knowing that Britons could now brandish them against the modern French other because their ancestors had formerly honed them in their (now resolved) internecine strife.[43]

Scott's willingness to repeat this winning formula is a testament not only to its resonance with a belligerent public, but also to his own desire for commercial success. As he made clear in his communications with Wordsworth, he had no use for the vision of a starving artist, casting works of genius on a philistine world. Scott had his own standards of artistic excellence, but his bardic ambitions required that he write for the existing public. In modern times, the only way to gauge the interest of anonymous readers was to calculate which books they were buying, in what quantity, and at what price. The modern epic, as Scott had discovered, was inex-tricably connected with the spread of print capitalism, whose mass pro-duction of common reading material brought together a vast audience into an imagined community of the (multi)-nation. In the case of Scott, however, this entrepreneurial bordering between print capitalism and artistic integrity was motivated not only by pride and patriotism, but also by social ambition, psychological insecurity, and his own increasingly extravagant consumer tastes.[44]

Indeed, no sooner was Scott flush with fame and money than he set himself up as one of the border lairds of whom he wrote. In 1812, he purchased an old farmhouse adjacent to a ruined abbey, with a command-ing prospect of the Tweed. This was but the first installment in a series of costly purchases of land for an estate which he would eventually call "Abbotsford." Here he began to build a large castellated mansion from which he and his descendants would dominate one stretch of the Anglo-Scottish border and preside in aristocratic splendor over a happy peasan-try. Yet for Scott, this road to the leisured life of a landed gentleman had to be paved with bourgeois self-discipline and relentless work. His writing

[43] JWS, I: 211–487.
[44] JWS, I: 213–15; Benedict Anderson, *Imagined Communities: Reflections on the Origin and Spread of Nationalism* (London, 1983), 1–46.

had to be squeezed in between the demands of his legal business and the hunting, socializing, and entertaining that his lordly aspirations required. To maintain his output, he had to budget his time, carefully measuring his productivity in pages per day. As more and more money rolled in, expenses mounted even faster. The broad acres of choice real estate that Scott sought did not come cheaply. The pseudo-medieval replica that he constructed was all the more costly because he wanted it fitted with all the most modern conveniences and amenities inside – plumbing, gas lighting, and water closets.[45]

To come up with the necessary cash for all these grandiose projects, Scott resorted to risky strategies: investing in the copyrights of other authors, editing classics such as Swift and Dryden, and speculating in what amounted to a futures market in his own unwritten work. From 1809 on, he poured more and more of his rapidly accumulating fortune into a secret publishing partnership with his printer, John Ballantyne. By controlling the entire process of literary production, he reckoned that he could eliminate the need for intermediaries between himself and the consumer, thereby increasing his profits on his own and others' creative works. Both from a personal and from a financial perspective, these investments turned out to be serious mistakes. The editorial work was thankless and time-consuming, and most of the publishing ventures were money-losing propositions from the start. Within a few years, the secret Scott–Ballantyne partnership had fallen dangerously into debt. During the economic recession of 1812–13, the firm was swept up in the credit crisis that was uprooting marginal enterprises of every kind. Only Scott's heroic efforts (and valuable copyrights) prevented his speculative activities from being publicized amid a tide of red ink.[46]

It was in this economic context that Scott made his decision to begin writing novels. The sales on his most recent poems, *Rokeby* and *Bridal of Triermain*, had shown signs of weakness. The consumer market was saturated. Byron had emerged as the latest hot poet, and Scott was desperately short of cash. By shifting his product line from poetry to prose fiction, he could still protect the brand name by publishing anonymously. As he sent his manuscript, *Waverley*, off to the printer, Scott anxiously awaited the market's verdict on this latest literary and

[45] Lockhart, *Life of Scott*, I: 189–236; JWS, I: 359–439; Sutherland, *Scott: A Critical Biography*, 154–74.

[46] Lockhart, *Life of Scott*, I: 189–215, 226–33; JWS, I: 359–453. Lockhart, *Life of Scott*, I: 150–317, II: 319–498; JWS, I: 389–453; Sutherland, *Scott: A Critical Biography*, 109–53; A. S. Collins, *The Profession of Letters: A Study of the Relation of Authors to Patrons, Publishers, and Public, 1780–1832* (London, 1928), 128–35, 155–60.

entrepreneurial move. Within a few months, it became clear that this risky gambit had paid off. During the first year, the book went through five editions and 6,000 copies. Over the next twenty years, 40,000 sets of the three-decker novel would be sold. The firm was saved, the family castle was secured, and a new literary genre, the historical novel, was created.[47]

4   The Waverley romances of Anglo-Scottish Union

In retrospect, of course, this all made perfect sense. Imperial Britain had undergone a fiery trial, and the meaning of "Union" had to be rethought. In his perusal of Maria Edgeworth's and Sydney Owenson's fiction, Scott saw the opportunity to accomplish what they could not – to project social and national conflict backward onto the retrospect of history, and thus to depict the British Union as a successfully finished fact. Stripped to its essentials, the new formula was simple enough: traditionalism need not be feared as a reactionary impediment to progress if it could be turned into a species of sentimental nostalgia. The tattered remnant of ancient feudalism might be defanged and made safe for industrial capitalism if it could be transformed from an outmoded social system into an arena of entertainment. Scottish nationality could be saved and updated if it could be refigured in the form of romance and recreation for a protean, expanding imperial polity.[48]

In a sense, all the difficult educative work which Edgeworth had assigned to the Anglo-Irish landlord (with such disappointing results), Scott now found already accomplished by the happy accidents of Anglo-Scottish history. Here, the extremes of revolution and reaction had already been avoided. The centrist path was available to those who embraced this history. Scott's genius lay in his understanding of the ways in which Scotland's rapid but uneven socio-economic development facilitated political unification and cultural reconciliation in a British frame. Having studied under Adam Ferguson and Dugald Stewart at Edinburgh University, he was well aware of their four-stage sequence from savagery, through barbarism, and agriculture, to commerce. However, the fiction-writer could romanticize, rather than problematize, the transitions between these stages so long as his artful recitation of the

---

[47] John Feather, *A History of British Publishing* (London, 1988), 1–584; Lockhart, *Life of Scott*, I: 243.

[48] Among modern critical studies of *Waverley*, two in particular impinge on the themes of this book: Duncan, *Modern Romance*, 52–105, and Saree Makdisi, *Romantic Imperialism: Universal Empire and the Culture of Modernity* (Cambridge, 1998), 70–99.

progress narrative was kept in a romantically adventureful mode. The swift integration of the (agricultural) Lowlands into Britain's national and imperial (commercial) economy is implicitly framed by the artistry of Scott, so that the Highlands appear as an isolated region of residual (but romantic) barbarism, which has now to be violently (albeit romantically) absorbed into the British modernizing machine. As a result of this uneven development, Scotland is shown to have experienced in a single generation a modernizing process that, in England, had been spread out over 250 years.[49] In Edgeworth's Ireland, such rapid change would have required the mandate of the landlord. In Scotland it seemed to have occurred on its own historical steam, albeit only after the Act of Union in 1707. Scott's aim, in his novel of 1745, was to embody "in imaginary scenes and fictitious characters" an account of how this real-world historical process had played out at the human, experiential level. By selling this romance to a predominantly English readership, he encouraged his English readers to identify imaginatively with the backward regions that they were absorbing, while he reminded Scots of the benefits of integration into the British Empire.[50]

The main character, Captain Waverley, is essentially a touristic vehicle for bringing the English reader into the backward Scottish interior, where spatial movement simultaneously tracks a trajectory of evolutionary change. The first stop is Tully Veolan, the estate of Baron Bradwardine, a pedantic, Latin-quoting Jacobite who clings to the tattered remnant of his feudal authority in a ramshackle family castle.[51] From the Baron's window Waverley notices the foothills of the Scottish Highlands. Here, he is told, feudalism exists, not as a mere antiquarian affectation, but as an all-too-palpable living reality. In this wilderness, where ancient clans pursue blood feuds and tribal vendettas, the military power of the ruling lairds is virtually unchecked. Their patriarchal authority over their tribes is subject only to the ancient customs that they have sworn to maintain. When he is invited up into the mountains, Waverley's childhood romances are spectacularly realized. Through a succession of brilliantly executed *tableaux* of ever more remote and exotic scenery, the reader is vicariously conducted into this Highlands "Heart of Darkness." For a heart-stopping chapter, he or she is left at the mercy of a desperate pack of social bandits before being rescued by the clan chieftain, Fergus MacIvor, who rules

---

[49] Adam Ferguson, *An Essay on the History of Civil Society* (Cambridge, 1995); Philip Shaw, *Waterloo and the Romantic Imagination* (New York, 2002), 35–66; SW, 492–4.
[50] SW, 493.   [51] SW, 63, 74–130.

despotically but paternalistically over his warriors and tenants, much as his ancestors have done for centuries.[52]

When the Young Pretender actually appears in the Scottish Highlands and mobilizes the lairds and Lowland barons to take up arms, Waverley responds with habitual indecision. His wavering enables the reader to continue the voyage, albeit at a more comfortable emotional distance from the now increasingly dangerous events. Inadvertently, Waverley ends up joining the rebels in their quixotic crusade. Hopes run high in the immediate aftermath of the Jacobite victory at Prestonpans. But as these romantic champions penetrate deeper into the hostile English countryside, their delusory fantasies begin to fade. Suddenly reawakened to the realization that he does not really belong with these dreamers, Waverley seeks a way back from political miscalculation to touristic adventuring. Separated from the Jacobite battalion as accidentally as he joined it, this temporary borderer returns to his own side and is assisted in obtaining a royal pardon for his treason by a family friend who holds a high army post.[53]

After the Jacobites have been utterly crushed, British law metes out its stern justice, tempered where possible by merciful humanity. The Lowland Baron is reprieved and even gets his estate back, albeit under modern private-property terms. Fergus, the practical feudalist, by contrast, is too dangerous to be released.[54] After his execution, the clans will finally break up. The surviving lairds will metamorphose into wool-growing (and tenant-expropriating) landowners, and the Highlands will be integrated into the British state as a tourist attraction. Back in England, Waverley will marry the Baron's daughter and combine her father's former fiefdom with his own family estates. He will become a great agrarian capitalist landlord, living happily ever after with his domesticated wife.[55] The ages of feudalism and tribalism are now gone forever, and we are all better off now that their poverty, their ignorance, and their violence can no longer tyrannize our lives. Yet feudalism and tribalism can survive in imagination, without any sacrifice of modern conveniences. Inasmuch as we can preserve the romantic vision of ancient exploits and atavistic loyalties by embodying them in stories like Scott's *Waverley*, we will momentarily bring these images of chivalry back to life. Safely, through

---

[52] SW, 123–228, quote on 129. Here, in particular, Scott's work shows the influence of Jane Porter, *The Scottish Chiefs* [1809] (New York, 1956).

[53] SW, 225–457. For an interesting analysis of the "feminization" of the passive hero, Waverley, see Duncan, "The Romance of Subjection: Scott's *Waverley*," in *Modern Romance*, 62–79.

[54] SW, 457–91.

[55] T. M. Devine, *Clanship to Crofter's War: The Social Transformation of the Scottish Highlands* (Manchester, 1994), 19–76.

commodified entertainment, we may again inhabit the bygone world in which the heroes once lived and died.

To understand the enormous impact of *Waverley*, we must recall that it was written in 1814, amid the final collapse of Napoleon's empire. It hit the bookstands about a month after the Bourbon restoration and rose to bestsellerdom against the dramatic backdrop of Waterloo. The wartime uncertainties within which Scott's early poetic epics had been published seemed to permit only a provisional celebration of attenuated British unity. But now the three nations appeared fully united in the patriotic glow of unconditional victory. Under these circumstances, Scott could openly celebrate the final creation of Britain: the British triumph of 1745 could now be portrayed as decisive because it was refracted in the even more definitive victories of 1815.[56] Yet, as Linda Colley has pointed out, this triumph brought hubristic risks. In a sense, the successful consummation of Britain only meant that the stakes of Britishness had been raised. Having solved the problems of internal integration, Britain was now ready for the global, imperial future that lay ahead. Meanwhile hitherto disenfranchised groups – workers, women, soldiers, colonials – had been mobilized in the war effort. Now they would expect repayment.[57]

The fact that peace was quickly followed by deflation, depression, and unemployment induced Scott to acknowledge the historical limits of his romance. The happy ending he had just provided for the crisis of 1745 disposed of one challenge to the progress narrative, but others were appearing on the horizon. So in 1815, he quickly wrote another novel, *Guy Mannering*, in which the contradictions of Union were approached in a different way. When the novel opens, in 1764, the Scotland of the post-Waverley generation remains still backward and impoverished. The ancient Bertram dynasty has survived into the modern era, but it has done so Rackrent-style, by squeezing peasants and undermining the very paternalism from which its ever-diminishing legitimacy is drawn. The outcome is a still backward, dysfunctional society in which Edgeworth's improving agenda is little to be found. Ignored, exploited, or summarily evicted, the villagers have been driven to ally with marauding criminals and to interbreed with itinerant gypsies. As a result, they exhibit dangerous symptoms of regression to a rootless barbarian state. As the novel proceeds, the Bertram heir is kidnapped, disinherited, and sent off to India, where he lays the foundation for winning his property back. Yet this does not occur

---

[56] Edwin Emerson, *A History of the Nineteenth Century, Year by Year*, 3 vols. (New York, 1902), I: 507–605.

[57] Linda Colley, *Britons: Forging the Nation, 1707–1837* (New Haven, 1992), 321–75.

through a proper Edgeworthian education in modernization, but through the literary conceits of an adventure-filled plot. Bertram and his English commander Mannering must learn to complement one another in a voluntary alliance. Warily, these borderers face off, back and forth across the Anglo-Scottish frontier. Eventually, pride and prejudice give way to mutual respect and understanding. When Bertram marries Mannering's heiress-daughter, England and Scotland are symbolically wed and backwardness evaporates.[58]

Aware of an oversimplistic resolution, Scott continued to worry over the questions of progress and union in *The Antiquary*, which advances the story into the 1790s. The Wardour dynasty is now presented as another family on the path of irreversible decline. But what will take their place in a revolutionary era? The traditional community has been broken up, and its bard, Edie Ochiltree, is reduced to the status of beggar. His delphic buffoonery suggests that the key to the future lies in the proper reading of a buried history. Jonathan Oldbuck, the Whig antiquarian, promises to find an answer, yet his old books offer but fragmentary glimpses into the past.[59] Without some sense of how to eliminate reaction from the right and radicalism from the left, cross-bordering serves no constructive purpose. Scotland, it seems, is not inherently exempt from the Irish specter of dysfunction. Modern union requires a vital center, which must itself be the product of a constructive history. Over the next three years, Scott used his fiction to conduct a sustained historical interrogation of exactly how this manly progressive center was forged.

In *Old Mortality* (1816), Scott goes back to the late seventeenth century, when this vital center was plainly absent. The novel opens in 1679, when Scotland is essentially a conquered colony, wracked internally with sectarian strife. On the right stands Claverhouse, the imperial proconsul sent up from London, whose ruthless troops trample property, search houses, arrest suspects, and terrorize the population on which they feed. From the left they are confronted by the fanatical Covenanters, whose radical ideology of spiritual freedom belies a program of worldly tyranny-from-below.[60] Between the extremes of these left and right fanaticisms, the Scottish nation stands – embodied in the hero, Henry Morton. Unlike the passive Waverley, Morton is presented as an active figure: a small laird who yearns for the peace and quiet of his farm, but who understands that, in the context of backward, seventeenth-century Scotland, no British vital center can yet be

---

[58] Walter Scott, *Guy Mannering* [1815] (London, 2003).
[59] Walter Scott, *The Antiquary* [1816] (London, 1998).
[60] Walter Scott, *Old Mortality* [1816] (London, 1999), 1–118.

achieved. Whether under the Puritan radicals, the Stuart reactionaries, or even the Williamite constitutional monarchists, Scotland is condemned to an essentially colonial relation to the English center until it can forge a civil society in its own terms. Scott's unsatisfactory ending, which simply brings Morton back as *aide de camp* to the new Whig monarch, again signals his failure to find an indigenous centrist path that had not yet been created in the Scotland of the late seventeenth century.[61]

In his next novel, *Rob Roy*, however, Scott had a breakthrough when he began to see how this centrist path had been blazed by the advent of a new kind of cross-border enterprise. The date is advanced to 1715; the Hanoverians have assumed the throne, and the Jacobites are plotting to overthrow the new regime. The Revolutionary Settlement and Anglo-Scottish Union – so recently secured – are both to be put to their first serious test.[62] Where *Old Mortality* explored the role of religion, ideology, and political oppression in impeding the British fusion, *Rob Roy* explores the role of capitalism, commerce, and communication in opening it up. Frank Osbaldistone, the son of a rich London merchant, is banished to the antiquated border estate of his rude country cousins as punishment for wasting his time with second-rate poetry when he was supposed to be working as an apprentice in his father's firm. By the end of the novel, Frank is cured of this infatuation by the realization that the modern romance *is* the romance of capitalism. He has (at least metaphorically) brought Scotland into the modern era, by demonstrating that the modern hero (and perhaps even the modern poet) has become a daring, audacious entrepreneur.[63]

The adventures that Frank undergoes to achieve this realization involve removing the reactionary forces on both sides of the border, which have impeded the coalescence of the two nations into a single commercial society. In Northumberland, he encounters the degenerate, pre-capitalist branch of his own family, sunk in ignorance, drunkenness, Roman Catholicism, and rural idiocy. Only his youngest cousin, Rashleigh, shows signs of intelligence – an intelligence that turns him into the evil genius of the plot. Usurping Frank's place in the London counting house, Rashleigh absconds with the firm's assets, decamping to Scotland, where he first assists and then betrays the Jacobite cause. To save his father's commercial honor, and to recoup the family business, Frank is forced to venture up north. In Scotland, he must recover the purloined promissory

---

[61] Scott, *Old Mortality*, 119–352. For the controversy over Scott's portrayal of the Covenanters, see Ferris, *Literary Authority*, 130–99.
[62] Millgate, *Walter Scott*, 107–51.   [63] SRR, *passim*.

notes that are owed to his father. He has only ten days remaining before his father's otherwise unpayable debts become due.[64]

Time is short, and travel is hard. The difficulties of communication (physical and cultural, as well as linguistic) between England and Scotland, and between the Highlands and the Lowlands, work to compound the hazards that bedevil the intrepid Frank. They also explain why the economic integration of these distant regions remains so precarious and incomplete.

The Union had, indeed, opened to Scotland the trade of the English colonies; but betwixt want of capital, and the national jealousy of the English, the merchants of Scotland were as yet excluded, in great measure, from the exercise of the privileges which that memorable treaty conferred on them. Glasgow lay on the wrong side of the Island for participating in the east country or continental trade, by which the trifling commerce as yet possessed by Scotland chiefly supported itself.[65]

This check to the expansion of the Clydeside economy of the western Lowlands was inextricably connected to the social crisis of overpopulation, pauperization, and underdevelopment, which was swiftly engulfing the Highlands and the northern isles. The romantic outlaws, so picturesquely delineated in *Waverley*, are now acknowledged as an economically marginalized population of 230,000 which can no longer support itself from infertile soil and inaccessible land. With nowhere to go, and with no viable commercial economy to absorb them, these rude Highlanders are compelled to live by their wits, by their arms, and by their martial traditions. Somehow they get by through a makeshift mixture of smuggling, blackmailing, and stealing from their Lowland neighbors, garnished with desperate plots and conspiracies against the fledgling Hanoverian state.[66] The only cure for these grim crises of social disorder and subsistence are new forms of employment and economic development, which will facilitate the transfer of this superfluous population to the Lowland south. The new paladins of this enterprise are the merchant and the capitalist, who must initiate the requisite investments, open up potential markets, and connect the primitive framework of Scottish trade and commerce with the larger British, European, and transatlantic economies. Two bold and resolute impresarios of the marketplace appear – Bailie Jarvie and his distant Highland kinsman Rob Roy MacGregor.

The merchant Jarvie's role is straightforward. By breaking into the West Indian sugar and North American tobacco trades, this Glaswegian

---

[64] SRR, 196–287.   [65] SRR, quote on 224.
[66] SRR, 266–329, especially 305; T. M. Devine, *The Scottish Nation* (New York, 1999), 170–245.

prefigures his city's glorious future as a great imperial center of commerce and industry.[67] More sensational is the role of economic mediator and political unifier that Scott assigns to Rob Roy, the outlaw Highland chief. Rob professes utter contempt for ignoble commerce, but he is a former cattle trader himself. Even more than Fergus, he is no feudal champion, but a perfect pragmatist. He is a go-between, a fixer, and a communicator in several languages. These skills enable him to mediate between people from vastly different social and ethnic backgrounds and to pass nimbly and noiselessly across multiple frontiers. Because he bears the taint of the dispossessed Highlander, Rob Roy can never himself be unambiguously enrolled in the British project. Condemned to remain outside the Anglo-Scotland that he (with Jarvie and Morton) has helped to create, he succeeds at last in evading the hangman, dying in his own bed at a ripe old age.[68]

Scott's *Rob Roy* was a major intellectual accomplishment inasmuch as it identified capitalist economic integration as the chief catalyst for centrist Unionism. At the same time, he also made it clear that the social consequences of capitalism were not entirely benevolent, and might even generate a new extremism of intra-national class conflict. In his next novel, *The Heart of Mid-Lothian* (1818), Scott conducted a full audit of costs and benefits in the progress narrative to produce his most sophisticated rendering of Unionist project.[69] The book begins in 1736, with the Hanoverian regime only precariously entrenched in Edinburgh and the bi-national relationship still fundamentally unequal and incomplete. Proud Scots (like proud Irish a century later) deeply distrust the royal agents who rule from Edinburgh Castle. They still resent the insolence of the British soldiery. The Jacobites, habitually disloyal, are still dreaming of a return to the old dynasty, while the radical Presbyterians are disillusioned by what they regard as a betrayal of the Whig revolution. To the lower classes, still economically depressed and impoverished, the magic of capitalism has not yet performed its meliorative, integrative work. Indeed, the old complaints about disenfranchisement and dispossession have now been joined by a new resentment of the increasingly long fiscal arm of the burgeoning British state. For many Scots, "liberty" is not so much a high-flown constitutional principle as Rob Roy's underground tradition of smuggling, tax evasion, and social banditry.[70]

---

[67] SRR, 298–304, 315–19.   [68] SRR, 266–318, 500–1.

[69] David Daiches, "Introduction," in Walter Scott, *The Heart of Mid-Lothian* (New York, 1948).

[70] SHML, 7–84.

The story is built around the experiences of a peasant family, the Deans. The father, David, is an old Covenanter, who looks back to the glory days of true religion but cannot adjust to the realities of an increasingly secularized, market world.[71] Lacking proper parental guidance, his daughter Effie joins the wrong crowd, becomes pregnant, and loses her child under mysterious circumstances of which she can give no satisfactory account. Only her elder sister, Jeanie, has the resources to deal with her family's tragedy. Somehow, she must cobble together a pragmatic and provisional strategy that will enable her to confront her hard choices without abandoning the moral values in which she has been schooled. Is it right to lie in order to save the life of her wrongly condemned sister? What recourse does someone in her position have against the operation of an unjust law?[72]

By insisting on right and truth in the matter of her sister, Jeanie expands moral space for the novel as a whole. She will not mock the law by lying to save Effie from its own injustice. Instead, she will make a pilgrimage to London, and appeal to the British King and Queen. By thus appealing to a higher "British" justice, she will offer the new state an opportunity to reveal its elevation as a locus in which the legitimate grievances of the Scottish nation can be redressed. By making his main character a woman in this novel, Scott sidesteps the awkward realization that the centrist path may not yet be fully traversible in masculine terms. At all events, Jeanie is Scott's truest borderer – the only one who ventures far enough south to experience English society fully, and thus to discern the full meaning of union (beyond politics or economics) on a moral plane.[73] As she penetrates southward from the heart of Midlothian to the heart of England, Jeanie's horizons are correspondingly enlarged. She learns to appreciate the English landscape, English villages, and English agriculture. She finds the language barrier less disabling than she had anticipated, and the people to be less alien and inhospitable than she had feared. Two-thirds of the way down to

---

[71] SHML, 75–97, 360–75. See also Brown, *Walter Scott*, 118–20.

[72] SHML, 98–162, 182–233, quote on 105. The sharply realistic Jeanie Deans forms a striking contrast to the two cartoonishly Amazonian heroines of *Rob Roy*, Die Vernon and Helen MacGregor, created a year earlier. For an analysis of *Heart of Mid-Lothian* as a series of legal and moral cases, see James Chandler, *England in 1819: The Politics of Literary Culture and the Case of Romantic Historicism* (Chicago, 1998), 309–21.

[73] SHML, 224–60, especially 249. She borrows money for the trip, makes arrangements for her lodgings, gets smugglers to write her a pass for protection against robbers, and uses an old family claim on the cause and clan of Campbell as a means of enlisting the intercession of the Duke of Argyle in helping her to gain an audience with the Queen. SHML, 253–90, 360–94.

London, she undergoes a dreadful ordeal that ends in a moment of revelation when she learns both the identity of her sister's seducer and the motives which led him to his desperate acts. He is the son of an Anglican clergyman, the inverse image of her own Presbyterian father. Both men are good, upstanding, and well-meaning Christians, but their one-sided and narrowly formulated national religions have left their children in moral jeopardy.[74]

As her mission to England reveals this other side of the British equation, Jeanie comes to recognize that her private tragedy has a public, political face. In the errors and *mésalliance* of two star-crossed lovers, she finds an analogue for the ruptures and misunderstandings of the two connected nations from which they came. The Anglo-Scottish Union must be completed on a psychological level, by acts of mutual recognition which will enable each side to imagine itself in the situation of the other. Jeanie knows that she comes from a poorer, less sophisticated country, and that the English have much to offer the Scots. But they cannot be allowed to dictate terms, or to abuse their power advantage. If Jeanie codes Scotland as the feminine partner in this union, then it is a partnership she will enter only on terms of equality.[75]

In the final portion of *The Heart of Mid-Lothian* – often dismissed as anti-climactic filler – Scott conducts an audacious thought experiment, exploring, in several different directions, exactly how the parable of Anglo-Scottish integration might be brought to a satisfactory close. Two separate and partly incompatible scenarios are considered, only to be melded together at the end. The first of these scenarios focuses on the future of Jeanie. After her return to Scotland, she is rewarded with the patronage of the Duke of Argyle, which enables her to marry her childhood sweetheart, to set him up as a (new model) Presbyterian minister, and to relocate her entire family (minus Effie) to the Isle of Roseneath, where the Duke has established a model farm. These Argyle model farms are a portent of Scotland's brighter British future and of the role of the enlightened chieftain (now a Whig aristocrat) in weaning his Highland tenants from their obsolete, dysfunctional ways. They must be brought down to Clydeside and integrated into the new market capitalism. Yet on Roseneath, the Highlanders split into two opposing camps: those under Duncan Knockdunder acquiesce in the Hanoverian supremacy and find their niche as frontier policemen for the British state. Duncan, however, has an outlaw double, the Gaelic fugitive Donacha dhu Dunaigh, who has retreated into the forests, where he

[74] SHML, 253–359.   [75] SHML, 349, 360–404.

gathers a motley crew of dispossessed peasants who eke by through robbery, smuggling, and extortion.[76]

Lest the reader simply dismiss these desperadoes as vestigal nuisances, Scott offers another, less auspicious scenario, which follows the fortunes of Effie. Instead of joining her family after her release from prison, she leaves Scotland to elope with her seducer, George Staunton, who stands to inherit a large English estate. Enormously wealthy, completely anglicized, and successfully evading her guilty past, Effie seems to have left behind all the traumas of Scotland until she returns as a tourist fifteen years later. Enthralled by the sublimity of a remote Highland vista and distracted by the grandeur of a magnificent waterfall, she loses her footing and is pulled toward the torrent down a rocky ravine. As she screams and looks upward, her stare is met by the black, begrimed face of an outlaw adolescent. He is one of Scotland's castaways, a follower of the chieftain of the banditti, Donacha. As we find out a few pages later (but she does not), he is her own long-lost illegitimate son.[77]

Here is the toughest challenge facing the Anglo-Scottish Union. Can the dispossessed child of Scotland's repudiated past, transformed by neglect into a dangerous savage, be reclaimed, even by his own upstart, anglicized mother, who cannot recognize him, speak his language, or even know his name? Scott remains committed to his romance of British reconciliation and integration, but he is enough of a realist to suspect that this reunion may not work. The savage boy retreats back into the thickets, only to re-emerge a few days later, when he (unwittingly) kills his father in a robbery attempt. Kidnapped and sold into slavery by his banditti brethren, he is shipped off to a Virginia plantation across the sea. There he runs away to join a band of wild Indians with whom, it is presumed, he spends the remainder of his days.[78]

By toying with these subversive counter-plots of British dis-union, Scott clouded this complex tale with sobering shadows. Yet it would be wrong to read *The Heart of Mid-Lothian* as a dirge for the failure of the British project. If Effie's abandoned boy is unable to join it, Jeanie's respectable, ambitious, and upwardly mobile children are happily enlisted in the final, overriding conclusion of the book. With the aid of their aristocratic aunt's patronage and money, they enter the professions, one joining the army and the other practicing law. True, they must give up their mother's

---

[76] SHML, 405–59, 484–9, 524–9. On the role of the Dukes of Argyle in the British integration of Scotland into eighteenth-century Britain, see Eric Cregeen, "The Changing Role of the House of Argyll in the Scottish Highlands," in N. T. Phillipson and Rosalind Mitchison (eds.), *Scotland in the Age of Improvement* (Edinburgh, 1970), 24–46.

[77] SHML, 496–523, especially 502–6.   [78] SHML, 524–30.

peasant legacy of plainspoken self-possession. But perhaps they might be recalled by books like *Waverley* to the romantic national heritage of the old Scottish world that they have lost.[79]

5   The reception of Scott's British Unionist romance

While *The Heart of Mid-Lothian* remained Walter Scott's most sophisti-cated exploration of Britishness, the problem of union continued to absorb his energies for the rest of his life. We can see this preoccupation in his post-*Waverley* series of novels on the unions involved in the making of Englishness, *Ivanhoe* (1819), *The Abbot* (1820), and *Kenilworth* (1821). It reappears in his late Scottish novels, as well as in his stage management of George IV's visit to Scotland, the first of any Hanoverian monarch. Most of all, we can see it in his *History of Napoleon* – a direct engagement with the French other of his own era, written at lightning speed to repay his creditors amid the commercial crisis of 1826. It was at this moment of personal danger, when Sir Walter met his own Waterloo and his sense of masculinity was impugned, that his most poignant brief for centrist patriotism was issued, together with his most testy warning that the English must not abuse the allegiance of their less wealthy north-ern neighbors. In his child's *History of Scotland* and in his *Malachi Malagrowther* letters, he finally insisted that the price of enduring political Union was some provision for the junior partner to retain the cultural trappings of her separate historical and national identity.[80]

Of course, we cannot assume that Scott's readers were equally preoc-cupied with these questions of union and bi-nationality. Nevertheless, reviews and surviving reader reactions were nearly universal in praising of his depiction of Scottish characters and his success in presenting Scotland to an English audience. Long after the volumes had been set aside, Jeanie Deans, Edie Ochiltree, Rob Roy, Fergus MacIvor, and Meg Merrilies remained alive in the minds of readers. Scarcely less memorable were the more homely personalities, whom readers could identify as distinctively "Scotch" – Rose Bradwardine, Bailie Jarvie, Jonathan Oldbuck, Godfrey Bertram, Henry Morton, and many more. "His portrait of the higher [Scottish] orders is the production of a master's hand," wrote an anony-mous commentator in the *Monthly Review*. "Yet it is inferior to the picture which he has sketched of the honest and humble industrious peasantry of

---

[79] SHML, 531–2.

[80] These matters will be treated in my article "Walter Scott and the Creation of Britishness" (in progress).

his native land; a picture which, though invariably favourable to their moral and civil excellence, bears about it no marks of exaggeration, and evinces no blindness to their faults and imperfections." Even Scott's extensive use of dialect, which made his stories sometimes difficult to follow, was a deliberate device to make the English reader pause. Confronted with the challenge of decryption, he or she was obliged to see the world momentarily through Scottish eyes. If Union required Scots to adapt to English progressive centrism, it also induced English readers to toy with fantasies of roguish Scottish extremists, now that they were safely buried underground.[81]

An astute reader like Henry Crabb Robinson grasped the way this experiment in cross-cultural transference worked. Although "the writer in his own person argues in favour of the Hanoverians," he presents "all the elements of national insurrections ... in a light which prevents all aversion. One almost wishes them success." Another reader who responded in this manner was George IV. As Prince Regent he became an instant fan of *Waverley* and its successor volumes, repeatedly wining and dining Scott, whom he believed to be their author, both before and after his ascent to the throne. Strangely attracted to the romance of the rebels who had tried to overthrow his great-grandfather, George was persuaded by Scott to appear on the streets of Edinburgh dressed in the formerly proscribed (and now ill-fitting) costume of a Highland chief.[82]

For most readers, however, it was unnecessary to reflect on an authorial strategy that remained all the more effective for being merely implied. Indeed, the touristic quality of all Scott's novels meant that the reader could subliminally register a good deal of their message simply by going along for the ride. As E. T. Channing put it in 1818, Scott "conducts us from time to time, as events may require, from one apartment to another ... We feel the changes of season, of day and night in their effect upon the prospect ... we carry from descriptions like this, feelings that spring from beholding the world, rather than reading of it." Scott himself was thoroughly conscious of the way he conducted his readers from class to class and from place to place. As he playfully noted in an anonymous review of his own books, "his chief characters are never actors, but acted upon"; this device enabled the author to draw "in the reader through the medium of the hero." In this way, the author could avoid "going into explanations and details which [if] addressed directly to the reader might appear tiresome and unnecessary," but which the reader would painlessly

[81] *Monthly Review*, 2nd ser., 87 (December 1818), 356–70.
[82] Edith J. Morley (ed.), *Henry Crabb Robinson on Books and their Writers* (London, 1938), I: 277.

and spontaneously assimilate "by exhibiting the effect they produce upon the principal person of his drama."[83]

By thus sending his heroes (and by extension, his readers) on bordering adventures that allegorized the vicissitudes of the Anglo-Scottish Union, Scott helped to channel patriotic feelings of Britishness that his audience had already instantiated in response to the events of their day. As the reader made his or her way through the Waverley series, he or she could follow the author's own voyage of intellectual discovery. The celebratory enthusiasm of the inaugural novel gave way to the probing explorations of its more sophisticated successors, which explored the roles of capitalism, culture, compromise, and reconfigured masculinity in forging the deeper channels of political centrism that were necessary for political Union to endure. Vicariously vanquishing retrograde extremes on both sides of the border, this centrist politics would render the old radicalism and repression obsolete, even as it endowed them with an appealing patina of romance. As the stakes of Britishness were ever more imperialistically raised, readers were reassured that they could manage their impending *Pax Britannica*, so long as their political center remained intact.

Indeed, for many of his most serious reviewers, Scott's valorization of the political center constituted his most important contribution. The note was first struck in the Whig *Edinburgh Review* by Francis Jeffrey, who gave all the Waverley novels respectful attention and praised the Tory Scott (as presumptive author) for the capaciousness of his narrative sympathies.[84] William Hazlitt, the radical, detested Scott's Toryism, yet he attested that "the candour of Sir Walter's historic pen levels our bristling prejudices on this score, and sees fair play between Roundheads and Cavaliers, between Protestant and Papist. He is a writer reconciling all the diversities of human nature to the reader. He does not enter into the distinctions of hostile sects or parties, but treats of the strength or infirmity of the human mind."[85]

According to another anonymous reviewer, Scott's personal prejudices did not "weaken his appreciation of the beauty . . . and self-consistency of his adversary's view." It was this even-handedness, S. T. Coleridge

---

[83] Anonymous review (attributed to Walter Scott) in *Quarterly Review* (April, 1817), reprinted in John O. Hayden (ed.), *Scott: The Critical Heritage* (New York, 1970), 113–43, quote on 115; E. T. Channing, review in *North American Review*, 1818, also reprinted in Hayden (ed.), *Critical Heritage*, 148–64, quote on 151.

[84] Francis Jeffrey, *Contributions to the Edinburgh Review*, 3 vols. (London, 1846), III: 32–102; P. H. Scott, "The Politics of Walter Scott," in J. H. Alexander and David Hewitt (eds.), *Scott and his Influence: The Papers of the Aberdeen Scott Conference, 1982* (Aberdeen, 1983), 208–17.

[85] William Hazlitt, "Scott and the Spirit of the Age," in Hayden (ed.), *Critical Heritage*, 279–89, quote on 286–7.

observed, that enabled Scott to adopt the historian's stance of impartial arbiter, summoning back to life all the forces of historical transformation. These novels embodied nothing less than "the contest between two great moving principles of social humanity: religious adherence to the past and the ancient, the desire and the admiration of permanence, on the one hand, and the passion for increase of knowledge, for truth ... in short, the mighty instincts of *progression* and *free agency*, on the other." As Harriet Martineau noted, this dispassionate assumption of the standpoint of Clio had a paradoxical result, for it turned Scott, the romantic Tory, nostalgic for the past, into a new kind of modern liberal, ready to advance the progressive causes of his own day.

He has exposed priestcraft and fanaticism, he has effectively satirized eccentricities, unamiablenesses, and follies; he has irresistibly recommended benignity in the survey of life, and indicated the glory of a higher benevolence; and finally, he has advocated the rights of women with a force all the greater for his being unaware of the import and tendency of what he was saying.[86]

If Scott was unaware of the ways in which he was inadvertently advancing the rights of women, he was thoroughly conscious of having created a new kind of capacious, hegemonic, centrist liberalism, a progress narrative that could transcend divisions of religion, ideology, class, and nationality, and in which even a Tory like himself could feel at ease. By granting nostalgia to a defeated foe, a minority faith, or a conquered nation, it was possible to master the past and move on in a mutually acceptable manner. Both sides could then enter the brave new world of industrial capitalism and the modern multi-national (imperial) state without losing touch with those ghostly ancestral voices which intoned the virtues and the values of a nobler, bygone age.

Scott's "establishment of literary authority," as the critic Ina Ferris has termed it, was greatly amplified by the enduring popularity of his books. Each of the five novels that he published in the aftermath of *Waverley* sold between 6,000 and 15,000 copies within its first year. Moreover, since many of these volumes were purchased by lending libraries, it is safe to infer that Scott's initial readers numbered in the tens of thousands, with perhaps hundreds of thousands or more worldwide. Through translations, popular plays, versifications, and operas, the stories were transmitted to an even wider audience, albeit in diluted form. Moreover,

---

[86] S. T. Coleridge, letter to Thomas Allsop, 1820, and "A Question of History" (attributed to G. P. R. James in *Fraser's Magazine*, 1847), both reprinted in Hayden (ed.), *Critical Heritage*, 178–81 and 382–93 respectively, quotes on 180, 386 respectively. Harriet Martineau, "Scott as Moral Hero," *Tait's Edinburgh Magazine* (1833), reprinted in Hayden (ed.), *Critical Heritage*, 340–4, quote on 340.

throughout the nineteenth century, Scott's popularity only increased. From the 1830s onward, the aggressive marketing of the (now illustrated) uniform edition – sold by Robert Cadell for 5s per volume – placed tens of thousands of copies of Scott's writings into middle-class households throughout the United Kingdom alone. In 1838, a survey of cheap circulating libraries in London revealed that there were more volumes of Scott and his knockoffs (166) than were in the entire catalogue of voyages, travels, history, and biography combined. When the copyright finally expired, in the 1860s, individual novels could be (and were) sold for as little as 3d apiece. By making Scott accessible to new generations of readers, Victorian publishers insured that his powerful amalgam of romanticized nostalgia and pragmatic modernism would continue its allure. The number of Waverley or Kenilworth streets, railway stations, towns, and overtures still extant testifies to the enduring appeal of these books.[87]

6   Conclusion: from British to imperial Union

As this chapter has shown, the power of Scott's consensus rested on his talent for drawing all the multiple resonances of "union" – political, national, social, economic, religious, cultural, marital, familial, psychological, and symbolic – into a protean, imaginative gestalt. By reading Scott's novels, Englishmen could wear the tartan, while Scots could access Britishness. Liberals could enjoy the luxury of sentimental nostalgia, while Tories could acknowledge the advantages of capitalist prosperity. Women gained vicarious access to the arenas of public action, while men enjoyed romantic fiction without taint of effeminacy. Indeed Scott's unions were by no means necessarily limited to Britain's domestic shores. He himself was happy to leave Ireland to Maria Edgeworth but, like most Scots, was extremely conscious of the opportunities that loomed in the farther distance of the overseas Empire. Many of his closest relatives, including all four brothers and his brother-in law, and several of his closest college friends, entered various branches of military or imperial service, as eventually did both of his sons. In a moment of discouragement, at the age of twenty-six, when his literary ambitions were yet unfulfilled, Scott himself had considered emigrating to India or some other colony.[88] His

---

[87] Richard D. Altick, *The English Common Reader* (Chicago, 1957), 217; Alexander and Hewitt (eds.), *Scott and his Influence*, 507–12; William St. Clair, *The Reading Nation in the Romantic Period* (Cambridge, 2004), 632–44.

[88] Lockhart, *Life of Scott*, I: 8, 9, 77–8, 192–3, 271, II: 345, 544, 581, 623–5; JWS, I: 56, 148– 51.

literary triumphs forestalled the necessity of exile, and the Empire was relegated to the margins of his books. Thus in *Guy Mannering*, the dispossessed heir of a decayed Scottish family is banished to India for most of the novel before returning to re-establish his ancestral estate. Correspondingly, West Indian and Virginian plantations fuel Jarvie's fortune in *Rob Roy*, but no preoccupation with slavery disturbs his stolid equanimity. In *St. Ronan's Well* (1823), we are given a border spa, economically distorted and physically disfigured by the influx of retired Indian nabobs, with their hordes of lakhs and "copper faces." Finally, in *The Chronicles of Canongate* (1826), Scott actually set a novella in India itself. The result was inauspicious, for this story, "The Surgeon's Daughter," is one of his weakest creations, filled with conventional stereotypes, which were already becoming clichés.[89]

Given the powerful romantic effects that James Fenimore Cooper achieved by transporting the *Waverley* formula to the wilds of America, it may seem surprising that Scott himself made so few comparable efforts in this direction. Indeed, in contemplating the surgeon's daughter, he has one of his pseudonymous selves exclaim,

Send her to India to be sure, That is the true place for a Scot to thrive in; and if you carry your story fifty years back, as there is nothing to hinder you, you will find as much shooting and stabbing as ever was in the wild Highlands. If you want rogues ... you have that gallant caste of adventurers, who laid down their consciences at the Cape of Good Hope as they went out to India, and forgot to take them up again when they returned. Then, for great exploits, you have the old history of India, before Europeans were numerous there, the most wonderful deeds, done by the least possible means, that perhaps the annals of world can afford.[90]

If we take the tone of this passage to be ironic, Scott's reluctance to extend his bordering romance to the Empire makes a good deal of sense. Perhaps he knew better than to spin tales about places he had never visited, whose history and culture he only superficially understood. Yet the knowledge that all too many other Scotsmen had left behind their consciences when traveling to such venues probably generated a sense of unease. Without the Anglo-Scottish happy ending of consensual union,

[89] SRR, 224; Scott, *Guy Mannering*; Scott, *St. Ronan's Well* [1823] (London, 1911); Scott, "The Surgeon's Daughter," in *The Waverley Novels* (London, 1909), XXII: 591–854. This latter story has been recently examined by James Watt, "Scott, the Scottish Enlightenment and Romantic Orientalism," in Leith Davis, Ian Duncan, and Janet Sorenson (eds.), *Scotland and the Borders of Romanticism* (Cambridge, 2004), 94–112.

[90] Walter Scott, preface to "The Surgeon's Daughter," 616; James Fenimore Cooper, *The Leatherstocking Tales* (New York, 1985), I. For Scott's meetings with Cooper, see JWS, II: 871, 999, 1002–3, 1039.

such adventures were likely to leave a bitter aftertaste of conquest, theft, and brutality. In the absence of the final result of progressive centrism or cross-cultural reciprocity, there was nothing particularly edifying about such uninvited bordering. Of course, the Edgeworths had offered an alternative model of how a technologically advanced commercial nation might legitimately impose its will on a backward, barbarized people who needed to be educated in the ways of capitalist modernity. Their experience in Ireland, however, demonstrates that this imposition was not likely to be favorably received. By rejecting the offer of compulsory improvement, recalcitrant colonial others had the power to call the bluff on liberal imperialism. Their mere resistance could pierce the philanthropic patina, exposing missionaries and educators as little different from the rapacious exploiters they purported to replace.

This, then, is the relevance of the progress narratives treated in this chapter to the liberal imperialism, which is the subject of the remainder of this book: the romances of British Union, attempted by Edgeworth and Owenson, and more successfully crafted by Scott, represented an ideal type, to which later romances of Empire could aspire. In particular three elements of this ideal type will be relevant to the ensuing discussion. First, it was necessary to establish a plausible account of why Britain and any given colonial dependency truly belonged together. It had to be shown that they were bound by a common historical past and linked together in a future destiny. These two conditions were of course related, since the history of domination precipitated hopes for a more perfect, progressive future union. Correspondingly, the presumption of a shared future animated a search for historical commonalities. In the romances of Scott these connections were self-evident. The English and the Scots were situated together on a single island, and were increasingly seen as possessing a common religion, language, and ethnicity. Yet, as Scott's novels show (and Edgeworth's or Owenson's even more), these commonalities were neither automatic nor universal, as differences of speech, of race, of sectarian allegiance, or of historic oppression sometimes created barriers, which had to be surmounted before Union could be achieved. To this end, the romances of Britishness purveyed by our authors had constant recourse to the language of real or symbolic kinship – marriage, brotherhood, cousinship, wardship, or paternity – that could either explain how those divided by the past could be united in future, or how those who subsisted as long-lost relations could use historical narratives to rediscover their consanguinity.

Second, the novels we have examined all trace the complex relationship between the trajectory of capitalist development and the romances of political, or cultural, unity. Scott's great discovery – articulated in *Waverley* and its successors – was that the stages of "progress" proceed

unevenly in neo-colonial settings. What might appear as slow, spontaneous evolution in the metropolis precipitates rapid, hothouse growth on
the periphery. Indeed, the periphery itself is profoundly fractured
between those social groups and geographical regions that relatively
easily fall in with the progress narrative and those which resist, are
excluded, or bear its costs. It is the former who constitute the natural
partners for consensual trans-imperial union, while the latter remain
difficult zones of opposition and resistance which unionist projects
must try to overcome. Thus the romance of imperial union must be
articulated simultaneously in two quite different registers. The first
seeks to identify the forces of progression (both peripheral and metropolitan), which are fit for the political centrism of modern masculinity.
The second lingers reproachfully on the zones of exclusion, where centrism is closed off by retrogressive men – radicals, reactionaries, savages,
or effeminates – who remain dysfunctionally trapped on the political
extremes.

Finally, the romance of multi-national union insists that the progress
narrative can be consummated only when it leaves sufficient room for
cultural autonomy. In Scott's narratives this requirement is omnipresent, underwriting bordering of every kind at the Anglo-Scottish interface. Englishmen must learn to appreciate Scotland. Scotsmen, to
remain manly, must command English respect. Scotland's defeats are
redeemed by the romantic glow that they lend to British history.
England's victories are softened by the political inclusion of the vanquished, or at least of those who prove capable of modern masculinity.
Here was the core of Scott's residual nationalism: economic development and political fusion do not erase cultural difference. Consensual
union is sustainable only in an atmosphere of mutual esteem. For the
liberal imperial unionists who would extend the progress narrative to
more distant nations, and different climes, this would be the biggest
challenge. Did the Anglo-Scottish romance offer a model for farther-
flung histories that might legitimize more distant imperial connections?
Could the progress narrative be enlarged so as to induce Britons to give
respect to the peoples they had conquered, while reconciling those
conquered to the advantages of *Pax Britannica*? Walter Scott was
canny enough to avoid these questions. His compatriots and successors
who pressed outward into the Empire were obliged to confront the
challenges that he evaded.

2　Imagining a British India: history and the reconstruction of Empire

The writings and records of the antient inhabitants of Hindoostan, it is probable, encircle most of the branches of human knowledge. The current learning, however, of its present inhabitants is contracted within very narrow bounds, from the operation of many causes ... It is, therefore, only from a diligent research into books that we can expect to become acquainted with the science and learning of the nations of the East.

> W. B. Bayley, student essay presented at Fort William College, Calcutta, February 6, 1801, in *Primitae Orientales*, 2 vols. (Calcutta, 1802–3), I: 40–1

This writer, it will be said, has never been in India; and ... [has little] acquaintance, with any of the languages of the East. I confess the facts; and will now proceed to mention the considerations, which led me, notwithstanding, to conclude that I might still produce a work of considerable utility, on the subject of India. In the first place, it appeared to me, that a sufficient stock of information was now collected in the languages of Europe, to enable the inquirer to ascertain every important point, in the history of India.

> James Mill, *The History of British India*, 6 vols. [1818] (New York, 1968), I: xx–xxi

In the still more important qualities, which constitute what we call the moral character, the Hindu, as we have already seen, ranks very low; and the Mahomedean is little, if at all above him. The same insincerity, mendacity and perfidy ... are conspicuous in both ... As all our knowledge is built upon experience, the recordation of the past for guidance of the future is one of the effects in which the utility of the art of writing principally consists. Of this important branch of literature the Hindus were totally destitute.

> James Mill, *History of British India*, II: 366, 369

Englishmen are not always incapable of shaking off insular prejudices, and governing another country according to its wants, and not according to common English habits and notions. It is what they have had to do in India; and those Englishmen who know something of India, are even now those who understand Ireland best.

> John Stuart Mill, *England and Ireland* [1868], *Collected Works*, VI (Toronto, 1982), 519

56

In the summer of 1811, Walter Scott received a letter from one John Malcolm, a Scotsman who had lived in India since the age of thirteen. Malcolm, who was now returning home after an absence of thirty years, was clearly angling for an invitation to Abbotsford. He solicited Scott's attention with three carefully calculated appeals. In the first place, he was a fan of *The Lay of the Last Minstrel* and its successor volumes. Second, he was a fellow borderer who hailed from the country where those epics had been staged. Finally, Malcolm enclosed a eulogy that he had delivered in Bombay at the funeral of Dr. John Leyden, a mutual friend. When Malcolm visited Abbotsford, a few months later, the two men found that they had many common interests and connections. The conversation perhaps began with encomiums to Leyden and the relationships between Scottish and Indian traditions suggested in his work. Fortified by their own mutual interests in bordering, folklore, antiquarianism, and history, Scott and Malcolm emerged from this encounter as lifelong correspondents. The Indian officer felt honored to be noticed by the famous writer, who clearly recognized that he had much to learn about oriental subjects. A year later, Scott apprised his new friend of a nearby property that was about to come on the market. While Malcolm's "mouth watered" at the prospect of joining Scott as a border laird, he explained that he could not afford retirement at this stage in his career.[1]

In fact, something more than money was at stake. For Malcolm was determined to return to India, this time as a governor or a general, to complete the imperial mission that he had begun as a lowly ensign three decades before. In youth, he too had dabbled in poetry, but circumstances had forced him into a life of action. Denied the repose of a romance writer, he had become an actor in a real-life historical romance far more sweeping and exciting than any product of Scott's imagination. His bordering had been stretched from the Indus to the Ganges, as the frontiers of British Hindustan had expanded during his period of service. Because this actual work of making India British was more astonishing than the plot of any Waverley fiction, the role that history had to play was correspondingly larger and more complex. For Scotland and England were physically adjacent, seemingly fated by geography and providence to become conjoined. Such a Union might require continual management and re-negotiation, but it was not difficult to visualize or understand. Britain and India, by contrast, were half a

---

[1] John Malcolm to Walter Scott, April 4, 1811, Scottish National Library, Edinburgh, MS 3881, fos. 101–5; John Malcolm, obituary for John Leyden, cutting from *Bombay Courier*, Scottish National Library, MS 3881, fo. 101; *DNB*, XI: 1094–5.

world apart, not only in geography and climate, but in culture, religion, and ethnicity too. Any union constructed imaginatively, only through the plotlines of a novel, would likely be dismissed as implausible.[2] Somehow an historical truth would have to be found that would reveal a bi-national connection, which was not merely accidental, or grounded in the naked reality of conquest.

This need for deeper and more liberal legitimation of the imperial connection was reinforced by the erosion of the older bonds of mercantilism on which British India had originally been built. So long as conquest was seen as indispensable to the national interest it might require no elaborate justification. But once Smithian liberalism began to call this assumption into question, the famed East India Company (hereafter referred to as EIC) began to look like just another illegitimate mercantilist corporation whose machinations had to be exposed and whose privileges ought to be checked. The fact that Indian conditions were rapidly forcing this entity to metamorphose from a trading company into an instrument of government only reinforced this ideological unease. If the EIC was destined to become the new locus for Anglo-Indian sovereignty, then this strange development seemed to require some explanation. In an era dominated by liberal principles, how was such alien, authoritarian governance to be justified?[3]

As both Malcolm and Scott recognized, the answer had to lie somewhere in the distant mists of history, and this was where their mutual friend John Leyden came in. For he had bridged the gap between the border-expanding of Malcolm and the border romancing of Scott. In youth, he had collected border ballads with the latter while training as a physician at the University of Edinburgh. Offered an EIC medical post, he grasped at this opportunity to combine ancient eastern wisdom with the modern knowledge of the west. During the voyage out, he studied Hebrew, Arabic, and Persian. These were followed by Sanskrit, Hindustani, and Bengali after his arrival. Armed with these tools, Leyden was able to enter the lists of orientalist scholarship, joining an enterprise of linguistic translation, historical reconstruction, and imperial legitimation that was more consequential than any tale from the author of *Waverley*'s pen.[4]

---

[2] For example, Sydney Owenson, *The Missionary: An Indian Tale* [1811] (Toronto, 2002).
[3] For the transformation of the EIC from a trading company to a colonial state, see P. J. Marshall, *Problems of Empire: Britain and India, 1757–1813* (London, 1968), and Sudipta Sen, *Distant Sovereignty: National Imperialism and the Origins of British India* (New York, 2002). Philip Lawson, *The East India Company: A History* (London, 1993), 86–144.
[4] Percival Spear, *The Oxford History of Modern India, 1740–1975* (Oxford, 1978), 21–84; P. J. Marshall (ed.), *The British Discovery of Hinduism in the Eighteenth Century* (Cambridge, 1970), 1–44; *DNB*, XI: 1094–5.

In this chapter, we will investigate the role of history and orientalism in the making of British India. In the first section, we will consider some of the reasons why the search for a progress narrative in Anglo-India should, paradoxically, have taken its earliest seekers back to the remotest depths of antiquity. Then we will consider the ways in which the expanding early nineteenth-century Raj called forth a novel brand of orientalism, which combined the neo-classical, linguistic skills of Leyden with the active bordering that was valorized by Scott. In particular, we will focus on the experience of James Tod, John Malcolm, and Mountstuart Elphinstone, whose successful Indian bordering paradoxically diminished the need for further adventures and paved the way for the creation of a more bureaucratic, utilitarian colonial state. This utilitarian polity, however, was ushered in through the culturally defamatory *History* of James Mill (another Scot), which made it worse than useless to many Indians. The progress narrative, Mill and his followers insisted, could be sustained only in anglocentric form. We will conclude with a look at Rammohun Roy – utilitarian, romantic orientalist, historian – whose Anglo-Indian bordering among these incipient genres gave promise of a new kind of progress narrative: one grounded in a syncretic vision of union that anticipated the challenges of the future.

1   Orientalism, old and new

That history would play an important role in making India British was evident from the very start. From the moment (1765) when the EIC became the *diwani* (ruler and tax-collector) of Bengal, it was obvious that its officials would have to obtain some knowledge of the legal conventions, land tenures, and inheritance customs of that country. During the 1770s, the Governor-General, Warren Hastings, elevated this necessity into a virtue when he determined that India, like England, should be governed by her own traditions of common law. From the very beginning, therefore, the project of British rule in India was connected with the discovery of a serviceable version of Indian history.[5] Given the unedifying but inescapable record of recent British conquest, Hastings hoped that the resources of philology, archaeology, and ethnology could be deployed to excavate a deeper history. This, he hoped, would convince Britons that Indians were not worthless savages to be mercilessly exploited, but heirs to a great civilization. Knowledge of this glorious past would thus "lessen the weight of the chain by which

[5] Warren Hastings, "Letter to Nathaniel Smith," in Marshall (ed.), *British Discovery of Hinduism*, 185–91, quote on 189; see also 60–72.

the natives were held in subjection" and reconcile them to benevolent British rule. To this end, Hastings sponsored three oriental scholars, John Hollwell, Nathaniel Halhead, and Charles Wilkins, to master the Sanscrit language and to gain the trust of the Hindu pandits, who retained a residual (albeit allegedly corrupted) understanding of the culture and institutions embedded in the ancient texts. When Wilkins translated the *Baghavad Gita* in 1874, Hastings declared it to be superior to the better parts of *Iliad*, *Odyssey* and *Paradise Lost*. Halhead's compilation of the *Gentoo Code*, which was intended to help English judges in interpreting the law, was claimed by its editor to be older than the Code of Moses and equal to any of the codes of ancient Greece.[6]

By all accounts, however, the greatest of these orientalists was the High Court Justice Sir William Jones. For Jones, the foundation-stone for modern Anglo-Indian union lay in the history of language itself. To show that Hindus could boast a playwright with the genius of Shakespeare, he translated Kalidasa's *Sakuntala* from Sanskrit into English. Then, through careful etymological analysis, he synchronized Indian with European chronologies to put the comparative history of east and west on a solid empirical frame. Finally, and most portentously, Jones demonstrated that Sanskrit was part of the same linguistic family as Persian, Greek, Latin, Celtic, and the Germanic tongues. All these languages, he inferred, were descended from a common (but now extinct) "Aryan" or "Scythian" (today called "Indo-European") root. From this epoch-making philological discovery Jones inferred that the genealogy of myths, religions, and legal institutions, and entire cultures, could be traced. These implications, he thought, ought to transform the relations between Britons and Indians since – appearances notwithstanding – they were distant cousins. Descended from the same prehistoric ancestors, they were now being reunited by British imperialism in modern times.[7]

---

[6] John Hollwell, "The Religious Tenets of the Gentoos," Charles Wilkins, "Translator's Preface to Bhagvat-Geeta," and Nathaniel Brassey Halhead, "The Translator's Preface to 'A Code of Gentoo Laws,'" in Marshall (ed.), *British Discovery of Hinduism*, 62–4, 192–5, and 162–8, respectively; Bernard S. Cohn, *Colonialism and its Forms of Knowledge: The British in India* (Princeton, 1996). The role of late eighteenth-century historians such as Nathaniel Halhead, Alexander Dow, Robert Orme, Mark Wilks, and William Hollingbery in mediating British understandings of India is treated in Sen, *Distant Sovereignty*, especially 27–56.

[7] William Jones, "On the Gods of Greece, Italy, and India," in Marshall (ed.), *British Discovery of Hinduism*, 196–245; Garland Cannon, *The Life and Mind of Oriental Jones: Sir William Jones, the Father of Modern Linguistics* (Cambridge, 1990); and S. N. Mukherjee, *Sir William Jones: A Study in Eighteenth Century British Attitudes to India* (Cambridge, 1968). On linguistic theory, see Colin Kidd, *British Identities before Nationalism: Ethnicity*

In recent years, discussion of orientalism has been cast in the long shadow of Edward Said. Said himself focused on the ways in which European scholars turned middle-eastern Islam into an allegedly inferior "other," against which they could construct a superior "West" for themselves. There has been considerable debate among Indian historians as to the relevance of Said's approach.[8] Given the respect with which Jones and his early followers treated their Sanskrit texts, one might almost draw the opposite conclusion; that Jones's "Aryan hypothesis" was intended to foster a new fusion of identity and interest between Britain's and India's elites. In Britain, a classically educated elite of landowning gentlemen might be persuaded by the orientalists to extend the boundaries of their classicism to encompass the ripest fruits of that ancient Aryan civilization that paralleled (and perhaps preceded) the classical civilizations of the west. In Calcutta, EIC policymakers hoped to precipitate something like a reciprocal process: here, the best of the native Aryan, classically educated elites would be transformed into British-style landlords by the Permanent Settlement of 1793, which granted them full title to their zamindari estates. Here was a vision of union stranger than Scott's, though seemingly confirmed by the facts of history. In ancient times, when Britons had been naked savages, the warming rays of civilization had risen in the east. Now, in the modern *Pax Britannica*, her imperial, aristocratic rulers would return the favor, bringing modern civilization to the Indians, who had fallen behind.

If this argument is at all correct, then it was the *failure* of the Permanent Settlement, rather than some inherent Eurocentric bias, which sealed the fate of Anglo-Indian orientalism. British ignorance of Bengali social relations, as well as official failures to grasp the patrimonial character of zamindar property, both combined to render the 1793 Settlement quite impermanent. So far from improving their estates, many of the zamindars used their windfalls to mortgage their properties, eventually selling out to urban speculators. In the end, Bengal's landlords bore less resemblance to England's gentlemen-capitalists than to Edgeworth's Irish absentees. Deprived of a credible class of independent Indian collaborators, British

---

and Nationhood in the Atlantic World, 1600–1800 (Cambridge, 1999), 1–74, Hans Aarsleff, *The Study of Language in England, 1780–1860* (Princeton, 1967), and Thomas Trautmann, *Aryans and British India* (Berkeley, 1997).

[8] Edward Said, *Orientalism* (New York, 1979); Ronald Inden, *Imagining India* (Oxford, 1990) makes the case for Said in the Indian context. The essays in Carol A. Breckinridge and Peter Van der Veer (eds.), *Orientalism and the Postcolonial Predicament: Perspectives on South Asia* (Philadelphia, 1993) and Vinayah Chaturvedi (ed.), *Mapping Subaltern Studies and the Postcolonial* (London, 2000) offer multiple perspectives; Trautmann, *Aryans* is mildly critical of Said.

officials were obliged to create their own coterie of indigenous dependants, who were incorporated directly into the colonial state. In particular, they drew on the services of the Hindu pandits, who assisted them in interpreting Indian customs and in administering the law.[9]

In the beginning, British orientalists professed a genuine respect for these native scholars. Jones, for example, paints an idyllic portrait of country life in his suburban cottage, composing Sanskrit verses as tiger-cubs played at his wife's feet. As the pandits became ever more financially dependent on EIC employment, however, their perspectives became subordinated to the agenda of the Raj. Talents that had been honed in the Brahman academies of Nadiya and Banares were harnessed to the task of reinforcing British rule. In this manner, orientalism began to take on a Eurocentric hue, as Indian intellectuals were enlisted to adapt indigenous traditions and to transform them into instruments of foreign hegemony. The command of language, as Bernard Cohn has argued, was becoming the instrument for a new kind of language of command. Bengali Brahmans were lured into collaboration with the British, only to find their orientalism converted from a Brahman tradition into a British technique. The final result was that orientalism began to shift from celebrating the glories of ancient India to excoriating the inadequacies of modern Indians, who were deemed to have fallen from their ancestors' heights. Progress was becoming an accomplishment so uniquely British as to warrant Britons' control over Indian history.[10]

This contempt for the Indians of the present mounted during the 1780s, as the expertise of a phalanx of munshis and pandits was deployed to produce grammars, dictionaries, readers, and translations, so that future generations of British officials would no longer have to rely so heavily on natives like themselves. By the 1790s, British orientalism had become almost self-sufficient. Traditional Indian intellectuals suddenly found themselves relegated to servile positions, as imperial Britons like John Leyden became the new avatars of Indian history. The Brahman officials who had once interpreted Hindu law and collected Company revenue were increasingly reduced to the status of minor functionaries. This pattern of intellectual exploitation and expropriation was institutionalized after 1800 in the College of Fort William, which was opened

---

[9] Ranajit Guha, *A Rule of Property for Bengal: An Essay on the Permanent Settlement* (Durham, 1996); S. Battacharya, "Eastern India," in Tapan Raychaudhuri and Irfan Habib (eds.), *The Cambridge Economic History of India*, 2 vols. (Cambridge, 1982–3), II: 270–332.

[10] Mukherjee, *William Jones*, 112–14; Trautmann, *Aryans*, 28–61; Cannon, *Oriental Jones*, 216, 219, 225, 227, 264–5, 274, 280, 287, 291, 346, 350–1; R. Rocher, "British Orientalism," in Breckenridge and Van der Veer (eds.), *Postcolonial Predicament*, 232–5; Cohn, *Colonialism*, 16–56.

in Calcutta by the new Governor-General, Lord Richard Wellesley, to train novice officers in the EIC in Indian languages and laws. The attitudes of these students, as expressed in their course essays, are very revealing of the direction in which British orientalism was headed. On the one hand, most of the students dutifully praised the high achievements of ancient Indian civilization. Yet these *pro forma* endorsements were usually offered as foils to show how far the modern Hindus had degenerated from the high civilization of their distant ancestors.[11]

It is somewhat ironic that, at the very moment when the Fort William students were composing these essays, their most distinguished professor, H. T. Colebrooke, was proving the equations British = modernity and Indian = backwardness to be factually incorrect. In a 1795 publication, he had argued that economic backwardness in Bengal was primarily the product of EIC mismanagement. The wealth of the people, which ought to be reinvested in agriculture, was being diverted and dissipated by British venality and greed. "If Bengal had a capital in the hands of enterprising proprietors ... the situation of the labourers would be less precarious ... Under a system of government which neither drained its wealth, nor curbed rational enterprise, Bengal could not fail to revive."[12] According to Colebrooke, this road to Bengali modernization lay not in the imposition of British Protestant values, but in a revitalization of classical Hindu learning, which had formerly made Indian civilization so great. Indian progress need not be built out of imported material, but could be grounded in foundations that had ancient Indian roots. Taking up the scholarly mantle of oriental research where Sir William Jones had left it off, Colebrooke delved more deeply into the canonical Sanskrit texts than any European had before. Ancient Indian astronomers and mathematicians, he argued, had reached a level of sophistication and understanding never equaled by the Greeks, the Arabs, or anyone else until Copernicus. In a series of pathbreaking articles, Colebrooke provided a detailed analysis of the four sacred Vedas, as well as the subsequent Shastras, Upanishads, and Vedantic philosophy that they spawned. In a series of further essays, he turned his

---

[11] *Primitae Orientales: Essays by Students of the College of Fort William*, 2 vols. (1802–3). See especially the essays by T. Hamilton, W. P. Elliot, W. B. Bayley, T. Newman, E. Wood, R. Jenkins, W. Chaplin, J. Hunter, and W. Oliver. See also David Kopf, *British Orientalism and the Bengal Renaissance: The Dynamics of Indian Modernization, 1773–1835* (Berkeley, 1969), 1–126; O. P. Kejariwal, *The Asiatic Society of Bengal, and the Discovery of India's Past, 1784–1838* (Oxford, 1988), 70–152; Sisir Kumar Das, *Sahibs and Munshis: An Account of the College at Fort William* (Calcutta, 1978).

[12] H. T. Colebrooke, *Remarks on the State of Husbandry and Commerce in Bengal* (Calcutta, 1795), quote on 29–30.

attention to the historical origin of the Jains, the Buddhists, and the Hindu caste system.[13]

While Colebrooke was concerned to demonstrate the antiquity of these Hindu accomplishments, he was no less interested in showing how they remained living traditions in the Hindu practice of his own day. In a set of essays on Hindu religion, he implicitly countered the ethnocentrism of his students, showing how the Vedic texts had generated a panoply of complex religious practices that endowed contemporary Indian life with a satisfying sense of coherence and dignity. Taking sharp issue with those who claimed that modern Indians had degenerated from the exalted level of their ancestors, Colebrooke determined to rescue the contemporary Hindu from the reproaches of his detractors. The upper-class Brahmans, he argued, exhibited a moral and spiritual elevation which would have done honor to the elites of any European country. The exalted monotheism celebrated in their time-honored scriptures stood in contrast to the degenerate polytheistic practices which had emerged among the lower classes only after the true and pure Hindusim had been dethroned.[14]

Had Bengal developed a wealthy, bi-culturally educated landed elite, such as Lord Cornwallis had hoped to establish through the Settlement of 1793, Colebrooke's program of neo-classical orientalist research might have provided the basis for a genuine collaboration between British officials and a native aristocracy. As it was, the finer points of Colebrooke's respect for Indian civilization were lost on the EIC cadets who had to listen to their professor's lectures. As he himself noted, this call for respect contradicted what they saw all around them: on one side, a conquering white race, whose ranks they expected to join, and on the other, a mass of disempowered, darker-skinned natives, who had been thrust into positions of humiliation and inferiority. "Never mixing with natives," Colebrooke complained, "an European is ignorant of their real character, which he, therefore, despises. When they meet it is with fear on one side, and arrogance on the other. Considered as a race of inferior beings . . . their sufferings meet no more compassion than those of a dog or monkey."[15]

Nevertheless, this stark dichotomy between colonized fear and imperial arrogance which characterized Anglo-Indian relations in Bengal

[13] H. T. Colebrooke, *Essays on the Religion and Philosophy of the Hindus* [1837] (Delhi, 1972), 1–69, 143–306; T. E. Colebrooke, *Life of H. T. Colebrooke*, I (London, 1873).

[14] Colebrooke, *Religion and Philosophy*, 70–142; Colebrooke, *Life of Colebrooke*.

[15] Colebrooke, *Life of Colebrooke*, 190–2, quote on 29; Kejariwal, *Asiatic Society*, 76–117; Das, *Sahibs and Munshis*, 12–13; Kopf, *British Orientalism*, 51, 87, 89.

had not yet permeated other parts of the subcontinent, where Briton and Indian continued to encounter one another on more equal terms. In the west lay the vast confederation of the Marathas, whose wealth and power probably exceeded that of British India during the 1790s. Here, a living, evolving Hindu society remained intact. To the north and south lay the even more formidable world of Muslim-controlled India. In Delhi, the Mughal Emperor still sat on his hereditary throne, however much his actual power and influence had diminished. By contrast, in Deccan, two highly militarized Muslim states formed a counterweight to British coastal rule. Where Hyderabad gradually drifted deeper into the EIC orbit, Mysore, under its Sultans, Hyder Ali and his son Tipu, was built up into an armed fortress of anti-British resistance committed to forming alliances with other native powers with a view to challenging British subcontinental hegemony.[16] In these Muslim states, as well as in the lands of the Marathas, Britons encountered Indians not as masters and conquerors but as ambassadors, military attachés, allies, antagonists, and traders – even as suppliants for royal favor and participants in court intrigues. This was a world where British merchants and envoys found themselves propelled by strong incentives to engage with upper-class Indians on terms of mutual respect and equality. The natural result was that some "went native" – dressing in Indian costume, patronizing mosques and temples, participating in festivals and pilgrimages, taking on Indian concubines, and, in a few cases, even marrying the daughters of highly placed Hindu or Muslim elites. "Progress" remained up for grabs in such settings, where Britons had not yet foreclosed the possibility that it might be achieved in indigenous terms.[17]

In 1799, the dramatic defeat of Tipu Sultan at Seringapatem radically altered this state of affairs. The Mysore territories were carved up, Tipu's army was disbanded, the French were expelled, and vast accessions were made to the territories directly governed by the EIC. Once proud, independent principalities, such as Hyderabad, Jaipur, Travancore, and Oudh, would henceforth be transformed into acquiescent British clients: ruled in name by bejeweled maharajahs, but in fact by British Residents directly outside the palace gates. Progress would henceforth be firmly in the hands of the British, and yet the need to cast it into an Indian idiom gave orientalism a new lease of life. As the

---

[16] Spear, *History of Modern India*, 37–103; Christopher Bayly, *Imperial Meridian: The British Empire and the World, 1780–1830* (London, 1989), 1–74; C. A. Bayly, *Indian Society and the Making of the British Empire* (Cambridge, 1988), 7–105.
[17] William Dalrymple, *White Mughals: Love and Betrayal in Eighteenth-Century India* (London, 2002).

process of Raj-construction that had begun in Bengal, Madras, and
Bombay was now repeated on a subcontinental stage, British India
became a more diverse and complicated place.[18] Correspondingly, the
character of oriental and historical studies, which underwrote its legitimacy, had to be expanded and rearranged. Where the old orientalism
had focused on a few ancient canonical Sanskrit texts, the new orientalism cast its net more widely through the mass of archaeological,
anthropological, topographical, historical, and statistical sources that
were piling up. Where the old orientalism had been designed to elicit
the collaboration of the Brahmans in running the Bengali state, the new
orientalism was deployed as a tool for managing the various modern
warlords and potentates whom British arms were defeating, but whose
full acquiescence had yet to be gained. In both cases, orientalism was
conceived primarily as an instrument of liberal imperialism, which had
been designed to justify a British hegemony that had originated in
violence but now needed to be recast in consensual terms.

2   Scottish orientalism and the romance of British India

One of the most striking features of the new orientalism was the extent
to which it was dominated by Scots. Indeed, with the exception of
Colebrooke, *all* the major contributors to historical scholarship in the
post-Jones generation were of Scottish origins.[19] To some extent this
simply reflected the general over-representation of Scots in the EIC,
which was due to the extensive patronage networks that had been
established during Henry Dundas's reign as political fixer for Pitt.
Thanks to Scotland's system of public education these recruits were
likely to be better educated than their English counterparts, and more
inclined to intellectualize about imperial affairs.[20] This was especially

---

[18] Bayly, *Imperial Meridian*, 75–256.

[19] The Scottish orientalists of this generation included N. B. Edmonstone (1765–1841),
William Erskine (1773–1852), Alexander Hamilton (1762–1824), Colin Mackenzie
(1753–1821), James Mackintosh (1765–1832), William Kirkpatrick (1754–1812),
William Hunter (1755–1812), John Gilchrist (1759–1841), Thomas Munro (1761–
1827), Mark Wilks (1760–1831, born in the Isle of Man), James Kirkpatrick (1764–
1805), John Malcolm (1769–1833), John Leyden (1775–1811), and Mountstuart
Elphinstone (1779–1859), to whom we may add the slightly younger John Crawfurd
(1783–1868) and Vans Kennedy (1784–1846). All have entries in either *DNB*, *ODNB*,
or both.

[20] T. C. Smout, *A History of the Scottish People, 1560–1830* (London, 1969), 81–8, 421–50;
T. M. Devine, *Scotland's Empire, 1600–1815* (London, 2004), especially 250–70. See also
Jane Rendall, "Scottish Orientalism: From Robertson to James Mill," *The Historical
Journal*, 25.1 (1982), 43–69. For a discussion of Malcolm, Elphinstone, and Munro,
see Diane McLaren, *British India and British Scotland, 1780–1830* (Akron, 2001).

true of those who had been able to take in a few years at one of the Scottish universities before their arrival in India. In the classrooms of Edinburgh or Glasgow they were exposed to the teaching of John Millar and Dugald Stewart, with the shades of Adam Ferguson, Adam Smith, David Hume, William Robertson, and Lord Kames still hovering in the atmosphere. Not surprisingly, the four-stage evolutionary model of societal development made a profound impression on all these indivi-duals, as it had on Walter Scott. In India, as in Scotland, uneven development had created dramatic juxtapositions of groups at every stage of development, from unlettered savages to commercial elites.[21] On the new imperial frontiers where these differences were most pro-nounced, British administrators faced three urgent questions, each of which could only be answered in the light of history. (1) How could British take-over (either formal or informal) be justified as the only means of rescuing colonial peoples from chaos and/or setting them on the road to modernity? (2) What mode of British governance and indigenous collaboration was most appropriate for each people? (3) How should law be administered, property be defined, and taxes be raised? Precisely because there were no universally correct answers to these questions, they had to be solved in relation to the circumstances of time and place.

To this end, Colin Mackenzie (1753–1821) was deputed to produce a survey of Mysore after the defeat of Tipu, so that the British could become acquainted with the lands that their conquests had gained. Carrying this assignment far beyond the call of duty, Mackenzie devoted the rest of his life (and much of his income) to accumulating a vast archive of manu-scripts, artifacts, inscriptions, and folklore from southern India. On the basis of this and other material, Mark Wilks (1760–1831) wrote his massive *Historical Sketches of South India*, with the triple purpose of excoriating the rapacity of Tipu's administration, justifying the necessity of a British take-over, and tracing the complexity of Deccan society over the historical *longue durée*. Dismissing simplistic notions of an oriental despotism, Wilks showed how traditional Hindu rulers – for all their chequered record of internecine conflict and periodic plunder – often ruled with justice, in the interest of their people. Correspondingly, he disputed the notion that traditional India did not support private property, thereby laying the foundation for the ryotwari land settle-ment that would be implemented a decade later by Thomas Munro

---

[21] Karen O'Brien, *Narratives of Enlightenment: Cosmopolitan History from Voltaire to Gibbon* (Cambridge, 1997); Ronald Meek, *Social Science and the Ignoble Savage* (Cambridge, 1976), 5–67, 99–229.

(1761–1827) in Madras.[22] Drawing in part on Wilks's evidence, Munro argued that the mistake of 1793 in Bengal need not be repeated. Thanks to his and other officials' campaigning on the basis of supposed customary right, the ryotwari peasant cultivator, rather than the zamindari landlord, was recognized as proprietor of the land through much of the subcontinent.[23]

By contrast, William Erskine (1773–1852) opened up the study of Mughal history to English readers by translating and annotating the memoirs of its founding Emperor, Babur. Working during his service as a Bombay magistrate, Erskine was fascinated by the history of the Mongols, a conglomeration of dispersed pastoralist tribes who periodically erupted out of their central Asian heartland to conquer the greatest civilizations of Europe, China, and India in succession. What made the Mongols so formidable in warfare, and yet so reluctant to abandon their primitive lifestyle? For Erskine, Babur was a critical transitional figure in the shift from nomadic simplicity to aristocratic polish, since he retained the barbarian mentality of his ancestors (Ghengis Khan from his mother, and Tamerlane from his father) while developing a refined taste for poetry, food, and theological speculation. This unique combination made him an effective warrior, even as it induced him to regard settled Delhi as an attractive target for conquest. The stage was thus set for his grandson Akbar whose own residue of barbarian shrewdness brought Mughal power to its ultimate apogee.[24]

It was, however, James Tod (1782–1835) who imported Walter Scott's historical romance most directly into India. Like Mackenzie, Tod was a surveyor, and he developed an interest in triangulating local culture, politics, and history alongside his maps. Swept up in the northwest frontier wars of the 1800–19 period, he became a great chronicler of, and advocate for, the Rajput noblemen and princes, whom he saw as natural allies of the British in their struggles against the Mughal and Maratha states. To counter those Britons who regarded the Indians as a people without history, Tod produced a massive compilation, *Annals*

[22] Cohn, *Colonialism*, 57–105; Kopf, *British Orientalism*, 127–214; Mark Wilks, *Historical Sketches of the South Indian History*, 4 vols. (New Delhi, 1980). For a sensitive examination of Mackenzie's archive creation, see Nicholas Dirks, *Castes of Mind: Colonialism and the Making of Modern India* (Princeton, 2001), 63–123.

[23] T. H. Beaglehole, *Thomas Munro and the Development of Administrative Policy in Madras, 1792–1818: The Origins of the "Munro System"* (Cambridge, 1966); Nilmani Mukherjee, *The Ryotwari System in Madras, 1792–1817* (Calcutta, 1962); and Burton Stein, *Thomas Munro, the Origins of the Colonial State, and his Vision of Empire* (Oxford, 1989).

[24] William Erskine (with John Leyden), *Memoirs of Zehir-ed-din Muhammed Báber, Emperor of Hindustan*, 2 vols. (London, 1826), with preface by Erskine. See also Erskine's two-volume *A History of Hindustan under Báber and Humáyan* (London, 1854), esp. 8–77.

and Antiquities of Rajasthan (1829–32). Drawing on ancient Sanskrit literature, and the kind of artifacts and manuscripts amassed by Mackenzie, Tod also found a wealth of information in the bardic epics that he encountered during his borderings on the marchlands between British and Maratha territory. As in the Scottish Highlands, he explained, every clan had its narrator poet, who purported to recount several thousand years of local history. Although their primary focus was on the martial exploits of noble families, these bards could also convey a more critical subtext, which might chronicle the failures and shortcomings of the leading dynasties. "There is not a petty state in Rajasthan that has not had its Thermopolaye, and scarcely a city that has not produced its Leonidas," Tod enthused. "But the mantle of ages has shrouded from view what the magic pen of the historian might have consecrated to endless admiration."[25]

Taking it upon himself to raise this historian's pen, Tod hoped to convey the Rajput romance to his western readers while convincing the Rajputs that the next chapter in their annals was to sign on as British allies. Aware of the difficulty inherent in forging this imagined community over a distance of so many languages, skin colors, and 8,000 miles, Tod explored the Anglo-Indian relationship on multiple levels in his book. The parallel between Hindu Rajputs and Scottish Highlanders was meaningful because "in the same stages of society the wants of men must everywhere be similar, and will produce the analogies which are observed to regulate Tatar hordes, or German tribes, Caledonian clans, the Rajpoot Cúla (race) or Jarega Bhyá (brotherhood)." At considerable length, and with great ingenuity, Tod argued that the system of social relations that had evolved in Rajasthan was essentially the same as the feudal system that dominated medieval Europe for many centuries. Lest the reader think that this is mere coincidence, or that it was insufficient to seal the bond of imaginative union between Britain and India, Tod excavated a deeper historical connection: Rajput legends, cosmologies, and divinities all bore a striking resemblance to biblical legends, Germanic folklore, and Greek myths. All were descended from a common ancestral culture that could be located somewhere back in prehistory if one dug deep enough.

If we can show the Germans to have been originally Scyths or Goths, a wide field of curiosity and inquiry is open to the origin of government, manners, etc. All the antiquities of Europe will assume a new appearance ... Scandinavia was

---

[25] James Tod, *Annals and Antiquities of Rajasthan*, 2 vols. [1829] (New Delhi, 2001), I: xviii. See also Tod's *Travels in Western India* (New Delhi, 1971); *DNB*, XIX: 904–5.

occupied by Scythians five hundred years before Christ ... In short, we are no other than a colony of Tatars.[26]

So Britons had to go to India to learn their own hidden history! Perhaps these long-lost cousins were not retrograde sluggards, but noble barbarians, who had preserved the virtues that the stay-at-home metropolitan Aryans had lost. "Extinguish the martial virtues" and "the Rajputs will soon cease to respect themselves. Sloth, low cunning and meanness will follow. What nation ever maintained its character that devolved upon the stronger the power of protection?" The problem, of course, was that Tod was trying to convince the Rajputs to accept the protection of (stronger) British authority. He might wax eloquent about "the struggles of a brave people for independence during a series of ages sacrificing whatever was dear to them for the maintenance of the religion of their forefathers, and sturdily defending to death and in spite of every temptation, their rights and national liberty." Unfortunately, in the coming age, the greatest threat to the independence of the Rajputs was not to come from their ancient Islamic or Maratha rivals, but from the British, who would henceforth tell them how to be free.[27]

Tod wrestled with some part of this dilemma in his diary. "Our position in the east has been and continues to be one in which conquest forces herself upon us." However, "we have the power, however late, to halt, and not anticipate her further orders to march." Walter Scott could get away with romanticizing Scottish feudalism because it had been decisively defeated by capitalist modernity. The romancer, in the very act of celebrating, revealed that it no longer posed any threat in reality. In Rajasthan, by contrast, the feudal remnant was all too palpably present. EIC policy-makers were scarcely inclined to glorify warlords whom they regarded as residual nuisances and potential rebels. Tod's rhapsodies on Rajput valor did not go over well with his superiors in Calcutta. Fearing that he was in danger of "going native," they recalled him and accused him of corruption and dishonesty. After clearing his name, Tod resigned in disgust, devoting the rest of his life, in England and on the continent, to sifting his ethnographic evidence and preparing his *Annals* for the press. Yet if Tod's was an extreme case, his romantic embrace of the manly, Hindu warrior was shared by other early nineteenth-century British officials. Like Scotland's Highlanders, these troublesome cavaliers had to be transformed from frontier pests into

---

[26] Tod, *Rajasthan*, I: 108, 51. For a critique, see Inden, *Imagining India*, 72–6.
[27] Tod, *Rajasthan*, I: xix, 104, 107–72.

loyal imperial soldiers, defending and extending further conquests. Equally inclined toward the romance, but more committed to its imperial outcome, was Tod's superior John Malcolm, whom we have already met at Abbotsford.[28]

3   John Malcolm and the romance of British India

Unlike Tod, Wilks, Colebrooke, and Mackenzie, all of whom came to India with some higher education, Ensign Malcolm landed in Madras, in 1783, at the age of thirteen. At the time there was nothing to distinguish him from the throng of impecunious Scotsmen whose families could offer them nothing but a passage to India as compensation for the dearth of employment opportunities at home. For the next eight years "Boy Malcolm" led the dissolute life of a typical junior officer until war with Tipu exposed him to broader views. Eight years before the founding of Fort William College, he had the wit to realize that the road to EIC advancement lay in linguistic proficiency and the ability to act as an Anglo-Indian go-between. The bordering propensities imbued by a Scottish childhood turned out to have value on the Indian frontier.[29]

So the young man taught himself Persian and Hindustani, and gained the trust of his native subordinates through his sunny disposition and sympathetic demeanor. At the court of Hyderabad and in the two sieges of Seringapatem, Malcolm learned how to play the game of Indian politics and made a strong impression on his own superiors, who quickly advanced him through the ranks. In 1798, the new star attracted the attention of Lord Wellesley and his brother (the future Duke of Wellington). Inspired by the Wellesleys' romantic, anti-Jacobin politics, he ardently embraced their vision of an invincible, globe-spanning British Empire, which could serve as a bulwark against the radicalism and fanaticism of revolutionary France. At the same time, Malcolm's own experiences in India taught him that while imperial strategy had to be conceived with a global compass, colonial expansion always advanced in a local context whose particular actors, issues, and etiquette had to be grasped in their own frame.[30]

---

[28] Tod, *Rajasthan*, I: 101; *ODNB*, LIV: 885–6; Norbert Peabody, "Tod's Rajasthan and the Boundaries of Imperial Rule in Nineteenth Century India," *Modern Asian Studies*, 30.1 (1996), 185–220.

[29] John William Kaye, *The Life and Correspondence of Major-General Sir John Malcolm, G.C.B.*, 2 vols. (London, 1856), I: 1–29; *DNB*, XII: 848–58.

[30] Kaye, *Life and Correspondence of Malcolm*, I: 30–104; Elizabeth Longford, *Wellington: The Years of the Sword* (New York, 1969), 45–105.

Sent out to Persia on a diplomatic mission in 1800, Malcolm came back with a treaty that he hoped would provide protection for India's western flank. Deputed to the Maratha court, he persuaded the Peshwa to place himself under British protection against the formidable warlords who contested his sovereignty. Moving to the rebel camp, he then negotiated the submission of the great warlord Daulet Rao Scindia, while simultaneously brokering an agreement between Jeswant Rao Holkar (the other leading Maratha warlord) and the leaders of the Sikhs. In all these discussions, a connecting thread can be discerned. First, Malcolm tried to win the confidence of his rival with a carefully chosen personal gesture in a style that he may have learned from the young Captain Tod. Unlike Tod, however, Malcolm's next move was to issue demands with an iron fist. "Negotiation," he once quipped, was best undertaken "at the head of an army." Finally, when his point had been gained, as it often (but not always) was, he would depart with some extravagant flourish of generosity toward his defeated rival, which usually implicated the EIC in a huge financial obligation. While this *noblesse oblige* made a good impression in India, it also enraged the EIC Directors in London, who began to regard Malcolm as an improvident hot-head, liable to land them in unwise commitments and unnecessary expense. After a second mission to Persia ended in failure in 1809, his career began to stall. As he saw younger but better-connected men promoted over him, Malcolm reckoned that his best hope was to take up the pen.[31]

Malcolm's turn to authorship was motivated by a mixture of personal frustration and political unease over the failure of the British public (including the EIC establishment) to understand the responsibilities that they had taken on in India. The seeming ease with which the British had conquered the subcontinent had led Britons mistakenly to view Indians (and Asians more generally) as people of little account. This was an understandable error. Malcolm later recollected "with shame" the time when he thought he was "very superior" to the Indians with whom he worked. "But as my knowledge of them and of myself improved, the distance between us lessened." According to Malcolm, the Indians tolerated (and occasionally welcomed) British conquest, not because they were weak or inferior, but because two

---

[31] Kaye, *Life and Correspondence of Malcolm*, I: 105–512, II: 1–96, quote on I: 313; J. W. Malcolm, *The Political History of India, 1784–1823* [1826], ed. N. Panikkar, 2 vols. (New Delhi, 1970). This is an expanded two-volume work, the first five chapters of which were published as *A Sketch of the Political History of India* in 1811. See also John Malcolm, *A Sketch of the Sikhs* (London, 1812).

centuries of political instability had destroyed their social fabric. British India, he insisted, was grounded on Indian opinion.[32] The solution, Malcolm might have concluded, was to figure out how to get the Indians working together. This however would have sent the likes of him packing back to Scotland, where – as fourth son of a bankrupt laird – he was likely to join the ranks of Walter Scott's romantic failures. Not surprisingly, Malcolm preferred to remain in India, where he could become an imperial war hero advancing the tried and true strategy of divide and rule.

In his 1812 publication *A Sketch of the Sikhs*, we can see Malcolm wrestling with the question of why Indians were unable to resolve their own divisions. The book introduces British audiences to the story of Nanak, the fifteenth-century reformer who had tried to synthesize Islam and Hinduism into a single syncretic creed. In principle, this union might have worked, but Nanak had the misfortune of preaching it on the Marchlands of the young Mughal Empire, to an audience of fierce warrior tribes. Malcolm then shows how Sikhism evolved over the next three centuries from the pacifism of its founder to a violent movement, which simply added more fuel to India's internal instability. In Malcolm's *Political History of India*, he reflected more directly on the emergence of the British Raj. Here he discovered an apparent paradox: the ability of the British to promote stability in India depended on their willingness to act with a firm hand. Those Viceroys who, like Cornwallis or Wellesley, were overtly militaristic brought peace and prosperity to the land. By contrast, those who, like Sir John Shore, exercised forbearance conveyed a message of weakness, which merely emboldened the enemies of Britain to act.[33]

Malcolm was disappointed by the poor response to his volumes, which fell stillborn from the press. Frustrated in his career, he took a furlough in Britain to grease the wheels of patronage, to visit his family, and – as we have already seen – to cultivate Walter Scott. Of course, Malcolm could not know that at the very moment when he was making Scott's acquaintance the poet was secretly transforming himself into the author of *Waverley*. Nevertheless, when Malcolm was recalled to

[32] John Malcolm, "Notes of Instructions Regarding Intercourse between European Officials and Natives," in John Briggs, *Letters Addressed to a Young Person in India* (London, 1828), 190–1, 193–4, quote on 196–7. For a critique of the British belief that eighteenth- and nineteenth-century India was really politically disordered and unstable, see Bayly, *Indian Society*, 1–105.

[33] Malcolm, *Political History of India*, I: 4, 109; Malcolm, *Sketch of the Sikhs*, 23. See also John Malcolm, *The History of Persia*, 2 vols. (London, 1815), II: 622, for his dire assessment of the negative consequences of Muslim rule.

India in 1816, he found himself thrust into the midst of *Waverley* adventures of his own. Assigned the task of wiping out lawlessness on the Maratha frontier, Malcolm's police operations quickly assumed more Herculean aims. When the warlord Holkar revolted, in what he perceived to be a moment of British weakness, the Peshwa (Baji Rao II) joined him in a full-scale anti-British attack. For the British, this was a perfect pretext for ridding themselves of the Marathas once and for all. After his success in conducting the military operations at Mehdipur, Malcolm deposed the Peshwa, while awarding him an £80,000 pension, which the furious EIC Directors were obliged to honor.[34]

Thwarted in his desire to become Governor of Bombay, Malcolm learned that his empire-building would be rewarded with another challenging assignment to pacify the northern portion of the now escheated Maratha lands. As he surveyed these vast tracts, which still swarmed with minor robber-barons and petty cattle thieves, Malcolm sent an entertaining letter to Walter Scott. "The largest folks are quiet, but the difficulty is to keep the Rob Roys under." He then related the story of one particularly savage local warlord whom he had (he hoped) successfully enlisted on the British side. Rob Roy, of course, was a criminal and a marauder. Yet by retelling and romanticizing his story, Scott had been able to show how the new conditions of commercial capitalism and Anglo-Scottish Union were transforming such law-breakers into indispensable mediators and go-betweens. In writing up his two-volume *Memoir of Central India*, Malcolm found himself drawn into the background of Maratha history. Starting out as Hindu guerilla fighters, these partisans initially depended on popular support for their work. Even as they conquered, they remained personally modest and egalitarian, more interested in the realities than in the trappings of power. No sooner did one set of leaders establish their authority than a fresh crop of upstarts rose to challenge their place. Throughout his bold career of conquest and territorial expansion, Mahadji Sindia retained "the manly simplicity of character which led him equally to despise the trappings and the allurements of luxury." His role was "marked by many acts of violence and oppression; but he was nevertheless a man of mild disposition, and particularly desirous of improving the countries he had conquered or usurped."[35]

From Malcolm's perspective, Sindia had only two deficiencies: (1) he was not quite capable of actually realizing his dream of central Asian pacification without European assistance, and (2) the European power

---

[34] Kaye, *Life and Correspondence of Malcolm*, II: 97–298, especially 237–66.
[35] Kaye, *Life and Correspondence of Malcolm*, II: 299–457, quote on 364–5; John Malcolm, *A Memoir of Central India, Including Malwa*, 2 vols. [1820] (New Delhi, 1970).

from which he sought this assistance was not Britain, but France. For a time, the British thought they could work with the Holkar family as a Maratha counterweight to Sindia, but its unreliability forced the EIC's hand. Like Scott's barbarian Highlanders and his own barbarian Sikhs, Malcolm's Maratha princes possess many fine heroic qualities of devotion and loyalty. They are, however, too uncivilized and erratic to absorb the complex ideas and institutions of progress on their own. Condemned to an endemic state of lawlessness, they are in need of the firm paternal guidance of the already progressive British, who can force them into the order that they cannot achieve on their own. As with seventeenth- and eighteenth-century Scotland, so with early nineteenth-century India, British expansion and integration is offered as an opportunity for barbarians who are capable of something better, but cannot quite achieve modern civilization by themselves. In this formula, British conquest brings order to the colonial hinterland and then enlists the conquered barbarians as fresh cannon fodder and fierce shock-troops, to be sent out for an even greater British conquest of more distant barbarians somewhere else.[36]

So far, Malcolm's British Indian romance was quite similar to that of Tod. There was however one important difference. For where Tod hoped to see the Rajputs remain independent, tied into a consensual union with Britain, Malcolm was enough of a realist to understand that such expectations were naive. Britain had no choice but to break up the Maratha state, decisively trouncing the warlords – sending some into exile while turning others into vassals of client principalities. But was it possible for a once-proud prince like Sindia to accept dependence on the British government without losing the aristocratic pride on which he formerly stood? All too often, in practice, Malcolm acknowledged, the princely "puppet" regimes that British suzerainty permitted were sad shells of their former selves, presided over by demoralized ex-potentates and sunk in indolence, ostentation, and gross sensuality. British Residents could try to persuade or pressure, but "when it [interference] descends to minute checks and interferences in the collection of the revenue [or] the administration of justice" nominal political independence becomes "not merely impolitic, but dangerous, as his [the Prince's] condition must be felt by himself and all attached to his person or family as a mockery and degradation."[37]

---

[36] Malcolm, *Central India*, I: 58–580; Malcolm, *Sketch of the Sikhs*, 131.
[37] John Malcolm, *The Government of India* (London, 1833), 31; Malcolm, *Central India*, I: 141. See also Kaye, *Life and Correspondence of Malcolm*, II: 340–1; John Malcolm, *Instructions on Intercourse* (London, 1828), 220–1.

No less than Tod, Malcolm wanted to apply the *Waverley* romance to India, but unlike Tod, he understood that British India was fundamentally different from Anglo-Scotland, where the cause of Union could draw on a common language, culture, economy, and geography.

The cause which has compelled, and will continue beyond all others to compel us to increase our dominion lies deep in the character of our power. We have, whenever our authority is in question, no retreat. Our situation is unlike that of a national government which is associated in language, prejudices, habits, and religion with the people it governs. This want of a natural root in the soil forces us to adopt a course of action, which a state differently circumstanced might avoid. The necessity of not injuring the impression upon which the very foundation of our authority rests, obliges Government to carry through, at all hazards, every dispute and contest with the inhabitants of our provinces, or those of any State which we protect.[38]

To make India British would be a vast, revolutionary undertaking of wholesale societal transformation that would necessarily meet with much internal resistance since it would entail overturning many of the most venerable traditions that the Indians held most dear. The cultural and political recognition that Scott had demanded as the price for Anglo-Scottish Union might have to be withheld from the indigenous Indians in this more difficult and distant case. Indians might not merely lose control of their past to scholar-imperialists like Malcolm. They would also lose control of their future to a new breed of British official, who favored much more direct colonial expansion and penetration on pragmatic, utilitarian grounds. Since India had porous eastern and western borders this new logic of control would likely require an indefinite course of further annexation. As British incursions destabilized frontier social relations and precipitated tribal warfare or resistance, this would then provide a further pretext for British power to intervene. Like Tod, Malcolm preferred to govern India indirectly through its traditional maharajahs and nobles, but he understood that this might prove to be impossible.

If forced by circumstances to depart from this course, better assume the direct sovereignty of the country at once than leave to the mock and degraded instruments of our power any means of avenging themselves upon a State which renders them the debased tools of its Government ... Territory is coming too fast upon us. We cannot prevent accessions, and the period may arrive when the whole peninsula will be under our immediate rule; but every consideration requires this period to be delayed, and every effort should be made to regulate a march in which we must proceed.[39]

[38] Malcolm, *Central India*, II: 267–8.
[39] Quoted in Kaye, *Life and Correspondence of Malcolm*, II: 373–4.

But the British Indian juggernaut had already left the Calcutta Station, and there was no way of knowing where and when it might stop. When Malcolm finally got his Governorship of Bombay in 1827, the India of his imagination was scarcely to be seen. The old borderer was not happy cooped up in the pinnacle of high office. The man who believed in government by patronage, victor's *largesse*, and *noblesse oblige* was forced to preside over a period of fiscal retrenchment, taking his marching orders from a cadre of EIC accountants who were determined that the runaway costs of government be reduced. The man who believed in decentralized local, aristocratic government was forced to preside over the construction of a centralized authoritarian state. Unhappy with the way things were going in India, Malcolm retired early from Bombay. The Britain to which he returned in 1830 was a strange country, and it had paid scant attention to the message of his books. Uninterested in the distant problems of India, it was obsessed with its own internal drama of industrial change. Malcolm's love of aristocracies, his worship of Wellington, and his deepening mood of misanthropic nostalgia all combined to turn him into a hidebound Tory – even as he continued to exhibit the manners of *cultural* liberality.[40]

4   **Mountstuart Elphinstone and the project of Indian modernization**

More adept at negotiating the currents of the post-1820 period was Malcom's friend and fellow Scotsman Mountstuart Elphinstone. The two had met during the Second Maratha War of 1803, when Elphinstone was a young attaché, fresh from Fort William College, assigned to General Wellesley's staff. Brilliant, well educated, and from aristocratic stock, Elphinstone had many of the advantages that Malcolm lacked. As the years passed, their friendship deepened, yet tensions also began to accumulate underneath. Malcolm's penchant for Indian princes, his worship of the Wellesleys, and his romantic Scottophilia all struck Elphinstone as over the top. Elphinstone was by no means immune to the romance of India, but his critical intellect and depressive personality made him skeptical of simple solutions in

---

[40] Malcolm, *Government of India*; "I will not compress the concerns of an empire into a ledger, or calculate its destinies like an account current," avowed Malcolm in a *Speech on East India Company Charter* (London, 1833), 5. But the bottom line was that this was what his EIC employers expected him to do. See also Kaye, *Life and Correspondence of Malcolm*, II: 495–621; McLaren, *British India and British Scotland*, 114–15.

which the welfare of India and the interests of Britain could supposedly be magically reconciled.[41]

Appointed as envoy to Afghanistan in 1808, he published a report in which he noted the "strong resemblance [of that country] to Scotland in ancient times." The primitive freedom and rough independence of the Afghans appealed to Elphinstone, and he forgave their habitual turbulence, dissimulation, and occasional cruelty. Although "there is scarcely a tribe ... that is not in a state of actual war or suspended hostility," the violent episodes were usually intermittent, and might be settled by customary rituals of propitiation by calling an inter-tribal Jurga (assembly) or by appeal to the higher authority of a Khan or a King. On the other hand, the Afghans' politeness, hospitality, religious observances, and treatment of women all struck Elphinstone as exemplary. The main danger to Afghanistan lay in meddlesome foreigners (perhaps including himself) who were liable to upset the delicate balance of internal affairs.[42]

By contrast, Elphinstone's perspective on India was quite different, for here Scottish social evolutionary theory suggested a different approach. Unlike Afghanistan, India was a sedentary, agricultural society in which the land had accumulated the improvements of many generations, and had spawned significant pools of commercial wealth. Here tribal unrest and endemic warlordism were not a viable way of life but a social catastrophe, which left whole swathes of villages pillaged, deserted, and burned. Given that the Asian alternative to chaos was oriental despotism, British intervention was morally justified to save Indians from themselves. In 1809, Elphinstone was appointed as Resident to the Maratha court at Pune, and he watched as it self-destructively imploded. Even more than Malcolm, Elphinstone was fascinated with the Marathas, and began to contemplate studying them with a full-dress history.

It would comprise the dissolution of the Mogul Empire, with the causes and formation of the present order of things ... The struggles of Sivajee and his successors, the splendid conquests and tremendous reverses of the first Peshwas, the re-establishment of their power by their adoption of the European art of war, the crimes and distractions of the succeeding period, and the final close of

---

[41] T. E. Colebrooke, *The Life of Mountstuart Elphinstone*, 2 vols. (London, 1884), I: 1–229, 315; R. D. Choksey, *Mountstuart Elphinstone: The Indian Years* (Bombay, 1971), 1–60.

[42] Mountstuart Elphinstone, *Account of the Kingdom of Cabul* [1815] (Oxford, 1972), 196–401, quotes on 217–18 and 230; Choksey, *Elphinstone*, 61–106.

the Maratha turbulence and Maratha greatness in the Treaty of Bassein [1802] would afford no bad material for a judicious historian.[43]

In the event, the treachery of the last Peshwa in 1817 obliged Elphinstone to defer his studies and to abandon the writing for the making of history. Once again, he was thrown together with Malcolm in a crisis that tested their resources of intelligence and tenacity. In the eyes of their superiors, Elphinstone's quick thinking, even more than Malcolm's generalship, saved the day. By anticipating Baji Rao's duplicity, he had prevented a massacre and facilitated the strategy by which the Peshwa was bloodlessly deposed. Deeply chagrined at this eclipse of his glory, Malcolm had to watch as his junior colleague was assigned the task of reorganizing the former Peshwa's territories and bringing them into the framework of British rule.[44]

Faced with this daunting and formidable challenge, Elphinstone abandoned all thoughts of his Maratha *History*. The Marathas were now gone, and the British directly or indirectly controlled most of the subcontinent. Under these circumstances, where Britain was responsible for India's future, it was no longer so easy to see the relevance of Indian history. The notion that the British could simply replace the Mughals or Marathas was now dismissed as completely erroneous. The British were not just another conqueror. Only by bringing India the benefits of social and economic progress could they justify their distant and improbable hegemony. At the same time, the road to socio-economic modernization was fraught with dangers, most of which were as yet unknown. Initially, Elphinstone hoped to preserve traditional Indian customs, institutions, and elites. Yet this was for him a pragmatic rather than an ideological goal. Faced with the daunting task of administering all 50,000 square miles of the former Maratha province, he tried a number of different experiments. In the end however most of the land was incorporated directly into British India. Here it was overseen by a cadre of British collectors who were endowed with near-dictatorial powers to raise revenue, try cases, and issue administrative decrees. While this entailed stripping traditional Indian elites of their former authority, it also involved training new western-educated native sub-officials to help the British collectors and assistants in

[43] Mountstuart Elphinstone, *Selections from the Minutes and Other Writings of the Honourable Mountstuart Elphinstone*, ed. George W. Forrest (London, 1884), 224–55, quoted in Colebrooke, *Life of Elphinstone*, I: 348–9; Choksey, *Elphinstone*, 107–51.

[44] Colebrooke, *Life of Elphinstone*, I: 230–340, II: 1–99; Choksey, *Elphinstone*, 152–212. For details of the events leading up to Baji Rao II's deposition, see R. D. Choksey (ed.), *The Last Phase: Selections from the Deccan Commissioner's Files, Peshwa Daftar, 1815–1818* (Bombay, 1948).

their bureaucratic work. In a clear departure from the Bengali model, minor litigation was handed over to native juries called *panchayats*, and the land was settled directly on ryotwari cultivators so that the former aristocratic landholders could be circumvented entirely.[45]

When he came to consider how to deal with refractory feudal hold-overs, disloyal landowners, and discharged soldiers of the former regime, Elphinstone turned neither to the pages of Sir Walter Scott nor to his own unwritten Maratha *History*. Rather, to his own surprise, he found guidance in the writings of Jeremy Bentham – a thinker whom he had previously found uncongenial, but whom he now came to respect and admire. What Elphinstone found attractive in Bentham was his utilitarian contempt for obstructive forms and conventionalities when they impeded the path of rational policy implementation. Perhaps in Britain, with its long-established progressive history and constitutional traditions, such restraints might be desirable as checks and balances against the risk of executive autocracy. In India, however, where these traditions were deemed reactionary – and where power was now being exercised by benevolent despots like himself – political centralization and administrative efficiency were more likely to promote the greatest happiness for the greatest number.[46]

These Benthamite tendencies were greatly reinforced after 1819, when Elphinstone's conquered districts were annexed to the Bombay Presidency, and he was appointed Governor (in preference to Malcolm) over both domains. At this time, the urban population of Bombay was approximately 200,000, having nearly tripled over the previous sixty years. Yet Elphinstone and other forward-looking British officials envisioned an even more spectacular future growth based on capitalist enter-prise. In this vision, the peasants of Gujarat and Maharashta would generate vast consignments of cotton, which Bombay merchants would sell to Lancashire in return for British manufactured goods. Not long detained by the disaster this would wreak on India's textile artisans, Elphinstone did recognize the state's obligation to create new, market-savvy colonial subjects through mass education. Here again, he found himself moving in directions that he had not originally anticipated. Instead of patronizing the old-style Hindu academies, left over from the days of Baji Rao, he decided to concentrate on urban secular

---

[45] Mountstuart Elphinstone, *Territories Conquered from the Paishwa: A Report* (Delhi, 1973), 1–106, 168–74. See also Kenneth Ballhatchet, *Social Policy and Social Change in Western India, 1817–1830* (Oxford, 1957), 1–134, 193–200, 234–47; Choksey, *Elphinstone*, 213–54.

[46] Elphinstone, *Territories Conquered from the Paishwa*, 146–73; Ballhatchet, *Social Policy*, 35–42, 77–83, 217–91.

education for the middle class. In 1818, a Bombay Education Society was founded, and plans for several schools were set afoot. Elphinstone agreed to provide modest subsidies for their operation, and the scheme met with almost instantaneous success. By the mid-1820s, a chain of lower and higher schools was in operation, and the only question was whether the latter should impart western learning in Indian vernaculars, or the teaching of advanced subjects should be confined to the English language.[47]

For his part, Elphinstone favored the first alternative, since he wished to educate not merely an *haute bourgeois* elite, but also a cadre of competent native teachers who would go out into the countryside and teach the peasants to read and write. Mass education, Elphinstone suggested, would remove popular prejudices against the British, by helping peasants to understand the new system and, where necessary, to defend their own rights. Through education, the peasant might learn the advantages of prudence, frugality, delayed marriage, and self-respect. These virtues, while making Indians more British, would not necessarily be conducive to indefinite British rule. "When the natives get more extended notions," he wrote to a friend, "they will expect first a share of their own Government and then the whole." Yet "it will be better," he concluded, "to lose the country by the effects of our liberality, than to keep it like Dutchmen or Spaniards."[48]

Elphinstone was of course unusually perceptive in his insight that the paradoxical result of making India British would be to facilitate her final independence from imperial rule. Nevertheless, by the 1820s and 1830s, many other British officials were beginning to draw the conclusion that the best way for modern India to move into the future would be to cast off the chains of her unfortunate history. "The diffusion of European knowledge and morals among the people of India" was "essential to their well being," argued the new Governor-General, Lord William Bentinck, in 1833. "The development of the natural resources of the country depends mainly on the introduction of European capital and skill."[49] Yet the transition from Brahma to Bentham might not be

---

[47] Elphinstone, *Selections from the Minutes*, 77–116; Ballhatchet, *Social Policy*, 135–262; Colebrooke, *Life of Elphinstone*, II: 100–200; Bayly, *Indian Society*, 69–71, 129–31.

[48] Ballhatchet, *Social Policy*, 250–5, 262–319, quote on 250. On the education controversy, see Bruce Tiebout McCully, *English Education and the Origins of Indian Nationalism* (Gloucester, 1966); M. A Laird, *Missionaries and Education in Bengal, 1793–1837* (Oxford, 1972); and Gaur. Viswanathan, *Masks of Conquest: Literary Study and British Rule in India* (Columbia, 1989); Choksey, *Elphinstone*, 255–401.

[49] Eric Stokes, *The English Utilitarians in India* (Oxford, 1959); John Rosselli, *Lord William Bentinck: The Making of a Liberal Imperialist, 1774–1839* (Berkeley, 1974), quote on 195.

quite so seamless as these words implied. As Bentinck himself well knew, it required one final, dispositive Scottish-Indian *History*.

5   James Mill and the British assault on Indian history

If books are not to be judged by authorial intentions but by audience effects, then James Mill's massive six-volume *History of British India* proved to be an extraordinarily influential work. Read by many leading politicians and policy-makers after its appearance in 1818, it became the set text for EIC training-school cadets. Even after 1844, when H. H. Wilson published a critical edition that noted its many flaws, the book continued to be the main source from which British readers got their Indian history. Arriving just when the Marathas were departing, Mill's *History* became, in fact, a tract for the times. Its arrogant indictment of Indian civilization corresponded all too well with the needs of an imperial power whose rapidly expanding might and influence had made it the dominant force in the subcontinent. Mill's great accomplishment was to puncture the prestige of orientalism. His role was to shatter the romance of EIC officials such as Malcolm and to dispel the allure of Indian history. To an increasingly self-confident and arrogant Raj, Mill offered a welcome ideological justification of unconditional British cultural and historical superiority. To a British administration that no longer felt the need to compromise with Indians, or even to placate the sensitivities of indigenous elites, Mill's *History* showed why it was neither necessary nor desirable to make such concessions.[50]

Mill's re-valuation of Indian civilization rests on a deconstruction of the work of Sir William Jones. Jones's exaggerated claims about the sophistication of ancient Hindu learning had been made on the basis of evidence whose provenance Mill thought questionable, at best. Men like Jones and Colebrooke had given the Indians too much credit out of a generous but misplaced sense of *noblesse oblige*.[51] Did the Hindus vaunt the subtlety of their Sanskrit language? Mill (who did not think it worth learning) dismissed it as "loose, vague, wavering, obscure and

[50] James Mill, *The History of British India*, 6 vols., notes by H. H. Wilson (New York, 1968). An abridged one-volume edition is also available, edited and with a good introduction by William Thomas, hereafter referred to as *British India* (Chicago, 1975). For a good general discussion of Mill's *History of British India*, see Javed Majeed, *Ungoverned Imaginings: James Mill's "The History of British India" and Orientalism* (Oxford, 1992); Lynn Zastoupil, *John Stuart Mill and India* (Stanford, 1994), 7–27; and C. H. Philips, "James Mill, Mountstuart Elphinstone and the History of India," in C. H. Philips (ed.), *Historians of India, Pakistan and Ceylon* (Oxford, 1961), 217–29.
[51] Mill, *British India*, especially 197–205, 216–38.

inconsistent." Did the Hindus exalt the purity and elevation of their religion? Mill condemned it as a farrago of absurd rituals and insane self-mortifications, "which subjects to its votaries the grossest images of sensual pleasure, and ... which ascribes to the supreme God an immense train of obscene acts." "Volumes would hardly suffice to depict at large a ritual which is more tedious, minute, and burthensome; and engrosses a greater portion of human life, than any which has been found to fetter and oppress any other portion of the human race." Was India reputed to be a land of great riches? This was an illusion, fostered by the superfluous profusion of unproductive gold and silver, which kept "the great body of the people" in "a state of poverty and wretchedness."[52]

As a Scottish student of Dugald Stewart, Mill well understood that both Britons and Indians had entered history as barbarians. Yet while Britain had moved upward to the heights of civilization, India (notwithstanding its own passage into agriculture and commerce) had remained in a state of *cultural* barbarism. Mill attributed this stagnation to the enduring dominance that the privileged Brahmans had exercised over the rest of society. "A whole race of men were set apart and exempted from the ordinary cares and labours of life." Establishing their influence "by artful contrivances for deceiving the people," these pernicious priests had devised the malignant caste system to maintain their inequitable system of degradation and profligacy. The result of this breathtaking imposition was the maintenance of the majority Hindu population in a state of gross ignorance and moral degeneracy. Indians, Mill complained, were habitually lazy and dishonest. Lacking courage and resolution, they resorted to lawsuits and perjury. Their treatment of women was disgraceful, the surest proof of barbarity.[53]

So closely did Mill's anathemas resonate with the ethnocentrism of Victorian imperialists that later readers may have assumed that he shared their elitist and anti-democratic views. In fact this was very far from the case. For Mill saw himself as a radical anti-imperialist, a principled believer in political democracy, and a staunch opponent of aristocratic privilege in all its forms. So far from being a racist, he was a steadfast

---

[52] Mill, *British India*, 151, 182, 210, 163, 242–5.
[53] Jennifer Pitts, *A Turn to Empire: The Rise of Imperial Liberalism in Britain and France* (Princeton, 2005), 123–33; Mill, *British India*, 3–250, quotes on 209. In contrast to Malcolm, who criticized the patriarchal excesses of Islam, Mill credits the "fierce, manly" Muslim invaders of the subcontinent with bringing India to the threshold of historical activity. Only the British, however, could bring full civilization. Mill, *British India*, 251–99; Bruce Mazlish, *James and John Stuart Mill: Father and Son in the Nineteenth Century* (New York, 1965), 116–45; Majeed, *Ungoverned Imaginings*, 195–200; Stokes, *Utilitarians in India*, 53–65, 86–93.

believer in human equality who repudiated all notions of biological inferiority. A vigorous proponent of nurture over nature, he insisted that human behavior was shaped entirely by environmental forces. With the benefit of proper education and training, he insisted, all people could achieve the same high level of civilization and morality. Yet this offer of *political* equality was made contingent on a *refusal* of recognition to Hindu culture. Mill's harsh indictment of Indians was thus intended to help them – to liberate them from the chains of their repellent history.[54] If progress in India was to be brought by Britons, it seemed only logical to make a clean break with indigenous tradition and to re-write the progress narrative in an anglocentric frame.

In fact, it is a slight oversimplification to describe Mill's *History* as "anglocentric," for he saw that the deadweight of a dysfunctional past also operated in Britain, impeding the triumph of reason and progress at home. Indeed, it has been argued that Mill's virulent assault on Hinduism was actually a displacement of his own hatred of the English aristocracy. By this theory, his attack on Brahman priestcraft was obliquely targeted at the Anglican establishment, and his acidic response to the oriental character was a cover for his frustration at ignorance and credulity in the metropolis.[55] In truth, Mill's projection of cowardice onto the defenseless Hindu his own cowardice, since he treated the same corruption with a good deal more deference when he encountered it in powerful vested interests at home. As a radical who had lived through the Age of Revolution, he knew the high costs of taking on the British establishment directly. In writing about India, he cleverly disguised the extremity of his own progress narrative, diverting it to a target that he knew was undefended and would not bring him into conflict with the powerful and the great. Mill may well have rationalized this prudential approach with the logic of his own felicific calculus: what, after all, was the modest unhappiness of ten million Britons against the abject misery of forty-five million benighted Indians, whose best hope for progress was to adopt the (admittedly still flawed) anglocentric way?[56]

---

[54] James Mill, *The Article Colony, Reprinted from the Encyclopedia Britannica* (London, n.d.); Mazlish, *James and John Stuart Mill*, 132–45. Majeed, *Ungoverned Imaginings*, 123–94, takes Mill's radicalism seriously, while Uday Singh Mehta, *Liberalism and Empire: A Study in Nineteenth-Century British Liberal Thought* (Chicago, 1999), 87–97, focuses on the exclusionary, even racist, side of his work. The challenge is to explain how these two contradictory strands could have co-existed in Mill's *History of British India*.

[55] Majeed, *Ungoverned Imaginings*; William Thomas, "Introduction," in Mill, *British India*, xxxiv–xxxviii; Joseph Hamburger, *James Mill and the Art of Revolution* (New Haven, 1963).

[56] Alexander Bain, *James Mill: A Biography* (London, 1882), 1–158.

That Mill's benevolence was not entirely disinterested – that a good deal of his own sense of self was at stake – can be seen in the venom and visceral hostility with which he calumniated all aspects of Hindu culture. Indeed, there is an irony in the way his animus against Indian civilization drives his own prose beyond the rationalism he espouses, into exactly the kind of rhetorical hysteria that he finds so objectionable in his image of "the east." It is clear from his language that Mill found something about India to be deeply and personally threatening. This ineffable specter, which eludes his diagnosis, is invariably conjured up under the catch-all label of "effeminacy." "The wild imaginings" and "wild eulogies and legends" of effeminate Hindus haunt the otherwise dry and deracinated pages of his *History*. They threaten to overspill the sober realm of utility and to escape any "coherent system of belief." If the Hindus were simple primitives, like the Native Americans or the Scottish Highlanders, they would pose no danger to the British masculinity of a man like Mill. It is because they insinuate the illusion of cultivation that their wiles must be aggressively resisted, and their "barbarism" ruthlessly exposed. In contrast to Elphinstone, who hoped to Britishize the Indians, Mill fears that they will orientalize their conquerors and render them effete. The only solution is that the Indians must completely give up their culture and embrace the anglicized version of Britishness to which he (a Scotsman) had acquiesced.[57]

At this point, it is instructive to compare Mill with that other struggling, aspiring writer with whom he shared the streets of Edinburgh during the 1790s. Young Walter Scott, as we have seen, learned to carve out a viable masculine identity by diverting the fires of revolution and crafting a centrist romance of bi-national unity. Swept up in the revolutionary fervor that Scott resisted, Mill abandoned first Scotland, then religion and political centrism, in favor of a cold, atheistic London literary exile. Having eschewed Scott's reconciliatory romance of Anglo-Scottish Union, he clung more desperately to the redeeming powers of reason, hazarding the hope that they could be purveyed to an English audience through the foil of an Indian *History*. To insure his rejection of fancy and imagination. Mill associated these qualities with alien, effeminizing (i.e. Indian) forms. Perhaps this explains why a penurious Scottish writer with a growing family in London would seek an English reputation by devoting twelve laborious years to writing a dry, unsympathetic Indian *History*.[58]

[57] Mill, *British India*, 13, 174, 176, 247.
[58] Bain, *James Mill*, 1–158; Mazlish, *James and John Stuart Mill*, 3–145; Eli Halevy, *The Growth of Philosophical Radicalism* (London, 1928), 313–514.

In a sense, Mill's gamble paid off brilliantly, and his labors were richly rewarded, enabling him to join the English intelligentsia of his day. Since English law was itself no ideal utilitarian model, reformers could do better by leaving England and setting to work on the blank slate of the east. Unfortunately, the early English nabobs had degenerated to the level of their new environment, and it was only with the Regulating Act of 1773 that the notion of turning the EIC into an instrument of progressive government was born. Twenty year later, the Permanent Settlement of Bengal showed just how rudderless and mistaken the EIC policy-makers remained when they set the interests of the few (zamindars) over those of the many (ryots). However, as Mill's narrative drew closer to the moment when its publication could enter (and alter) the narrative itself, its author looked more favorably on the potential of the EIC.

> In regard to *intention*, I know no government, either in past or present times that can be placed equally high with that of the East India Company. I know no government which has on all occasions shown so much of a disposition to make sacrifices of its own interests to the interests of the people whom it governed ... but that they have never erred so much, as when, distrusting its [*sic*] own knowledge, they have followed the directions of men whom they unhappily thought wiser than themselves, viz. Practical Statesmen and Lawyers.[59]

Written by a statesman and lawyer *manqué*, this was taken as a job application. A year later, in 1819, Mill was appointed to the post of Assistant Examiner. Regularly promoted over the ensuing decade, he was made Examiner in 1830. Mill's co-optation into Indian decision-making not only did wonders for his masculine self-esteem, but also convinced him that a new spirit of utilitarian rationalism was about to become dominant in the formulation of policy. No doubt it was flattering to be publicly told by Lord William Bentinck at his departure for India in 1833, "I am going to British India, but I shall not be Governor General. It is you who will be Governor General." In fact, as most recent historians have concluded, the importation of Benthamite utilitarianism into India during the 1830s effected no immediate revolution in imperial government. It was Indian conditions, much more than official intentions, which dictated how policies would play out on the ground. When economic transformation finally began, in the 1850s, it proceeded more by technology transfer and capital investment than through the animating force of bureaucratic policy. While the ryotwari land settlement was increasingly favored by policy-makers, Mill was

[59] Mill, *British India*, 396, 409, 579, quote on 583.

mistaken to imagine that it constituted a radical experiment that would plough Ricardian rent back into government coffers to promote indigenous economic development and peasant autonomy.[60]

Seen in this light, Mill's gestures of ultra-rationalist self-congratulation appear at least partly as exercises in self-delusion. His attack on Indian culture did less to promote the triumph of universal values than to reinforce the narrow prejudices of the new English ruling elite. Privately, Mill must have viewed Indian developments during the years of his EIC employment with a certain amount of wonderment and unease: a reformist government, animated by hostility to orientalist extravagance and wedded to principles of administrative centralization, was becoming a chrysalis for the gestation of a new kind of hard-edged, racially exclusionary anglocentric arrogance. A liberal imperialism, committed to westernization and "manly" empowerment, was becoming the instrument for removing Indians from responsible positions in self-government and degrading them to the status of an inferior breed. What did Mill the democrat and anti-imperialist really think of the new Greater British Leviathan that was imposing its weight everywhere around the world? How did Mill the atheist feel when the loudest and most effective advocates of his radical principles turned out to be not secular reformers, but Christian missionaries? It is hard to believe that he was utterly blind to these contradictions between the aims he professed and the results he achieved.[61]

Not everyone was enamored with Mill's anglicization of the progress narrative, and at least a few of the older orientalists worried that his performance in trashing Indian culture was the surest way to alienate Indians from British progress. In an obscure Bombay publication, Vans Kennedy, a very different type of Scot, shredded Mill's claim that ignorance of India, its language, and its culture was an advantage in promoting understanding and objectivity. Drawing on his own background as an EIC official who had lived long in India, Kennedy showed how Mill had misconstrued or neglected most of his sources. Even worse, he had made the elementary mistake of equating the Hindu way of life with Brahman ideology. It was quite impossible for a culture as vicious and dysfunctional as Mill had depicted to survive for several thousand years. What India needed was knowledgeable and sympathetic Britons who were willing and able to translate her alien features into

---

[60] Bain, *James Mill*, 343–9; quoted in Rosselli, *Lord William Bentinck*, 84. Stokes, *Utilitarians in India*, especially 81–139; Bayly, *Indian Society*, 106–35.

[61] Stokes, *Utilitarians in India*, 50–2, 87–93, 173–9, 193–6; Zastoupil, *Mill and India*, 7–27; Pitts, *A Turn to Empire*, 123–33.

terms that a metropolitan audience could appreciate and understand.[62] When he contemplated the matter from his London retirement, Mountstuart Elphinstone was quietly inclined to agree. While he did not publicly dispute Mill's conclusion, he privately expressed his dismay at the tone of Mill's book. "Nothing is more common," he noted, "than to pronounce hastily and decidedly on the national character of a nation: Yet how different it is to form a correct judgment on such a subject." Gradually, reluctantly, Elphinstone was persuaded to write a different *History of India* that would provide an alternative to Mill's misbegotten work.[63]

Although this project was never completed, the first two volumes appeared in 1841. They concentrate on traditional India, before the British arrived. Without offering any strong endorsement to Hindu (or Muslim) culture, Elphinstone pleads that Indians be understood in the context of their history. The ancient Code of Manu was not appealing to a modern reader, but would Englishmen like to be judged by the witchcraft statutes of Elizabeth? Conducting a thorough review of the evidence, Elphinstone reinforces the orientalist conclusion that the ancient Indians were more advanced than any other civilization, including those of Europe and Greece. If this lead had been lost in recent centuries, Indians remained at least as intelligent and capable as any other people. India's failure to initiate its own modernization is regarded by Elphinstone as largely accidental, and not indicative of any deficiency in its elite. In contrast to Mill's corrupt, parasitic, and intellectually obfuscating Brahman, Elphinstone's is a fastidious and spiritual ascetic, whose prescribed life "is one of laborious study as well as of austerity and refinement." If modern Brahmans have departed from the ways of their ancestors and can be found in a wider range of activities and occupations, this is merely evidence of their flexibility and their self-refashioning for conditions of modernity.[64]

In his treatment of Hindu religion, Elphinstone emphasizes its noble, elevating monotheistic elements. At the same time he praises rather than blames the Hindus for incorporating pagan, idolatrous elements of popular worship into orthodox religion. The notion that the Hindus are

---

[62] Vans Kennedy, "Remarks on the Sixth and Seventh Chapters in Mill's History of British India," in *Transactions of the Literary Society of Bombay* (London, 1823), III: 124–82. *ODNB*, XXXI: 273–4.

[63] Colebrooke, *Life of Elphinstone*, II: 353, 355; Mountstuart Elphinstone, "On the Moral Character of Hindus as Described in Mill's British India," British Library, London, European MSS, 128, fo. 218.

[64] Mountstuart Elphinstone, *The History of India: Hindu and Mahometan Periods* (Allahabad, 1966), 10–85, quote on 12.

(or were) effeminate, Elphinstone counters with a depiction of the grandeur and brilliance of a Sepoy cavalry. "Nothing can be more magnificent
than this sort of charge: The thunder of the ground, the flashing of their
arms, the brandishing of their spears, the agitation of their banners rush-
ing through the wind."[65] Elphinstone throws his greatest challenge to the
imagination of British readers in his discussion of Indian drama and
poetry. "A person unacquainted Shanscrit [sic]," he avows, "scarcely
possesses the means of forming an opinion on the poetry of the Hindus."

What ideas can we derive from being told that a maiden's lips are a bandujiva
flower and that the luster of the madhuca beams on her cheeks? ... Yet those
figures may be as expressive to those who understand the allusions, as our own
comparisons of a youthful beauty to an opening rose, or for one that pines for
love to a neglected primrose.

As antidote to the culture-blindness and earth-abstraction of Mill,
Elphinstone tries to transport his readers

to the deep shade of a grove, where the dark tamála mixes its branches with the
pale foliage of the nimba, and the mangoe tree extends its ancient arms among
the quivering leaves of the lofty pípala, some creeper twines round the jambu,
and flings out its floating tendrils from the topmost bough. The asóca hangs
down the long clusters of its glowing flowers, the madhavi exhibits its snow-white
petals, and other trees pour showers of blossoms from their loaded branches.
The air is filled with fragrance, and is still, but for the hum of bees and the
rippling of the passing rill.[66]

Even in India, Elphinstone notes, it is difficult for Britons fully to enter
into the cultural and imaginative world of Indians. "Religion and manners
put bars to our intimacy with the natives, and limit the number of transactions as well as the free communication of opinions. We know nothing
of the interior of the families but by report; and have no share in those
numerous occurrences of life in which the amiable parts of character are
most exhibited." And yet Elphinstone believed that, if British India were
really to cohere over the long run, these barriers would have to be surmounted, and a much higher level of sympathy and mutual understanding
would have to be achieved. It was here that history had an indispensable
role to play. Yet Mill's ethnocentric *History* had the opposite effect. Its
"sneers and sarcastic expressions" could only increase the distance
between Briton and Indian and inflame the prejudices of both alike.[67]

---

[65] Elphinstone, *History of India*, 183, 187–91, 196–7, quote on 81.
[66] Elphinstone, *History of India*, 147, 151–2.
[67] Colebrooke, *Life of Elphinstone*, II: 353, quote on 355. See also Elphinstone, "On the
Moral Character of Hindus" and Elphinstone, *History of India*, 193–4.

In his private journal, Elphinstone noted that "the most desirable course for events in that country [India] is that European opinions and knowledge should spread until the nation becomes capable of founding a government of its own, on principles of which Europe has long had exclusive possession." Yet this goal (of which Mill also approved) would become possible only if the Indians could formulate their own distinctive way of absorbing Britishness into an authentically Indian idiom. Once again, Elphinstone placed great hopes on the creative powers of history to provide a vehicle for bi-cultural dialogue and mutual recognition in which both Indian and Briton could learn to revise their one-sided self-narratives and craft together a more balanced (and more mutually integrated) Greater British history. Having dismissed the value of Mill's work in initiating this dialogue, he had no illusions about the long-term utility of his own corrective *History*. On the other hand, he placed great hope in the fledgling efforts of a new breed of "Europeanized Indians" – and most notably in the works of the Brahman reformer and translator *par excellence*, Rammohun Roy.[68]

6   Rammohun Roy's Union of Anglo-Indian history

Born eleven months before James Mill, Rammohun Roy was raised in a devout Bengali Brahman family that exhibited many of the features which Mill would later so stridently decry: child marriage, ritual purification, and habitual abasement before a pantheon of household gods all marked the rhythms of daily domestic life. Initially dutiful and preternaturally religious, young Rammohun grew uneasy about many aspects of his father's creed. The study of Persian and Arabic gained him access to the Koran and opened his eyes to the monotheistic religion of the Muslims, which seemed more rational and satisfying than his own ancestral faith. Further studies of the Vedas, Vedanta, and Hindu reformers like Nanak, however, convinced him that there was an alternative, superior tradition within Hinduism. At the same time, he realized that the recovery of this purer original mode of worship would require abandoning the idolatry and superstition that most Hindus actually practiced.[69]

---

[68] Colebrooke, *Life of Elphinstone*, II: 344–5.
[69] CLR. In addition to Collet's original research, much of the value of this volume comes from the research of the editors, published as supplements to each chapter. See also Rammmohun Roy, "Autobiographical Sketch," in *The English Works of Rammohun Roy*, ed. Jogendra Chunder Ghose [1906], 4 vols. (New Delhi, 1982), I: 223–5; A. K. Majumdar, "Religion of Rammohun Roy," in V. C. Joshi (ed.), *Rammohun Roy and the Process of Modernization in India* (New Delhi, 1975), 69–88.

When Rammohun's widening spiritual horizons brought him into conflict with his father, the boy left home at age fifteen. Pressed by the need to make money, he became a successful moneylender and banker servicing the needs of high-living British officers and zamindari elites. Although the details of Rammohun's life during this phase of his life are sketchy, it appears that he made a great deal of money and saved up enough to live independently for the remainder of his life. Apprenticing himself to an EIC collector, Roy perfected his English, made himself master of the details of the Bengali revenue system, and worked for a time as a collector himself. This job gave him a window into the degradation of so many among his zamindar class.[70]

This apogee of Rammohun Roy's secular anglicization corresponded with his spiritual discovery of Jesus Christ. Adding Greek, Latin, and Hebrew to his linguistic armory, he made a close study of the Gospels and the Old Testament. When he read such passages as the Sermon on the Mount, he realized that the essence of Jesus's message was exactly the same as that conveyed by the more elevated portions of the Vedas or the Koran. When Roy published a pamphlet entitled *Precepts of Jesus: The Guide to Peace and Happiness*, the leaders of the British community in Calcutta rejoiced that he seemed ready to embrace Christianity. Yet when the pamphlet appeared in 1820, they found that they had misjudged their man. For Roy took considerable pains to distinguish the deep truths enunciated by the *prophet* Jesus from the corrupt shell of Christian dogma, sectarian ritual, and theological absurdity that had developed around the subsequent practices of European Christianity. In this bold, audacious effort to turn the tables on British discourse, all the charges that were made against degenerate Hinduism were now reversed by this linguistically omnicompetent Hindu who saw exactly the same pattern in the history of Christianity. When the Baptist missionaries tried to dismiss Roy's arguments in their *Friend of India*, their Indian friend shot back with another pamphlet, *An Appeal to the Christian Public in Defense of "The Precepts of Jesus"*, in which his argument was restated more forcefully. In two further "Appeals" to additional rebuttals, Roy politely, but determinedly, refused to concede an inch of ground.[71]

Rammohun Roy was clearly accomplishing in the sphere of religion what he had accomplished in the secular realm a decade earlier: he was challenging the British masters on their own imperial territory, and then

---

[70] CLR, 1–58; Asok Sen, "The Bengal Economy and Rammohun Roy," in Joshi (ed.), *Rammohun Roy and Modernization*, 103–35.

[71] CLR, 59–107.

forcing them to engage with him on Indian terms. All the defects which Christians found in his religion were equally evident in their own. How was the Christian Trinity of Father, Son, and Holy Spirit any different from the Hindu trinity of Brahma, Vishnu, and Siva? If Hindu idolatry and superstition were vicious, then the Christian equivalents were equally vicious. Hinduism, Islam, and Christianity, Roy now concluded, each represented different approaches to the same underlying universal truths: God was one, omnipotent, and indivisible. He was the lord and creator of all nature, and had endowed all human beings with the same morally grounded precept to "love thy neighbor." In their laudable efforts to make religion comprehensible to the uneducated, the early expositors of all three religions had made too many compromises with the bigotry, superstition, and idolatry of the masses. Everywhere, this produced the same lamentable results: preposterous fables, degrading rituals, sectarian hatreds, and irrational beliefs. Yet in an era of global enlightenment, it should be possible for diverse cultures to exchange their religions, much as Jones had proposed that they should exchange their classical texts. Separating the chaff of latter-day corruptions from the core of deep spiritual truths underneath, each religion could be ransacked and fused in a higher unity. In this task, Christian, Hindu, and Muslim (not to mention Buddhist, Sikh, Confucian, and Jew) were all equally placed. Eschewing insular ethnocentrism and arrogant presumptions of superiority or inferiority, the new synthesis could provide the spiritual foundations for a trans-national, trans-racial union of east and west.[72]

Given the reality of British–Indian power relations, Rammohun Roy was not permitted to indulge in this naive ecumenical formulation for very long. His desire to encompass everyone seemed to satisfy no one. Unimpressed with the boldness of his rhetorical sallies against the English master, orthodox Hindus fixed instead on what they perceived as his manifest apostasy. His original rebellion against his paterfamilias was never forgiven, and his very existence posed a challenge to the verities of Brahman conventionality. Meanwhile, the Muslims (like the Christians) did not know what to make of this man who had worked for the British, venerated Jesus, called himself a Hindu, was hated by the pandits, routinely quoted the Koran, and publicly appeared in Islamic dress. This confusion, moreover, did not end with Rammohun Roy's death. Over the years, he has been variously depicted as an apologist

---

[72] CLR, 107–66; Roy, "The Precepts of Jesus: The Guide to Peace and Happiness," in *English Works*, III: 482–544, IV: 545–874; "A Present to the Believers in One God," in *English Works*, IV: 940–58.

for the British Raj, a forerunner of Indian nationalism, a romantic pantheist in the style of Goethe, and a prefiguration of the twentieth-century "guru" who peddles "eastern wisdom" to the pocketbooks of the west. As a result, there has been a tendency to play down Roy's significance – either to exalt him as unique original or to dismiss him as an unclassifiable freak.[73] Viewed against the backdrop of nineteenth-century liberal imperialism, however, he may be considered in relation to the other figures in this chapter. With James Mill, he could be scathing about the degradation of modern Hindus, but with Henry Colebrooke, he lovingly resurrected the ancient classics from which they had diverged. With John Malcolm he could wax eloquent about the preservation of Indian traditions, yet with Mountstuart Elphinstone he could seek an Indian path to modernization that could never be articulated in the English language alone. In short, Rammohun Roy was the British–Indian other – the sympathetic but alien interlocutor whom liberal imperialism would have to accommodate if it were ever to achieve true union on an imperial scale.

Staking out this new space for liberal imperial discourse was an act of considerable originality that could only have been attempted by a man, like Roy, of multiple hybridities. As an anglicized Indian, a Hinduized Briton, a modernizing traditionalist, a romantic rationalist, a bourgeois intellectual, and a scholar-aristocrat, Roy had precisely the right combination of material and conceptual resources to invent a new kind of "bordering." Unlike the bordering that we have so far considered, that of Roy did not flow from metropolis to the margins. Rather, it grasped the gravitational situation of the center from the eccentric vantage of an orbital periphery. To make useful calculations from so unstable a location required a man of great acuity who was also fast on his feet. Moreover, Roy's work involved an enormous amount of literal as well as figurative translation – interpreting Britons to Indians and *vice versa*. Here Roy's vast linguistic skills and familiarity with the canonical texts of every sect and denomination stood him in good stead. His substantial wealth allowed him to initiate projects that others would not sponsor and to prime the pump of inter-cultural communication. At various points in his career he financed a succession of papers and journals, in English, Bengali, Persian, and other languages, publishing articles not only in his own name, but also in a range of pseudonymous disguises, which enabled

---

[73] For a range of different interpretations of Rammohun Roy, see the essays in Joshi (ed.), *Rammohun Roy and Modernization*; Ramananda Chaterjee, *Rammohun Roy and Modern India* (Calcutta, 1918); and Iqbal Singh, *Rammohun Roy: A Biographical Inquiry into the Making of Modern India* (Bombay, 1958).

him to float trial balloons or indulge in playful parody.[74] In this manner, over a period of twenty years, he was able to accomplish two seemingly contradictory feats. In the first place, he was able to gain acceptance as a British imperialist, without sacrificing his reputation as an Indian patriot. Second, he was able to continue to identify as a practicing Hindu, without ever flagging in his commitment to British modernity. Let us consider these dual accomplishments in turn.

To understand Roy's trajectory as a British imperialist, it is first necessary to ask why his global, even cosmic, bordering – with its transcendent vision of universal spirituality – should ever have assumed a distinctively British imperial face. Indeed, during his youth, Roy's political and spiritual aspirations had been more open-ended. Like many European intellectuals, he had been inspired by the ideals of the French Revolution, and he identified with the cause of oppressed peoples in Italy, Greece, Latin America, Ireland, and everywhere else around the world. Initially attracted to Napoleon, he was ultimately repelled by that dictator's penchant for violence and tyranny. In the meantime, Roy's EIC work, and his later friendships with Britons (usually Scotsmen) like David Hare, Alexander Duff, and William Adam, left him with a growing respect for British liberal culture. Finally, the unconditional British triumphs of the 1815–20 period, both in Europe and in India, left no really viable practical alternative for the gestation of a nascent Indian national identity. By bringing peace, prosperity, and western education, the British, according to Roy, had differentiated themselves from all of India's previous conquerors.

Divine Providence at last, in its abundant mercy, stirred up the English [sic] nation to break the yoke of those tyrants, and to receive the oppressed Natives of Bengal under its protection. Having made Calcutta the capital of their dominions, the English distinguished this city by such peculiar marks of favor, as a free people would be expected to bestow, in establishing an English Court of Judicature, and granting to all within its jurisdiction, the same civil rights as every Briton enjoys in his native country; thus putting the Natives of India in possession of such privileges as their forefathers never expected to attain, even under Hindu rulers.[75]

---

[74] CLR, 128–9, 138–52, 167–208, especially 132–6, 171–7. Collet notes that in the early 1820s, Roy was editor of the bilingual *Sambad Kanmundi*, the Persian *Mirat-ul-Akhbar*, the *Brahminical Magazine*, and a Unitarian Press. CLR, 128–9, 171–7, 132–6. See also Wilhelm Halbfass, *India and Europe: An Essay in Understanding* (Albany, 1988), 197–216. On colonial hybridity in postmodern discourse, see Robert J. C. Young, *Colonial Desire: Hybridity in Theory, Culture and Race* (London, 1995), and Homi K. Bhabha, *The Location of Culture* (London, 1994).

[75] CLR, 163, 172–4, 233, 267, 306, 335, 396; Roy, "Appeal to the King in Council," in *English Works*, II: 446.

Such panegyrics, which might seem exaggerated, even slavish, in reality posed a challenge to the triumphant Briton, setting forth a high standard of Indian expectation that they too must be made the beneficiaries of this vaunted English liberty. Thus, when censorship of the Calcutta press was imposed, Roy (now the proprietor of several papers, in multiple languages) penned the solemn and eloquent protest from which the above-quoted passage is drawn.

The second great duty that Roy enjoins on the British imperial masters is the obligation to provide their subjects with a western education so that they would in future be empowered to modernize themselves. In a letter to the Governor-General, Roy registered his opposition to government endowment of ancient Sanskrit learning, which he seemed to disparage in almost Millite tones. His objection was not to the Sanskrit learning, however, but to the *state* endowment of religious curricula, at the expense of the practical, scientific, and technological education that Indians would need to acquire if their descendants were to stand on their own. Sharing Elphinstone's prophesy of a future independent India, Roy saw no reason why "the connection between Great Britain and India" should not remain "on a solid and permanent footing," even after Indians gained self-government. Within the framework of some voluntary federal constitutional structure, "India may then for an unlimited period enjoy union with England, and the advantage of her enlightened Government; and in return contribute to support the greatness of this country." But even if "events should occur to effect a separation between the two countries," then a fully modernized, self-reliant nation of Muslims, Hindus, and Christian European settlers could follow the American example of independence, creating a distinctively Asian descendant of the British patrimony.[76]

For the moment, Roy was not inclined to press Indian claims to enfranchisement (which he doubtless regarded as inopportune). Instead he cast his voice with the English reform movement, which was gathering steam in the mother country. When the House of Lords threatened to throw out the Reform Bill, Roy angrily exclaimed, "In the event of the Reform Bill being defeated I would renounce my connection with this country," and declared that he would shift his moral allegiance to the United States. But after the great measure finally passed, he jubilantly exclaimed, "Thank Heaven, I can now feel proud of being one of your fellow subjects." These comments – which might on one level be read as a subordination of Indian liberty to

[76] Roy, "A Letter on English Education," in *English Works*, III: 471–7; "Remarks on the Settlement in India by Europeans," in *English Works*, II: 315–20.

English liberalism – can also be read as a bold insistence that Indians had a voice in the English polity. It was a measure of Roy's self-confidence (not to mention his elevated class privilege) that he was able to assert – against the denials of the racists – that he too was a Greater British citizen. Even more tellingly, it was a measure of his self-possession that he could deflect Mill's fears of the effeminate Brahman with a proud assertion of his own patrimonial legacy.[77]

This was not an easy maneuver, and it required much sureness of foot. From the very outset, Roy had announced his principled opposition to the caste system. Yet in practice he never fully broke with his Brahmanical entitlements, and always took care that his multiple transgressions – socializing with foreigners, traveling across the ocean, and patronizing social inferiors – never went so far as to enable his high-caste brethren to repudiate him entirely. To European friends he represented this as a pragmatic compromise that was necessary to preserve his effectiveness in Indian society. On a deeper level, it seems to have been a psychologically necessary device to prevent him from losing touch with his own identity. So far from abandoning Hindu tradition, Roy put a great deal of thought into envisioning how it might be reconciled with modern progress. At the height of the Education Controversy, when he was publicly attacking the propriety of government support for Sanskrit learning, he also privately endowed a Vedantic Academy, in which just such a curriculum was explicitly retained. Not surprisingly, these tensions emerged most sharply on the inflammatory question of sati. Having witnessed this horror within his own family, Roy developed a lifelong aversion to this and other lesser expressions of gender oppression and inequality. However, he was ambivalent about Bentinck's decision to proscribe sati, believing that it would be better for Hindus to come to this decision on their own.[78]

How long Rammohun Roy would have been able to maintain this balancing act if he had not died prematurely is difficult to tell. It is clear however that he could not have regenerated the cause of liberal imperialism all alone. Ultimately, success or failure in Indianizing the progress narrative could not depend on one man, howsoever brilliant. Rather (*pace* Elphinstone) it would require the energies of an entire class of western-educated Indians. Here too, Roy paved the way, with the formation of Brahmo Samaj, an

---

[77] CLR, 308–9, 330–6, quote on 334.
[78] CLR, 98, 189–92, 251–301; Ashis Nandy, "Sati, a Nineteenth Century Tale of Women, Violence and Protest," in Joshi (ed.), *Rammohun Roy and Modernization*, 168–94. See also Roy, "Conference between and Advocate for and an Opponent of the Practice of Burning Widows Alive," "A Second Conference," and "Abstract of the Arguments Regarding the Burning of Widows," in *English Works*, II: 321–72; and Lata Mani, *Contentious Traditions: The Debate on Sati in Colonial India* (Berkeley, 1998).

organization dedicated to advancing his universalistic ideals. It is characteristic that this organization should have emerged from the failure of the Calcutta Unitarian Committee during the 1820s. So long as Unitarianism retained its vestigial Christian and anglocentric overtones, it elicited only lukewarm Indian support. Yet in 1828, when Roy took leadership of the committee, the interest of western-educated Brahmans was awakened as he translated it into a more authentically Indian cultural idiom, and recast its ecumenicism in Vedic terms. Over the next two generations, nearly all the leading Bengali bhadralok (i.e. respectable, middle-class) families would contribute one or more members to Brahmo Samaj.[79]

Nevertheless, the success of this voluntary association in incubating an organically indigenous Indian bourgeois ideology would depend on two things. First, these rising families of merchants, financiers, landlords, and lawyers would have to succeed far more effectively than their zamindari predecessors in integrating themselves into Greater Britain's burgeoning world economy, carving out an autonomous space of economic empowerment, which would be free of the EIC's imperial and political control. Second, such an urbanized Indian bourgeoisie would have to meet with a new breed of metropolitan interlocutors who would follow Roy in recognizing the integrity of Indian culture: a new cohort of British administrators and intellectuals, receptive to experiments in syncretism, through which a more inclusive Greater British citizenship might someday emerge. These two requirements were tall orders. On their fulfillment, however, the future of nineteenth-century liberal imperialism would depend.[80]

7   Conclusion

With Rammohun Roy and Brahmo Samaj, we come full circle to the original orientalist vision that sought to mediate the British–Indian Union

[79] This included the Banerjis, Boses, Chakrabartys, Chatterjees, Dasses, Dattas, Debs, Dutts, Mitras, Sens, Roys, and Tagores, to name only the most important. CLR, 209–50, 275–9; David Kopf, *Brahmo Samaj and the Shaping of the Modern Indian Mind* (Princeton, 1979). The organization was originally named Brahmo Sabha. It was officially changed to Brahmo Samaj in 1843. Kopf, *Brahmo Samaj*, 1–153; Nemai Sadhan Bose, *Indian Awakening and Bengal* (Calcutta, 1976), 31–133; and Partha Chatterjee, *The Nation and its Fragments: Colonial and Postcolonial Histories* (Princeton, 1993), 35–75.
[80] CLR, 130–3, 164–5, 209–30. For studies of Brahmo Samaj and other "westernized" Bengali intellectuals of the pre-Congress era, see Kopf, *Brahmo Samaj*; J. K. Majumdar (ed.), *Rammohun Roy and Progressive Movements in India: A Selection from Records, 1775–1845* (Calcutta, 1941); McCully, *English Education*; F. Max Muller, *Biographical Essays* (New York, 1884); and Tapan Raychaudhuri, *Europe Reconsidered: Perceptions of the West in Nineteenth Century Bengal* (Oxford, 1988).

through interpretations of history. That eighteenth-century neo-classical version had proven too narrow, and too dependent on aristocratic elites. By contrast, the romantic, Scottish orientalism of the 1800–20 period succeeded so well in taming the frontier lands of British India that it put itself out of a job. Mill's counter-orientalist utilitarian recipe for British–Indian progress was more consistent with capitalist modernization, but it could never underwrite any genuine vision of imperial Union because it mandated the obliteration of Indian culture and history. Rammohun Roy tried to synthesize what was best in all these approaches, but history placed limits on what he could do. Unlike Walter Scott, he could not romanticize the old imperial history of violence and oppression, because that history was not yet a closed book. The new Empire that the British unleashed during the early nineteenth century in India showed that the violence of conquest and oppression had not yet run its course. So the great syncretist looked to a brighter political future and a deeper spiritual past. Britain and India had to come together, he portentously warned a friend, because India – like Ireland – would have a say in Britain's fate. "From her remote situation, her riches and her vast population, [she would prove] either useful and profitable as a willing province of the British Empire, or troublesome and annoying as a determined enemy."[81]

The words today sound impressively prophetic, but at the time they were something of an audacious bluff. Unlike India's defeated warlords, her indebted zamindars, and her salaried pandits (not to mention her millions of overtaxed peasants and degraded artisans), Roy could afford to issue this challenge because he had become financially independent of the Raj. Liberal capitalism and the progress narrative, he hoped, would create many others like himself. No less fervently, he hoped that it would create a more cosmopolitan class of Britons who might view their Empire more ecumenically, transcending its inherited anglocentric frame. In the next chapter we will see how metropolitan liberal imperialists rose to this challenge, by examining the contributions of the Evangelical Zachary Macaulay and those of T. B. Macaulay, his historian son.

[81] CLR, quote on 385–6.

3 Imagining a Greater Britain: the Macaulays and the liberal romance of Empire

> In England we can have no other feeling than that of respect for men who stood up in bad times to maintain the independence of their country against unjust aggression ... No greater calamity could have befallen England than if, for want of such men [William Wallace and Robert Bruce] she had been able to place on Scotland the yoke she abhorred, and to have her, even down to this time perhaps, a conquered nation ... I say it would have been a happy thing for the British Empire if Ireland had her Wallace and her Bruce, if it had not in those dark ages come by conquest under the arbitrary yoke of England, but had like Scotland gradually amalgamated with England by pacific measures.
>
> T. B. Macaulay, toast to Calcutta Scottish Society, Dec. 1, 1834, quoted in
> S. C. Sanial, "Macaulay in Lower Bengal," *Calcutta Review*, 244 (1906), 306

> We are trying ... to give a good government to a people to whom we cannot give a free government ... We have to engraft on despotism those blessings which are the natural fruits of liberty ... It may be that the public mind of India may expand under our system till it has outgrown that system; that by good government we may educate our subjects into a capacity for better government: that having been instructed in European knowledge, they may in some future age, demand European institutions. Whether such a day will ever come I know not. But never will I attempt to avert or retard it. Whenever it comes, it will be the proudest day in English history. To have found a great people sunk in the lowest depths of slavery and superstition, to have ruled them as to have made them desirous and capable of all the privileges of citizens, would indeed be a title to glory all our own.
>
> T. B. Macaulay, speech to House of Commons,
> July 10, 1833, in MMW, 557, 572

In 1784, while Walter Scott and John Malcolm were contemplating their futures, another young Scotsman, three years their senior, struck out for the empire of the west. Like Scott, Zachary Macaulay had dreamed of a life in literature. However, as one among thirteen children of an impecunious Presbyterian minister, he knew that this was not to be. Apprenticed to a Glasgow merchant at the age of fourteen, Zachary decided, two years later, that he had no future in Scotland. Lacking the patronage that might have drawn him to India, he felt no choice but to

99

book a passage to Jamaica on his own. Forced by circumstances to take work as a plantation under-manager, he confessed to a friend, "you would hardly know [me] were you to view me in a field of canes, amidst perhaps a hundred of the sable race, cursing and bawling, while the noise of the whip resounding on their shoulders, and the cries of the poor wretches, would make you imagine that some unlucky accident had carried you to the doleful shades." Determined to work his way out of this perdition, after five long years Zachary was able to return home. To his pleasant surprise, upon arrival in England, he discovered that a family connection with Thomas Babington had brought him into the orbit of the leading coterie of Anglican evangelical elites. Seeing the chance to make something good out of his time in Jamaica, he eagerly joined their burgeoning anti-slavery campaign.[1]

Zachary's move from the coercive extreme of the first British Empire to the metropolitan center of its prospective liberal successor set in motion a two-generational saga that this chapter will trace. The romance of freedom that Zachary forged as an anti-slavery activist was fittingly completed (and rhetorically trumped) by the grand progress narrative penned decades later by his son. Yet if the Macaulays were prime makers of the romance of liberal imperialism, in no small part this was because the experience of liberalizing the Empire provided both of them with the upward mobility by which they made themselves. This personal stake in the liberalization of the entire Empire gave both men a unique vantage that had been unavailable to those predecessors who had conceptualized union in a more limited bi-national frame: Anglo-Scottish, Anglo-Irish, or British-Indian. Linking British expansion to the universal van of human progress, and identifying empire as the agent for transmitting improvement to every distant clime, the Macaulays forged a comprehensive ideological framework that equated the liberalization of the Empire with the ascendancy of Britain and saw the ascent of Britain (also their own personal ascent) as inextricably connected to the creation of a liberal Empire. In both cases, however, as this chapter will demonstrate, these rhetorical achievements were obtained at a price – equating progress (both personal and global) with anglocentric assimilation, and obliging colonial others to abandon those national identities of cultural difference that both Walter Scott and the orientalists had regarded as necessary to ease the passage from backwardness into modernity.

---

[1] Viscountess Knutsford, *The Life and Letters of Zachary Macaulay* (London, 1900), 1–12, quote on 8. For the origins of Anglican anti-slavery see Christopher Brown, *Moral Capital: Foundations of British Abolitionism* (Chapel Hill, 2006).

1   The first Macaulay and the second British Empire

If Zachary Macaulay believed that evangelical Christianity was his salvation, he also knew that the deliverance was not merely spiritual. Conversion to Christianity meant upward mobility, the embrace of political centrism, and a more refined version of masculinity. The oath-swearing, slave-driving Jamaican gambler became a hard-working evangelical reformer, equally at home in the Negro village or fashionable drawing room. Surrounded, for the first time, by a domestic circle of pious, intelligent women, Zachary learned to be a respectable, virtuous man. With enthusiasm, he internalized his mentors' strategy of working within the existing system – advancing moderate reform as the expedient alternative to the dangers of radicalism and reaction at the political extremes.[2] Of necessity, this commitment to respectability and moderation enjoined patience and forbearance, since reform had to find its own pace. When the campaign against the slave trade was consumed in the fires of revolution during the 1790s, the Evangelicals turned their attention away from the House of Commons and looked for modest, provisional solutions on the ground. During the American wars, a group of Negroes had already gained their freedom by fighting on the loyalist side. Settled unsatisfactorily in London or Nova Scotia, they were now to be sent to Africa, where they could obtain the land that they had once been promised. Here, in the slavers' heart of darkness, they could form a model community of freedmen-farmers that would demonstrate the superiority of free labor, and gradually obtain increments of self-government as they demonstrated rising levels of industriousness and self-control.[3]

Offered a position as Governor of this Sierra Leone colony, Zachary eagerly accepted, regarding himself as tailor-made for this sort of challenging but redemptive work. Situated about midway between the freedmen who were being sponsored and the evangelical elites who were sponsoring them, he seemed a logical choice to mediate between the two. In some respects, Zachary proved to be a successful leader, since he was able to

[2] Knutsford, *Zachary Macaulay*, 13–25; CM, 3–20. For Evangelicals see Ford K. Brown, *Fathers of the Victorians: The Age of Wilberforce* (Cambridge, 1961); D. W. Bebbington, *Evangelicalism in Modern Britain: A History from the 1730s to the 1980s* (London, 1989); Reginald Coupland, *Wilberforce: A Narrative* (Oxford, 1923). For anti-slavery see David Brion Davis, *The Problem of Slavery in the Age of Revolution* (Ithaca, 1975). See also Seymour Drescher, *Capitalism and Anti-Slavery: British Mobilization in Comparative Perspective* (Oxford, 1987); and Robin Blackburn, *The Overthrow of Colonial Slavery, 1776–1848* (London, 1988).
[3] Drescher, *Capitalism and Anti-Slavery*, 67–88; Christopher Fyfe, *A History of Sierra Leone* (Oxford, 1962), 1–37; Mary Louise Clifford, *From Slavery to Freetown: Black Loyalists after the American Revolution* (Jefferson, 1999).

identify with the predicament of his charges, and he was remarkably free of racial prejudice. Yet he was also rigid and dictatorial and had been placed by his employers in what turned out to be an impossible situation. While it appeared to be an attractive proposition on paper, the colony was, in reality, a money-losing proposition from the start. It was simply impossible to keep faith with the settlers when the shareholders expected that dividends would be paid. Subjected to demands for rent, the colonists complained about the betrayal of pledges that they would be given their own land. Denied the representative government that they had been promised, they were driven to the edge of revolt. In the end, it was the very piety and spiritual fervor of the black settlers that made life miserable for Macaulay. He had gone to Africa inspired by the most noble philanthropic motives. Now he had to endure the ingratitude of his charges, who accused him of tyranny and hypocrisy for his pains.[4]

By 1799, Macaulay had become fed up with the Sierra Leone experiment and – partly chastened – returned home. Setting himself up in London as a merchant with Africa, he continued to devote the bulk of his time and energy to evangelical causes. In particular, he remained passionately committed to the campaign against the slave trade, doing a good deal of the organizational and agitational legwork that enabled the more elite movement leaders, such as Babington and William Wilberforce, to become household names. In 1807, when the British slave trade was abolished, Macaulay and his "Saints" shifted their attention to the evils of the institution of bondage itself. New committees were formed, new petition campaigns were organized, and new politicians were cultivated to introduce new bills. By 1833, when slavery was finally proscribed throughout the British Empire, Macaulay was old, infirm, and nearly bankrupt. Preoccupied with the work of emancipation, he had neglected his own business. In 1826, his financial affairs were thrown into disarray in the same credit crisis which had felled Sir Walter Scott.[5]

How are we to explain Macaulay's lifelong preoccupation with slavery, especially as his own youthful encounter with the Jamaican plantation had begun to fade? One answer was offered on the epitaph of his

---

[4] Fyfe, *History of Sierra Leone*, 1–87; Knutsford, *Zachary Macaulay*, 26–57, 86–115, 121, 127–8, 164–6, 174, 196–215; Clifford, *Slavery to Freetown*, 105–215; John Peterson, *Province of Freedom: A History of Sierra Leone, 1787–1870* (Evanston, 1969), 13–31. Zachary's experience in Sierra Leone is examined more thoroughly in the supplementary notes to this volume, and in Catherine Hall's forthcoming work on the Macaulays.

[5] Knutsford, *Zachary Macaulay*, 216–489, especially 241–2; Brown, *Fathers of the Victorians*, 372–82; Coupland, *Wilberforce*, 228–494.

gravestone, which praises a life devoted "to the diffusion of Christianity, and the relief of human wretchedness," which "during forty successive years ... rescued Africa from the woes, and the British Empire from the guilt of slavery and the slave trade." If we take this memorial seriously, then we must place this desire to save and reconstruct the British Empire at the center of our attention. The original mercantilist Empire, the epitaph seems to say, was built on a foundation that is no longer tenable. Grounded in plantation slavery, it now produces only misery and guilt. To save Africa from woe, and Britain from perdition, it is necessary to reconstruct the Empire on a new foundation. For Macaulay and his evangelical friends, it was the transforming power of Christian faith that provided the animating principle on which a new understanding of Empire could arise.[6]

In the old Empire, choices had been relatively limited, and roles comparatively fixed. The dissenter was a second-class citizen. The conquered Catholic and Indian were third-class. The black man (with a few exceptions) was predestined to slavery. The man with a Scottish brogue had the chance to become a slave-driver. If (like Malcolm and Elphinstone) he had friends and family in high places, he might find a more elevated and genteel position involving less brutal forms of rule. In the new British Empire, these outward badges of hierarchy remained significant, but their meaning had been destabilized by enhanced prospects for individual freedom and mobility. Black people were no longer to be treated only as beasts of burden. White men like Zachary now had the chance of a career that would reform them, rather than beat them, in hopes that their descendants might rise to positions like their own. This modicum of mobility opened the way to new freedoms and aspirations, but it also created new anxieties, ambiguities, and problems of recognition. In a world where impecunious Scotsmen could go out to become colonial governors and then send the sons of African chiefs to be educated in London schools, the old system of inherited ranks and fixed statuses was breaking down. If outward marks no longer made the man, then inner qualities became more important. Evangelical Christianity provided a language in which the aspiring individual could monitor his own conscience, and find a standard for judging others around him.[7]

Above and beyond these personal considerations, Christianity's greatest merit, in Macaulay's eyes, lay in its universality. Daunted by the

---

[6] Quoted in Knutsford, *Zachary Macaulay*, 489.

[7] Zachary Macaulay was enough of a *parvenu* that he deeply felt this individualist religion of discipline and conscience. But he was enough of an elitist to seek its incorporation within the established institutions of Church and State. Knutsford, *Zachary Macaulay*, 250–68.

bewildering variety of circumstances and conditions that confronted British rulers in places as diverse as Africa, India, the West Indies, Ireland, and the white settler colonies, evangelical Christianity presented itself as a potentially powerful common denominator. It offered a universal standard of recognition that seemed to solve the problem of imperial union without any laborious efforts at translation. In place of a multitude of different ethnic, class, and gender self-understandings which had to be translated from one cultural idiom into the next, Christianity offered a simple act of conversion that promised to bind colonized and colonizers together in a single moral community.

This hope can be seen in the pages of *The Christian Observer,* one of Macaulay's many projects, which he edited and published (and substantially wrote) himself. In a single year (1809), there was a long review of conditions in Haiti, a retrospect on the American Revolution, and an essay on the prospects for British India.[8] Given Haiti's dark history of enslavement and rebellion, it was here that Macaulay paradoxically placed his highest Christian hopes. In spite of the brutality to which they had been subjected, the black freedmen were acquiring both religion and education. In twenty years, he prophesied, they "would be the most literate peasantry in the world." By contrast, the Anglo-Saxons of the northern ex-colonies were not always wise in exercising the freedom to which they had been born. Still, the British editor strove to understand their point of view. "As a colony grows in strength it will gradually become more disposed to contend for its interests," but unless these interests were cavalierly disregarded, the "thousand ties of sentiment and affection" which attached it to the mother country ought to prevent it from breaking away.

I suspect that there is in all communities, more particularly in growing colonies, a certain period, during which, as in domestic life, and for nearly the same reasons, government is an affair of great delicacy. The period is that when the consciousness of newly acquired strength first produces a tendency to insubordination; when the awe of long-established authority begins to wear away; and knowledge has generated presumption, but has not yet softened into wisdom ... This period immediately precedes real maturity ... After the crisis has passed, I apprehend authority is easily preserved, though it will naturally have assumed a less arbitrary character.[9]

There was nothing original in Zacharay's use of the family metaphor to characterize the relationship of these white, North American

---

[8] *The Christian Observer,* 8 (1809), 781–92.
[9] *The Christian Observer,* 8 (1809), 21–2 and 25–6.

adolescents to their mother country. What was new was his (and his fellow Evangelicals') belief that this language of "family" was also applicable to the relationship between the metropolis and the colored colonies. However, the spiritual brotherhood of Christianity was especially necessary here as a symbolic substitute for the absent biological connections of race.[10] This led Evangelicals like Zachary into a profound error, which became most evident in their approach to India. All the orientalists considered in Chapter 2 were deeply cognizant of the dangers of trying to foist Christianity on a culture that had different, historically rooted religious traditions. "The sense of degradation," warned John Malcolm, "which they [Indians] must feel as a conquered people is soothed by the uninterrupted enjoyment of religious tenets and ceremonies handed down from their forefathers." Attack these, he presciently prophesied, and the Indians would instantly unite (Hindus and Muslims together) in a joint campaign of religious grievance that they would never be able to organize in the secular political realm.[11] Mountstuart Elphinstone and Rammohun Roy had each, in different ways, reinforced the same point. Yet Macaulay took his cues from a fellow Evangelical, Charles Grant, who had also served in India. The Hindus, Grant argued, were like ill-disposed children who had been raised in the bad environment of a degenerate home. "Discord, hatred, abuses, slanders" were the normative principles of such a society. The natural affection of parents for children, husbands for wives, and *vice versa* was suppressed. Child marriage yoked couples together like "animals of a lower species," children were sold into slavery, and women were brutally exploited and oppressed.[12]

To assert Protestant Christianity as the solution to these evils was not merely to criticize a few dysfunctional institutions. It was, *à la* James Mill, to condemn an entire culture (and the people who practiced it) as

---

[10] For a recent discussion of the relationship between religion and race see Colin Kidd, *British Identities before Nationalism: Ethnicity and Nationhood in the Atlantic World, 1600–1800* (Cambridge, 1999), and his more recent *The Forging of Races: Race and Scripture in the Protestant Atlantic World, 1600–2000* (Cambridge, 2006). Yet where Kidd sees the Bible and biblical identity as alternatives to biological racial categories (at least before the later nineteenth century), the case of Macaulay and the Evangelicals draws attention rather to the ways in which religious blinders (e.g. Protestant Christian identity) limited and constrained the capacity for imagining a trans-racial family of man.

[11] John Malcolm, *The Political History of India, 1784–1823* [1826], ed. N. Panikkar, 2 vols. (New Delhi, 1970), II: 151.

[12] Eric Stokes, *The English Utilitarians and India* (Oxford, 1989), 1–24; Ainslie Thomas Embree, *Charles Grant and British Rule in India* (Columbia, 1962); Charles Grant, "Observations on the State of Society among the Asiatic Subjects of Great Britain, Particularly with Respect to Morals and on the Means of Improving It," *Parliamentary Papers*, 10.282 (1812–13), 1–112, quotes on 27–9.

backward, irrational, and uncivilized – incapable of achieving modernity without disciplines imposed from outside. A Walter Scott would never have fallen into the error of depicting the vanquished other in such humiliating and infantilizing language. Even the Edgeworths, for all their condescension, well understood the incendiary consequences of casting Protestant proselytism as proper antidote for the disease of Catholic Irish peasant backwardness. Yet if Protestant religion could not provide a viable basis for consensual union in an Empire that was riven with a staggering array of cultural, confessional, and racial diversity, perhaps the desired result could be achieved through a more secular vision of progressive, world-encompassing British history. Zachary Macaulay was completely unsuited to creating such a synoptic British and imperial history. But inadvertently, without understanding what he was doing, he planted the seed of the man who would try.

2   The second Macaulay and the historian's Empire

In 1799, after his return from Sierra Leone, Zachary Macaulay was married. In 1800, Thomas Babington, the first of nine children, was born. Almost immediately, it became clear that the boy was extremely precocious. He possessed a photographic memory, began to read at the age of three, and by the age of seven was already at work on a "Universal History." Zachary was of course proud. But he worried about the lad's spiritual state, fearing that excessive adult adulation might go to his head. Determined to provide a salutary counterweight of discipline and correction, he admonished young Tom about the dangers of laziness and obstinacy.[13] Subjected to the same incessant exhortation as the Sierra Leone colonists, young Tom responded in a similar way. Outwardly, he was dutiful and minimally compliant, but inwardly, he resolved to follow his own path. Fortunately, Zachary was frequently away on business, so that the tenor of the household was set by his wife,

---

[13] There are several important biographies of Macaulay. The first (TLL) was by his nephew and was followed more recently by that of John Clive (CM), which carries the story to 1839. Robert E. Sullivan's *Macaulay: The Tragedy of Power* (Cambridge, MA, 2009) was released just as the present book went to press. Therefore, it has not been integrated into my account. Among shorter biographies, Owen Dudley Edwards's *Macaulay* (New York, 1988) is insightful. Another way to follow Macaulay's life is to read his own correspondence, now gathered, expertly edited, annotated, and introduced by Thomas Pinney in the six volumes of PLM. This can now be supplemented by William Thomas's five-volume edition of *The Journals of Thomas Babington Macaulay* (London, 2008). A now somewhat dated bibliographic survey of the more specialized secondary literature, by John Clive and Thomas Pinney, can be found in David J. DeLaura (ed.), *Victorian Prose: A Guide to Research* (New York, 1973), 17–30.

Selina. This bright, vivacious woman, with a touch of whimsy, was the temperamental opposite of her overbearing husband. Under her influence, home life at Clapham was full of wit and wordplay, high spirits and imagination. Like his mother, Tom became a voracious reader and, as his intelligence and erudition grew, he would entertain his younger sisters with wonderful romances drawn from his own studies of history. Although Zachary was concerned about Tom's neglect of subjects that did not amuse him (e.g. mathematics), he could not deny that the child was giving himself a magnificent literary, classical, and historical education.[14]

In fact, by the time Tom went to Cambridge, in 1818, father and son had reached an uneasy rapprochement. Zachary was not, after all, unaware of the dangers of adolescent rebellion. The problem was not so much that he had high expectations for his son, but that these expectations were mutually incompatible. On the one hand, he wanted his heir to enjoy the advantages he had lacked – wealth, social position, and a university education – all the calling cards for full-fledged membership in the British governing class. At the same time, he wanted the boy to replicate his own sense of evangelical mission to raise the downtrodden and reform society. Tom might have resented his father's contradictory expectations, but he took them as a challenge instead. He would find his own way to square this circle. To do so, he discovered, entailed transcending his father's entire Christian world vision. All the great works and vast multi-national communions that the father had sought in Christ were now to be rediscovered by the son in the secular progressions of history.[15]

Since the younger Macaulay's deification of historical progress can be traced back to the age of seven, it is important to examine the way this notion evolved in his mind. Unlike his father's monolithic Christian conversion, its development consisted of three successive strata of historiographical consciousness, each of which left its own conceptual (and emotional) residue. The first stratum was the history that Tom learned *en famille*, with his mother and sisters, through stories, romances, novels, and popular historical works. We should not assume that this most fundamental stratum was in any way facile or superficial, since it included not only Edgeworth's fictions, but also the entire corpus of Walter Scott's books. Indeed, the epic poems and novels that we surveyed in Chapter 1 all appeared during the formative years of Tom Macaulay's youth and adolescence. They were eagerly purchased, read, and discussed in the

[14] CM, 21–35; TLL, I: 17–77; PLM, I: 3–98.
[15] CM, 36–60; TLL, I: 78–108; PLM, I: 99–203.

Macaulay household. Scott's historical romance of an Anglo-Scottish Great Britain was something Macaulay simply took for granted (and assumed in his own readers) in later years.[16]

Overlaid on this "feminized" romantic, domestic history was the "serious" masculine, public history which Macaulay read as he got older, in erudite, scholarly works. This was the history of great wars, eloquent speeches, and heroic deeds. It was the history of epochal imperial cycles: conquests and defeats, rises and falls. In Macaulay's time this genre was still heavily dominated by the classical authors, read and studied in their original Greek and Latin. So far from being considered a detour into useless esotericism, this classical curriculum was widely championed as the most appropriate school for the soldiers and statesmen of the coming generation. Britain, after all, was the Greece and/or Rome of the modern era, as Edward Gibbon had well understood. The best way to learn the techniques of imperial rule and senatorial decorum was to study the way the Greeks and Romans had done it, and then make the appropriate adjustments for differences of time and place.[17]

Finally, there was the much more amorphous field of "modern" history, which covered more or less everything from the middle ages onward. This was the most embryonic and open-ended genre. Here were no definitive models, but great opportunities for a contemporary historian of the first rank. The progress narrative, with its four-stage sequence, had of course gained a considerable following in Scotland. But elsewhere, it had been rather slow to penetrate into mainstream histories. This meant that many key questions about the dynamics of modern progress had been addressed only on a general level in treatises (or in fiction), but had never been given the detailed exposition that came with close attention to this or that particular case. Yet without such detailed case-by-case accounting, it was impossible to answer the big questions in an informed and intellectually responsible way. What were the determinate mechanisms of progress? By what means was it propagated from one society to the next? How did it apply to (and presumably integrate with) the various arenas of human endeavor, such as politics, economics, culture, religion, or social structure? Why did some societies

---

[16] For an interesting discussion of Macaulay's relationship to Scott and the epic tradition, see Edwards, *Macaulay*, especially 54–82.

[17] "History," in MMW, 133–59; MEL, 313–14; CM, 21–60; TLL, I: 17–108. For examinations of the role of the Greek and Roman classics in nineteenth-century British intellectual life, see Frank M. Turner, *The Greek Heritage in Victorian Britain* (New Haven, 1981); Richard Jenkyns, *The Victorians and Ancient Greece* (Cambridge, 1980); and Norman Vance, *The Victorians and Ancient Rome* (Oxford, 1997).

progress more quickly than others? What could be done to prod the laggards along?[18]

In 1828, with his formal education finished, Tom Macaulay gathered his maturing thoughts into an essay on "History." So far from being the acolyte's obeisance to illustrious progenitors, this essay reads like a sprinter's handicap sheet: to write a truly great work of history, the novice announces, would be "the rarest of intellectual distinction." Indeed, no existing history "approaches to our notion of what a history ought to be." The reason, he avows, is that history, among all the disciplines, is unique in being "under the jurisdiction of two hostile powers ... reason and imagination." Whatever their original intentions, all historians had ended by leaning to one side or the other. None had entirely succeeded in bridging the divide.[19] The failure of the eighteenth century's philosophical historians to give full scope to their imaginative faculties had opened the way for the rise of the novel. Refused entry by the scientific historian in search of truth, the imaginative spirit of romance had found its home in the genre of fiction. The writer who came closest to bringing romance back into history was no historian, of course, but the novelist Sir Walter Scott. He had "used those fragments of truth which historians had thrown behind them in a manner which may well excite their envy." But "the truly great historian," the young acolyte anticipates, "will reclaim those materials which the novelist has appropriated."[20]

This challenge, Macaulay recognized, was all the more difficult inasmuch as modern society was more complex and multifarious than its ancient predecessor. In a warrior-dominated aristocratic society, it seemed reasonable to restrict the scope of history to the annals of courts and camps. But now, in a diverse, pluralistic, and progressive society, many other histories needed to be written: histories of ideas, of science, of religion, of economic development, of manners, morals,

---

[18] Ronald Meek, *Social Science and the Ignoble Savage* (Cambridge, 1976); J. G. A. Pocock, *Virtue, Commerce, and History: Essays on Political Thought and History, Chiefly in the Eighteenth Century* (Cambridge, 1985), 215–310; J. G. A. Pocock, *Barbarism and Religion: Narratives of Civil Government* (Cambridge, 1999).

[19] "History," in MMW, 133–59, quote on 133. See also 139. For an analysis of the ways Macaulay combined rationalism and romanticism see Rosemary Jann, *The Art and Science of Victorian History* (Columbus, 1985), 66–104; and William Thomas, *The Quarrel of Macaulay and Croker: Politics and History in the Age of Reform* (Oxford, 2000), 59–92.

[20] "History," MMW, 157, 158. See also "Hallam," in MEL, 51–2. Macaulay also spoke of Jane Austen as an influence. Edwards, *Macaulay*, 127. On the relationship between Macaulay and Scott, see Mark Phillips, "Macaulay, Scott, and the Literary Challenge to Historiography," *Journal of the History of Ideas*, 50.1 (1989), 117–33; and Frank Palmieri, "The Capacity of Narrative: Scott and Macaulay on Scottish Highlanders," *Clio*, 22.1 (1992), 37–52.

of domesticity, and of the middle and lower classes.[21] In such an environment, moreover, historians were no longer just patriarchal citizens in a neo-classical republic of letters. They now had to write for profit and (like novelists) peddle their goods in the literary marketplace.

The "perfect historian" would not only be a great synthesizer, examining life in its "ten thousand different aspects": "He shows us the court, the camp and the Senate. But he shows us also the nation. He considers no anecdote, no peculiarity, no familiar saying as too insignificant for his notice which is not too insignificant to illustrate the operation of laws, of religion, and of education, and to mark the progress of the human mind." Like the novelist, the perfect historian would have to appeal to a new mass audience, including middle-class women, now the most avid consumers of books. As for himself, Macaulay left no doubt as to the extent of his own ambitions. Many years later, when he was writing his great history of British political and social transformation, he confessed to his publisher that "I shall not be satisfied, unless I produce something which shall for a few days supercede the last fashionable novel on the tables of young ladies."[22]

Macaulay's confidence that his great, masculine *History* was a book that young ladies would prefer to the novel was deeply rooted in his character and experience. It stemmed from the fact that, even after he graduated to the manly world of action and erudition, in a deeper sense, he never left home. At Cambridge, he had pined for his mother and sisters. After obtaining his degree, he simply returned to London and took up residence in the parental home. In later years, he continued to live close to his sisters, usually contriving to have at least one of them in (or near) his household.[23] Macaulay's odd relationship to women has often been noted. He never married and appears to have had little interest in or contact with women outside his own family. Yet his relationship with Hannah and Margaret, his two youngest sisters, gradually developed into an intimate, almost incestuous, liaison that became the most important and powerful emotional connection of his life. "My affection to my sisters," he frankly admitted, "has prevented me from forming any serious attachment. But for them, I should be quite alone in the world." With his sisters, in the safety of his intimate family circle, he could indulge all his formidable powers of romantic daydreaming and fantasy. It was from this family circle romancing that his *History of England* would later emerge. The vivid word-pictures and set pieces

---

[21] "History," in MMW, 156–9.
[22] TBM to M. Napier, November 5, 1841, in PLM, IV: 15.   [23] CM, 256–88.

that would delight hundreds of thousands of readers nearly all had their origins in the parlor games and breakfast badinage of the Macaulay household.[24]

For Macaulay, then, the romance of history was always, first and foremost, an emotionally freighted family romance. Nearly a decade before he officially began his researches, in a letter to Margaret, he revealingly confessed: "A slight fact, a sentence, a word are of importance in my romance. Pepys's *Diary* found almost inexhaustible food for my fancy ... The conversations which I compose between great people of the time are long and sufficiently animated in the style, if not the merits of Sir Walter Scott." Years later, when these "conversations" were set down, polished up, and narratively structured, permanently fixed in print between the covers of his *History*, Macaulay could enter the literary marketplace with confidence, knowing that his book had already passed muster "on the tables of [at least two particularly discriminating] young ladies."[25]

If Macaulay's feminized family romance gave him access to the romantic history that could trump Sir Walter Scott, he understood, like Scott, that this was not enough. To become a "real man" and a "perfect historian," he would have to return to the more strenuous genres of public history and rigorous scholarship, which, even more than the historical novel, had long been almost exclusively a masculine domain. Yet, even more than Walter Scott, Tom Macaulay was on his own in making this re-masculinizing move. The old genres of manly history – most notably the stately, classical (or neo-classical) narratives that traced the rise and fall of great empires – were incapable of capturing either the multi-dimensionality or the directionality of modern experience. They were inadequate for the kind of dynamic, romantic history that this ambitious young scholar hoped to write. The history of modern society was no longer a recurrent history of rises and falls, but an upthrusting linear history of development and progress – of economic growth and techno-logical improvement. Even more (if more problematically) it was the

---

[24] TBM to M. Macaulay, November 26, 1832, in PLM, II: 203; CM, 260–8. The relationship between Macaulay's domestic arrangements and his historical writings is sensitively examined in Bonnie Smith, *The Gender of History: Men, Women, and Historical Practice* (Cambridge, 1998), 70–7; and Catherine Hall, "At Home with History: Macaulay and the History of England," in C. Hall and S. Rose (eds.), *At Home with the Empire: Metropolitan Culture and the Imperial World* (Cambridge, 2006), 32–52. See also Theodore Koditschek, "T. B. Macaulay, Whig History and the Romance of Empire," in T. Brotherstone, A. Clark, and K. Whelan (eds.), *These Fissured Isles: Ireland, Scotland and the Making of Modern Britain* (Edinburgh, 2005), 61–84.

[25] Quoted in CM, 263. See also John Clive, *Not by Fact Alone: Essays on the Writing and Reading of History* (Boston, 1989), 220–7; and Edwards, *Macaulay*, 8–9.

history of moral advance and political elevation through an ever-extending penumbra of intelligence and liberty.[26]

Of course, in figuring out how to historicize the progress narrative, Macaulay understood that the old classical historiographical traditions could still be of use. At his father's knee, he had learned that Britain possessed an Empire. But he had also learned that it was a new kind of moral, post-classical (and hopefully indestructible) Empire, grounded in the logic of progress and freedom.[27] While these reflections were never set down in systematic fashion, they surface again and again at various points in the younger Macaulay's writings. They are admirably encapsulated in an engraving by Gustave Doré, "The New Zealander," which was inspired by a passing comment in one of the historian's review essays. The image of the New Zealander was a passing fancy, but it was the kind of fancy in which Macaulay was wont to indulge at critical moments in his life.[28] Having long reflected on the transience of the ancient empires, his mind must have proceeded through a sequence of recurrent images, a succession of imperial cycles with their attendant epic historians – men whose literary monuments alone can endure the ravages of time and decay: the Greek Polybius, with the Roman victors, musing over the ruins of Carthage, and imagining that Rome might someday suffer the same fate; then Gibbon musing over the ruins of Rome, and wondering about their implications for the British Empire of his own day; and finally, the New Zealander of the distant future, musing over the decadence and grandeur that had been Britain, perhaps inspired by Macaulay's now-venerable text.[29]

Macaulay's hope, to put it in a nutshell, was to show how and why the Empire of Britain might escape the fate of its predecessors. Where Roman expansion had been limited by geography and technology, British expansion was grounded in the premise of constant improvement, subject to no necessary geographical limit. Unlike Rome, which ultimately collapsed under the weight of its social and economic contradictions, Britain might

---

[26] Ann Douglas, *The Feminization of American Culture* (New York, 1988), especially 165–99.

[27] For example, see TBM to K. Macaulay, April 4, 1807; to C. Hudson, August 30, 1815; and to Z. Macaulay, February 2, 1813, May 8, 1813, May 14, 1816, November 16, 1816, February 5, 1819, and September 1819, in PLM, I: 5, 17–18, 30–1, 66–7, 77–9, 84–5, 118–21, 132–4.

[28] Macaulay notes his frequent indulgence in such fantasies in his journal entry for November 22, 1838, quoted in TLL, I: 458.

[29] See *The Histories of Polybius*, trans. Evelyn S. Shuckburgh, 2 vols. (Bloomington, 1962), II: 528–30, for Polybius's eyewitness account of the burning of Carthage, in which he reports the Roman general Scipio's fears that Rome might eventually be sacked in a comparable manner. For Gibbon in Rome see Edward Gibbon, *Autobiography* (New York, 1961), 154, and, of course, Edward Gibbon, *The Decline and Fall of the Roman Empire*, 3 vols. (New York, n.d.).

catalyze virtually inexhaustible economic growth and social advancement almost anywhere around the globe. Within the framework of a flexible, dynamic constitution, it might reconcile progress with order in a free society.[30] Even if the colonial children eventually chose the path of political independence, the Empire of a common civilization would remain. To tell the story of this limitless, progressive Empire would require a completely original historian, writing more open-ended forms of history. Macaulay hoped to become that historian. In the course of figuring out how to do full justice to this story, he would take up (in altered form) his father's project of making it come true.

3   Frustrations in Whig politics

Although the history of progress became something of a secular religion for Macaulay, his early efforts to trump his father's evangelical Christianity had first to be conducted on narrower political and occupational terrain. Although never exactly a radical, Tom had enraged his father when in 1819 he expressed sympathy for the victims of Peterloo.[31] Yet during the 1820s, the dynamics of the family shifted as Zachary found himself falling into line with his son's Whiggish views. As the Tory Party grew increasingly reactionary and dependent on the West Indian interests, Zachary found that his own anti-slavery politics were bringing him into the orbit of advanced Whigs like Henry Brougham. Brougham, for his part, was greatly impressed with Tom's talents, and encouraged the youth to think of a political career in the Whig Party. That Tom needed to find a career in which he could earn a living was becoming inescapable, for Zachary's financial embarrassments were mounting, just as the cost of educating his children was reaching its peak. So far from resenting this burden of financial responsibility for the family, Tom saw it as a golden opportunity to strike off on his own.[32] The breakthrough came in 1825, when the younger Macaulay published a brilliant analytical essay on Milton in the prestigious *Edinburgh Review*. Over the next few years, there were further *Edinburgh Review* essays, and the identity of the anonymous author became widely known. In educated, liberal families across the nation, the name

---

[30] No concept is more central to Macaulay's vision of history than "improvement," defined as mankind's steadily increasing mastery over the material world. Different forms of government can promote or retard but never entirely halt the march of improvement. For an astute analysis of the general role (and limits) of utilitarianism in Macaulay's thinking, see Thomas, *Macaulay and Croker*, 69–74, 83–92.
[31] TBM to Z. Macaulay, September, 1819, in PLM, I: 131–4.
[32] Knutsford, *Zacharay Macaulay*, 460–89; CM, 96–288; TLL, I: 117–19.

"T. B. Macaulay" became a household word. Lady Holland adopted the Young Turk and enlisted him as a fixture in her London salon. There he met all the leading Whig patricians and politicians, many of whom he greatly impressed. In February 1830, Lord Landsowne, one of the leading Whig grandees, offered Tom a seat in the House of Commons for the pocket borough of Calne.[33]

As the young Macaulay penetrated these Whig aristocratic circles, he learned to moderate the expression of his anti-establishment views. In the essay on Milton, he had valorized dissenters and rebels. The heroes of history were those courageous individuals, like the blind poet, who had been willing to stand up to despots and tyrants. Through their brave sacrifices such men had advanced the cause of progress, and had secured the rights and privileges that their descendants enjoyed. As his career advanced and his historical understanding deepened, however, the young Macaulay was weaned from these immature views. No longer answering to the authority of his father, he found himself wrestling with the more formidable historiographical revisionism of David Hume. In his highly influential *History of England*, this conservative *philosophe* had painted a distinctively un-Whiggish picture of the relationship between progress and liberty. The most extensive liberty had prevailed during the backward middle ages, when political decentralization and feudal license had plunged Europe into a millennium of plunder and anarchy. Modern progress was thus dependent on the appearance of strong centralized states during the sixteenth and seventeenth centuries.[34]

From this perspective, the Stuarts were depicted no longer as tyrants, but as order-promising authorities whose real sin was their inability to deliver the goods. By contrast, the Whig heroes of the early modern period were refigured in Hume's imagination as troublesome pests. The English revolutionaries of the 1640s, or the Scottish Presbyterian Covenanters of the 1670s, were, to a man, either fanatics or lunatics in Hume's estimation. Progress depended on the defeat and confinement of such fractious meddlers. To be sure, the history of absolutism demonstrated that this authoritarian reaction also needed to be kept within bounds. The ideal solution was the kind of long-established mixed government that had been gradually evolving throughout western

---

[33] CM, 96–141, 145, 206–21; TLL, I: 117, 130. *Edinburgh Review* essays were published anonymously, but the identities of authors (especially popular authors) were spread through the grapevine. See John Clive, *Scotch Reviewers: The "Edinburgh Review", 1802–1815* (Cambridge, 1957).

[34] David Hume, *The History of England from the Invasion of Julius Caesar to the Abdication of James II*, 6 vols. (Philadelphia, n.d.), V and VI.

Europe, but which had achieved near perfection on the British Isles during the eighteenth century.[35]

While Macaulay could never accept Hume's Tory interpretation of progress, he was troubled by the cogency of this "law and order" view. The conventional Whig glorification of dissenters and martyrs, he concluded, would have to be revised. Their struggles and sufferings had advanced the cause of progress only when their resistance to authority had been combined with a respect for law and property.[36] Modern "liberty" was therefore a relative rather than an absolute term. So far from being an unconditional entitlement or "English" birthright, modern liberty was simply the means to a higher progressive end. That higher end was the vision of moral and material progress on which all right-minded people could agree. Political participation and active citizenship were therefore not absolute rights, but *contingent* entitlements in which the precise lines of inclusion and exclusion would always have to be drawn in a *provisional* way. Whether at home or in England, Scotland, Ireland, or the Empire, these lines could never be permanently fixed. Rather, they were fluid and could be expected to widen as material prosperity and moral progress advanced. Those who were included today might have been inadmissible in an earlier era. Those who were inadmissible today might be included in some future epoch. Great Britain was a dynamic formation that history was rendering progressively greater, not merely because new territories were added, but because the stakes of citizenship were constantly being raised.

With his own entry into the House of Commons, amid the crisis of 1830, young Macaulay suddenly found himself well placed to articulate this expansive constitutional-historical vision, not only to his fellow law-makers, but also to the newspaper-reading public at large. This was indeed a moment of extraordinary ferment in British politics. Civic rights for dissenters and Catholic Emancipation had just been wrested from a moribund Tory Government, which had resisted every step of the way. England seethed with anger and discontent. Urban workers, demanding constitutional reform, were forming themselves into political unions. Rural incendiaries, inflamed by high prices and starvation wages, were marauding through the countryside under the banner of "Swing." In Paris, there was another French Revolution. Finally, by the end of the

---

[35] Nicholas Phillipson, *Hume* (New York, 1989), 53–141; Duncan Forbes, *Hume's Philosophical Politics* (Cambridge, 1975); CM, 85–9.

[36] For conventional Whig history before Macaulay, see Pocock, *Virtue, Commerce, and History*, 215–310; John Burrow, *A Liberal Descent: Victorian Historians and the English Past* (Cambridge, 1981), 1–35; and Bridget Hill, *The Republican Virago: The Life and Times of Catherine Macaulay, Historian* (Oxford, 1992).

year, a Whig ministry forced its way into power, promising to reform the political system from end to end.[37]

On March 1, 1831, Lord John Russell introduced the Reform Bill into the House of Commons. On the next night, Macaulay electrified the House. The existing system of representation, he argued, had been laid down in the middle ages. Since then, however, society had progressed. As a result, the political system had grown corrupt and unresponsive to enlightened public opinion. Parliament was dominated by a few powerful aristocrats, while the rising middle classes were vastly under-represented. Many of the most thriving and dynamic of the new industrial cities had no representation at all. "This is not government by property, it is government by certain detached portions and fragments of property, selected from the rest, on no rational principle whatever." The British governing classes were faced with a choice: either they could admit to full political citizenship those whom it was safe to admit, or they risked disorder, tumult, and revolution.

Save property divided against itself. Save the multitude, endangered by its own ungovernable passions. Save the aristocracy, endangered by its own unpopular power. Save the greatest, and fairest, and most civilized community that ever existed, from calamities which may in a few days sweep away all the rich heritage of so many ages of wisdom and glory. The danger is terrible. The time is short.

What was most impressive about Macaulay's speech was not this histrionic peroration, but the way in which the argument situated the Reform Bill crisis of Britain in the 1830s within the broader sweep of British and human history.

All history is full of revolutions, produced by causes similar to those which are now operating in England. A portion of the community which had been of no account expands and becomes strong. It demands a place in the system, suited not to its former weakness, but to its present power. If this is granted, all is well. If this is refused, then comes the struggle between the young energy of one class and the ancient privileges of another. Such was the struggle between the Plebeians and the Patricians of Rome ... Such was the struggle which the Third Estate of France maintained against the aristocracy of birth. Such was the struggle which the Roman Catholics of Ireland maintained against the aristocracy of creed. Such is the struggle which the free people of colour in Jamaica are now maintaining against

[37] Eric Hobsbawm and George Rude, *Captain Swing: A Social History of the Great English Agricultural Uprising of 1830* (New York, 1968); W. N. Molesworth, *The History of the Reform Bill of 1832* (London, 1865); Joseph Hamburger, *James Mill and the Art of Revolution* (New Haven, 1963); Vincent Starzinger, *Middlingness: Juste Milieu Political Theory in France and England: 1815–48* (Charlottesville, 1965).

the aristocracy of skin. Such finally is the struggle which the middle classes of England are waging against an aristocracy of mere locality.[38]

Anyone familiar with the opening lines of the *Communist Manifesto*, written sixteen years later, will immediately recognize the source from which Marx and Engels cribbed their own curtain-raiser. There is, of course, one crucial difference. Marx and Engels invoked this image of progress through social conflict to insist on the inevitability of class struggle. Macaulay, by contrast, had been at pains to argue that class struggle could be avoided if ruling elites granted concessions in a timely, responsible way. Ironically, at the very moment when his public voice was soaring to these oratorical heights, the private man was painfully uncertain as to the political prudence and sagacity of the British aristocracy of his day. Five months later, when he learned that the Lords were likely to reject the Reform Bill, he angrily confided his dark vision of the future to his sister.[39]

Even more alarming than the open reaction of the Tories, he charged, was the vacillation and timidity of his own Whig party leaders, who, after raising the hopes of the people, now seemed all too willing to jump ship and capitulate. "Nothing remained," he sharply upbraided his patron, Lord Landsowne, "but an insolent oligarchy on the one side, and an infuriated people on the other." Over the next few weeks, he lobbied tirelessly behind the scenes. "*Entre nous*," he bragged to his closest male friend, "they would have made a poor hand of it without me ... I really believe that, but for the stir which I made among our county-members, the ministers would have resigned." Yet instead of rewarding him adequately for his services, the Whig grandees were fobbing him off with minor offices and vague promises for the future.[40] Like the middle classes, whom he wished to induct into political citizenship, Macaulay himself was knocking in vain at the portals of power. Moreover, the eventual passage of the Reform Act did little to strengthen the ministers' backs. Two years later, when Irish Church reform and the abolition of colonial slavery were being debated, the Whig leaders seemed on the verge of another *volte-face*. "I see nothing before us," Macaulay lamented to his sister, "but a frantic conflict between extreme opinions – a short period of oppression,

---

[38] MMW, 486–7, 492.
[39] Karl Marx and Friederich Engels, *The Communist Manifesto* (New York, 1948), 9. "Reform or Revolution. One or the other I am sure must and shall have. I assure you that the violence of the people, the bigotry of the Lords and the stupidity and weakness of the ministers alarms me so much that even my rest is disturbed by vexation and uneasy forebodings" (TBM to Hannah Macaulay, September 15, 1831, in PLM, II: 99).
[40] TBM to Hannah Macaulay, September 15, 1831, in PLM, II: 100; TBM to Thomas F. Ellis, October 17, 1831, in PLM, II: 106.

then a tremendous crash of the funds, the Church, the peerage, and the Throne."[41]

4   Encounter with colonial India

Like so many other *parvenus* whose centrist aspirations were frustrated in Britain, Macaulay solved his problem by seeking opportunity on the imperial periphery. In 1833, he participated in the revision of the EIC Charter and accepted an appointment to go to India in the newly created post of Legal Member of the Supreme Council. Many of his London colleagues expressed surprise that so promising a politician would abandon the Westminster scene. In India, Macaulay explained, his salary would be huge. If he survived the climate, he could return home financially independent after a few years.[42] Given his father's imperial past, however, we may assume that more was at stake. Indeed, in a powerful speech, delivered in the debate over EIC Charter reform, he laid out the significance of India for Britain in the liberal, industrial capitalist age.

Though historical accident had originally thrust them together, Britain and India now needed one another, and were fated to move together into the coming era of free trade. The principles of the British Reform Act were not yet appropriate for backward India, yet the existing Anglo-Indian administration could not continue in its old anachronistic way. Having evolved from a privileged mercantilist corporation into a free trading instrument of imperial sovereignty, the EIC had to be converted into an effective utilitarian vehicle for pressing India forward along a path of accelerated socio-economic progress. Even from the most narrowly selfish perspective, Macaulay told his parliamentary colleagues, it was in Britain's interest to end the last vestiges of monopoly, and to promote India's social and economic development. In the age of British industrialization, Britain had much more to gain by turning Indians into prosperous consumers of her manufactures than to squeeze a scant revenue out of the impoverished peasants whom she had inherited from the subcontinent's despotic past. It would be idiotic "to keep a hundred millions of men from being our customers, in order that they may continue to be our slaves."[43]

---

[41] TBM to Hannah Macaulay, June 17, 1831, in PLM, II: 257. The theme of Macaulay's politics and his relationship to Whiggism is exhaustively treated in Joseph Hamburger, *Macaulay and the Whig Tradition* (Chicago, 1976).

[42] CM, 233–7.

[43] MMW, 551–72. In his private correspondence, Macaulay was somewhat less certain about the benevolence of British intentions in India and more uneasy about the moral warrant of her rule.

So far, Macaulay had done no more than to restate forcefully the modernizing agenda for British India, which his father, Mountstuart Elphinstone, and James Mill had already formulated in a less florid way. Where Macaulay broke new ground was in his willingness to acknowledge the likely political consequences of Indian modernization. British India, he frankly avowed, was a despotism, and would have to remain so for some time. Yet if the vast mass of Indians were not ready for representative institutions, the small (but rapidly growing) westernized elite should be offered responsible posts in the EIC administration, and should be promoted in a manner consistent with their ability. With English education performing its magic, the orator closed with his famous prophesy of that future "proudest day" of English history (quoted at the head of this chapter) when Indians would enjoy all the institutions of representative government that England had pioneered.

As he uttered this stirring vision of metamorphic union, the younger Macaulay could justly have reflected on the ways in which his own historical approach to liberal imperialism was a signal advance on his father's more restricted creed. Where Zachary would fix the colonial child in a permanent state of arrested development, his son now acknowledged that the nonage must be limited, and that the colonial child would someday achieve autonomy. Where Zachary envisioned civic independence as emerging from Protestant foundations, his son now recognized that it was actually the product of secular forces of progressive history. Where Zachary sought the bond of union between center and periphery in the Bible, his son found it in education, law, and history. Though India's government would remain for a time colonial and despotic, it would not rule arbitrarily, but through a system of enlightened, codified jurisprudence. As Legal Member of Council, therefore, T. B. Macaulay anticipated playing a central role. Although his position was advisory, he believed he would enjoy the confidence of Governor-General Bentinck and might influence the shape of India for generations to come. As he busied himself for departure, according to one mordant observer, he "rather gave himself the airs of a Lycurgus; and spoke as if he were about to bestow on the swarming millions of India, the blessings of rudimentary legislation."[44]

In India, the bulk of Macaulay's energies were absorbed in the laborious work of drafting a new legal code, essentially taking up this project from the point where Mountstuart Elphinstone had left off. This involved organizing and consolidating existing Anglo-Indian legal practice,

[44] CM, 289–478, quote on 235–6.

winnowing out those traditional customs deemed unacceptable, and giving the rest a rational foundation and a universal gloss. At the same time, Macaulay was concerned, as far as possible, to plant seeds from which future liberal institutions could grow. Thus he persuaded Bentinck to lift press censorship. More controversially, he pushed through a series of proposals that subjected white European residents of Calcutta to the same courts (and native judges) which had jurisdiction over Indians in the town.[45]

Yet Macaulay's championing of Indian constitutional rights and abstract principles of equality before the law did not mean that he found India a congenial place. For personal reasons, his Indian tenure was a period of trauma, when he lost both of his beloved sisters (one to death, the other to marriage) and became emotionally closed in on himself. Yet he also found India to be an alarmingly voluptuous environment, in which the extremes of climate and behavior abounded, and the Whig *via media* was nowhere to be found. "To be in such a land," he remarked upon arrival, "nothing but dark faces and bodies with white turbans and flowing robes – the trees not our trees – the very smell of the atmosphere like that of a hothouse – the architecture as strange as the vegetation. I was quite stunned." The exoticism that so appealed to adventurous borderers like Malcolm and Elphinstone left the mentally rigid Macaulay perplexed. On one level, he could see why so many British officials became acclimatized to life in India and even dreaded their return home. In Calcutta, they were able "to entertain guests, to buy horses, to keep a mistress or two, to maintain fifteen or twenty servants who bow to the ground every time they meet him, and suffer him to kick and abuse them to his heart's content . . . The case with me is very different. I have not yet become reconciled to the change from English to Indian habits."[46]

This accurately depicts the behavior of all too many British officials, and testifies that Macaulay practiced the liberalism he preached, but it utterly fails to comprehend what sensitive men like Malcolm and Elphinstone found so appealing in Indian life. This failure of imagination is revealingly displayed in his picture of a dysfunctional household, in which repulsively servile and effeminate Indian abjection elicits a correspondingly repellent, hyper-masculinist British response. For a man like Macaulay, whose sense of his own manhood was so imbued with the ideal of chaste moderation, these stark antinomies were alarming. By keeping his English heart at home, in his domestic family circle, he could hold fast to a psychic space

---

[45] CM, 289–341, 427–78.
[46] TBM to Mrs. E. Cropper, June 5, 1834, in PLM, III: 37; TBM to C. Macaulay, December 5, 1836, in PLM, III: 203–4.

where private romance remained compatible with (and formed a counter-part to) liberal and egalitarian relations in the public arena. By contrast, in India, the principle of exaggerated patriarchy seemed to saturate every institution and encounter in both public and private life. The huge extremes and outsize dimensions of everything in India – its dramatic contrasts between mastery and servitude, wealth and poverty – struck him not merely as abuses to be rectified, but as dangerous symptoms of an effeminizing infection, which threatened to dissolve his self-image of sober, equable English masculinity.

In the small world of Westminster politics, Macaulay's relations with James Mill had been complicated. There was perhaps an Oedipal ele-ment when the young Whig eviscerated the older dogmatic utilitarian with a vehemence that could not be safely directed against the older dogmatic Evangelical at home. In India, however, Macaulay behaved quite differently, since he believed that dogmatic utilitarianism was exactly what the wanton Indians required. Carefully reading Mill's *History* and EIC dispatches, Macaulay envisioned his role as quasi-Benthamite man-on-the-spot who could actually implement the policies that the London bureaucrat had abstractly advised. Indeed, on the key question of education, Macaulay carried anglocentrism one step beyond Mill. Not only did he recommend that the government support "useful" western knowledge over "worthless" oriental erudition, but he insisted that this support be offered to English-language instruction alone.[47]

With its sneering contempt for "astronomy which would move laughter in girls at an English boarding school – History, abounding with kings thirty feet high," Macaulay's infamous *Minute on Education* is often cited as the very model of Eurocentric arrogance. His claim that "a single shelf of a good European library was worth the whole native literature of India and Arabia" has assumed its own life as a discreditable soundbite that resonates loudly in the postcolonial cybersphere of our day. Yet if we read the *Minute* carefully, we must acknowledge that it is also a radical docu-ment in its presumption that English and Bengali boys have equal intel-lectual potential, and that Britain will default on her imperial obligations if she fails to provide the latter with the infrastructural wherewithal to catch up with the former. "Had our [British] ancestors neglected the language of Cicero and Tacitus," Macaulay observes, "had they confined their attention to the old dialects of our own island ... would England have been where she now is?" Yet "what the Greek and Latin were to the

---

[47] CM, 342–99.

contemporaries of More and Ascham, our tongue is to the people of India today."[48]

As Macaulay saw it, his efforts to anglicize higher education in India were simply part and parcel of the universal vision of gradualist reform that he had eloquently articulated in his parliamentary speeches. In Britain, this reform might come directly from free institutions of representative government. In India – less advanced along the path of development – political freedom could come only indirectly, through *educational* means. But not for him the nuanced synergism of Rammohun Roy, which would have Britons and Indians learning from one another. In Macaulay's schoolroom, as in that of the Edgeworths, the lessons traveled in one direction alone. There was simply nothing of value in the smothering nightmare of Indian history. All the laws and customs of India, he contended, had been forcibly imposed by alien invaders and were institutionalized by fraudulent means. At first the British had appeared as just another set of plunderers. But now that policy was dominated by utilitarian reformers such as Mill, Bentinck, and himself, Macaulay believed that the character of British rule had changed. His own work on the penal code had been an exercise in frustration since he could do little more than systematize three inherently defective (and contradictory) legal traditions, papering them over with a rationalist gloss. India's incipient middle class was not to be emancipated by such legalistic evasions, but rather by the advantages of an English education. Through such education – the one Macaulay himself had obtained – they would gain access to a vast mass of both useful and ennobling knowledge. This would enable them to emancipate themselves. Britain's mission in India, as he famously put it, was "to form a class who may be interpreters between us and the millions whom we govern; a class of persons Indian in blood and color, but English in taste, in opinions, in morals and in intellect."[49]

But what exactly should this curriculum of colonial anglicization teach? In one of his last letters to his father, Macaulay assured the ailing Evangelical that a secular English education in "astronomy, geography

[48] T. B. Macaulay, "Minute on Education," in J. G. Aggarwal (ed.), *Landmarks in the History of Indian Education* (New Delhi, 1993), 11, quote on 4–6. For the contemporary reception of Macaulay's *Minute*, see the documents in H. Sharp (ed.), *Selection from Educational Records*, I, *1781–1839* (Calcutta, 1920), 102–42.

[49] C. K. Darkhar (ed.), *Macaulay's Legislative Minutes* (Madras, 1946), 65–141, 235–71, especially 260; CM, 427–78; Macaulay, "Minute on Education," 11; on Macaulay and the work of codification, see Elizabeth Kolsky, "Codification and the Rule of Colonial Difference: Criminal Procedure in British India," *Law and History Review*, 23 (2005), 631–83.

[and] natural history" would destroy Indians' attachment to Hinduism. Yet he was careful *not* to add that this would open the way for their Christian conversion, since the younger Macaulay believed nothing of the sort. But if Christianity were not to form the basis for moral, political, and literary education, what was the secular alternative? Macaulay's suggested reading lists were cautiously vague. Top students should be rewarded with a string of canonic texts: "Bacon's *Essays*, Hume's *England*, Gibbon's *Rome*, Robertson's *Charles V*, *Scotland*, and *America*, *Gulliver*, *R. Crusoe*, Shakespeare, *Paradise Lost*."[50] Yet surely something was missing from the historians on this list. Was English history really to be handed over to the Tory Hume? Explicit discussion of India's history lessons was left to Macaulay's brother-in-law Charles Trevelyan, who worked alongside him in the education debates. In a book that was published three years later, Trevelyan took up the argument where Macaulay's *Minute* left it off. "The existing connection between two such distant countries as England and India cannot be permanent," Trevelyan explained. When Indians had learned their lessons in English history and culture, they would want the same self-government that England possessed.

But there are two ways of arriving at this point. One is through the medium of revolution; the other through that of reform ... The only means at our disposal for preventing the one and securing the other is to set the natives on a process of European improvement to which they are already sufficiently inclined. They will then cease to desire and aim at independence on the old footing. A sudden change will then be impossible, and a long continuation of our present connection with India will even be assured to us ... The political education of a nation must be the work of time; and while it is in progress we shall be as safe as it will be possible for us to be. The natives will not rise against us because we shall stoop to raise them up.[51]

5   **Progressive (English) history as liberal (imperial) politics by other means**

Macaulay could hardly hear these echoes of his own Reform Bill oratory without recalling his youthful ambitions to become the perfect historian – an ambition that he had shelved, but never entirely given up. Of course,

[50] TBM to Z. Macaulay, October 12, 1837, in PLM, III: 193. The same point is made, less colorfully, in the *Minute on Education*. See also letter to John Tytler, January 28, 1835, in PLM, III: 122–3. Because he regarded Islam as less retrograde than Hinduism, Macaulay was less sanguine about the success of British imperialism in undermining it. See CM, 342–426, quotes on 402–3.

[51] Charles Trevelyan, *On the Education of the People of India* (London, 1838), quote on 192–3.

we cannot know exactly what he was thinking, but we can gain a window into his internal reflections if we look closely at what he did and wrote during 1835, when the final battle for Indian education was joined. The year opened with a brief and traumatic nervous breakdown, precipitated by news of his sister Margaret's death. Sanity was preserved only by a headlong plunge into his administrative duties and by a rigorous "recreational" course of re-reading the Greek and Roman classics that had so enchanted him in youth. Somewhat to his surprise, Macaulay discovered that his tastes had changed. Reading with the eyes of a mature man of political accomplishment, he was particularly captivated by Thucydides, whom he now pronounced "the greatest historian that ever lived."[52] Of course, Macaulay had not forgotten his own youthful ambitions to best Thucydides as the perfect historian, combining all three levels of historical enquiry – the classical (cyclical), the modern (progressive), and the romantic (domestic) – in some transcendent, synoptic work. However, circumstantial evidence suggests that, until his Indian educational work got him thinking about gaps in the modern secular curriculum, he had set these ambitions aside. In part, this was simply because the daily press of politics and administration left little time for sustained intellectual production beyond the review essays that regularly issued from his fluent pen. However, there is also reason to think that, during his years as a rising politician, Macaulay had harbored doubts about whether conditions would make it possible for him to realize his ambitions to write the perfect (and perfectly gradualist) history that would promote the cause of reform over that of revolution, and would provide the political education that both English and Indians required.

These doubts can be detected as early as 1824, when he had dashed off a parodic *jeu d'esprit* about the fate of "The Wellingtonian," a great English epic, which he imagined as being written in the year 2824 by an Anglo-Chinese poet, Richard Quongti. In this caprice, the Macaulayite role of critical reviewer was assigned to one Kissey Kikey, a black professor at the world's most eminent (and clearly anglophone) institution of higher learning, the University of Timbuctoo. The literary conceit in this piece of "prophetic" juvenalia lay in the prospect that nineteenth-century British history might survive the next millennium only in a garbled and mythified form.[53] Even if this nightmare of the New Zealander was not to be taken seriously, Macaulay's essay on Milton, written a year later, showed that he still harbored doubts about whether

---

[52] CM, 256–478; TLL, I: 333–430; TBM to T. F. Ellis, February 8, 1835, and to Richard Sharp, February 11, 1835, in PLM, III: 130, 137, respectively.
[53] MMW, 80–6.

progress was actually achievable in a steady, incremental way. In lieu of the "perfect historian" his readers were here offered the supreme English poet, who had successfully straddled the distance between critical prose and epic poetry in a manner unequaled before or since. Yet Milton's genius had not been entirely *sui generis*, since it had partaken of the heroic and revolutionary (and freedom-enhancing) conditions that his generation faced:

> He [Milton] lived at one of the most memorable eras in the history of mankind. That great battle [between] liberty and despotism, reason and prejudice ... was fought for no single generation, for no single land. The destinies of the human race were staked on the same cast with the freedom of the English people. Then were first proclaimed those mighty principles which have since worked their way into the depths of the American forests, which have roused Greece from the degradation and slavery of two thousand years, and which, from one end of Europe to the other, have kindled an unquenchable fire in the hearts of the oppressed, and loosed the knees of the oppressors with an unwonted fear.[54]

Three years later, however, the radical reviewer (Macaulay) had become a Whig politician, and his views on revolution and poetry had begun to change. So far from bringing freedom and progress, revolution was now deemed a dangerous paroxysm of chaos and anarchy. Perhaps spurred on by the shades of Burke and Hume, Macaulay refigured violent "revolution" from a link in the chain of human freedom to a disaster of discontinuity, in which history spirals out of control and the progress narrative is arrested. In this chastened mood of prosaic, anti-revolutionary disenchantment, he began an abortive *History of the French Revolution*, which explored the dysfunctional dialectic that was unleashed when the skein of continuity was ruptured, and the political center no longer held: in 1789, tyrannical oppression had sparked a bloody insurrection, which was subsequently stanched by an equally brutal dictatorship, which (after the interlude of a failed restoration) precipitated another sanguinary revolution in turn.[55]

In all these disparate historiographical fragments and experiments, a common anxiety over historical discontinuity can be discerned: lost lays, fractured epics, failed fusions, violent revolutions, and aborted narratives all betoken the miscarriage of a continuous historical progression, in which the past foreshadows the future, and the present illuminates

---

[54] "Milton," in MEL, 14. In 1820, at the age of twenty, Macaulay wrote a bloodcurdling (but possibly tongue-in-cheek) "Radical War Song," in MMW, 436–7.

[55] T. B. Macaulay, *Napoleon and the Restoration of the Bourbons*, ed. Joseph Hamburger (Columbia, 1977), especially 46–75.

the past.[56] Discontinuity was to be feared because it foreclosed the possibility of manly political centrism, leaving society exposed to the extremes of left and right. By the end of 1834, however, Macaulay had convinced himself that the history of England (as it became Britain) was different, since the events of the late seventeenth century had broken through the cycles of dysfunction and had set these metamorphic nations on an upward path of irreversible improvement. "The History of England is emphatically the history of progress," he averred in a review of James Mackintosh's earlier attempt to grasp it whole. "It is a history of the constant movement of the public mind, of a constant change in the institutions of a great society." When examined in small separate portions, it may with more propriety be called a history of actions and reactions, he acknowledged, but "we must carefully distinguish between that recoil which regularly follows every advance, and a great ebb. If we take short intervals ... we find a retrogression. But if we take the centuries ... we cannot doubt in which direction society is proceeding."[57]

This ebbing and flowing of actions and reactions might, at moments, appear to betoken French-like alternations of sharp political extremes. Over the *longue durée*, however, the triumph of England/Britain was that the center always won out. As Macaulay processed the personal losses that he suffered immediately after writing these words, it seems likely that he found comfort in this discovery that his father's manly centrism was the overarching theme of secular British history. For this insight enabled him simultaneously to discharge his Oedipal impulses and to actualize his long-nurtured aspirations to attempt the perfect *History*. It convinced him that the saga of his own nation was indeed special: it offered the gift of education in political gradualism to all peoples, as well as a golden opportunity for the perfect historian to conjoin modern improvement with neo-classical narration – to fuse imaginative romance with the critical reviewer's analytical skills.

As he immersed himself in the dispute over Indian education during the spring of 1835, Macaulay's discovery of the redemptive powers of English history may well have assumed an even greater significance in his mind. Here indeed was England's gift to India: not his father's Christianity, but a history of limitless secular progress radiating out from the metropolitan

---

[56] Macaulay's preoccupation with the catastrophic consequences of historical discontinuity during this period is most poignantly illustrated by his composition of the *Lays of Ancient Rome*. These were imaginary reconstructions of the lost heroic ballads that Livy and Polybius had used for their classical histories. In 1842 the *Lays* were published to great acclaim and huge sales. TBM to Macvey Napier, July 20, 1838, in PLM, III: 252; C. H. Firth, *A Commentary on Macaulay's History of England* (London, 1964), 58–9.

[57] Quote from Macaulay, "Mackintosh's History of the Revolution," in MEL, 325–6.

center and providing a template for freedom everywhere around the globe. England offered the record of a modern civilization that might be enhanced and extended, but could no longer be destroyed or over-thrown.[58] While we cannot penetrate Macaulay's inner thinking, by the end of the year, he announced to a friend that he had "more than half-determined to abandon politics" and to devote himself fully "to undertake some great historical work which may be at once the business and amuse-ment of my life." As he contemplated the prospect of his return to England, the rough-and-tumble of party politics began to lose its attrac-tions. "What strange infatuation," he wondered, "leads men who can do something better to squander their intellect, their health, their energy on such objects as those which most statesmen are engaged in pursuing."

That a man before whom the two paths of literature and politics lie open, and who might hope for eminence in either, should chuse politics and quit literature seems to me madness. On the one side is health, leisure, peace of mind, the search after truth, and all the enjoyments of friendship and conversation. On the other side is almost certain ruin to the constitution, constant labour, constant anxiety. Every friendship which a man may have becomes precarious as soon as he engages in politics.[59]

So far from providing a royal road to freedom and fulfillment, a suc-cessful politician "consents to make himself as much a prisoner as if he were within the rules of the Fleet. Who can look back on the Life of Burke, and not regret that the years which he passed in ruining his health and temper by political exertions were not passed in the composition of some great and durable work?" In Macaulay's mind, a striking role reversal and gender inversion are taking place. The politician who controls the desti-nies of millions has been recast as a prisoner of forms, a slave of evanescent circumstances, who can only temporize amid the flux of events. By con-trast, it is now the modern historian, no longer in the forum but in the domestic privacy of his study, who has assumed the authority of universal arbiter and educator, with his Olympian "high grave, impartial summing up."[60]

After his return to England in 1838, Macaulay was tempted again by the lure of political ambition. Reluctantly drafted to represent Edinburgh in Parliament, he agreed to join Lord Melbourne's 1839 government as Minister of War. Yet the battle-worn veteran now found the summits of political power to be oddly anti-climactic. Faced with Chartist agitators,

[58] It was probably no accident that this breakthrough came to Macaulay during his time in India, when he was wrestling with the curriculum for Calcutta's future university.
[59] TBM to Thomas F. Ellis, December 30, 1835, in PLM, III: 158–9.
[60] PLM, II: 159; "History," in MMW, 133–59.

Canadian rebels, South African resisters, and Chinese drug interdictors, Macaulay found himself part of a Whig government whose policies of repression, coercion, and exclusion seemed to belie all his own rhetorical and ideological aims.[61] By returning to his original historians' avocation, however, he could re-animate the Whig romance of inclusion and liberty. The ideal of union, not yet viable for the imperial politician, was fully available to the imperial educator-cum-historian, who might raise the coming generation to a nobler purpose, both in Britain and in the colonies. The provincial middle-class constituents whom Macaulay represented in the Commons needed to be weaned from their narrow philistinism and elevated to the *gravitas* of civic responsibility.[62] Beyond them lay the great disenfranchised masses of multiple nationalities. The romantic historical epic originally intended for the night tables of English ladies might serve an imperial purpose as well. It might convince the half-educated Indian, the half-emancipated Jamaican, and the half-emaciated proletarian at home that the English Constitution, from which they were being excluded, was an accomplishment worthy of admiration and a political ambition towards which they could aspire. By writing a history of English continuity, the continuity of British and imperial history might be preserved. The course of progress, temporarily obstructed, might be reopened by remembrance of the progress on which it stood. If Whig politics was not advancing along the trajectory that it promised, Whig history might allow its continuation by other means.[63]

Yet in reducing the progress narrative to a tale of anglicization (and *vice versa*), Macaulay saddled both with ponderous encumbrances, which diminished their ability to serve the hegemonic purposes towards which he aimed. Anglicization had indeed been the road to freedom and upward mobility for himself, his father, and James Mill – ex-Scotsmen whose embrace of metropolitan Englishness really did open the door to Greater British imperial opportunity and power. But for the Hindu (or Muslim) boy who might want to follow in the Macaulays' footsteps, it was highly unlikely that the same anglocentric road would lead to a comparable advance. Yet in the name of some distant, psychically disruptive future benefit, this boy was being asked to abandon his home, his beliefs, his

---

[61] CM, 236; TLL, I: 464–8, II: 17–42; MMW, 598–608, 623–30.

[62] See Macaulay's correspondence with John Howison and Duncan McLaren in PLM, IV: 26, 91–2, 108–11, 113, 185–91. See also Burrow, *A Liberal Descent*, 61–93.

[63] See, for example, the remarkable civics lesson, panegyric of the Whig Party, and preview of what would become the basic argument of his *History*, which he delivered to his Edinburgh constituents at the very moment when he was contemplating beginning work on that book, in MMW, 583–4. Again, it is the theme of continuity that shines through. "A great party which has, through many generations, preserved its identity."

caste, and his customs, all in the name of slavishly imitating an alien civilizational world-view. In public, Macaulay could be a legislator, a proconsul, and a utilitarian improver. But then, in the privacy of his "English" domestic circle, safely ensconced with his beloved sisters, the public man allowed himself the romantic indulgence of daydreams. So far from being seen as incompatible with the public world of manly reason and action, Macaulay's romances were valorized as operating congruently and symbiotically in a separate but parallel sphere. Attached in this manner to the cause of progress, Macaulay's *History* would make him rich and famous. But his English romance might serve only to reinforce the inferiority of disenfranchised others – women, workers, Irish, Indians, and Africans – who were still very far from their "proudest day."

6   The historical romance of the British center

"The *History*," Macaulay informed his editor, as he set himself in harness in 1838, "would then be an entire view of all the transactions which took place between the revolution which brought the crown into harmony with parliament [1688] and the revolution which brought parliament into harmony with the nation [1832]." Here we are promised a grand cycle of the Constitution, which also traces an upward arc of progress in society. In the event, Macaulay delivered nothing so classically proportioned, and his grand epic shows many fissures, sutures, and strains. In part this is because he died prematurely and his five volumes cover only the first fifteen years of his projected 147-year span. More tellingly, however, volume I reveals Macaulay's uncertainty about how to begin the story. In fact, the book has four beginnings that fit uneasily into the epician's saga, but are deemed necessary parts of the pedagogue's lesson plan. The first (chapter 1, parts 1–34) begins with an analysis of the ways in which western Europe wrested civilization out of the barbarism of the middle ages, through the development of powerful early modern nation-states. Only in England, however, did the state become sufficiently flexible to combine civilization with liberty.[64] The second prefatory "essay" (chapter 1, parts 35–70, and chapter 2) focuses on the ways in which this fragile fusion of freedom with order was threatened during the period 1640–85. Here the violent revolution of the 1640s is depicted as a

---

[64] Quote in PLM, III: 252; MHE, I: 1–112. On December 18, 1838 Macaulay confided to his journal, "The great difficulty of a work of this kind is the beginning. How is it to be joined on to the preceding events. Where am I to begin?" But "after much consideration" his anxiety abated: "I think that I can manage by the help of an introductory chapter or two to glide imperceptibly into the full current of my narrative" (*Journals*, I: 107–8; see also II: 38).

regrettable, but probably unavoidable, mistake. Taken over by Puritan extremists, it had to be suppressed by military dictatorship, and was finally resolved by a corrupt and cynical restoration that endangered liberty in the opposite way. The implication is left that England required a second moderate revolution before she could enjoy the benefits of continuous progress and liberty. However, before Macaulay begins his full-dress narrative, he inserts another 53,000-word essay that contrasts the social economic and cultural condition of England in the 1680s with its condition in Macaulay's day.

> During a hundred years there has been in our Island no tumult of sufficient importance to be called an insurrection. The law has never been borne down either by popular fury or by regal tyranny. Public credit has been held sacred. The administration of justice has been pure ... Every man has felt entire confidence that the state would protect him in possession of what had been earned by his diligence and hoarded by his self-denial.

In agriculture, new scientific methods of animal breeding, crop rotation, and fertilization had been adopted since 1685, as farmers and landlords had responded to market incentives to improve their lands. The result had been a vast increase in output, and a national population at once much larger and yet better fed. In urban districts, which had expanded as a result of this population explosion, the changes had been even more visible and dramatic. Though all classes had benefited from these improvements, the most dramatic gains had been realized by the working classes and the poor. Living standards, diets, and medical care had been ameliorated, while manners and morals (both high and low) had been purified and refined. "The factory child, the Hindu widow and the negro slave" now enjoyed comforts, protections, and prospects of which their ancestors had never dreamed.[65]

This third chapter, which is sometimes hailed as a pioneering attempt at social history, is in fact an early symptom of trouble in Macaulay's perfect history. Having embedded his argument about modernization within a neo-classical narrative, he finds himself in need of this awkward interpolation to provide the didactic before-and-after contrasts that the narrative itself does not provide. In chapter 4, however, he returns to his narrative, launching into the line of detailed set-piece episodes that will carry him through the remaining four and a half volumes of the book. But this neo-classical narrative is conceived so narrowly that the *modern progress* narrative can scarcely make its case. Largely a chronicle of courts and camps, this story of high politics does not "show us the nation," much less

---

[65] MHE, I: 210–322, especially 252, 317, 321–2.

"society in ten thousand aspects." The "operation of laws, of religion, and of education" scarcely registers on a surface that utterly fails "to mark the progress of the human mind." Macaulay's whole procedure implies a claim that the material progress outlined in his third chapter is the direct product of the political events between about 1685 and 1700, detailed in the remainder of the book. To sustain such a claim, however, would require an apparatus of hypothesis testing, interpretation, and explanation, which is alien to the epic format in which he fatally miscast his book.[66]

Dimly aware that his narrative will have to do some heavy analytical lifting, Macaulay tries to fortify it with a series of symbolic tropes, most notably gendered images of "masculinity" and "effeminacy." As the story grows more entangled with contingent detail, these gender tropes loom ever larger as generalized metaphors for political health and disease. Extremism is presented as a kind of hysteria, in which gender-appropriate behavior becomes disarranged. Progress flows from the deeds of "real men," who express their masculinity and advance the national interest by charting a harmonious middle path between the extremes of right and left. Between these two shoals, both ever present although alternating with one another in their relative danger and intensity, the Macaulayite hero must steer the ship of state.[67] If the more blatant forms of absolutist tyranny and Puritan hysteria had been defeated during the reign of Charles II, the danger of extremism still remained at the time of his death. Two "false men" now enter the drama: the Duke of Monmouth from the left and James II from the right, each attempting to seduce the real men of England from their proper middle path. In a sense, these false men are even more dangerous than their predecessors, precisely because their gender disorders are not so openly displayed. The historical task of the next three years (1685–8), as Macaulay depicts it, will be to unmask these dissemblers in so decisive a manner that the English, Scots, and Welsh – in the course of making themselves into Britons – will never have to learn this fundamental lesson in liberty again.

In 1685, then, Macaulay situates his readers at the political impasse between a Catholic king, who is as yet an unknown quantity, and a failed revolution, whose radical ghost still haunts the atmosphere. The radicals,

---

[66] For a critique which faults him for retreating first into cultural history and then into political narrative, narrowly conceived, see P. R. Ghosh, "Macaulay and the Heritage of the Enlightenment," *English Historical Review*, 112.446 (April, 1997), 358–95.

[67] A range of commentators, from John Morley to John Burrow, have noted this trope in Macaulay's writing. Burrow, *A Liberal Descent*, 72–7. Its centrality to Macaulay's discursive strategy, however, deserves more systematic attention. See also Koditschek, "Macaulay, Whig History," 68–72.

exiled by the Exclusion Crisis, have fastened on the Protestant pretender Monmouth as their best hope for getting the dreaded despot dethroned. From the very beginning, however, we are made to know that trouble is brewing by the language of false manliness in which Monmouth and his associates are described. He is a bastard, an imposter, a usurper, an adventurer, born on the wrong side of the monarchial bed. When he "invaded" the Somerset coast without adequate troops and without preparation, he issued a *pronunciamiento* which disclosed the unworthiness of his cause. Over the next few weeks, as he advanced into Devon, he attracted a motley crowd of plebeians. And yet this mob was neither morally fit to participate in the political nation nor militarily fit to vanquish the aristocratic cavalry. When the forces engaged at Sedgemoor (July 6, 1685) the rebellion was rapidly and definitively crushed. Defeated, unhorsed, and hunted by bloodhounds, the royal impersonator was finally apprehended: "a gaunt figure" dressed like a workingman, and his discovery "hidden in a ditch."[68] Over the next few months, the rebels were rounded up, and Judge Jeffreys's Bloody Assizes conveniently converted what had been a dangerous rabble into mangled, tortured fodder for the Whig martyrology.

With the hyper-masculine radicals of the left immobilized and defeated, Macaulay turns to the dangers of an effeminate king. Now it is James who becomes the vacillating, destabilizing radical, encroaching on the sanctity of private property and trampling on the liberties of freeborn Englishmen. The legitimate embodiment of stability and order is now wreaking havoc and disorder. He is undermining the very *status quo* of which he ought to be the head. For two full years, his loyal subjects endure these headaches and assaults without complaint. It is only after James's frontal attack on the Anglican Church, and after his procreation of a questionable heir, that the gentlemen of England, Scotland, and Wales are forced to act. When the king symbolically abdicates, throwing the Great Seal into the Thames, the nation is reduced *de facto* to a state of nature. This is the great test of political maturity, which the English people pass with flying colors. On the night of December 11, 1688, when they might have descended into barbarism and anarchy, they demonstrate instead their aptitude for civil society. Despite a number of riots by irreclaimable rabble, a spontaneous calm prevails through most of the realm. "Never within the memory of man had there been so near an approach to concord among all intelligent Englishmen as at that conjuncture: and never had concord been more needed."

[68] MHE, I: 323–506, especially 440, 434–5, 467.

England has proven herself to be capable of political centrism and historical continuity. Therefore she is fit for constitutional government. The story of how she achieved that fitness is her greatest gift to the rest of mankind. Macaulay concludes his second volume with a seven-page civics lesson for his readers – a panegyric on the English historicizing genius which first showed the world how to combine order with liberty:

> This Revolution, of all revolutions the least violent, has been of all revolutions the most beneficent . . . It is because we had a preserving revolution in the seventeenth century that we have not had a destroying revolution in the nineteenth. It is because we have had freedom in the midst of servitude, that we [now] have order in the midst of anarchy.[69]

With the consummation of this "preserving" revolution of 1688, Macaulay's epic is transported to a more capacious moral and physical space. The text remains, for the most part, devoted to narrative, but it reveals an additional subtextual layer, as the political history of England is transformed into a romance of British expansion and unity. As the energies of the English people are released from their internecine struggles, the constitutional historian can become the celebrator of an entirely new and dynamic kind of national-cum-imperial polity. At a time when today's historians are justly criticized for issuing histories of Britain which limit themselves to England, it is striking to encounter the opposite phenomenon in Macaulay: a *History of England* which becomes, from 1689 onward, a genuinely British history. The title is, of course, significant, for it reflects Macaulay's anglocentric understanding of the way in which constitutionalist-cum-nationalist (and eventually imperialist) expansion must proceed. The creation of a larger British polity provides the framework for Scotsmen, provincials, and dissenters (perhaps presaging the Indians, Irishmen, and proletarians of the future) to create their own versions of "English" accommodation with the newly established, metropolitan Whig regime.[70]

It is in his handling of these themes of multi-national fusion, sociopolitical accommodation, and reconciliation that Macaulay borrows most decisively and creatively from the fictional romances of Scott. In Scott's novels, these reunions, reconciliations, and national expansions

[69] MHE, II: 1–425, quote on 425.
[70] MHE, II: 510. But see also James Vernon, "Narrating the Constitution: The Discourse of 'the Real' and the Fantasies of Nineteenth-Century Constitutional History," in James Vernon (ed.), *Re-Reading the Constitution: New Narratives in the Political History of England's Long Nineteenth Century* (Cambridge, 1996), 219–22. It is of course significant that volumes I and II of Macaulay's *History* were published at the end of 1848, the year of revolution throughout continental Europe, but not in Britain.

are invoked by a plot device. In his *History*, Macaulay draws on Scott's intra-ethnic and multi-national emplotment to bring coherence to a cascade of confusing real-world incidents and events. In this manner, his English constitutionalist narrative is refigured into a far-flung archipelagic story that moves beyond the metropole, to the Celtic fringe. Here, the dynamic commercial capitalism, which has already established a foothold in England, must still do battle with the residual vestiges of a barbarous feudal past. The more limited and familiar political or religious party antagonisms – Court versus Country, Royalist versus Parliamentarian, Anglican versus Presbyterian – are superimposed upon a more elemental contradiction between civilization and savagery.[71]

Yet as the drama moves beyond Anglo-Scotland, Macaulay's inspiration falters, and his account of the expansion of Britishness becomes more disjointed and confused. This can be seen in his handling of the character of William, who is the closest thing to a hero in the book. Initially, William appears as a cold, inscrutable foreigner. Yet in making himself British, he becomes the manly Englishman *par excellence*. Resourceful, intrepid – a man of grand visions but few words – William is the very paragon of balanced masculinity. In the Macaulayite romance, it is his job to eschew personal aggrandizement and to sacrifice his self-interests to the needs of his adopted country. His role is that of referee or honest broker – connecting antagonistic factions that must be brought to co-operate if the absolutist danger is to be removed. Arriving in England, he unites Episcopalians with Puritans, and Whigs with Tories, while patiently waiting for the English Parliament to call him to the throne. Duly crowned, he then travels north to Scotland, patiently waiting for the Scottish Parliament to make him King on their terms. No doubt, this cautious, consensus-seeking, constitutionalist punctilio resulted in the anomaly which made all subsequent "British" monarchs Presbyterians north of the border, and Anglicans south of the Tweed. Nevertheless, Macaulay argues, it was the pragmatic wisdom that permitted this religious anomaly which also made it possible for full political Union between the two British kingdoms to proceed.[72]

Yet, as constitutionalist narrative morphs into nationalist romance (volume III), William figures ever more centrally as an almost magical character – a real-life Waverley – who inadvertently calls up an entire nation and imperial mission in his wake. At moments, there seems to be nothing that this conjurer cannot do:

Under his dextrous management the hereditary enemies of his house had helped him to mount a throne; and the persecutors of his religion had helped him to

---

[71] MHE, III, *passim*.   [72] MHE, III: 194–237, especially 205.

rescue his religion from persecution. Fleets and armies, collected to withstand him, had without a struggle, submitted to his orders. Factions and sects, divided by mortal antipathies, had recognised him as their common head ... In a few weeks he had changed the relative position of all the states in Europe, and had restored the equilibrium which the preponderance of one power had destroyed.[73]

This over-reliance on the mystique of the manly, plenipotent William is symptomatic of a deeper problem in Macaulay's epic strategy: for "William" has almost ceased to be a real historical actor. He is in danger of becoming an artificial plot device, invoked to negotiate the treacherous currents of the 1689–99 period, and for banishing the dread specter of renewed popular agency.[74] Macaulay's own death in 1859 – just after he had buried William in his book – meant that we cannot say how he would have extended his continuitarian narrative of English/British progress without the binding glue of William to make the center hold. Yet in the later volumes that he lived to complete, we can already see the problems that such a work would have faced. All the vicissitudes of the 1690s – the French Wars, the 1692 Bubble, the renewal of the EIC Charter, and the Darien Fiasco of 1698 – gravely challenge Macaulay's romance of the *via media*. Once Whig and Tory factionalism re-emerge on the narrative surface, we may legitimately question what enduring gains 1688 has achieved.[75]

While Macaulay's mature essays on the Augustan and Georgian periods, "War of Succession in Spain" (1833), "Horace Walpole" (substantially about Robert Walpole, 1833), "Chatham" (1844), and "William Pitt" (1859), are no substitutes for the epic narrative that remained unwritten, they give us some idea of how he might have treated the developments of the eighteenth century. In each case there is a more or less unsatisfactory effort to find an heroic manly figure who can advance the linear ascent of progress through a corrupt and confusing age.[76] So far from propelling the continuitarian narrative, however, these essays only

[73] MHE, II: 205, 422–506, III: 1–101, 196–299, quote on 38. Macaulay had been reflecting on the historical role of William since 1822, when he had written a college prize essay on the subject, "Essay on the Life and Character of King William III," printed with editorial comment by A. N. L. Munby in the *Times Literary Supplement* (London), May 1, 1969, 468–9.

[74] MHE, III: 38. See also Macaulay's description of William's heroism on the battlefield, in MHE, III: 502.

[75] MHE, IV, V, *passim*. The one partial exception here is in the handling of the Bubble and recession of 1692, which is masterful, considering the time when it was written.

[76] "War of Succession in Spain," "Horace Walpole," and "Chatham" (William Pitt the Elder), in MEL, 238–66, 267–87, 288–313 respectively, and "William Pitt" (the Younger), in MMW, 395–436. For other relevant essays on eighteenth-century English themes see "Boswell's 'Life of Johnson'" and "Life and Writings of Addison," in MEL, 160–85 and 699–744 respectively, and "Samuel Johnson," in MMW, 372–95.

serve to reinforce the conclusion that the modern (nineteenth-century) progress that Macaulay celebrated at the start of his book was *not* the direct result of 1688. On the contrary, it represented a much later reaction against the corruption and degeneracy of the eighteenth century. Yet to acknowledge these inglorious eighteenth-century realities openly would have cast doubt on the significance of 1688 in setting a vital center in continuous motion, or of putting the nation on an inevitable path of social and political improvement. The only essays that seem to work in this way are the two that Macaulay wrote on Robert Clive and Warren Hastings between 1839 and 1841, just as his work on the *History* was getting underway.

7   Peripheral nightmares: the Indian and Irish centers do not hold

That Macaulay fell so easily into the romance of Clive and Hastings was, in no small part, because their story was his own. As ambitious young aspirants who were compelled to seek their fortunes in India because of the dearth of opportunities available at home, they were eighteenth-century precursors of himself. In 1743, Clive shipped out without resources or prospects. Seventeen years later, he returned in a shower of riches, having transformed the EIC into the ruler of Bengal. Clive's triumph, Macaulay shows, was partly a matter of luck and timing. But it was also a consequence of his qualities of truculence and daring that emboldened him to seize every opportunity that came his way. Like all Macaulay heroes, Clive is presented as a paragon of manly self-possession. He was prepared to take risks to achieve great objects, but he was always hard-headed, even-tempered, and disinclined toward needless extravagance. The story of Hastings, a generation later, was similar, although by now the British were more firmly entrenched. In contrast to Clive, who was primarily a soldier, Hastings was a scholar and an administrator who secured British control over Indian institutions and (perhaps most importantly) made the Indian Empire pay. Equally adept at commanding troops, managing subordinates, drafting position papers, and vanquishing opponents in policy debates, Hastings also embodied those manly qualities of self-assurance that enabled true Englishmen to dominate those who (like the native Bengalis) were feckless and irresolute.[77]

One of the most striking features of these two essays is the way Macaulay makes it clear from the first sentence that they are intended

---

[77] "Clive," in MEL, 502–47; "Hastings," in MEL, 602–67.

for metropolitan audiences. Whereas the author of the epic of 1688 envisions a universal readership, in "Clive" he explicitly enjoins his fellow Britons to take an interest in "the actions of our great countrymen in the East." Contrasting the British conquest of India with the Spanish conquest of America, he notes that "the people of India, when we subdued them, were ten times as numerous as the Americans whom the Spaniards had vanquished, and were at the same time quite as highly civilized as the victorious Spaniards." In contrast to the blanket denunciations of Mill, Macaulay emphasizes the wealth and sophistication of Mughal India. "They had reared cities larger and fairer than Saragossa or Toledo, and buildings more beautiful and costly than the cathedral of Seville."[78] Indeed, India's weakness was its over-civilization during the early modern period, a decadence reminiscent of the Roman Empire just before its collapse: "A succession of nominal sovereigns, sunk in indolence and debauchery, sauntered away life in secluded palaces, chewing bang, fondling concubines and listening to buffoons. A succession of ferocious invaders descended through the western passes to prey on the defenseless wealth of Hindustan."[79]

It was thus to spare the Indians a millennium of dark ages that the British intervened on the subcontinent during the eighteenth century. In the beginning, Macaulay acknowledges, the first generation of Britons who appeared in India were scarcely distinguishable from the horde of other plunderers and predators who picked at the corpse of the Mughal regime. The role of Clive and Hastings in Macaulay's imperial romance is to effect the necessary transformation in Britain's Indian administration from the first Empire of pillaging freebooters to his own second Empire of improvement and utility.[80] Since these men could not be depicted as both tyrants and liberators, Macaulay's vacillation between the characterizations imparts an undertone of defensiveness into his account of their glorious escapades. Was Clive's conquest of Bengal really undertaken for the cause of justice, or so that he could appropriate "between two and three hundred thousand pounds," and then be "astonished at his own moderation"? His reorganization of the Bengali government under direct British rule was followed within three years by a devastating famine in which a third of the population died. Were the new British officials in any way responsible for this disaster, or did British profiteers benefit from

[78] "Clive," in MEL, 502–25, quote on 645. Note how Macaulay effortlessly locates eighteenth-century India in the scale of civilization as a bit more civilized than sixteenth-century Spain. Thus he accomplishes *en passant* (and rather more favorably to the Indians) the laborious task that took James Mill six tedious volumes.

[79] "Clive," in MEL, 507.

[80] "Clive," in MEL, 502–47; "Hastings," in MEL, 636.

starvation and dearth? "There is no reason," Macaulay avows, "for thinking that they either profited or aggravated an evil which physical causes
sufficiently explain." In the case of Hastings, the gap between aspiration
and achievement was even more striking. Lover of oriental literature and
learning, he accumulated a thick dossier of peculation, evidence tamper-
ing, and judicial murder along the way to his impeachment trial.[81]

Notwithstanding these lapses (which were scarcely minor), Macaulay is
determined to praise Clive and Hastings for introducing honesty into
Indian politics for the first time.

English valour and English intelligence have done less to extend and preserve our
Oriental empire than English veracity. All that we could do by imitating the
doublings, the evasions, the fictions, the perjuries which have been employed
against us, is as nothing, when compared with what we have gained by being the
one power in India on whose word reliance can be placed.

And yet were Clive and Hastings actually honest? Macaulay has to
acknowledge that, in practice, they were not. "He [Clive] knew that the
standard of morality among the natives of India differed widely from that
established in England. He knew that he had to deal with men destitute of
what in Europe is called honor, with men who would give any promise
without hesitation, and break any promise without shame." And so, in
India, Clive and Hastings became as deceitful and duplicitous as the
people they ruled.[82]

Unable to reclaim his heroes for the causes of truth and justice, the
historian can only attribute their shortcomings to the polluted environment in which they worked.

The physical organization of the Bengali is feeble even to the point of effeminacy.
He lives in a constant vapour bath. His pursuits are sedentary, limbs delicate,
his movements languid ... During many ages he has been trampled upon by
men of bolder and more hardy breeds. [He] shrinks from bodily exertion; and
though voluble in dispute and singularly pertinacious in the war of chicane, he
seldom engages in personal conflict, and scarcely ever enlists as a soldier ... There
never, perhaps, existed a people so thoroughly fitted by nature and habit for a
foreign yoke.[83]

If we recall Macaulay's *Minute*, with its dismissal of racial differences
and its aspiration to make moral Englishmen out of "Indians in colour
and blood," these insinuations of the inherent servility of Bengalis come as
a shock. They strike a false note in the author's celebrations of British

[81] "Clive," in MEL, 502–47, and "Hastings," in MEL, 602–68, quotes on 527, 542, and
543–4.
[82] "Clive," in MEL, 521, 526.   [83] "Clive," in MEL, 517; "Hastings," in MEL, 611.

India. Did he secretly doubt the beneficence of its own administration, or its utilitarian power to bring Indians the gift of modernity? Could some fatality in the extremes of India's hothouse environment leave the British themselves un-manned and de-centered, once they too acclimatized to this torrid periphery? In the privacy of a letter to his sister, Macaulay acknowledged "the truth that every enemy is formidable in India. We are strangers there. We are as one in two or three thousand to the natives. The higher classes whom we have deprived of their power would do anything to throw off our yoke. A serious check in any part of India would raise half the country against us."[84]

After Hastings, Macaulay had little more to say about India, and it was with relief that he turned from these conundrums of imperial coercion to his metropolitan romance of English liberty. Yet the two could not be quite so easily separated. By the time he reached volume III of his epic, he found that the Irish Question had rudely intruded on the Glorous Revolution in the home country. "When the historian ... turns to Ireland," he reluctantly acknowledged, "his task becomes peculiarly difficult and delicate. The seventeenth century has, in that unhappy country, left to the nineteenth a fatal heritage of malignant passions." In a judicious show of apparent impartiality, Macaulay avows that "neither of the hostile castes can justly be absolved from blame." Yet the historian knows that the crux of this problem is that the two sides were unevenly matched. "Though four fifths of the population of Ireland were Celtic and Roman Catholic, more than four fifths of the property of Ireland belonged to the Protestant Englishry."[85]

In his youth, Macaulay might have interpreted these inequalities as the creative basis for class struggle – an opportunity to redress the grievances of a rising subject people, through an auspicious dose of progressive reform. In Parliament, he had vociferously defended the rights of Irish Catholics, and supported their demands for equality before the law. But now, in his *History*, the mature Macaulay seems immobilized by the Irish conflict, which appears as a hopeless labyrinth, in which progress does not advance, and the center does not hold. Although Macaulay makes a judicious show in assigning both sides responsibility for this disaster, he exculpates Britain's Glorious Revolutionaries for this inglorious disaster that plays out on Irish ground. On the contrary, it is the Irish Catholics who precipitated the catastrophe of 1690 by indulging in a reactionary conspiracy to bring back the Stuarts.[86] For thus allowing themselves to be made into the dupes of a despot (James II), Ireland's Catholics were

---

[84] TBM to E. Cropper, June 27, 1834, in PLM, III: 50.
[85] Quotes in MHE, II: 97, and III: 123.   [86] MHE, II: 104–5.

reduced to a condition of despotism. In Macaulay's eyes, this despotism can be explained, if not entirely justified, by emphasizing the cultural backwardness of the victims, even by dropping hints of their innate inferiority. "No man of English blood then regarded the aboriginal Irish as his countrymen. They did not belong to our branch of the great human family. They were distinguished from us by more than one moral and intellectual peculiarity, which the difference of situation and of education ... do not seem altogether to explain."

In 1690, when these barbarians rose up to throw off the yoke of their Anglo-Saxon liberators, their true incapacity for self-government was revealed for all to see.

The destruction of property which took place within a few weeks would be incredible if it were not attested by witnesses unconnected with each other ... All agreed in declaring that it would take many years to repair the waste ... The Protestants described with contemptuous disgust the strange gluttony of their newly liberated slaves. The carcasses, half raw, and half burned to cinders, sometimes still bleeding, sometimes in a state of loathsome decay, were torn to pieces and swallowed without salt, bread, or herbs.[87]

These brutal creatures, scarcely superior to the animals that they bestialized, could only gain from the sometimes-less-than-benevolent despotism that Protestant Anglo-Saxon settlers re-imposed. Macaulay will not quite defend their colonial rule of insolence and injustice, but their "power [was] derived from superior intelligence," from their exceptional "knowledge, energy, and perseverance," which concentrated the best qualities of the lands from which they came. It is striking how Macaulay's English Puritans and Scots Presbyterians – the very men who had been troublemakers and "austere fanatics" in the broils of the mother country – suddenly transformed themselves into stalwart, resourceful frontiersmen at the moment when they usefully emigrated across the Irish Sea.[88] In Macaulay's account of the brutal Irish War, with its heroic climax in the siege of Londonderry, his romance of liberal imperialism suddenly takes an unexpected turn. In Scotland, in America, and perhaps even in India, the colonized natives are becoming candidates for civilization. In Ireland, however, they are denigrated as hereditary inferiors – menials to be subjected more or less indefinitely to an authoritarian power. What can account for this sudden reversal of rhetoric?

One obvious explanation is that Macaulay is angry at the Irish for having spoiled his Glorious Revolution: for having forced him (and his readers) reluctantly to see that the deliverance and emancipation of England (and/

[87] MHE, II: 325–6, III: 125–6.   [88] MHE, III: 152–3.

or Britain) is inextricably interconnected with the conquest and subjugation of the periphery. Yet Macaulay might have chosen to separate his
narratives, walling off his Irish story from the British main event. In this
reading, William's victory over James would continue to be celebrated.
But the subsequent penal laws and decades of religious persecution could
be written off as a regrettable instance of imperialist oppression, all too
much of a piece with the retrogressive Empire of the mercantilist age.[89]
Here the rhetorical strategy would be to point out all the ways in which the
Anglo-Irish connection had been transformed and liberalized by the nineteenth century: the repeal of the penal laws, the Act of Union, Catholic
Emancipation, the rise of O'Connell, the appearance of benevolent
Protestant landlords like the Edgeworths. Macaulay was perfectly well
aware of all these arguments, for he had articulated them many times in
his Parliamentary speeches over the years. In the 1820s, he had been
a staunch supporter of Catholic Emancipation. Yet Ireland remained an
anomaly. Culturally and economically too remote to be fully incorporated
into Britain, it remained physically too close to be romanticized away as
some exotic jewel in the Imperial Crown.[90]

Then, in the late 1840s, just as he was preparing to write his account of
the Irish War of 1690, the Great Famine struck. It seems likely that the
tenor of his account in the *History* was as much affected by the events of
the 1840s as by those of the 1690s. In the late summer of 1849, Macaulay
paid a visit to Ireland to gather materials for the coming volume of his
History. He was profoundly disturbed by what he saw.

From Limerick to Killarney, and from Killarney to Cork, I hardly knew whether to
laugh or cry. Hundreds of dwellings in ruins, abandoned by the late inmates, who
have fled to America; the labouring people dressed literally, not rhetorically, worse
than the scarecrows of England; the children of whole villages turning out to beg of
every coach and every car that goes by.[91]

How was this catastrophe in modern Ireland to be explained? The country
had now enjoyed over two centuries of Anglo-Saxon tutelage. The Union
of 1800 had afforded political and economic integration into the multi-
national British, imperial state. The legitimate grievances long nursed by
Irish Catholics had, for the most part, been satisfactorily redressed. For

---

[89] "The State of Ireland," in MMW, 642–7. Hall, "At Home with History," notes that "the
Empire was banished to the margins of his [Macaulay's] volumes" (49). On the other
hand, his account of the Irish campaign reflects his recognition that the two could not be
separated.
[90] See, for example, Macaulay's speeches on pre-famine Ireland: "Union with Ireland,"
"State of Ireland," "Maynooth," and "Church of Ireland," in MMW, 535–43, 641–57,
680–700; CM, 229–30.
[91] Quoted in TLL, II: 202. See also Macaulay, *Journals*, II: 125–45.

decades, the Irish had enjoyed the benefits of full access to the British economic miracle with its open sesame of migration and emancipated trade. What had been the consequences of these advantages? A blight of biblical proportions, which had reduced the population to starvation and savagery!

Who was responsible for this incomprehensible disaster? Such a question was bound to bring out all of Macaulay's unctuous defensiveness. Certainly not the British governments that he had so effectively served. Certainly not his own brother-in-law, Charles Trevelyan, who was now the senior Treasury official in charge of emergency famine relief. Trevelyan was the best of the rising generation of colonial administrators with whom Macaulay had worked closely in India. At considerable emotional cost, he had given his sister away to this man in marriage. In the famine, Trevelyan had done everything consistent with humanity and sound policy to relieve distress. For this disaster, the Irish could have only themselves to blame. "I cannot mend this state of things," he sententiously closed his description, "and so there is no use in breaking my heart about it."[92] Since the British imperialist could not accept responsibility for the fruits of his dominance, the dominated had to be impugned and the victims had to be blamed. If the Catholic Celt had been unable to benefit from eight generations of British opportunity, then the explanation must be that he suffers from some irremediable cultural or organic deficiency. The secret source of the Irish disaster of the 1840s had not lain in the Irish War of the 1690s. The Irish peasant was starving not because his ancestors had been conquered. On the contrary, both the starvation and the conquest could be interpreted as outward badges of his inherent inferiority.

From his account of the "Inglorious Revolution" in seventeenth-century Ireland, no less than from his own reaction to the Great Famine of the nineteenth century, Macaulay might have questioned some of his most fundamental assumptions: that British identity opened the path to economic emancipation; that British imperial expansion was the recipe for the universalization of English liberty. In his mind, however, the cases of Ireland and, to a lesser extent, India always remained troubling anomalies. The reverberations of brutal revolt with sharp repression, which had resounded the discordant note of Irish and Indian discontinuity, had to be seen as deviations from the consensual norms of unilinear British history. To explain these deviations from the "manly" center, Indians and Irishmen had to be cast as either infantile or

---

[92] For a recent study of British governmental response to the famine see Peter Gray, *Famine, Land and Politics: British Government and Irish Society, 1843–1850* (Dublin, 1999).

effeminate – which attributes were then taken as justifications for their exclusion from English liberty.

8   The reception of Macaulay's *History*

On December 2, 1848, a crowd of eager customers gathered at the offices of Longmans in Paternoster Row, awaiting the first two volumes of Macaulay's *History of England from the Accession of James the Second*. Within three months, 13,000 copies had been sold in Britain, and 100,000 in the United States. To a world still reeling from the shock of revolution, this paean to consensus came as a welcome relief. Indeed, the enthusiasm that greeted the book's appearance seems astonishing to our jaded, media-saturated age. "The first volume was cut and read aloud after breakfast without a break until luncheon hour," Lady Frances Balfour later recalled, "after which the reading was resumed until the shades of evening drew on." Mary Ann Evans (George Eliot) found the *History* "delightful." Thackeray thought it as beguiling as a sparkling dinner party. Lord Auckland resented a friend who interrupted his reading. The fifteen-year-old future Lord Acton read it four times. Even as far away as County Longford, the eighty-two-year-old Maria Edgeworth pronounced it a most enjoyable book.[93]

Within fairly short order, Macaulay's *History* was translated into all the major European languages. When the third and fourth volumes were published, in 1855, there was another, even more spectacular explosion of sales. By 1863, in Britain alone, 267,000 volumes had been sold. By 1875, when a new wave of cheap editions had begun to appear, 133,653 copies of volume I were in circulation. Meanwhile, the *Collected Essays and Speeches* were selling nearly as well.[94] By the end of the century, it seems likely that over 1,000,000 volumes by Macaulay had been placed in circulation. To say that Macaulay's books were bestsellers then is something of an understatement. The numbers alone make it clear that they replaced the novel not only on the night tables of ladies, but in the armchairs of many other readers as well. When we consider that many of these

---

[93] Amy Cruse, *The Victorians and their Reading* (Boston, 1935), 314–15; TLL, II: 204–6; Gertrude Himmelfarb, *Lord Acton: A Study in Conscience and Politics* (Chicago, 1952), 25; Hugh MacDonald, *Racial Myth in English History: Trojans, Teutons and Anglo-Saxons* (Hanover, 1982), 108. For Macaulay's own reaction to the acclaim, see *Journals*, II: 10–34, 46–9, 65–71.

[94] TLL, II: 182–90; Edwards, *Macaulay*, 50; Thomas Pinney, "Preface," in PLM, V: vii–ix; Richard D. Altick, *The English Common Reader: A Social History of the Mass Reading Public, 1800–1900* (Chicago, 1957), 296, 310, 388. According to *Blackwood's*, the *History* had "been read by almost every person in the three kingdoms pretending to intelligence"; see *Blackwood's Edinburgh Magazine*, 490.80 (Edinburgh, 1856), 126–41, quote on 128.

copies were purchased by lending libraries, and were passed along through many hands, it is clear that Macaulay's readership went beyond the middle class. In Manchester, a group of workers voted him thanks "for having written a history which working men can understand." The availability of cheap editions, from the 1860s onward, also made it a book that working men could afford. "From Eton and Harrow down to an elementary school in St. Giles and Bethnal Green," declared John Morley in 1881, "Macaulay's *Essays* are a textbook."[95]

What did these readers, from so many different backgrounds, geographical locales, and walks of life, make of Macaulay's works? The first, overwhelming reaction was simply to be seduced by the brilliant sparkle of the romance. If we understand both the *History* and the later *Essays* not simply as calculated political and historiographical interventions, but also as subliminal love letters to his departed sisters – graven monuments to the memory of happier days – this reaction begins to make more sense. Macaulay had poured all his formidable emotional, intellectual, and rhetorical powers into producing works that would be both instructive and entertaining. The overwhelming response from the public indicated how well he had succeeded in this aim. The rolling periods, the thrusting narration, the telling juxtapositions, and the middlebrow sensibility were each enormously seductive. His ability to paint vivid word-pictures, to place his common readers in the company of the powerful and at the center of events, all contributed to his appeal.[96]

Drawn in by the lure of Macaulay's romance, it was all too easy to assent implicitly to the message that was being transmitted to the various outsiders, who stood some paces back behind the author, outside the Establishment's gates. "A people which takes no pride in the noble achievements of remote ancestors," Macaulay reminded these aspirants, "will never achieve anything worthy to be remembered with pride by remote descendants." It mattered little that all the Macaulayite heroes – Sydney, William, Bentinck, and Fox – were not the biological ancestors of his readers.[97] In buying the romance, they were grandfathered into the progress narrative that it expressed. Instructed in the path that led to enfranchisement, these others would be emboldened to the deeds of political consequence that their own descendants (biological or otherwise) would, in future, recount with pride. Thus understood, history became a call to action. What the British gentry had gained in 1688, and the British

---

[95] Cruse, *Victorians and their Reading*, 127, quote on 295; Altick, *English Common Reader*, 160–1, 182, 296; Clive, *Not by Fact Alone*, 83–4; John Morley, *Nineteenth Century Essays* (Chicago, 1970), 73–97, quote on 74.
[96] Clive, *Not by Fact Alone*, 83–5.   [97] MHE, III: 191.

middle class had gained in 1832, would, in future, be extended to other subordinate social classes and colonial social groups. To appreciate the true potential for Anglo-India, Anglo-Jamaica, Anglo-Africa, and even Anglo-Ireland, it was sufficient to look back to the Glorious Revolution, to see what Whiggism, plus capitalism, plus Anglo-Scotland had wrought. In harnessing past remembrance to the circumstances of the present, a reassuring insight into the future was obtainable by drawing a line of continuity between all three. In this sense, Macaulay's *History* was its own last chapter, an achievement as glorious as the accomplishments it recounts.

To the Africans, Indians, West Indians, Irish Catholics, and English workingmen who were queuing up for citizenship in the Greater Britain of the future, Macaulay's message was one of patience and self-control. From his books and essays they could obtain a better understanding of the privileges toward which they were striving, an illustration of why these were worth having, and a delineation of the deficiencies that they would have to overcome. From this perspective, Macaulay's works could be seen as educational and civilizational ventures. In order to discern the prospects for the coming generations it was necessary to learn the lessons that Whig imperial history taught. Through British imperial expansion, outsiders everywhere could be turned into insiders. Potential trouble-makers and ideologically overwrought radicals at home could be turned into national heroes and colonial adventurers abroad. Political crises in the expanding capitalist state could be resolved without recourse to revolutionary violence. Savages and barbarians could be brought within the orbit of civilization, while retrograde, effeminate peoples, groaning under the yoke of oriental despots, could be reclaimed for the modern world of manly respectability. In the Macaulayite Whig and imperial romance there was no longer any need for subordinated groups to revolt or to organize collectively, because the path for individual advancement and assimilation would remain open so long as the larger capitalist and imperial system was able to expand. Class struggle could be banished from the Macaulayite arsenal of explanation because the Empire was becoming a paradise for the *parvenu*. Yesterday Clive and Hastings. Today Macaulay. Tomorrow the remasculinized Indian, West Indian, and African, all English in taste, intellect, and opinion, whatever their color or blood.

Such, I believe, is the message that Macaulay wanted his readers to take away from his books. Fortunately, the books themselves were not so seamlessly monolithic, and readers, especially colonial readers, were able to pick and choose among the messages themselves. Outside Britain those most eager and able to embrace the English constitutional romance were Anglo-Saxon readers in the white settler colonies who were looking for new ways, in their alien environment, to re-negotiate imaginative links with the mother country. In Melbourne, 300 copies were initially ordered – one for every 323 households in Victoria province – and yet the entire consignment was immediately sold. Some decades later, a traveler to the outback reported that, along with Shakespeare and the Bible, a copy of Macaulay's *Essays* was to be found on every squatter's shelf. Because these early Victorian heirs of Pym and Sydney were just then successfully agitating to obtain self-government, Macaulay's volumes acquired a special relevance and immediacy. When W. C. Wentworth proposed to add a hereditary upper house to New South Wales's fledgling constitution in 1852, the left Liberal Henry Parkes simply quoted Macaulay's indictment of the original turncoat Wentworth, who had betrayed the cause of liberty in the sixteenth century.[98]

In India and Ceylon, by contrast, Macaulay's romance required a good deal of translation (both literal and figurative) before it could be assimilated to subaltern needs. As he doubtless hoped (and perhaps expected), Macaulay's writings quickly entered the curriculum of English-language higher education in both countries. Victorian memoirs give a picture of precocious youths eagerly dissecting his volumes in search of eloquent passages that might polish their writing and rhetorical maneuvers that would help them in training for the Bar. On March 9, 1861, the Colombo Academy Debating Society deliberated on "the character of Cromwell" (his admirers won). A few weeks later, they disputed whether Macaulay or Dickens was the greater writer (Macaulay won).[99] The problem here is that too slavish an imitation of Macaulay produced not Cromwells, but men whose contempt for their own language and culture separated them from the masses, and subverted their own search for any authentic voice. For this reason, more serious (and ambitious) intellectuals tended to be more ambivalent about Macaulay's effects. The early Indian nationalist Rajnarian Bose had been raised to admire Macaulay and continued to appreciate him even after his attitudes towards the Raj changed. The great Bengali novelist Bankimchandra Chattopadhyay was perfectly willing to countenance Macaulay's writings, so long as his Indian essays were placed in

[98] John Holroyd, *George Robertson of Melbourne: 1825–1898, Pioneer Bookseller and Publisher* (Melbourne, 1968), 17; Morley, *Nineteenth Century Essays*, 74; Bruce McCully, *English Education and the Origins of Indian Nationalism* (Gloucester, 1966), 209. Parkes is quoted in Neville Meany, "'In History's Page': Identity and Myth," in Deryck Schreuder and Stuart Ward (eds.), *Australia's Empire* (Oxford, 2008), 365.
[99] Yasmine Gooneratne, *English Literature in Ceylon, 1815–1878* (Dehiwala, Ceylon, 1968), 24–6, 74–88, 128–52.

the "fiction" category. As a mature man, Nirad Chaudhuri was enraged by Macaulay's depiction of Bengali men. Nevertheless, he never forgot his discovery of the essay on Milton as a child, when he thrilled at the depiction of the poet "as a stern, unbending and powerful champion of liberty."[100]

Some sixty years after Macaulay's departure from Calcutta, the local historian S. C. Sanial published a series of essays on his Indian work. Amid all the criticisms which were then gathering steam, Sanial insisted that Macaulay be remembered for his critiques of racial discrimination, and for his "lofty aim" of "fitting the population of India to govern themselves." Ignoring the causal anti-Hindu slanders that disfigured the famous *Minute*, Sanial emphasized just how much attention Macaulay had given to the practical details of Indian higher education, improving curricula, advocating the merits of a non-sectarian system, and opening up schools to native teachers and students of all ages. One former Hindu College pupil, Bholanath Chander, still retained a physical image of Macaulay passing along the corridor, on his way to a recitation of student essays, with a bundle of books in hand. "Forgetting the libeler in the benefactor," Chander mused, "I now regard my having had a sight of him as an epoch in my life."[101]

Not surprisingly, perhaps, it was in Scotland and Ireland that the most overtly critical responses to Macaulay appeared in print. The *Irish Quarterly Review* acknowledged that, on first impression, the *History* went down like a novel. However, "on re-perusal and reflection [we] were reluctantly compelled to admit that it lacks the chief ingredient, without which history becomes a romance – Truth." Macaulay's glorification of William and his hostility to James, as well as his visceral denigration of the culture of Irish Catholics and Highland Scots, all gave this reviewer great offense. "Notwithstanding his great reputation in politics, eloquence and literature," the writer continued,

His book is a political romance, a work of genius, it is true, but of imagination, also, a perfect illustration of HOW NOT TO DO IT; very agreeable to read, very unprofitable to study, an invaluable book for a circulating library, but a worthless

---

[100] Tapan Raychaudhuri, *Europe Reconsidered: Perceptions of the West in Nineteenth Century Bengal* (Oxford, 2001), 124, 175; Sudipta Kaviraj, *The Unhappy Consciousness: Bankimchandra Chattopadhyay and the Formation of Nationalist Discourse in India* (Oxford, 1995), 35, 104, 110, 117; Nirad Chaudhuri, *The Autobiography of an Unknown Indian* (Reading, 1951), 100–1; Nirad Chaudhuri, *Clive of India: A Political and Psychological Essay* (London, 1975), 7–8; David Kopf, *The Brahmo Samaj and the Shaping of the Modern Indian Mind* (Princeton, 1979), 192.
[101] S. C. Sanial, "Macaulay in Lower Bengal," *Calcutta Review*, 244 (1906), 291–312; 245 (1906), 463–81, quotes on 463, 480–1; 247 (1907), 77–109.

addition to the collection of a student; false in its facts, uncandid in its criticisms, illogical in its reasoning, and unjust in its conclusions.[102]

Another response, published in the *Dublin Review*, made similar points in a less polemical way. Given Macaulay's public criticisms of the Protestant Ascendancy, Irish Catholics had hoped for fairer treatment in his *History*. In the event, they had been disappointed by the prejudice and partiality that the historian displayed. Yet the *Dublin Review* astutely recognized the way Macaulay's disparaging treatment of the Irish was connected with his determination to glorify the English Revolution of 1688. The historian "has but one end and object – the exaltation of the English Revolution. The principles of the English Revolution are his principles. The enemies of the English Revolution are his enemies." In England Macaulay's paeans to freedom have been justly earned, "But transfer the cause of the Revolution to Ireland, and how does it stand? . . . Principles, parties, men were all reversed . . . The same men [who had professed liberty in England], when they crossed the channel with William in his Irish campaign, turned their backs on all these professions."[103]

Macaulay's failure to confront these contradictions left it to his colonial readers to strike their own balance between skepticism and enjoyment as they negotiated the unresolved instabilities of his text. In general, it is fair to say that his choice in privileging the dictates of romance and epic over those of analysis and argument did exact a substantial intellectual cost.[104] This meant that the contradictions of British and imperial history tended to get papered over, or even completely suppressed. Short-shrifting the eighteenth century, with its legacies of conquest and corruption, oppression, and discrimination, may have made the romance glitter more brightly, but it telescoped the first into the second British Empire, and it pre-empted qualifications that would have complicated Macaulay's argument but might have strengthened his case. As we have seen, this left his actual treatment of colonial history exceptionally vulnerable. To look at Clive and Hastings from the perspective of the Indian, or at William from the perspective of the Irish, was to see not a manly hero, but a ferocious oppressor, who actually foreclosed the Whig gradualism that Macaulay espoused.[105]

---

[102] *Irish Quarterly Review*, 7 (1857), 192–242, quotes on 192, 242.
[103] *Dublin Review*, 40 (1856), 156–200, quotes on 168, 169.
[104] "The colour and movement of Macaulay daily transported me," the factory worker Kathleen Woodward wrote. In retrospect, however, she was moved to add that "my pleasure [had not then] been spoiled by any awareness of his prejudices or inaccuracies." Quoted in Jonathan Rose, *The Intellectual Life of the British Working Classes* (New Haven, 2001), 33, 42, 51–2, 83, 130–2, 164, 239, 368, 376.
[105] *Irish Quarterly Review*, 7 (1857), 192–242.

As we saw in Chapter 1, Walter Scott's solution to this problem was to romanticize the dark history of oppression and conquest. Safe in the conviction that this era had now ended, he could assume that successful integration into anglocentric capitalism now enabled most Scots to leave their bitterness behind. But this was less of an option for the Irishman or the Indian (or even for the male British proletarian), who had seen scant benefits from modern capitalism, and who saw the cult of the manly Englishman vaunt itself at his (masculine) expense. So far from attempting to sooth these troubled waters, Macaulay poured oil on them, with his inflammatory demand that the colonial other give up his infantile, outmoded romances, expunge all feeling for his obsolescent religion, and refigure the once glorious civilization of his ancestors as a paltry and negligible barbarian creed.

Caught up in the psychological needs of his own project, Macaulay failed to see just how subliminally invested he was in feeling superior to the Indians, Irishmen, and English proletarians, who stood behind him in the Greater British queue. As a result, he made a demand of these class and colonial others that he never would have accepted himself. To attain the age of reason, respectability, and manly self-possession, they would have to give up their indigenous romances, and buy into his own. Here, we must conclude that Macaulay's secular historical progress narrative did not so much transcend as replicate the limitations of his father's evangelical Protestantism. To many members of the British working class and, even more, to the colored men and women under British rule, the supposed universalism of both Macaulayite ideologies seemed equally hypocritical and false. In that sense, the most important long-term effect of T. B. Macaulay's historical romances may have been to reinforce the smug complacency of his English readers (including Anglo-Saxon settlers in the colonies). Confirming these people in their ethnocentric prejudices, his limited liberalism only fortified their illusion of cultural superiority. For all his ostensible belief in the equality of all races, Macaulay's romance sent a subliminal message to these Anglo-Saxon readers that they need not negotiate with colonial (or class) others on any terms but their own. As such, his romance left them ill prepared for the challenges of the post-1857 period, and may even have contributed to their retreat from liberal imperial principles in the later Victorian age.

9   Conclusion

In the end, then, it is the fragility and insularity of Macaulay's presumptively timeless, universal masterwork that impresses us today. Because of its anglocentric narrowness and explanatory impoverishment, it could not underwrite a genuinely inclusive version of British and imperial progress that might satisfactorily encompass the vast agglomeration of far-flung peoples, which the second British Empire was collecting around the globe. The ringing phrases of Macaulay's epics and essays sounded well on first hearing, but they were belied by the contradictions, which they all too often either ignored or suppressed. His disparagement of "backward" cultures and his emasculating demands for the deferral of citizenship all undercut the rhetorical paeans to an abstract "liberty" that was, in practice, being denied. In his own darker, more depressive moments, Macaulay contemplated the collapse of his vision, and the prospect of an empireless (and prematurely democratized) Britain in which greatness had been lost.

There would be many millions of human beings, crowded in a narrow space, deprived of all those resources which alone had made it possible for them to exist in so narrow a space; trade gone; manufactures gone; credit gone. What could they do but fight for the mere sustenance of nature, and tear each other to pieces till famine, and pestilence following in the train of famine, came to turn the terrible commotion into a more terrible repose.[106]

Macaulay, however, was an optimist by nature. Even the end of Empire would not necessarily be disastrous if her peoples continued to re-read his volumes and if that Empire were wound up in a proper English way. After all, the loss of the thirteen North American colonies had not marred the more permanent economic and cultural connections between these two nations, even after the violence and bad blood of 1775–83. How much better might be those "proudest days" of the future when the second British Empire realized its purpose by peacefully and spontaneously devolving into a commonwealth of independent states. Here was a happier image of the New Zealander – contemplating no ruin, but a still-bustling mother metropolis, perhaps with a volume of Macaulay in his hand!

The sceptre may pass away from us. Unforeseen accidents may derange our most profound schemes of policy. Victory may be inconstant to our arms. But there are triumphs which are followed by no reverse. There is an empire exempt from all natural causes of decay. Those are the pacific triumphs of reason over barbarism; that empire is the imperishable empire of our arts and our morals, our literature and our law.[107]

---

[106] MMW, 629. See other references to similar statements in Burrow, *A Liberal Descent*, 68. But see also Macaulay in a happier mood, imagining the England of 1930: "There would be a population of fifty million ... Better fed, clad, and lodged." Quoted in Hamburger, *Macaulay and the Whig Tradition*, 129.

[107] MMW, 572.

4 Re-imagining a Greater Britain: J. A. Froude: counter-romance and controversy

> He [Macaulay] was the creation and representative of his age ... launched into life when the fever of revolution was recommencing. Once more the enthusiastic and hopeful part of the world was beginning to believe that an extension of political power to the masses of the people was a panacea for all the woes which afflicted society ... The commercial organization was in its most wholesome condition when every individual was pursuing his own interests in an enlightened manner. The same principle was extended to every province of human activity. The interest of the community was said to be identical with the interest of the individual ... A better state of society might be anticipated from the unshackled efforts of every single person to improve his own condition than had ever been arrived at under the paternal authority of the best kings or aristocracies.
>
> J. A. Froude, "Lord Macaulay," *Fraser's Magazine*, NS, 13 (June, 1876), 675–94, quotes at 679, 681[1]

When James Anthony Froude published this retrospective on Macaulay, he wrote in confidence that the spirit of the age had changed. Society no longer automatically acceded to individual self-interest when its collective survival was deemed to be at stake. The cants of liberty and progress were no longer allowed to pass without question. "What kind of liberty," people now asked, "liberty to the good, or liberty to the fool and knave? The liberty of anarchy, or the liberty of wisdom and self-restraint?"[2] Froude himself could feel some pride at his own role in putting these questions back on the political agenda. In this chapter, we will explore their impact for the Empire and for the writing of history. What would happen to the progress narrative when the basic premises of Macaulayite liberal imperialism were cast into doubt? Macaulay himself had issued qualifications as to how far liberalism might apply in colonial settings. Froude would now extend these qualifications, and use them as the basis for a very different multi-volume *History of England* that sought to define Britons' relation to their past for a new generation.

[1] See also J. A. Froude on "Progress," *Fraser's Magazine*, NS, 2 (December, 1870), 671–90.
[2] J. A. Froude, "Lord Macaulay," *Fraser's Magazine*, NS, 13 (June, 1876), 680.

Where Macaulay's *History* had exalted the liberty of the subject, Froude's would extol the security of the state. Where the peaceable consensus of 1688 had been the crux of Macaulay's drama, Froude would find his turning point in the violent defeat of the Spanish Armada in 1588. Where Macaulay celebrated the rise of freedom and constitutionalism, Froude would give thanks for those providential autocrats who, like Henry VIII, brought order and stability to a dangerous world. The glories of Protestantism and the evils of Papism – which Macaulay had downplayed – would assume pride of place in Froude's overtly nationalistic account. The Empire, which Macaulay had treated as an open expanse of backward, expectant peoples waiting to receive the boons of British progress, would now be envisioned by Froude as a necessary perimeter, providing outlets for Britain's surplus population and ramparts in her struggles against alien powers. If Macaulay's contradictions subverted his inclusionary master-narrative and eroded liberal imperialism from within, Froude would belligerently trumpet these contradictions, laying them down as an antithetical foundation on which a new kind of exclusionary imperialism could be raised. And yet Froude would not sever all his links with liberalism, even as he embarked on this very different project.

1   Froudian whips

James Anthony Froude was born in 1818, the fourth son and eighth child of a Devonshire country vicar. When he was two, Froude's mother died, setting in motion a chain of disasters that marked him for life. Froude's father was a typical old fashioned "squarson" who performed his clerical duties, but whose primary interests were his paint-brushes, his dogs, and the hunt. Both as magistrate and as father, he was a coldly stoic and silent man. As the youngest child in a motherless home, Anthony was much left in the care of older siblings. Delicate, studious, averse to the rough-and-tumble of boy life, he had to endure constant mockery and humiliation throughout his youth. In particular, his oldest brother, Hurrell, fifteen years his senior, was a merciless bully who taunted him incessantly. So far from interfering to stop this maltreatment, the Revd. Froude reinforced it, finding fault with his youngest offspring whenever he could. Shortly before his mother's death, the boy endured his first whipping, and throughout the rest of his childhood, the beatings continued. For a brief time, school offered a respite from these torments but, at the age of eleven, Anthony was packed off to Westminster College, where the conditions were even worse than at home. Bullied, caned, and starved by the older pupils and headmaster, the boy arrived back at the Rectory four years later in utter disgrace. After a few listless years of trying to educate the boy at home, Froude's father finally dismissed him to Oxford, doubtful that he would ever come to any good.[3]

Yet when Anthony enrolled in Oriel College, at the age of eighteen, his life took a dramatic turn for the better. Suddenly, all the qualities for which he had been formerly punished and derided now became the sources of pleasure and popularity. Plunging with zest into university life, he developed a reputation for witty conversation, pleasant manners, and erudition, lightly worn. He made friends, went on vacation reading parties, and fell in love. But undergraduate life was not all smooth sailing, for Anthony's father closely monitored his expenses and behavior, while the ghost of the recently deceased Hurrell returned to haunt him anew. Hurrell had preceded Anthony at Oriel College, where he had cut a wide swath by dint of his heroic virtue and piety. Together with three other junior fellows of the college – J. H. Newman, John Keble, and E. B. Pusey – Hurrell had created an informal lay brotherhood, dedicated to revitalizing their clerical vocation by re-catholicizing the Anglican Church from within. Devastated by the loss of Hurrell, these Tractarians, as they were now called, looked with interest on the arrival of his younger brother, and hoped he would prove worthy of being inducted into their fraternity.[4]

For his part, young Anthony was flattered by the attentions of these influential college leaders. Nevertheless, he was put off by the intensity of their male bonding rituals and by their dogmatic tone of exaggerated religiosity. The homoerotic desires and sadomasochistic fantasies that he glimpsed in his dead brother's journals merely repelled the new undergraduate's emerging sense of masculinity. A moment of decision came when Newman invited young Anthony to contribute to a multi-authored *Lives of the English Saints*. Froude was attracted by the idea of tracing England's national religious traditions, but he was troubled by Newman's casuistry and cavalier approach to historical evidence. The Catholic mind, as embodied in these anchorites, struck him as un-manly and un-English – at once prostrating truth to disreputable fables and subjugating the nation to an alien yoke.[5]

---

[3] There may never be an adequate biography of Froude, since the bulk of his papers appear to have been destroyed by his daughter. DF is serviceable, though hagiographic, and includes a previously unpublished autobiographical sketch by Froude himself in volume I. Herbert Paul's older *Life of Froude* (New York, 1905) is still useful and contains some documentary materials that have since disappeared. MJAF is good on relations with the Carlyles.

[4] DF, I: 47–61. For Hurrell Froude and the early Tractarians see Frank M. Turner, *John Henry Newman: The Challenge to Evangelical Religion* (New Haven, 2002); R. W. Church, *The Oxford Movement* (Chicago, 1970); and Piers Brendon, *Hurrell Froude and the Oxford Movement* (London, 1974).

[5] DF, I: 75–80; *DNB*, XXIII: 680.

These reflections were reinforced by visits in 1840 and 1845 to Ireland, where Anthony was able to see modern Catholicism at work. The Irish, he perceived, were a conquered people, thoroughly beaten by English brawn. Nevertheless, in their defeat, they "multiplied like rabbits," and compensated for their worldly submission by living in a dream world of miracles and myths. Froude's reaction to the Irish was profoundly ambivalent. On the one hand, he was attracted to what he perceived as their child-like qualities of loyalty and imagination. On the other hand, he was appalled by their poverty, their credulity, and their fluctuation between outward compliance and inward fantasies of violent revolt. British rule in Ireland was like a powder-keg in a volcano. The very servants of Protestant elites were covertly sworn to slit the throats of masters, should the insurrectionary signal ever be proclaimed. Taken in by a Protestant clergyman's family, Froude came to admire, in this dangerous colonial outpost, the intrepid evangelical spirit that he had been taught to disparage in his own High Church college and his family home.

Face to face with the old enemy, with the practical effects of Romanism in the midst of the most superstitious, the most imaginative and inflammable people in Europe, the faith of the serious among the Protestants took the shape inevitably of the Protestantism which had fought for the Reformation in the sixteenth and seventeenth centuries. Their position was dangerous and they knew it. They had nothing to hope from the Government. Each year, in deference to the Catholic vote, their privileges were cut short and their endowments diminished. But their spirit rose with their difficulties.[6]

Fired up by this new vision of Protestant patriotism, Froude returned to the hallowed halls of Oxford, where his sudden resolution proved difficult to sustain. To gain election to a fellowship at Exeter College, it was necessary for him to take orders as an Anglican clergyman, while his continued dalliances with the now overtly Roman Catholic Newman rendered him suspect in conventional circles and renewed his own uncertainties about his spiritual state. Indeed, his perusals of Robert Chambers's *Vestiges of the Natural History of Creation*, and other scientific works, led him secretly to question the veracity of the Bible and to doubt his capacity for Christian faith of any kind. Meanwhile, at Dartington Rectory, the elder Revd. Froude continued to venerate the memory of the brilliant Hurrell and to find fresh faults in the disobedient Anthony. Anthony's response to this paternal judgment was to publish a pseudonymous *roman à clef* containing a thinly veiled portrait of his father as a controlling, abusive despot.[7]

[6] DF, I: 62–71, 86–92, quotes on 64, 87.   [7] DF, I: 93–106; MJAF, 14–15, 30–5.

So life went on for the next few years, as Anthony lurched unsatisfactorily from one abortive project to the next: he would emigrate to the colonies, study medicine, seek an Irish professorship, or enter the Republic of Letters as a novelist or essay writer. "So matters stood," he recollected, until "Europe was suddenly shaken as with an electric stroke, by the Paris Revolution of 26, February, 1848." Without any effective moral or political compass, Froude tried to respond to these stirring events. The freethinking of George Sand and the socialism of Louis Blanc appealed to his youthful romantic ardor, but horror of social disorder on the continent – and the specter of Irish rebellion at home – left him quickly diving back into the folds of orthodoxy. And yet this very renewed appreciation of the virtues of the Oxford establishment forced him to acknowledge that he could never be a reliable Anglican clergyman; that his faith would always be inadequate; and that candor would someday trap him into some inopportune burst of heresy. By so casually drifting into the Exeter College fellowship, indelibly "dip[ping] his fingers in the ecclesiastical ink," he had made the most catastrophic decision of his life.[8]

Vacillating, once again, he returned to rural Ireland and holed himself in a picturesque lakefront cottage "*en communiste*, with an Irish peasant family, consisting of man, wife, maid, four children, four cows, calves, etc." Inspired by this idyllic setting, a second novel spontaneously poured out, published this time under his own name, as *The Nemesis of Faith*. Like a philosophical treatise cast in the style of a cheap romance, *Nemesis* is the partly autobiographical story of a young Anglican who drifts thoughtlessly into clerical orders, where he undergoes a painful crisis of faith. Forced by his bishop to resign his benefice, he falls in love with a married woman, who dies of mortification from the ensuing disgrace. The exclergyman, meanwhile, resolves his dilemma by stifling his theological doubts and converting to Roman Catholicism, where he is conveniently absolved of his sins. If Froude had any hankerings to adopt his novel's solution, its publication in 1849 assured that this option would be foreclosed. "From all sides," he explained, "came a cry of execration":

By the Liberals I was regarded as a reproach to their cause, and they washed their hands of me. By the orthodox, if I had been the devil in person, I could not have been thought more horrible. Sewell, the senior Tutor at my own College, publicly burnt the book in hall before the assembled undergraduates. A preemptory demand was communicated to me from the Rector and the College authorities for the resignation of my fellowship.[9]

[8] DF, I: 72–85, 93–121, quotes on 95, 97.
[9] DF, I: 120–48, quotes on 124, 147; James Anthony Froude, *The Nemesis of Faith* (London, 1849).

Froude put a gallant face on the scandal. Unlike his lead character, he had manfully confronted his dilemma, and had thrown over a corrupt profession that subordinated the pursuit of truth to the practice of dishonesty. "I never felt lighter or happier than in the months which now followed," he bravely proclaimed. The reality was considerably bleaker: he had burned his bridges with the Church and the universities. All other establishment professions were closed to such apostates. Friends fell away, and respectable people shrank in horror, while his father finally disinherited him, once and for all. Even the offer of a teaching job in Tasmania was rescinded, from fear of this dangerous heretical purveyor of immorality.

The outcry against me meanwhile had been so violent that reasonable people had begun to ask themselves what I had done to deserve retribution so excessive. The book after all had been but a cry of pain. It might have been better to bear pain silently, but even with a bad toothache an occasional groan may be forgiven. There was nothing wicked in it that for having written it I should be crushed like a rat.[10]

In fact, British liberals had not deserted Froude to the degree that he claimed. On the contrary, they watched with mounting indignation as this spirited, articulate scion of the Oxford establishment was destroyed by his elders for the crime of integrity. In London, he was wined and dined by the German ambassador, Baron Bunsen, who exposed him to German criticism, Zoarastrianism, and ancient Indian philosophy. Introduced to John Chapman, Mary Ann Evans (George Eliot), and G. H. Lewes, he was offered entry into the portals of the *Westminster Review* coterie. In the summer of 1849, he was invited up to Manchester as tutor to a wealthy Nonconformist solicitor's family. Here he met all the leading Unitarian writers and intellectuals, the Martineaus, the Gaskells, and Geraldine Jewsbury. For a time, it appeared that Froude would be absorbed into this milieu – that he would join the liberal free-trading anti-clerical intelligentsia, marry the daughter of a Manchester magnate, and live happily and comfortably for the rest of his life. Yet there was something in Froude that resisted this outcome, something that made him shrink from these avatars of industrial capitalism, and drove him away from their liberal individualist ideology.[11]

Try as he might, he could not expunge a longing for the world of his father – the manly, stalwart Protestant world of old England's provincial gentry, which had so profoundly shaped the nation's development and

---

[10] DF, I: 130–50, quote on 148.

[11] DF, I: 151–67; MJAF, 45–81. See also Froude's essay "Progress" for some indications of what he found objectionable in the ideology of Manchester liberalism.

history. The Manchester marriage was called off, and Froude proposed to the daughter of a gentry family instead. As the sister-in-law of his friend, the budding Anglican clergyman-novelist Charles Kingsley, this woman brought with her a new set of associates, more conservative, more nationalistic, and more rooted in the countryside. Froude, it now appeared, had finally discovered his bearings – his own personal, authentic route to virile, adult English masculinity. He was not to travel this route alone, however. Guiding, goading, inspiring, and correcting him along the way was the towering figure of a powerful father-substitute: that irascible, inescapable Victorian prophet Thomas Carlyle.[12]

Froude had first encountered Carlyle's *Heroes, Past and Present* and *French Revolution* in 1842. In all his spiritual perplexities, the young man turned to what he took as the message of these books. "The question Carlyle asked of every institution, secular or religious, was not is it true? But is it alive? Life is not truth, but the embodiment in time and morality of a spiritual or animating principle." But how could one distinguish genuine "life" from the multitude of fraudulent crotchets and "pig philosophies" in which modern liberal relativism habitually wallowed? Carlyle, with his vehement style and strident voice, never seemed to be in any doubt. Froude eagerly lapped up all the older man's judgments, crediting him with dispelling the radical allurements of 1848. Finally, in June of 1849, the two men met. Perhaps inevitably, Carlyle began their relationship with a drubbing censure of Froude's recent book: "What on earth is the use of a wretched mortal's vomiting up all his interior crudities, dubitations, and spiritual, agonizing bellyaches, into the view of the public?" the Sage of Chelsea demanded. Froude's accommodating reaction to this corrective strapping, however, put the Sage in a genial mood. He, after all, had survived a similar youthful spiritual crisis, which had been resolved by the very insight that Froude had astutely detected in his works.[13]

The two men quickly became friends, finding a thread of common experience in their reaction to Ireland, which Carlyle had visited in 1846 (and would visit again in the summer of 1849). The Irish, both men agreed, were an impossible people who (in Carlyle's words) "unfortunately speak a partially intelligible dialect of the English language, and having a white skin and European features, cannot be prevented from circulating among us." Strategically and geographically contiguous to Britain, Ireland had proven to be culturally unassimilable and had therefore to be politically ruled with an iron fist. If the Irish could not be

---

[12] DF, I: 151–67; MJAF, 45–81.
[13] DF, I: 72–5, 111–13, 154–6, 194–201, quotes on 73, 94; MJAF, quote on 59.

civilized, Carlyle ranted, they could at least be compelled to work. All Irish paupers should be put under military discipline and forced to undertake bog reclamation. Troublemakers could be isolated and locked up.[14] A few months later, Carlyle began a series of *Latter-Day Pamphlets* that were even more extravagantly reactionary in tone: Britain herself had fallen into the hands of irresolute politicians who had lost their way in a fog of sentimental liberalism. Policy had been taken over by bleeding-heart drivellers; a myriad of "Sluggard and Scoundrel Protection Societies" had won the day. His *coup de grâce*, however, was delivered in his *Occasional Discourse on the Nigger Question*, which excoriated the figure of Quashee, the West-Indian ex-slave, who dared to abandon plantation work. "A swift, supple ... grinning dancing, affectionate kind of creature" when under white discipline, Quashee was degenerating into an ugly ungovernable savage who might have to be brought back under the whip, if only for his own good.[15]

The fact that Froude encountered Carlyle when he was at the depth of his furious descent into reaction was to have portentous consequences for the futures of both men. Having alienated his mainstream audience with these vicious diatribes, Carlyle became increasingly dependent on the two younger disciples – Froude and Ruskin – who were prepared to follow him in his infernal plunge. Froude, for his part, saw that his own reactionary predispositions were being magnified and reinforced by his new-found mentor; the anarchy of democracy was just around the corner; England was in danger; the barbarians were at the gate. Strong, virile, white men were the one thing needful for order to be restored, and society to be saved. This was the only "truth" that was authentically "alive" in the modern era. Whatever rational reservations Froude might harbor at the harshness of these formulae were dispelled by the authoritarian memories and lessons of his youth. Carlyle was just finishing his study of Oliver Cromwell and was about to embark on an even more ambitious biography of Frederick the Great. These resolute Protestant heroes of modernity had arrived at critical moments to restore honor and discipline to elect Anglo-Saxon peoples who had lost their godly way.[16]

---

[14] Thomas Carlyle, *Reminiscences of my Irish Journey in 1849* (London, 1882), especially 33–5.

[15] Thomas Carlyle, *Oliver Cromwell's Letters and Speeches: With Elucidations*, 5 vols. (London, n.d.). For Carlyle's assessment of Cromwell's activities in Ireland, see II: 141–6 and 203–7. On the West Indies, see Thomas Carlyle, "Occasional Discourse on the Negro Question," *Fraser's Magazine*, 40 (December, 1849), 670–9, expanded and republished as *Occasional Discourse on the Nigger Question* (London, 1853), in Eugene R. August (ed.), *Carlyle, the Nigger Question; Mill, the Negro Question* (New York, 1971), 1–37, quote on 12.

[16] Fred Kaplan, *Thomas Carlyle: A Biography* (Ithaca, 1983), 334–457.

Yet history and biography were not really genres to Carlyle's liking. He lacked the patience and (truth be told) the skill and judgment to spend years in dank archives, sifting documents, tracing lines of connection, and synthesizing the results of meticulous research. Here was an arena in which Froude could dutifully follow the inspiration of the master, while simultaneously surpassing the Sage in the actual performance of literary work. As he applied the Carlylean formula to the history of his own nation, powerful patterns began to take shape. The middle ages had been the childhood of the English, when (as with every primitive people) their quest for truth had been enmired in a poetic atmosphere of fable and myth. The Reformation had opened up a path to maturity, culminating in the achievement of British power and the ascendancy of the modern British imperial state. Yet this triumph of national and imperial maturation had been won at a price. Childish fables had to be abandoned, submission had to be made at the altar of empirical realism, discipline had to be instilled by the heavy hand of benevolent despots, and lesser, backward peoples had to be forcibly yoked to the van of Anglo-Saxon mastery.[17]

So Froude gathered his wife and newborn children and prepared himself to research and to write. To save money, the family moved to the Welsh wilderness (following the earlier example of the young Carlyles). Subsisting on his wife's small annuity and the money he could earn from reviewing, Froude began gathering materials for a full-dress *History of England* in the sixteenth century. A widely circulated essay on "England's Forgotten Worthies" surveyed the territory, while correspondence with Kingsley provided a venue for exploring possible themes. Returning to London in 1854 to gain access to the major (and largely unexamined) archive collections, Froude took up the historian's pen. In 1856, the first two volumes of *The History of England from the Fall of Wolsey to the Defeat of the Spanish Armada* were published. Although the sales were scarcely on the order of Macaulay, reaction was generally favorable, and Froude was encouraged to proceed. In 1858, volumes III and IV were issued; then, in 1860, the next two volumes appeared. In 1864, another two volumes began with the accession of Elizabeth. In 1866, yet another two appeared, and, finally, in 1870, the last two of the twelve-volume set were completed.[18]

[17] For Froude's account of Carlyle's work on these books, see his books *Thomas Carlyle: A History of his Life in London, 1834–81*, 2 vols. (New York, 1892) and *My Relations with Carlyle* (London, 1903). See also John Burrow, *A Liberal Descent: Victorian Historians and the English Past* (Cambridge, 1981), 231–85.

[18] DF, I: 168–98, 211–12, II: 263–325; MJAF, 83–127; J. A. Froude, "England's Forgotten Worthies," in *Short Studies on Great Subjects*, I (New York, 1894), 358–405.

2   Henrician flips

In his opening chapter, "The Social Condition of England in the Sixteenth Century," Froude stakes his claim as a counter-Macaulay. Where the Whig's analogous "State of England in 1685" saw a nation on the verge of great progressive changes, Froude depicts a stable and healthy traditional society which has no inner desire for fundamental change. The population, he contends (quite incorrectly), was stationary. The economy neither grew nor contracted. In social relations, a happy balance had been struck between aristocratic paternalism and peasant independence. Yet, from a distance, beyond the confines of this insular commonwealth, "a change was coming upon the world ... The paths trodden by the footsteps of ages was broken up: old things were passing away, and the faith and life of ten centuries were dissolving like a dream."[19] Here was a vision of historical transformation that comported ill with the progress narrative. It was, Froude suggests, a strange and largely negative revolution, which suffused all Europe in selfishness, amoralism, and mutual slaughter for nearly two centuries. Amid the chaos and the carnage, however, a uniquely English form of progress did emerge, since England alone wrested spiritual reformation from the revolutionary vortex in which the rest of the civilized world was consumed. In so doing, she transformed herself from a marginal medieval kingdom into a dynamic redeemer nation, predestined to create a world empire and to spread her new gospels of Anglo-Saxonism, work, and power everywhere around the globe.

Froude's narrative begins in 1528, when England was faced with a crisis that was at once dynastic, religious, and political: to forestall a return to the civil wars of the fifteenth century, Henry VIII was duty-bound to produce a male heir. This imperative in turn obliged him to break with the Pope. The recent emergence of two super-states to the south and east – France and the protoplasmic Habsburg Empire – underlined the necessity of internal English unity. On the other sides, the presence on the north and west of two unstable frontier lands – Scotland and Ireland – presented endless opportunities for the meddling of foreign powers. What made this situation truly alarming in Froude's eyes was that the moral energies of the English people were being sapped from within. The fabric of the old Church – which had organized the spiritual life of the nation for a millennium – was irremediably rotten. In the royal divorce crisis of 1528, England's spiritual and geo-political crises became portentously intertwined.[20]

---

[19] FHE, I: 1–91, quote on 61.   [20] FHE, I: 93–370, II: 1–122.

From this point on, Froude's epic becomes a stage for the interaction of three main actors, who are destined to save England and forge Britain: first, an old, reactionary clerical order which is impotent and dying; second, a problematically virile king, who is determined to do his political duty; and finally, a spiritually aroused elect, recruited from the ranks of the people, who are trying to convince the King to lead them in the godly direction they have divined on their own. In a manner strikingly different from that of Macaulay, Froude traces the shifting relationship between these actors in gendered metaphors. The old Church is depicted as impotent and effeminate, personified in the cold, barren figure of Catherine of Aragon, or the Nun of Kent, who is fraudulent, hysterical, and out of control. Yet after these easy targets have been removed, the Catholic Church reveals its hidden strengths: it is an institutionally entrenched (but morally degenerate) male clerical establishment, which wages a slow guerilla war against the triumph of the new faith. Cardinals Reginald Pole and David Beton personify these intransigent clerics. Connected by birth to the old Catholic aristocracies, they are powerful and dangerous masters of dissembling and intrigue. Incapable of any genuine fecundity, they devote their formidable skills to destroying the Protestant reformers' creative energies.[21]

To find the taproots of this new, irrepressible Protestant spirit, Froude must descend into the ranks of the people, where he finds "a little band of enthusiasts, armed only with truth and fearlessness." Empowered with these feeble weapons, they rise up to challenge two estates of gentlemen and a millennium of orthodoxy.

No common daring was required in those who would stand out at such a time in defence of such a cause. The bishops might seize them on mere suspicion . . . Every officer from the lord chancellor to the parish constable was sworn to seek them out and destroy them . . . hunted like wild beasts from hiding-place to hiding place; decimated by the stake . . . beset by informers, imprisoned, racked, and scourged . . . earning for themselves martyrdom, for us, the free England in which we live and breathe.[22]

Macaulay, the liberal, dismissed such people as "austere fanatics," but the conservative Froude does not see them in this light. Their lowly origins and extremism are redeemed by their undaunted courage in the face of very long odds. This is no longer the masculinity of the self-restraining centrist, but that of the self-certain militant, who is willing to wager body and soul on the chance that he is the harbinger of the future and the

[21] FHE, II: 123–247. For Catherine of Aragon, see I: 106, 146–62, 339–41, 398–413, 454–85, II: 161–80, 478–81; for the Nun of Kent, see I: 317, 317–36, 403, II: 165–219; for Pole, see III: 23–57, 189–208, 227–32, IV: 541–57; for Beton, see IV: 21, 50, 202–47, 305–21, 470–9.
[22] FHE, II: 1–115, quote on 37–8.

elect of God. Yet in his paeans of praise to the early Protestant radicals, Froude issues an important caveat: they were not tainted by the sin of revolutionary presumption. As far as possible, they were not sectarians and radicals, but moral exemplars and martyrs. In this lay their historical significance and strength.

When the break with the pope was made irreparable ... the fortunes of the Protestants entered a new phase. The persecution ceased, and those who but lately were carrying fagots in the streets, or hiding for their lives, passed at once by a sudden alternation into the sunshine of political favour. The summer was but a brief one, followed soon by returning winter; but Cromwell and Latimer together had caught the moment as it went by; and before it was over, a work had been done in England which, when it was accomplished once, was accomplished forever.[23]

Of course, behind Cromwell and Latimer, in "catching the moment," was the true impresario of the Divorce Crisis, the King. Froude's attempt to rehabilitate the reputation of Henry VIII constitutes his most striking historiographical innovation. Yet it was a dangerously overdetermined achievement. One need not be a Freudian to see that he identified Henry with his own father – or rather with the man he wished his father had been. Henry understood that occasional harshness and cruelty were necessary to navigate amid the treacherous cross-currents of an unstable world. With Scotland and Ireland in flames, all the monarchs of Europe against him, the Pope and his minions hell-bent on bringing England down, Henry did not have the luxury of leniency and kindness. "Executions for high treason," Froude reminds his comfortable readers, "bear necessarily a character of cruelty when the peril which conspiracies create has passed away." Ironically, it was Henry's very success in sniffing out traitors that helped to create the conditions of political stability in which his behavior would be harshly judged.[24]

Yet as his father's son, Froude cannot entirely suppress the many gratuitous bloodstains that blot Henry's record. Perhaps, like Revd. Froude, he thrashed his children because he lacked the political skill to inspire spontaneous obedience and consent. Viewed through the lens of conventional masculinity, Henry's record leaves something to be desired: twice cuckolded, thrice divorced, at various times estranged from all his literal and figurative children, dying without a satisfactory heir, Henry might be seen as a patriarchal failure. In order to rescue the King from these charges of impotence and incompetence, Froude invokes (albeit subliminally) an

---

[23] FHE, II: 34, 94–5.

[24] FHE, I: 343, III: 336–7, 343–5, quote on 336–7. See also FHE, II: 246, 341, IX: 304, 405, X: 251, 271, and 457, among many other examples of Froude's contention that hard, intolerant times required stern, intolerant methods.

alternative scenario in its place: Henry's true marriage was not so much with his wives as with the Protestant reformers, who alone had the power to consummate his sovereign status by enabling him to make their project of self-fabrication his own. The truest issue of this union was neither Edward, nor Mary, nor even Elizabeth, but the Protestant nationalism, around which a distinctively English (and then British) national identity could congeal.[25]

Somewhat troubled by evidence showing that the King "was divided against himself" on the question of religion, Froude grudgingly allows that a matchmaker, Thomas Cromwell, was required to bring the union of authority with Protestantism to fruition.[26] From this point on, however, Froude renders Henry's relation to Protestantism as essentially familial. Seizure of the monastic lands opened the way for ambitious (and lamentably abortive) schemes for the education and welfare of the national family. In foreign relations, the Reformation necessitated an equally far-reaching reconfiguration in England's relationship with her external kin. The old imperatives to absorb Scotland and Wales and to conquer Ireland were greatly intensified. At the same time, the new family logic enjoined Henry to give up his retrograde alliances with Charles V and Francis II, his monarchical pseudo-brothers. Far better if he had forged a grand Protestant alliance with his princely Germanic cousins, uniting under the banner of spiritual freedom all the far-flung branches of the advancing Teutonic tribes.[27]

To be sure, Froude does not fault Henry for his refusal to buy the Reformation hook, line, and sinker. He is, after all, the father, and he knows best. It is his job to restrain the excessive idealism of his spouse's and his children's utopian visions. It falls to him to introduce the necessary note of realism and correction when they become wayward or anarchic. Cromwell got too big for his britches, and so he had to be executed. By 1540, "the Reformers had overshot their healthy growth. They required to be toned down by renewed persecution."[28] In 1547, when Henry was struck down, the rising generation was still too immature to assume direct control. The result was twelve years of much more extreme (perhaps Froude-like) zigging and zagging under the titular reigns of Edward VI and Mary. By trying to force his radical utopian agenda, the boy-king's uncle, the Lord Protector Somerset, brought Protestantism itself into disrepute.

Needless to say, the collapse of this naive and puerile vision (followed by the even more criminal Protestant imposter, the Duke of Northumberland) precipitated a drastic swing to the right. Froude in no way regrets Queen Mary's six-year papistical reign of terror, inasmuch as it purified the ranks

[25] FHE, I: 91–121, 418–22, II 480–541, III: 260–75, 464–522, IV: 121–38.
[26] FHE, II: 206.   [27] FHE, II: 406–25, III: 367, 450.   [28] FHE, II: 421, III: 473.

of the reformers, and rooted out the careerists and time-servers among them. By embarking on their bloody rampage, burning heretics, and selling out the national interest, she and her papistical inquisitor, Cardinal Pole, created that deathless honor roll of martyrs from whose ashes an enduring Protestantism would arise.[29]

3   Victorian anxieties and Elizabethan adventures

Froude's reassessment of the character of Henry VIII, his refigurations of hard masculinity, his fixation with Irish backwardness, and his allergic reaction to Roman Catholicism are all sufficiently explained by his personal biography. Indeed, the publication of the early volumes of his magnum opus released an enormous emotional weight, inasmuch as they became the means of reconciling him with his father. During the final years of the old man's life, the pair spent long, happy hours discussing the origins of British Protestantism and the need for stern national discipline in the sixteenth century.[30] But how did Froude's contemporary readers respond to his remarkable historiographical reassessment? Because they had no part in the Froude family drama, their receptivity depended on changes in the climate of opinion after 1848.

Several factors may have contributed to this change in opinion. The Crimean War of 1854–5 reawakened a strain of British national chauvinism that had lain dormant, at least since 1815. The shocking revelations of military inefficiency which war opened up did even more to convince many Britons that national defense had been neglected, and that the state needed a strong leader at the helm.[31] The 1857 electoral defeat of Richard Cobden and John Bright in the liberal, industrial strongholds of Huddersfield and Manchester, respectively, suggested that liberal orthodoxy was being questioned, even by the entrepreneurial middle class. As industrial capitalism spread to the continent, manufacturers were becoming alarmed at the threat of foreign competition. If this was not to be expected from Russia, the still slumbering giant, it might well come from a revitalized France, or from a nascent Germany. On another (but not unrelated) level, the recent emigration of nearly a quarter-million Irish famine victims to Britain precipitated a wave of xenophobic nativism from the late 1840s onward that shocked many liberals, who regarded such expressions as things of the past. The advent of illustrated

[29] FHE, V: 1–515, VI: 1–534.   [30] DF, I: 200–1.
[31] Asa Briggs, *Victorian People: A Reassessment of Persons and Themes, 1851–67* (Chicago, 1955), 52–86; Olive Anderson, *A Liberal State at War: English Politics and Economics during the Crimean War* (London, 1967).

publications like *Punch*, together with a cheap, sensationalist mass-market press, circulated derogatory images of dangerous, bestial "Paddies" throwing bombs, lowering wages, and infusing their primitive savagery into the heart of the mother isle. The ecclesiastical titles controversy of 1850 came as a match to light these combustible materials. An innocuous papal plan to divide Britain into diocesan districts unexpectedly detonated a recessive strain of Anglo-Protestant anti-Catholicism of a virulence that had not been seen since the eighteenth century.[32]

However, far and away the gravest affront to Britons' sense of national integrity came from the Indian Revolt of 1857, which shook the very foundations of the British Empire. Whereas Frenchmen, Russians, the Irish, and even the Pope were Europeans, the Indians had been regarded as slavish and effeminate orientals, incapable of manly action, and therefore properly held under British control. The sudden eruption of these distant menials onto the pages of British newspapers was therefore a humiliating event, which provoked metropolitan readers to a contradictory response: on the one hand, they were outraged at the ingratitude of miscreants who so violently rejected the British civilizing mission, while on the other hand, they were shocked at the audacity of subordinates, whose ability to seize their independence had to be taken seriously. Initially, the revolt precipitated critiques of British misgovernment. After the Kanpur massacre in July 1857, however, reaction took a more hysterical, racist tone.[33] Even sane, sophisticated intellectuals began to represent Indians as brutal, rapacious beasts. The Earl of Shaftesbury broadcast (false) reports of children impaled on swords and of women raped, with eyes, ears, and noses cut out. "The mother's, the maiden's

---

[32] David S. Landes, *The Unbound Prometheus: Technological Change and Industrial Development in Western Europe from 1750 to the Present* (Cambridge, 1972), 124–230; Paul M. Kennedy, *The Rise of the Anglo-German Antagonism, 1860–1914* (London, 1980); Martin Wiener, *English Culture and the Decline of the Industrial Spirit: 1850–1980* (Cambridge, 1981). See also James S. Donnelly Jr., *The Great Irish Potato Famine* (Stroud, Gloucestershire, 2002); Lynn Lees, *Exiles of Erin: Irish Migrants in Victorian London* (Ithaca, 1979); D. G. Paz, *Popular Anti-Catholicism in Mid-Victorian England* (Stanford, 1992); Briggs, *Victorian People*, 15–51.

[33] G. B. Malleson, *The Mutiny in the Bengal Army: A Historical Narrative by One who has Served* (London, 1858); Charles Ball, *History of the Indian Mutiny*, 2 vols. (London, 1859). For British responses to the Revolt, see F. Byrne, "British Opinion and the Indian Revolt," in P. C. Joshi, *Rebellion, 1857* (Calcutta, 1986); Eugenie Palmegiano, "The Indian Mutiny in the Mid-Victorian Press," *Journal of Newspaper and Periodical History*, 7 (1991), 3–11; Jenny Sharpe, "The Unspeakable Limits of Rape: Colonial Violence and Counter-Insurgency," *Genders*, 10 (1991), 25–46; Heather Streets, *Martial Races: The Military, Race, and Masculinity in British Imperial Culture, 1857–1914* (Manchester, 1994), 18–51; Gautam Chakravarty, *The Indian Mutiny and the British Imagination* (Cambridge, 2005); Patrick Brantlinger, *Rule of Darkness: British Literature and Imperialism, 1830–1914* (Ithaca, 1988), 199–296.

wild scream of despair" was rhymed in *Punch* to "the agonized wail of babies [which] sickens the air." Charles Dickens fantasized about being able "to exterminate the [oriental] Race upon whom the stain of the late cruelties rested." Even Macaulay, ill and nearing the end of his life, was appalled that "the cruelty of the sepoys" had turned English opinion into "one terrible cry for revenge." Worse yet, "the universal feeling that not a single sepoy within the walls of Delhi should be spared" was a sentiment "with which I can not help sympathizing."[34]

For younger, more robust liberals, like Goldwin Smith, however, the gravest danger of the mutiny lay in the backlash that it generated within Britain, and in the bloody retribution that was exacted in its wake: men's heads blown off at the mouths of cannons; summary courts martial and executions throughout the subcontinent; civilian towns, cities, and villages looted and pillaged. If British soldiers were allowed to inflict such wanton lawlessness in a distant colony, what repercussions would this have for civil liberties at home? In this volatile climate, the publication of Froude's *History* could not but have damaging effects. In particular, Smith objected to Froude's celebration of Henry VIII, and his eagerness to excuse that monarch's most indefensibly repressive acts. Like the lawless British soldiers in Victorian India, Smith depicted Henry as a sanguinary despot who habitually resorted to repression and murder to fuel his wanton ambitions and lusts. By repeatedly excusing Henry's depredations as "reasons of state," Froude was paving the way for a revival of dictatorship in modern times. "A conviction on the unsupported evidence of the counsel of the Crown seems to him a perfectly conclusive, though harsh mode of condemnation ... The most tainted witness is good enough to convict a 'traitor' ... if 'the pressure of the times' means a conviction is useful." To Catherine of Aragon, Anne Boleyn, Thomas More, Thomas Cromwell – to both Catholics and Protestants at varying times – Henry had only one message: "It is not the obedience of the outward act only that the king requires, but the obedience of the soul. To hang draw and quarter you is a 'necessity' ... you are on the wrong side. You are 'guilty of not being able to read the signs of the times.'"[35]

---

[34] Quote from Shaftesbury in Chakravarty, *Indian Mutiny*, 37; from *Punch* and Dickens in Brantlinger, *Rule of Darkness*, 205 and 207, respectively; from Macaulay in TLL, II: 359–60. Laura Peters, "'Double-Dyed Traitors and Infernal Villains': *Illustrated London News*, *Household Words*, Charles Dickens and the Indian Rebellion," in David Finkelstein and Douglas Peers (eds.), *Negotiating India in the Nineteenth-Century Media* (London, 2000), 110–34; Nancy Paxton, *Writing under the Raj: Gender, Race, and Rape in the British Colonial Imagination* (New Brunswick, 1999), 109–65; Rudranishu Mukherjee, "'Satan Let Loose upon Earth': The Kanpur Massacres of 1857," *Past and Present*, 128 (1990), 92–116.

[35] Goldwin Smith, "Review of Froude's *History of England*," *Edinburgh Review*, 219 (July, 1858), 206–52, quotes on 210 and 242.

Convinced that he had correctly read the signs of the times, Froude responded to Smith's criticisms in the September 1858 issue of *Fraser's Magazine*. Mawkish liberals like Smith took for granted the freedoms that others had previously earned with their blood. In saving the nation from civil war, Henry's harsh measures had preserved more victims than they had destroyed. Imagine, Froude asks his readers, what would have happened if the Chartist radicals, Irish rebels, and French revolutionaries had been able to join forces in 1848? "Very strong measures of repression would without doubt have been resorted to." Imagine, he challenges them again, what will be the future of consequences of a better-organized Indian Mutiny? Russia would almost certainly take advantage of Britain's discomfiture. "Let the conspiracy have spread along the frontiers; let Persians and Afghans on one side, let the Burmese on the other, have entered into the same scheme." Would any responsible British Viceroy desist from the most strenuous measures? "God forbid that any man be sent to govern India who would hesitate at such a crisis to adopt any measures of repression which would prove really effective." Yet Froude feared that the actual mutiny would soon be forgotten. British opinion would again subside into flaccid complacency, and meaningful measures of imperial security would be abandoned, "held up as willful tyranny, an enormous oppression of which the mutiny was the legitimate consequence."[36]

This dispute between Smith and Froude was symptomatic of a fundamental change in attitude that can be detected in many other quarters as well. The liberal imperialism of the previous half-century was not necessarily rejected, but it was increasingly questioned as an expensive luxury that a beleaguered power like Britain could not always afford. In this new political and intellectual climate, a historian like Froude could enjoy a rhetorical advantage over one like Macaulay, since the imperial violence that drove the latter to defensiveness and extenuation could be simply accepted by the former as the way of the world. To Froude's thinking, Empire was inherently coercive, sustained by threat of violence and grounded in conquest. Liberals who believed otherwise were simply deluding themselves and endangering national and imperial security with their naiveté. Progress and peace might indeed be attained in the long run, but they could be achieved only through the exercise of benevolent despotism.[37] For the historian, this recognition of the

---

[36] J. A. Froude, "The *Edinburgh Review* and Mr. Froude's History," *Fraser's Magazine*, 58 (September, 1858), 359–78, quotes on 375, 376–7, and 377. See also Goldwin Smith's counter-rebuttal in *Edinburgh Review*, 220 (October, 1858), 586–94.

[37] Froude, "Progress," 671–90.

continuity of the British Empire had a felicitous and empowering effect. It meant that the *history* of the nation and its Empire would always be relevant to the *future* of the nation and its Empire in a direct and unmediated way. The harsh lessons of the past must not be forgotten, because the world remained a harsh and unforgiving place.

Froude's interest in the Empire rose in direct proportion as he came to appreciate that it represented a necessary bulwark against (and a distraction from) the broils of Europe. Yet before Froude could set his narrative sails into the Atlantic, he had to return to the Westminster court in 1558, to take the measure of the new Virgin Queen. In "Forgotten Worthies," he had cast Elizabeth as successor to her father's heroic role. "The figure of this solitary woman braving and ruling the tempest, surrounded by conspiracies, the special hate of the Catholic world, and pursued in her grave by the foulest calumnies, made intelligible to me the enthusiasm with which she was worshipped by the noblest of her subjects." Yet as Froude pursued his researches deeper into the archives, he became increasingly disenchanted with this woman at the helm. On a personal level, she was moody and dangerously indecisive. In contrast to her father's strategic tackings between right and left, Elizabeth's vacillations appeared as marks of weakness. Her brilliant playing-off of one potential husband against another failed to impress Froude, who was obsessed with the need for a legitimate heir.[38]

For Froude, Elizabeth was most satisfactory as a monarch when she deferred to her ablest Protestant male advisors – especially William Cecil, but also Francis Walsingham, Henry Sidney, Francis Bacon, and the Scottish Earls of Morton and Murray. Yet these stolid *politiques* could never become the dominant figures that Macaulay would have made them. Ever searching for the *via media* – the rationalist center – these stay-at-home bureaucrats, howsoever brilliant, were lacking in the requisite Froudian adventurousness and panache. In "Forgotten Worthies," Froude had looked to the great privateering seamen Thomas Cobham, Richard Grenville, Walter Raleigh, the Hawkins brothers, and Francis Drake to lend heroic stature to the Elizabethan epoch. Bold, audacious, and romantically amoral, these Devonshire countrymen did seem poised to launch a new narrative by circumnavigating the globe. Operating on their own, they served both themselves and the nation by seizing the ill-gotten gains of the enemy and by bearding the Spaniard on the bounding blue: "The Sword of Spain was forged in the gold-mines of Peru; the legions of Alva were only to be disarmed by intercepting

---

[38] Froude, "England's Forgotten Worthies," quote from Froude's autobiographical fragment in DF, I: 172; FHE, VII: 1–540, VIII: 1–483.

the gold-ships on their passage ... Thus, from a combination of causes, the whole force and energy of the age was directed towards the sea." This appealing romance of patriotic swashbuckling would be taken to the hilt by Froude's brother-in-law Charles Kingsley, in his novel *Westward Ho!* Yet for Froude the historian, following the lead of his sources, a more complex and circuitous journey was required. England's way out into the imperial future ran through the British archipelago, where the forces of chaos and retrogression still raged uncontrolled.[39]

4   Protestantism and the British Union

Although Froude regarded the creation of Britain as one of the greatest achievements in human history, he did not delude either himself or his readers into believing that it arose from benevolent motives. England had habitually meddled in the affairs of its Celtic neighbors throughout the middle ages, but the imperatives to do so greatly increased during the sixteenth and seventeenth centuries. It was the break with Rome and the rise of French and Spanish super-states that suddenly transformed these frontier kingdoms into zones of contestation. They now became vulnerable marchlands that Protestant England would have to master, or else risk being perpetually threatened, invaded, and undermined by them. In Froude's Elizabethan narrative this imperative becomes so powerful that it reshapes the very meaning of Protestantism itself. The spiritual force that we first encountered in the reign of Henry now re-emerges as a binding *political* instrument, which draws Scotland and England together so as to prevent the northern kingdom from falling into the French, Catholic camp.

As always, Henry had tried to lay the foundations with his great victories at Flodden (1513) and Solway Moss (1542). However, his proposals for a marital union of the crowns was rebuffed by the Scottish nobles, who were still trapped in a feudal mentality.[40] It was only the spread of Presbyterianism among the Scottish middle class that brought the goal of Anglo-Scottish Union back into view from the 1560s onward. "What Kings and Parliament had done in England, in Scotland had to be accomplished by the people, and was accomplished therefore with the passionate features of a revolt against authority." Under the

---

[39] Froude, "England's Forgotten Worthies," 370–1; Charles Kingsley, *Westward Ho!* [1855] (London, n.d.).

[40] For Froude's treatment of Anglo-Scottish relations see FHE, IV: 1–6, 30–46, 105–228, 306, V: 31–98, VII: 101–3, 121, 159, 165, 177–200, 258, 269, 324–5, 359–90, 531, VIII: 154–67, 168, 176, 247, 261–8, 284, 295, 334–71, IX: 1–297, 403, 546–98, X: 456, 460, 468–70, XI: 130, 266–310, 462–558, XII: 91–120, 203, 204–343.

leadership of Knox and other charismatic preachers, however, this revolt was diverted from destructive, revolutionary channels into a new kind of creative political nationalism, "with relations too close now to be disowned."[41] In Ireland, by contrast, the path of union proved infinitely more painful. From the outset, all of Froude's anti-Celtic prejudices are on display. The Irish population's refusal to embrace the Reformation is taken as a mark of their intrinsically savage character. For them, Catholicism is less a religion than a form of idolatry – of a piece with their retention of Brehon Law, their incessant feuding, and their congenital idleness. The trade-off for turning Protestantism into the political glue of Anglo-Scottish union is that difference of religion in Ireland will always remain a barrier against any future fusion of civilization and polity. Where Scotland was the country that could be absorbed but never conquered, Ireland became the country that had to be repeatedly conquered, because it could not be absorbed. Where the Scots were fierce warriors, transformed into bulwarks of Britain, the Irish remained ungovernable savages whose proximity portended a dark future of British disunity.

Yet Froude's relentless assault on the character and culture of the Irish is subtly subverted by a secret desire for the very disorder and enchantment that Ireland is made to represent. Ireland is not merely chaotic; it is also seductive, and therefore destructive of English sobriety. In England and Scotland, the Saxons and Normans conquered the Celts. In Ireland, however, the conquering Normans and Saxons were Celticized.[42] What accounts for this Irish seduction? Unable to answer this question, Froude can only lament that Ireland is a problem that England will never resolve. Since they can neither absorb nor abandon the neighboring island, the English are condemned to reconquering it again and again. In Ireland, even the great Henry met his match. "Sadder history in the compass of the world's great chronicle there is none," the historian shakes his head, "so courageous, yet so like cowards; so interesting yet so resolute to forfeit all honorable claims to interest." "The Irish spirit," he writes with more genuine understanding, was attractive "in virtue of representing certain perennial tendencies of humanity which are latent in all mankind ... an impatience of control, a deliberate preference for disorder, a determination in each individual man to go his own way, whether it was a good way or a bad, and a reckless hatred of industry."[43]

---

[41] FHE, IV: 55, VII: 104, 159, IX: 236.   [42] FHE, IV: 66.
[43] FHE, II: 248–326, IV: 66–105, V: 414–36, X: 477–561, XI: 173–265, quotes on II: 258, 320; see also X: 477.

To Froude, everything that was wrong with Elizabethan Ireland – and the Irish – was encapsulated in the figure of the Ulster chieftain Shan O'Neil. Shan had risen within his clan under suspicious circumstances. He retained the old Brehon Law, and his power rested on resistance to English practices of primogeniture. Worse yet, he retained the old system of communal property in the land. According to Froude, Shan spent most of his time feuding with other chieftains, burning and plundering their peoples' crops, and intriguing to marry their daughters and wives. Unlike the Earl of Ormond, who deferred with cringing servility to the English masters, and the Earl of Desmond, who rose in glorious, futile revolt, Shan utterly defied the Tudors' (and Froude's) anglocentric agenda. When it was in his interest, he co-operated with the English, while secretly conspiring with the Spanish and French. When it suited, he could play the suffering Catholic, while simultaneously providing aid and cover to the Protestant corsairs – whom he resembled more than any other figure in Froude's book.[44] Yet where Froude's pulse ardently quickens with the adventures of the sea-rovers, his blood pressure merely explodes at the impertinences of Shan. When the English Deputy, Sussex, sent an army to gain control of lawless Ulster, Shan was forced to go to London, where he wooed the Queen with impudent letters, begging for forgiveness and reminding her that he was only a poor savage who wanted to become civilized. In 1563, restored and forgiven, Shan quickly returned to his habitual ways. Confronted with a conventional military assault by the new Deputy, Sidney, he remade himself into an effective guerilla warrior, disappearing into the countryside whenever the troops approached.[45]

In the end, of course, Shan went too far. Once his head was safely perched atop the gate of Dublin Castle, however, the English imperialists had to consider how to prevent any successor from replicating his feats. For Ireland's Highland warriors there would be no Scott-like romance of reconciliation or inclusionary British future. As the Elizabethan statesmen contemplated their conundrum they saw only one solution to the Irish morass: wholesale colonization by enterprising English or Scottish Protestant immigrants, who would either civilize the natives or root them out.

The exclusive right of a savage population over lands which they will not cultivate is always disputable. The Irish chiefs might be held to have forfeited such title as they possessed by their repeated rebellions, and might be fairly required to surrender a part of their domains as the price of their pardon. A thousand English soldiers

---

[44] FHE, VIII: 1–57, 372–421.   [45] FHE, VIII: 385–421, 38–9.

who had been just dismissed were ready made for the purpose; there were many "husbandmen, ploughwrights, cartwrights, smiths, and carpenters" among them.[46]

The Irish, according to this program, "were to become 'civil' and 'industrious,' or else 'through idleness would offend and die.'" When Irish nobles, like the hitherto loyal Butlers, objected to such proceedings, the colonists simply massacred their families wholesale. Though indefensible, such behavior was not illogical, as Froude points out. "The dead do not come back; and if the mothers and babies are slaughtered with the men, the race gives no further trouble."[47]

Faced with such genocidal scenes and sentiments, even Froude is eventually moved to disgust: "It cannot be said that England deserved to keep a country which it mismanaged so disastrously. The Irish were not to be blamed if they looked to the Pope, to Spain, to France, to any friend on earth or heaven, to deliver them from a Power which discharged no single duty that rulers owe to subjects."[48] Yet this momentary recognition of England's inhumanity is quickly quashed by Froude's overriding obsession with England's security. In the dangerous world of the Counter-Reformation, English liberty depends on Irish subjugation. It therefore follows that Irish subjugation must be accomplished by any means.

Froude's incontrovertibly unhappy Irish ending, I believe, explains the importance that he attaches to the derring-do of Hawkins, Drake, and the other seafaring buccaneers. For both historian and subjects, the Atlantic affords an escape from the bitter hatreds and insoluble problems of sixteenth-century Europe. It opens the way for a happier, healthier, more uniformly Protestant Greater Britain than was possible within the confines of the British Isles. The fact that this transatlantic empire would be actually achieved in the future only makes it more rhetorically serviceable to Froude. He can use his account of the great buccaneering exploits to gesture toward an outcome that his readers already know. In this manner, he can evoke the triumphant *telos* of British America, which will somehow redeem the contradictions, abuses, and atrocities that actually accompanied that imperializing project.[49] Lest his readers notice the parallels between pirates like Cobham, Hawkins, or Drake and the disorderly Irish who are being excoriated on alternate pages, Froude emphasizes the distinctively "Protestant" character of the former.

---

[46] FHE, X: 484.   [47] FHE, X: 477–563, quotes on 491 and 509.   [48] FHE, X: 517.
[49] FHE, V: 135–40, VIII: 423–83, IX: 359–71, X: 1, 107–9, 240, 257, 488, XI: 1–15, 368–406. Froude felt a deep personal connection to the sea. He was a skilled and inveterate yachtsman. Whenever possible, he spent holidays taking sailing trips, even helping to pilot a vessel to Norway when he was in his mid-sixties. DF, II: 505–13; Paul, *Froude*, 17, 115, 127, 337, 377–8.

To themselves they appeared as the elect, to whom God had given the heathen for an inheritance; they were men of stern intellect and a fanatical faith, who believing themselves the favourites of providence, imitated the example and assumed the privileges of a chosen people, and for their wildest and worst acts they could claim the sanction of religious conviction.[50]

Of course, the danger of turning Protestantism into a justification for plunder and slaughter is that Froude risks further debasing its "spiritual" content and turning it into a mere instrument of nationalist propaganda and *political* expediency. Never mind; once Froude's narrative sail catches the wind of his rhetoric there is no turning back.

The merchant of a seaport was driven by his occupation to comprehend and utilise the knowledge which was breaking upon mankind. To him to live by custom was bankruptcy and ruin. Unless he could grow with the times, unless he could distinguish fact from imagination, and laws of nature from theories of faith, he was left behind in the race by keener and less devout competitors ... The stars were now the mariner's patrons, and the tables of longitude and latitude were his Liturgy.[51]

In this vision of Weber, *avant la lettre*, the sea-roving Calvinist becomes a prime agent of modernity. Indeed, when the Elizabethan Protestant betakes himself to the expanse of the ocean, the Victorian historian momentarily seems to embrace that optimistic progress narrative that Macaulay had associated with Greater Britain unconditionally.

A restless impetuous energy, inventing, expanding, pressing forward into the future, regarding what has been achieved only as a step or landing-place upwards and onwards to higher conquests ... A sense that we shall be unworthy of our ancestors if we do not eclipse them in all that they touched, if we do not draw larger circles round the compass of their knowledge, and extend our power over nature, over the world, and over ourselves.[52]

Yet Froude remains enough of a conservative realist to recognize that he cannot redeem the predatory piracy of the Elizabethan age. The sixteenth-century English sea-rovers were secondary parasites who fed on the primary predations of the bullionist Spanish Empire. The fact that Spaniards had already robbed what the English stole from them hardly justifies the latter activity. In a soberer mood, Froude himself understands that the only sustainable defense of the depredations of the sea-rovers is – as with every disagreeable feature of the sixteenth century – reason of state. At a time when the English state was still beleaguered and weak, the seamen provided an effective – and officially deniable – means of diverting some small portion of the vast wealth of Spanish America into Protestant, English channels. While Elizabeth,

[50] FHE, VIII: 480.   [51] FHE, X: 108.   [52] FHE, VIII: 422–3.

the Queen, was buttering up her Spanish "brother," Elizabeth, the private investor, was raking in her share of the gold bars which had been purloined from Philip by Hawkins and Drake. From this secondary theft of what the Spanish Empire itself had stolen, it is a long way not only to modern capitalism, but even to a British maritime Empire that could be economically productive in a broadly mercantilist, rather than narrowly bullionist, frame.[53]

Nevertheless, in one respect – by pioneering the slave trade – the sea-rovers began to evolve new forms of plunder that did prefigure the nascent forms of surplus extraction, which would become characteristic of the coming mercantilist age. In a scant fifteen pages, Froude tries to explain away this further blot on Elizabethan Protestant morality.[54] In the end, Froude's sea-rovers enable his *History* to go out in a blaze of glory, with the defeat of the Spanish Armada in 1588. It is telling, however, that he chose not to continue his story beyond this dramatic victory as he had originally intended. Indeed, by bringing a modicum of safety and security to British Protestantism, the triumph of 1588 opened the way for a new atmosphere in which the harsh repressive measures of the Tudors would no longer be required. Macaulay's story of the struggle for liberty against obsolete absolutism, however, is not one that Froude was interested in taking up. His heart remained in the dark era of the sixteenth century, when liberty was but a promise, and absolutism was still required. This was a world of violence and dogmatism, of nightmarish disorder and autocratic dreams. It was a world of grotesque heresy hunts, of roasting, burning bodies; of genocidal butcherings of women and children; and of men screaming under the torture of the rack or the quartering knife.[55] Yet it was a world in which Froude felt psychologically at home. Victorian liberals might imagine that this world had been long superseded. Froude would now try to convince them otherwise.

5   Froude's Greater British Victorian vision

When Froude completed the last volume of his *History*, he was middle-aged and successful, earning over £1,400 per year. In 1861 he had been tapped as the editor of *Fraser's* – a monthly magazine with a circulation of over 3,000 which weighed in on all the important public issues of the day.

---

[53] FHE, XI: 368–406. For a recent historiographical perspective, see J. H. Elliott, *Empires of the Atlantic World: Britain and Spain in America, 1492–1830* (New Haven, 2006).
[54] FHE, VIII: 464–83, especially 470, IX: 358–80.
[55] On several occasions Froude acknowledges that Protestants, especially Protestant theologians, could be as bigoted, dogmatic, and authoritarian as their Catholic counterparts. FHE, V: 291, VII: 29, 381, VIII: 310, IX: 304, 405.

No less significantly, his historical research in the Cecil family archives brought him into a close epistolary friendship with Lady Salisbury, who included him in many high-class breakfasts and dinners, at which he was introduced to the leading politicians of both political parties. Indeed, when re-marriage transformed this hostess into the fifteenth Countess of Derby, Froude found himself closely connected with both the Stanleys and the Cecils – the two most distinguished and powerful Tory aristocratic dynasties in the land.[56]

In this new capacity, as a pillar of the literary establishment, Froude tried to moderate the tone of his writing for at least a few years. The American Civil War generated much uncertainty in Britain. Though Froude had friends on both sides, his main sympathies lay with the Confederates. Slavery, he argued, in a private letter, "is a thing to be allowed to wear itself gradually away as civilization advances. You cannot treat an institution as old as mankind as a crime to be put out by force."[57] In 1865, when Jamaica's Governor Eyre violently repressed what he deemed to be a black insurrection, Froude, as *Fraser's* editor, remained publicly neutral. When Carlyle, Ruskin, and others organized a committee to defend Eyre against charges of murder, they drew on the Henry VIII defense: Eyre had done what seemed necessary in an emergency situation. The results were not pretty, but the colony had been saved. Privately, silently, Froude sympathized.[58]

So in the Victorian present, as in his Tudor *History*, Froude sought to excuse the ugly, repressive side of empire by purveying a happy vision of stalwart Anglo-Saxons heading out across the seas. As as antidote to the fractured union with the racial other, Froude juxtaposed the image of a better, racially homogeneous union, which would unite old England into a global federation with her consanguineous colonies. On page 1 of the issue of *Fraser's* for January, 1870 (catalogued as volume I, no. 1 of the New Series) he published a manifesto envisioning a Greater Britain

[56] Lord Stanley (fifteenth Earl of Derby) makes fairly frequent reference to Froude in his extensive diaries, indicating periodic social contact as well as a steady interest in Froude's published works. In general, Stanley finds the writings clever, but not always practical, and overly influenced by Carlyle's authoritarianism. See, for examples, the following volumes edited by John Vincent: *Disraeli, Derby and the Conservative Party: Journals and Memoirs of Edward Henry, Lord Stanley: 1849–1869* (New York, 1978), 219–20, 252, 259; *A Selection from the Diaries of Edward Henry Stanley, 15th Earl of Derby, 1869–78* (London, 1994), 55, 70, 76, 194, 211, 242, 329, 521; *The Diaries of Edward Henry Stanley, Fifteenth Earl of Derby, between 1878 and 1893* (Oxford, 2003), 128, 268, 321, 328, 379, 414–15, 471–2, 526, 863–4.

[57] DF, II: 326–50, quote on 342; MJAF, 86–99.

[58] Bernard Semmel, *The Governor Eyre Controversy* (London, 1962); Thomas C. Holt, *The Problem of Freedom: Race, Labor and Politics in Jamaica and Britain, 1832–1938* (Baltimore, 1992), 263–309; DF, II: 314–16.

of the future, which would be grounded in a new relationship between the metropole and her Anglo-Saxon settler colonies. Though much had changed since the sixteenth century, Froude thought that his Victorian contemporaries had much to learn from the Tudors on the subject of Empire. As in the time of Henry VIII, the nation was facing new economic threats and geo-political challenges, this time on a truly global rather than merely European scale. Once again, the rise of other powers threatened to reduce Britain to a second- or third-class country.[59]

In a manner that also paralleled the sixteenth century, the social fabric of industrial Britain was rotting inside. A rapidly rising population was crowded into urban slums, where it was consigned to low-paid, injurious work. Two equally undesirable outcomes loomed. On the one hand, the urban population might become enervated and degenerate. Alternatively, its strength might be channeled into aggressive trade unions that would foment destructive conflicts of class against class. To forge an alternative to these dismal scenarios, Froude offered colonial emigration as a virtual panacea that might satisfactorily resolve all these problems at once: "We want land on which to plant English families where they may thrive and multiply without ceasing to be Englishmen. The land lies ready to our hand. The colonies contain virgin soil sufficient to employ and feed five times as many people as are now crowded into Great Britain and Ireland."[60]

The "settler" tradition that Britain had pioneered in Ireland, and perfected in the New World, was even more relevant in an urban industrial age. Modern liberals would wager Britain's greatness on her future as an industrial producer, but this gamble was too risky on its own. "It is against all experience that any nation can long remain great which does not possess, or having possessed has once lost, a hardy and abundant peasantry." By seeding the wilds of Canada, Australia, and New Zealand with "stout hearted" yeomen, Britain could rediscover the glory of her heroic Tudor age. "We have conquered our present position because the English are a race of unusual vigour both of body and mind," Froude contended. "If we are to preserve our place, we must preserve the qualities [industry, courage, and ingenuity] that won it."[61]

[59] J. A. Froude, "England and her Colonies," *Fraser's Magazine*, NS, 1 (January, 1870), 1–16; "The Colonies Once More," *Fraser's Magazine*, NS, 2 (January, 1870), 267–87. For a survey of other contemporaneous books and essays expressing concern about Britain's relation to her colonies (especially the white settler colonies), see C. C. Eldridge, *England's Mission: The Imperial Idea in the Age of Gladstone and Disraeli, 1868–1880* (London, 1973), 92–142.

[60] Froude, "England and her Colonies," 13.

[61] Froude, "England and her Colonies," 10–11.

Froude was especially concerned that during the previous quarter century, "Nearly four million British subjects . . . have become citizens, more or less prosperous, of the United States." By thus exporting its surplus population to that burgeoning trans-continental republic, Britain was recklessly fortifying a potential rival that might one day challenge the British Empire and leave it economically outpaced. The Liberal government of Gladstone and Granville, in particular, was dogmatically enslaved to the anti-patriotic logic of Adam Smith. On the assumption that people would migrate wherever the labor market led them, formal colonies might well appear as expensive burdens, rather than as bulwarks of national greatness. As soon as possible, they should be encouraged to become self-reliant and go their separate ways.[62]

Had this matter involved only the Home Island, such a neglectful imperial policy would be damaging enough. Once Ireland was factored into the equation, however, the peril was greatly increased. Indeed, no part of the Liberal program of 1868–70 alarmed Froude more than the concessions that it made to Irish Catholics. The disestablishment of the Irish Church and the empowerment of the Irish tenant were precisely the sort of precipitous surrenders that emboldened malcontents to demand ever more.

The Irish Church was reduced to a voluntary communion. Tenants and landlords were made joint owners of their lands – ill-mated companions set to sleep in a single bed, from which one or the other before long was likely to be ejected. Ireland made its usual response; and within two years the state of Westmeath became so serious that the Cabinet, which was to have won the Irish heart was obliged . . . to consider how the administration was to be carried on.[63]

The harsh truth was that Ireland remained overpopulated, even after the Great Famine. Here too, Froude invoked his panacea of colonial emigration. If the imperial government assisted the surplus Irish to resettle in the antipodes, they would become grateful and loyal. Years of hard, honest work would turn them into steadfast and productive British subjects at last. Even if they retained their Catholic religion, their inner spirit would be changed. The Australian sun would burn Protestant values and work discipline into them once and for all. Yet were the Gladstonian Liberals capable of such a sane and sensible policy? No, they consigned the Irish emigrant to his own devices, leaving him embittered, disloyal, and obliged to emigrate to the United States. Cast adrift in the Yankee Republic, he would find his feelings of anti-British grievance magnified.[64]

---

[62] Froude, "England and her Colonies," 1–16.
[63] J. A. Froude, *The Earl of Beaconsfield* (London, 1914), 211.
[64] Froude, "The Colonies Once More," 279–82.

Gradually, again, almost against his will, Froude found that his Greater British Unionist logic was dragging him back into the Irish morass. He had wanted to take a tour of New Zealand and Australia to gather material for a new book. Yet across the Atlantic, America beckoned, in the form of Fenian propagandists such as O'Donovan Rossa, who were blackening the reputation of Britain and hatching conspiracies to invade the homeland they had betrayed. Would the United States become the staging ground for a new Irish revolt, much as Spain and France had been in earlier centuries? Against the advice of his best friends, Froude crossed the Atlantic to deliver a series of anti-Fenian lectures. In America he was picketed, boycotted, strenuously controverted, and persuaded, for reasons of safety, to return home. Yet Froude was never one to back out of a fight. Back in Britain, he decided to expand his lectures into a three-volume historical study, entitled *The English in Ireland in the Eighteenth Century*.[65]

6   Froude revises Anglo-Irish history

Notwithstanding its narrower title, Froude begins his new book with a sweeping survey of Anglo-Irish relations since the Norman Conquest. Amid all the minutiae he discerns a simple pattern underneath: England has repeatedly conquered Ireland, but she has never understood how to manage this conquest.

To her misfortune [England] has never been able to persevere long in any one policy towards Ireland. She tries coercion, till impatience with the cost, and a sense of the discredit, produce hope that coercion is no longer needed ... Conciliation follows, and compromise, and concession, and apology. The stain is taken off, the anarchy revives, and again, with monotonous uniformity, there is a fresh appeal to the sword.[66]

After briefly reviewing the medieval phase of this cycle, Froude returns to his familiar early modern epoch. Why had the Tudor reconquest, which he had traced in his previous study, failed to break the pattern? The Elizabethans had seemed to be winning the battle, and with the elimination of the last O'Neil (Earl of Tyrone) in 1607, a new epoch seemed to open up. Ulster was seized by the Crown, and its native aristocracy was extinguished. On half a million fertile acres, the first great wave of Anglo-Saxon exodus commenced.

The long peace in England and the vast expansion of practical energy which followed the Reformation had produced hundreds of thousands of active, enterprising men, who were looking to push their fortunes. They had been turning

[65] FEI.   [66] FEI, I: 36–7.

their thoughts to America, but here in Ireland was an America at their own doors, with the soil ready for the plough. The grants were eagerly taken up. Unlike the Norman conquerors, who were merely military leaders, the new colonists were farmers, weavers, mechanics, and laborers. They went over to earn a living by labor, in a land which had produced hitherto little but banditti. They built towns and villages; they established trades and manufactures; they enclosed fields, raised farm-houses and homesteads where till then there had been but robbers' castles, wattled huts, and mud cabins, or holes in the earth like rabbit burrows.[67]

The remainder of Froude's book could be described as a long disquisition on how and why this promising experiment in the Anglo-Saxonization of Ireland had failed. The first blow was the uprising of 1641, when the natives took advantage of civil conflict in Britain to try to throw the hated intruder out. Froude offers many grizzly atrocity stories of burned houses, slaughtered children, and families left naked to perish of exposure on the roads. Eight years later, however, these dark days were redeemed by the Cromwellian re-conquest. Between 1649 and 1658, according to Froude, there was a real chance that anglicization might be institutionalized.

For the first and last time a government was about to be established in Ireland which, for the ten years that it endured, was to administer the country in the sole interests of honest labor – where the toiler was to reap the fruit of his toil, the idle and the vicious to reap the fruit of their devices ... Ulster, Munster, and Leinster would be the exclusive possession of Protestant English and Protestant Scots, reinforced, it might be by Calvinist fugitives from the Continent. The Irish peasantry might be trusted to remain under their new masters, if the chiefs of their own blood were removed; and with peace, order, and good government, and protected from spoilation, they might be expected to conform at no distant time, to the habits, language, and religion of their conquerors.[68]

For Froude, the great tragedy of Anglo-Irish history was that this Cromwellian experiment was never given time to work. With the Restoration, in 1660, the Catholic priests and old aristocrats trickled back in. In 1691, once again, Ireland had to be re-conquered, but within a few years, she reverted back to her habitual ways. The officially Protestant new establishment was riddled with lethargy and corruption, which allowed Catholicism to creep back in and fostered a disrespect for order and law. Overtaxed and excluded from the benefits of imperial commerce, eighteenth-century Ireland remained demoralized and impoverished while England and Scotland were making their great leap forward into the urban industrial age.[69]

[67] FEI, I: 1–73, quote on 69.   [68] FEI, I: 74–218, quotes on 121, 133.
[69] FEI, I: 219–634, II: 1–272.

According to Froude, this sad result was the direct consequence of the irresolution of English liberals, who lacked the will to revolutionize Ireland once and for all. Like their predecessors, the new class of Anglican, landlord rulers were losing touch with their English origins and were (like the early Edgeworths) becoming slowly Irishized. The Ulster Presbyterians, who might have given backbone to the new Protestant order, were feared, distrusted, and (according to Froude) repressed more thoroughly than the Catholics, whom they alone would have been able to uproot. It is in this context of misgovernment and self-delusion that Froude situates the Protestant "patriots" of 1782. Instead of buckling down to the hard work of anglicizing and civilizing Ireland, these parliamentary windbags spewed out dangerous Franco-American nonsense about "national independence." Instead of rallying loyally around the British imperial standard, they filled the people with unrealistic expectations, which undermined their own legitimacy. The result, predictably enough, was the 1798 debacle, when another fit of Irish anarchy exploded, and the island had to be reconquered by England all over again.[70]

Had the 1800 Act of Union finally resolved the Irish Question? Writing from the vantage of the 1870s, Froude saw the same dysfunctional cycle repeating itself once more. When they appeased seditious demagogues like O'Connell, or indulged thriftless Celtic peasants in their spoliation of landlord property, English liberals of the nineteenth century were repeating the mistakes of their predecessors. "Were England, even now, at this eleventh hour, to say that she recognized the state of Ireland to be a disgrace," the Union might be saved. But the government would have to be willing to suspend the Constitution for half a century, and govern the three southern provinces by dictatorial means. "Quiet people would recover confidence, and the law its authority ... Enterprise would take heart again and capital flow into the soil, and the shameful past would be forgotten like a black dream."[71]

Could Froude have failed to see the irony in this extraordinary claim? By raking over "the shameful past" with such inflammatory eloquence, and by enlisting it in the political reaction of his own day, he did as much as any Englishman of his generation to insure that this unhappy history would *not* be forgotten, but would be harnessed to the ideological struggles of the late Victorian age. Yet, in contrast to the seventeenth and eighteenth centuries, when the anglocentric voice had pronounced unopposed, now, in the 1870s, there were many diverse Irish nationalist speakers, with access to public media, who could tell their side of the

[70] FEI, II: 273–520, III: 1–533.   [71] FEI, III: 532.

story. According to the Irish historian J. P. Prendergast, who wrote a series of stinging reviews for *The Nation*, most of the atrocity stories which Froude uncritically recycled were either unreliable or demonstrably false. By contrast, the Cromwellian re-occupation, which Froude so glibly defended, had been explicitly dedicated to the genocidal extermination of the entire Celtic race.[72] These charges of falsification and whitewash were echoed by the Fenian radical John Mitchel, who issued his counter-blast from exile in the United States. Like Prendergast, Mitchel excoriated Froude for his brazen distortions, although he also expressed a sneaking admiration for this straight-talking Englishman, who dispensed with the usual evasions of liberal cant: "We have you down," he lampooned, "stripped, disarmed, garotted: our treatment of you and of your country has been stupid, and a scandal: it is going to be in the future what it has been in the past: and now, what are you going to do about it?"[73]

For those who were alarmed by what Mitchel and the Fenians were going to do about it, a more temperate response to Froude was offered by the Catholic priest T. N. Burke. Burke had encountered Froude in America, and had organized a series of counter-lectures to refute the English historian's claims. After the publication of Froude's book, the controversy was pursued in print. Like Prendergast and Mitchel, Burke disputed Froude's account of the 1640s and 1650s. But even worse than these factual errors was the contemptuous arrogance with which Froude (like most Englishmen) disparaged the Irish people as an inferior race. Although the Irish had been conquered and defeated, Burke believed that they were morally superior to those whom they served. Irishmen could not have perpetrated the alleged 1641 massacres because they were incapable of behaving in this way. More deeply attached to the Catholic Church than any other people, they were ready to suffer in silence for their religion, but would never persecute others on religious grounds. Beaten down, brutally oppressed by English aggression, Burke's Irishmen were, by nature, always loyal and even-tempered – ever ready to be generous and forgiving, in the image of Christ.[74]

---

[72] Donal McCartney, "James Anthony Froude and Ireland: A Historiographical Controversy of the Nineteenth Century," in T. P. Williams (ed.), *Historical Studies* (Dublin, 1971), 171–91, especially 176–81. Because he had helped Froude gain access to documentary materials on the 1641 uprising, Prendergast was particularly outraged at what he regarded as the culpable bias of Froude's published account of that event.

[73] John Mitchel, *The Crusade of the Period: And Last Conquest of Ireland (Perhaps)* (New York, 1878), 17; Bryan McGovern, "John Mitchel: Irish Nationalist and Southern Secessionist in Mid-Nineteenth Century America," PhD thesis, University of Missouri, Columbia (2003).

[74] Father T. N. Burke, *Ireland's Case Stated, in Reply to Mr. Froude* (New York, 1873).

Where Froude had depicted the English in Ireland as engaged in an endless struggle against Celtic disorder, Burke refigured Ireland under the English as the model of dignity in defeat. The old Brehon laws, which Froude deemed irrational and anarchic but which centuries of English rule had failed to extirpate, were represented by Burke as the archtypes of social cohesion. They reflected the genius of an ancient freedom-loving people. Through the system of communal landownership, every tribe remained a family, while the election of chieftains gave scope to individual initiative and solidified the sense of clan loyalty. The judges were learned men, trained in colleges, while the minstrels inculcated communal values of heroism and liberty. "The Catholic religion," Father Burke reminded his readers, "flourished in Ireland for six hundred years and more before the Anglo-Normans invaded her coasts ... Men came from every country in the known world to light the lamps of knowledge and sanctity at the sacred fire upon the altars of Ireland." "We Irish," Burke avowed, "are naturally a proud people."

The antiquity of our race, the purity of our blood, preserved through the ancient form of government by clans or families, the fact that serfdom never existed in any form in Ireland, the consciousness of intellectual gifts and power, the strange imaginativeness with which we are endowed, our romantic, though unfortunate history, so full of disaster yet so full of glory; all these, and other causes, have made us the proudest people on earth.[75]

Burke's defense of the Irish on the basis of their racial qualities, as well as Prendergast's assertion of their eternal victimhood, shows just how problematic liberal discourse had become by the 1870s. Absent Macaulay's confident progress narrative, could it offer nothing assertive with which to counter Froude? Froude seemed to have flattened Irish history into a succession of recurrent cycles, which repetitively vaunted the order and industry of Anglo-Saxons while maligning habitual Irish disorder and sloth. In the face of this revisionism, Prendergast could merely reiterate the disastrousness of Irish conjunctures, while Burke replicated Froude's race-essentialism with the valences reversed. Yet it would be a mistake to assume that liberal history had no constructive answer to Froude. On the contrary, his Irish *History* provoked one quite formidable exercise in counter-revisionism from a young, independent Irish scholar, W. E. H. Lecky, who never attracted as many readers but who produced a more enduring body of work.[76]

---

[75] Burke, *Ireland's Case Stated*, quotes on 18, 29.
[76] Donal McCartney, *W. E. H. Lecky, Historian and Politician, 1838–1903* (Dublin, 1994), 1–57. See also Elizabeth Lecky, *A Memoir of the Right Hon. William Edward Hartpole Lecky, by his Wife* (London, 1909); H. M. Hyde (ed.), *A Victorian Historian: Private Letters of W. E. H. Lecky, 1859–1878* (London, 1947); and Jeffrey Von Arx, *Progress and Pessimism: Religion, Politics, and History in Late Nineteenth-Century Britain* (Harvard, 1985), 64–123.

7   **W. E. H. Lecky's Anglo-Irish counter-history**

As heir to a wealthy Protestant landlord family, William Edward Hartpole Lecky felt an almost Edgeworthian sense of duty to benefit the country-men from whom his income was drawn. Yet where Edgeworth returned to the countryside to educate his tenants, Lecky (three generations later) haunted the libraries of Dublin to give the nation its first substantial empirical history. Lecky's decision to devote himself to historical scholar-ship was inspired by H. T. Buckle's *History of Civilization*, which he read as a Trinity College undergraduate in 1857, when it first appeared. Like many others of the same generation, Lecky was staggered by Buckle's audacious claim that history could be turned into a science that might definitively trace the development of civilizations and explain the trans-formation of societies in structural terms. Thus, at the moment when Macaulay's luster was fading, Buckle arose with an alternative version of the progress narrative – no longer conceived as a romance that might sour, but as a scientifically demonstrable inevitability.[77]

Like everyone else who addressed this question of progress, Buckle realized that the challenge was to explain why it appeared in so many different local guises, and why its velocity varied so greatly, depending on locality. His originality lay in the acuity with which he attributed these differences to environmental factors, thereby offering an alternative deter-minism that was diametrically opposed to Froude's increasing reliance on the determinism of race. Among backward, primitive (mostly tropical) peoples, according to Buckle, an early hothouse burst of civilizational development gradually slowed to a sluggish pace because heat, moisture, and luxuriant crops fostered a lethargic, low-energy environment, with diminishing incentives for continued improvement. By contrast, northern, temperate communities rose out of barbarism more slowly, but progressed more quickly thereafter, once physical environment ceased to be a barrier, and intellectual environment regulated the pace of advance. Those soci-eties that clung to blind faith and enforced tradition tended to stagnate and fall behind those that put a premium on experiment and innovation and were willing to break with timeworn institutions and creeds.[78]

Buckle's premature death in 1862 left grave doubts as to whether his project was feasible, but it also opened the way for ambitious acolytes like Lecky to make the theory their own, providing the detailed elabo-ration and documentation that Buckle had left unfulfilled. During the 1860s, Lecky published two books that developed parts of the Buckle

---

[77] H. T. Buckle, *History of Civilization in England*, 2 vols. [1857, 1861] (New York, 1897).
[78] Buckle, *History of Civilization*, I: 1–672.

thesis – *The Rise and Influence of the Spirit of Rationalism in Europe* (1865) and the *History of European Morals from Augustus to Charlemagne* (1869). Surveying his ground in a bold, sweeping manner, Lecky argued that European progress had been slow during the clerically dominated middle ages, but that the spread of the Renaissance and Reformation to the northwestern regions speeded it up.[79] But where did Ireland fit into this general picture? Like Froude, Lecky thought that the dead weight of Catholic credulity had retarded her development. But unlike Froude, he also attributed this backwardness to colonial exploitation. What Ireland needed, according to Lecky, was the fusion of secularism with patriotism that had momentarily been forged during the eighteenth century by men like Richard Edgeworth – the most advanced and enlightened of his own Protestant landlord elite. In 1861, Lecky had published a book, *Leaders of Public Opinion in Ireland*, that articulated this position. A decade later, when he learned that Froude was at work on eighteenth-century Ireland, he reissued the book.[80]

Since Lecky struck up a casual friendship with Froude in London, he probably had some notion of the drift of that historian's book. However, when *The English in Ireland* actually appeared, its inflammatory content came as a shock. Froude's perspective was "more fitted for the latitude of Russia than of England," complained this disciple of Buckle, and had a religious mentality "more fitted for the middle ages than for the nineteenth century." Yet Froude should not be pegged as a simple reactionary, driven by nostalgia for the supposed glories of a bygone age. On the contrary, when his rhetoric was stripped bare, he was exposed as an adherent of the ever-cynical doctrine that "might makes right."[81] This amoral perspective, Lecky noted, was indistinguishable from the opportunism of Ireland's radical separatist revolutionaries. Froude's brazen exaggeration of Catholic violence and his curt dismissal of Protestant atrocities were simply the mirror images of the Fenian distortions that he purported to refute. The two men shared a common interest in

---

[79] W. E. H. Lecky, *History of the Rise and Influence of the Spirit of Rationalism in Europe*, 2 vols. [1865] (London, 1913); *History of European Morals from Augustus to Charlemagne*, 2 vols. [1869] (New York, 1879).

[80] Ireland was mentioned in only nine of the 376 pages of Lecky's *Rationalism in Europe*. However, immediately before publishing this book, he had written two volumes on Irish history, *Religious Tendencies of the Age* (London, 1860) and *The Leaders of Public Opinion in Ireland*, 1st edn. (London, 1861). See McCartney, *Lecky, Historian and Politician*, 4–26, 57–84.

[81] McCartney, *Lecky, Historian and Politician*, 1–25, 57–8; W. E. H. Lecky, "Mr. Froude's English in Ireland," *Macmillan's Magazine*, 27 (1873), 246–63, quotes on 246–7. See also Lecky's review of Froude's second Irish history volume, also in *Macmillan's Magazine*, 30 (1874), 166–84.

misusing history to inflame sectarian antagonisms, and both stood to lose if a moderate centrist nationalism (and a careful scholarly neutrality) should prevail. In the context of 1873, the appearance of Froude's book was doubly unfortunate. For the first time in almost a century, Gladstone's Irish reforms of 1869–70 had generated an atmosphere of hopeful expectation that a spirit of moderation might take hold. In an age when liberal opinion and national self-determination were gaining ground all over Europe, the Irish were slowly recovering their civic identity. The long dark night of sectarian strife seemed to be waning, and was giving way to a mounting spirit of patriotic unity.[82]

Under these favorable circumstances, the principal danger came from irresponsible publicists who, like Froude, stiffened English intransigence to progressive change. This then fanned the flames of Fenian extremism both in Ireland and in America. It supported agitators' claims that the English were incapable of justice and could not learn from past mistakes. Froude professed to fear for the future of the Empire, but this future in fact depended on the creation of a more decentralized and egalitarian constitutional frame. In an era when public opinion had become sovereign, "no government would ever command the real affection of the [Irish] people which is not, in some degree, national, administered in great measure by Irishmen, through Irish institutions."[83] Of course, Lecky understood that to make this linkage between Froude's *History* and imperial misgovernment was to place on himself the burden of advancing the cause of good government, by producing a better, more balanced Anglo-Irish *History*. The monumental task would take him nineteen years and five volumes. The result, however, was the first really even-handed attempt to tell the Irish story – a book so comprehensive and carefully researched that it is still sometimes cited by historians today.[84]

---

[82] W. E. H. Lecky, *The Leaders of Public Opinion in Ireland*, 2nd edn. (London, 1871). Lecky's subsequent relation to the Home Rule movement was complex. See McCartney, *Lecky, Historian and Politician*, 57–185.

[83] Lecky, *Leaders*, 2nd edn., xiv–xvi, quotes on xviii and xix.

[84] LHI, compiled from an original eight-volume work that also encompassed aspects of English history. Lecky responded to Froude's "racial" interpretation of Irish history in the following way: "Without denying that there are some innate differences of character between the subdivisions of the great Aryan race, there is, I think, abundant evidence that they have been enormously exaggerated. Ethnologically the distribution and even the distinction of Celts and Teutons are questions which are far from settled ... Nations change profoundly in the very respects which their characters might be thought most indelible, and the theory of race is met at every turn by perplexing exceptions" (I: 397). Lecky's massive work has been abridged into a single volume by L. P. Curtis, who also provides a very useful introduction: W. E. H. Lecky, *A History of Ireland in the Eighteenth Century*, ed. L. P. Curtis (Chicago, 1972), 1–36, especially 35. Unless otherwise noted, all subsequent references are to the original edition.

Lecky begins his opening chapter on the "Protestant Ascendancy" by a counterfactual comparison of the Irish with the Scottish case. "The history of Scotland in the eighteenth century furnishes us with one of the most remarkable instances on record of the efficacy of wise legislation in developing the prosperity and ameliorating the character of nations." In the history of Ireland, however, "we may trace with singular clearness the perverting and degrading influences of great legislative injustices, and the manner in which they affect every element of national well-being." All the evils that Froude had identified as inherent in the Irish character – sloth, venality, lawlessness, and deceit – Lecky diagnoses as secondary consequences of the penal code's official violence.[85] Given that they were unable to participate in politics, to own land, to worship freely, and to educate their children in their ancestral creed, it is hardly surprising that Catholics should have become hypocritical, underhanded, and disloyal. With the Irish Parliament and government disempowered by unconstitutional laws that subordinated these institutions to supervisory oversight from Westminster, it was hardly to be wondered that they should grow corpulent, corrupt, and unrepresentative of even the relatively privileged Protestant minority. Excluded from British and colonial markets by alien laws designed to protect English merchants and manufacturers, the Irish people would become economically dependent, and frequently impoverished, as a generalized condition of underdevelopment took hold.[86]

Where Froude depicts eighteenth-century Ireland as a land of fatality, doomed to repeat the same dysfunctional cycle of the sixteenth and seventeenth centuries, Lecky restores it to the realm of conjuncture – an era fraught with opportunities for progress-advancing new departures that might have altered the course of history. As in his earlier book *Leaders*, Lecky concretizes the method of Buckle by focusing on the handful of enlightened, forward-looking Protestant leaders – Swift, Flood, and Grattan – who sought to break the shackles of Ireland's credulous, colonial confinement and to create a new trans-class, trans-sectarian national identity. The greatest of these heroes is Henry Grattan, whom Froude had dismissed as a bombastic malcontent. Borne high on the tide of his eloquence and the strength of 100,000 armed Volunteers, Grattan effected a bloodless constitutional revolution, which placed Irishmen in charge of their own destiny. Acting as citizens rather than as Protestants or as landlords, he and his colleagues clearly understood that the national independence that they had half-extracted from London would remain nugatory so long as Catholics remained disenfranchised.[87]

---

[85] LHI, I: 1–12, 13–241, quote on 1.   [86] LHI, I: 136–421.
[87] LHI, II: 136–517; Lecky, *Leaders*, 2nd edn., 104–222.

With his eyes very much on the constitutional crises of the 1870s, Lecky identified 1795 as the previous point of decision, when Irish history had taken a reactionary turn: had the patriotic Protestant landlords of that era succeeded in their plan to redress Catholic grievances, the course of history would have changed. The uprising of 1798 would have been averted, with all the horrors and atrocities that followed in its wake. Men like Richard Edgeworth would have risen to positions of national leadership, and Ireland might have become one of the most prosperous and enlightened countries in the world.

With the removal of the few remaining religious disabilities, a settlement of tithes, and a moderate reform of Parliament, it seemed still probable that Ireland, under the guidance of her resident gentry, might have contributed at least as much as Scotland to the prosperity of the Empire. But from the day when Pitt recalled Lord Fitzwilliam, the course of her history was changed. Intense and growing hatred of England, revived religious and class animosities, a savage rebellion, savagely repressed, a legislative union prematurely and corruptly carried, mark the closing years of the eighteenth century, and after ninety years of direct British government, the condition of Ireland is universally recognized as the chief scandal and the chief weakness of the Empire.[88]

Pitt is in many ways the evil genius of Lecky's Irish history books. Like some malignant forerunner of Froude, he typified the well-intentioned but arrogant English imperialist who barged into Ireland, knowing little of her real history, with some ill-designed panacea that inevitably made a bad situation worse. In particular, Pitt's scheme to strengthen the British Empire by forcing Ireland into the Union of 1800 had produced disastrous results. Over seven decades, it had weakened the Empire by humiliating and emasculating Ireland's natural Protestant gentry leaders, without reconciling Catholics to continued British rule. By destroying the Irish patriotism of the Protestants while selling out the Catholics, Pitt had left a legacy of political dysfunction that would be difficult to overcome.[89] Under these circumstances, the task of preserving Irish nationalism in a British imperial frame had fallen to the charismatic Catholic Daniel O'Connell. Eloquent and courageous, but also irresponsible and demagogic, O'Connell is a flawed hero in Lecky's account. The Great Emancipator's identification with underdogs everywhere, his principled commitment to non-violent mass action, and his keen

[88] LHI, III: 1–324, quote on 324.
[89] LHI, III: 325–547, IV: 1–473, V: 1–494; Lecky, *Leaders*, 2nd edn., 143–96. "Carried as it was prematurely, in defiance of the national sentiment of the people and the protests of the unbridled talent of the country, it [Act of Union] has deranged the whole course of political development, driven a large proportion of the people into sullen disloyalty, and has almost destroyed healthy public opinion" (195).

identification with Ireland as a national community all redeem him in Lecky's eyes. Yet O'Connell's deference to the Catholic hierarchy and his pandering to the unwashed masses had filled the Protestant gentry with anxiety and fear.[90]

In his 1871 introduction to *Leaders*, as well as in his subsequent Anglo-Irish *History*, Lecky acknowledged that some form of union between Ireland and Britain was inevitable, since "nature and a long and inextricable union of interests have made it imperatively necessary for the two countries to continue under the same rule."

No reasonable man who considers their relative positions can believe that England would ever voluntarily relinquish the government of Ireland, or that Ireland could ever establish her independence in opposition to England, unless the English [sic] navy were utterly shattered. Even in the event of the dissolution of the Empire, Irish separation could only be achieved at the expense of a civil war.

Nevertheless, Pitt's version of Union had equated amalgamation with centralization and the crushing of local and national sub-imperial autonomy. By devolving power "from the overworked Parliament of the Empire" to regional and national institutions, "the political talent of the country" could be activated safely, radical separatists could be marginalized, and "a sound public opinion may be gradually formed."[91]

The best hope for Victorian Ireland, in Lecky's estimation, was a new Fitzwilliam, an English statesman (perhaps Gladstone) willing to atone for the sins of his predecessors; and a new Grattan, an Irish gentleman-patriot (perhaps himself) willing to forge a genuinely national movement, enlisting Irishmen of every race and creed. This historiographically derived program to save the British Empire by re-negotiating its Union as a voluntary federation of different but equal nationalities was a bold new departure in conceptual terms. Rejecting Froude's (or even Macaulay's) recipe of integration through anglicization, it was predicated on the frank acknowledgement that political autonomy and cultural difference afforded the only basis for a lasting bond between peoples. Such future intertwinement would become possible only through a painful reckoning with their divided, divisive, and exploitative history.[92]

Yet at the very moment when Lecky the Irish historian was elaborating this vision, Lecky the Protestant landlord began to get cold feet. As work on his multi-volume *History* dragged on into the late 1870s and 1880s, he not only saw that the political landscape was changing, but that his own political reactions were beginning to shift. In particular, the rise of

---

[90] Lecky, *Leaders*, 2nd edn., 223–320.   [91] Lecky, *Leaders*, 2nd edn., xv, xx.
[92] McCartney, *Lecky, Historian and Politician*, 85–136.

the Land League and of Parnell as nationalist leader struck Lecky as dangerous developments which sought to divert the national movement into violence and illegality. "Whatever else Parnell and his satellites have done," he wrote, in 1879, to a friend,

they have, at least in my opinion killed home rule by demonstrating in the clearest manner that the classes who possess political power in Ireland are radically unfit for self-government. That a set of political adventurers who go about the country openly advocating robbery and by implication murder ... appears to me a most conclusive proof that the very rudiments of political morality have still to be taught ... Whatever else government has to do, *the protection of life and property* is its first duty.[93]

In another letter, Lecky acknowledged that he was beginning "to take a much more landlord view than you do of Irish affairs." A few years later, he was making remarks that went ever further against the grain of his published works. "So far from things tending toward home rule, I think you will soon find the opinion growing up on all sides that Ireland is unfit for the amount of representative government she possesses, and that a government rather on the Indian model may become necessary."[94] Irish nationalism may have remained Lecky's goal in theory, but Irish nationalism, as it actually appeared in the 1880s, elicited a reaction that was scarcely distinguishable from that of his historiographical opponent, Froude.

8   Ethnic evolution and Froude's imperial scheme

Though Froude could not have read Lecky's self-subverting letters – acquiescing *de facto* in the Froudian vision of history – their contents would not have surprised him. For this English historian it was axiomatic that every member of the propertied classes (which included Lecky) would at some point have to abandon highflown constitutional rhetoric and rally round the realpolitik imperative to preserve society. By the mid-1870s, Froude had reason to think that the British public in general was coming around to his point of view. In 1874, Gladstone and the Liberals were defeated and were replaced by the Tories, under Disraeli, who had pledged his party to the preservation of the Empire. Although a plan to bring Froude into Parliament fell through, he had aristocratic friends in high places, most notably Lords Derby and Carnarvon, who were the

---

[93] Quoted in McCartney, *Lecky, Historian and Politician*, 95–6.
[94] Quoted in McCartney, *Lecky, Historian and Politician*, 98–9. For a general discussion of late Victorian fears of Anglo-Saxon race degeneration, see Daniel Pick, *Faces of Degeneration: A European Disorder, c.1848–c.1910* (Cambridge, 1989), 155–221.

new Foreign and Colonial Secretaries, respectively. Froude had long wanted to take a tour of the antipodes, to report on the triumph of the Anglo-Saxon, but Carnarvon persuaded him to go on a fact-finding mission to South Africa instead. The Canadian provinces had recently been confederated under a unified Crown government, and it was hoped that the South Africans might be persuaded to do the same.[95]

Froude could work up an interest in South Africa only by envisioning it as a target for Anglo-Saxon emigration. When he stepped out onto the streets of Cape Town, however, he was forced to confront an environment that was far more fluid and complex. The British settlers, he discovered, were less interested in farming than in cashing in on the diamond-mining bonanza, which was just then opening up. Much closer to his ideal of the Anglo-Saxon yeoman farmer were the Boers of the interior. Unfortunately, these hard-bitten Dutch racial cousins wanted no part of his Greater British imperial dream. Froude attributed their hostility to high-handed mismanagement. He found it regrettable that their aspiration was not for imperial federation but for republican autonomy. Even more baffling to Froude's metropolitan eyes was the complex tapestry of South Africa's indigenous ethnic groups – Xhosa, Khoi, Zulu, Sotha, Tswana – each of which claimed part of the land and stood in a different relation to the various expanding white settler communities. Oblivious to the finer anthropological distinctions between these indigenous cultures, Froude lumped them all together as "Kaffirs" and deplored their occupation of arable lands for which Boers or Britons were predestined.[96]

After exploring the Cape Colony, Froude made his way to Natal. Here, on the imperial frontier, there were confused reports of a near rebellion by the natives or, alternatively, of a terrible atrocity of official repression on the scale of Governor Eyre. Carnarvon wanted to know what had actually happened. Froude obliged with long missives, posted every few days, on the fruits of his investigation. The trouble had begun

---

[95] Froude was deliberately cryptic about his political party allegiance. In 1875, the Liberal Parliamentary Whip asked if he would be willing to stand as a Liberal candidate for Glasgow and Aberdeen Universities. Froude's Tory friends in the Cabinet (notably Lord Carnarvon) and the Prime Minister, Disraeli, expressed enthusiasm for this scheme, and indicated that they would be happy to let the election go uncontested. In the meantime, the Liberal leaders began to realize that Froude shared few of their positions, and withdrew their offer. From this we may infer that, by the 1870s, Froude was essentially a Tory, although both he and the party leaders preferred not to advertise this fact. See DF, II: 419.

[96] J. A. Froude, "Leaves from a South African Journal," in *Short Studies on Great Subjects*, III (New York, 1893), 343–400, especially 350, 357, 363; J. A. Froude, *Two Lectures on South Africa* (London, 1880).

in the mines, which had recruited black labor and paid the workers in ammunition and guns. One tribe, the Hlubi, under the leadership of a chief, Langalabalele, had secreted their weapons, for fear that they would be confiscated. Rumors spread, and the British settlers were provoked into a panic of mayhem, wreaking wholesale plunder and carnage on the offending tribe.[97] Froude's initial reaction was not, as might be expected, his own published Henry VIII defense. His enquiries revealed not a shred of evidence that the Hlubi were planning to revolt, or to use their guns for anything other than hunting. Yet this flimsy charge had become the pretext for a government-sponsored rampage in which Hlubi property had been stolen, the tribe had been scattered, and hundreds of innocent people – including many women and children – had been slaughtered in cold blood. What Froude found most astonishing about this episode was its casual acceptance by all sectors of the white community. People simply shrugged their shoulders, explaining that this was how the Blacks had to be treated, according to the precepts of their own "Kaffir Law."[98]

After several weeks of listening to such comments, however, Froude began to fall in with the necessity of accepting this view. A public investigation might serve the dictates of justice, but, from the perspective of imperial policy, it would lead to disastrous results. In the first place, it would embolden the Blacks not to revolts or outrages, but to sauciness, indiscipline, and the migratory habits to which they were naturally prone. Even worse, however, it would inflame white opinion against interfering liberals from London, and completely stifle any chance of getting the Boer republics to agree to the imperial federation that was Carnarvon's (and Froude's) ultimate aim. The Boers were essential, not merely because they constituted the majority of the white population, but because they had rooted themselves organically in the South African soil, in ways that the recent British settlers had yet to learn. Their treatment of the natives was exemplary, Froude believed: all migratory tribes were expelled from their territories, and Blacks were permitted to live among them only as laborers in their homes and on their farms. The British, by contrast, oscillated between a false philanthropy that rewarded

[97] Edgar Brookes and Colin De B. Webb, *A History of Natal* (Pietermaritzburg, 1965); George W. Cox, *The Life of John William Colenso, Bishop of Natal*, 2 vols. (London, 1888), II: 313–448.
[98] Froude, "South African Journal," 363, 345, 368; Carnarvon Papers, British Library, London, Add. MSS, 60798, Carnarvon to Froude, November 4, 1874, December 24, 1874; Froude to Carnarvon, February 16, 1875, June 21, 1875, September 11, 1875, September 20, 1875, October 4, 1875.

idleness and a violent brutality to expunge the problems that false philan-thropy had spawned.[99]

As in Ireland, Froude's understanding of the colony derived from his fixation with a fateful encounter between seventeenth-century Protestant settlers and a civilization-resistant, work-averse population of indigenes. To prise moral victory of the former over the latter, it was necessary to hold back the tide of progress and play the progress narrative in reverse. In South Africa, the association of early Protestantism with the spirit of productive capitalism was no longer to be seen. The bordering role, once imbued with the glamour of Scott's characters, who could wander across frontiers, pass easily between cultures, and mediate opposing creeds, was now to be associated with the "backward" natives and anathematized in hostile tones. By contrast, the Boers were praised for their steadfast racial endurance, their determination to hold onto timeworn values, and their stubborn resistance to the cant of modernity. All the old qualities of the Tudor yeoman were embodied in these living fossils, stuck in the mind-set of the sixteenth century. Their treks were taken not for novelty or adventure, but to escape the maws of a metastasizing market, so that they might replicate the ways of their grandfathers in a new country.

He comes on the ground in a wagon. He builds sheds or pens for his stock ... The garden being planted, he builds a modest house ... In his hall he places his old tables, which his father brought from the Colony ... He has generally but one book – a large clasped Bible, with the births, deaths and marriages of the family for half a dozen generations on the flyleaf ... There he lives and begets a huge family ... When a son or daughter marries, another house is built for them on the property; fresh land is brought under tillage, and the Transvaal is thus being gradually filled up in patriarchal fashion by a people who know nothing of the [outside] world.[100]

By contrast the black pastoralists had to be forbidden from continuing in the ways of *their* peripatetic forefathers. They had to be forced to adapt to a white settler world that represented the arrested development of early modern European society. "Under his own chief in the forest," Froude allowed, the Negro warrior "is at least a man."

Trained and disciplined under European authority he might become as fine a specimen of manhood as an English or Irish policeman ... Do we think the black races so superior to Europeans that they can improve without training? Our grandfathers treated them like cattle; we treat them as if it were a sin to lay them under the same restraint as our own children. Our cruelty and our tenderness are alike fatal to them; the second, perhaps, is the most fatal of the two.[101]

---

[99] Carnarvon Papers, Froude to Carnarvon, October 20, 1875, December 1, 1875.
[100] Froude, *Two Lectures*, 35–6.   [101] Froude, "South African Journal," 362.

9   Racial exclusion and Froude's oceanic dream

When Froude returned to London after two trips to South Africa, he was disillusioned and exhausted. The mission to promote South African federation had accomplished nothing. Through ill-timed speeches and injudicious statements, he had made himself *persona non grata* throughout the region, and had alienated all the relevant ethnic groups. Never again would he be tempted to give up writing for active politics. Yet even Froude's writing was becoming a source of frustration. Between 1881 and 1884, his masculinity was tested, as he discharged his responsibilities as Carlyle's biographer while simultaneously absorbing the ire of those hero-worshippers who could not bear to admit that the Sage of Chelsea had feet of clay. Did the dutiful disciple feel a slight twinge of oedipal satisfaction as he outed Carlyle for his impotence, his anti-Semitism, and his mistreatment of Jane? Froude, by contrast, had enjoyed two happy, productive marriages, channeled his ethnic stereotypes into his writing, and delighted in conversation with exotics of every kind.[102]

Yet as he passed middle age, Froude's temperament soured and his alienation from contemporary life increased. The world had not listened to his prophecies, and the evils he had predicted were now at hand. Amid class divisions and democratic demagoguery, everything good in the English heritage seemed to be at risk.

What England was to become was to be seen already in the enormously extended suburbs of London and our great manufacturing cities; miles upon miles of squalid lanes, each house the duplicate of its neighbour: the dirty street in front, the dirty yard behind, the fetid smell from ill-made sewers, the public house at the street corners. Here with no sight of a green field, with no knowledge of flowers or forest, the blue heavens themselves dirtied with soot.[103]

Trapped within this putrid and phthisic environment, the stalwart sons of Albion would gradually lose their manly vigor, turn unavailingly against their betters, and usher in the degeneration of the Anglo-Saxon race. Fortunately, the solution to all these problems was evident, if only the governing classes would return to their responsibilities. In her far-flung Empire, Britain had achieved a providential perimeter, which offered both the means of protecting herself in great power struggles and a safety valve for the surplus population crowding within the Home Island. Once again, it was the wisdom of Britain's sixteenth-century rulers that made it possible for her nineteenth-century crisis to be resolved.

[102] DF, II: 471–500; MJAF, 153–208.   [103] J. A. Froude, *Oceana* (New York, 1886), 8.

It appeared as if the genius of England, anticipating the inevitable increase [of population and industry] had provided beforehand for the distribution of it. English enterprise had occupied the fairest spots upon the globe where there was still soil and sunshine boundless and life-giving; where the race might for ages renew its mighty youth, bring forth as many millions as it would, and would still have the means to breed and rear them strong as the best which she had produced in her early prime.[104]

Here we have not merely another celebration of genius of the Tudors, but a tacit admission that Froude could apprehend his own era only through plotlines originally devised for his Tudor *History*. Though the books of his final decade sold well, they were superficial reprises of his youthful epic, in which the sectarian broils of the sixteenth-century England were inflated to reappear as racial struggles on a nineteenth-century global stage. Having graduated from their early modern racial adolescence, the Anglo-Saxons had been loosed upon the seas to conquer the earth. Other, lesser peoples, who were behindhand in these qualities, would either be eliminated in the struggle for survival or be compelled by the conquering Saxon to surrender and submit. In earlier times, such racial inferiors might be left to wallow in their preternatural back-wardness. The nineteenth century, however (like the Tudor period, on a smaller scale), was an era of mounting competition in a crowded world. For this reason, the defense of Britain required her expansion. Manly Britons of the coming generation were enjoined to go out and master the many-hued native inferiors to be found in myriad Asian, African, and Indian habitats. After centuries of subjugation to the bracing power of Anglo-Saxon work discipline and imperial control, perhaps they too would finally graduate into the sunlight of freedom.[105]

In this complacent mood, Froude was freed to take his long-deferred Australasian tour. The trip that he had planned nearly forty years earlier as an undergraduate he now undertook as a sixty-six year old, in the company of his youngest son. This was indeed an emotionally freighted voyage, encompassing all the worlds that the historian had lost and that the nation might gain. Here, at last, he hoped to find virgin territories for the transplantation of Anglo-Saxon kin, where the racial and historical complexities of Ireland and Africa could be kept at bay. He decided to entitle the record of his travels *Oceana* – at once a tribute to Harrington's seventeenth-century old English utopia and a consecration of the New Britain that his descendants were now constructing across the seas.[106]

[104] Froude, *Oceana*, 10.
[105] J. A. Froude, *The English in the West Indies, or The Bow of Ulysses* [1888] (New York, 1890).
[106] Froude, *Oceana*.

In the pages of this book, Froude worked hard to fit the reality of Australasia into the mold of these expectations. Adelaide reminded him of England. The Melbourne coast was reminiscent of the Suffolk shore-line. English oaks were adapting well to the new climate. The lawn tennis at Government House might have been played by English gentility. The ministers would have done credit to a Cabinet in London. The crisis in Sudan had elicited a troop of bronzed volunteers. In New Zealand, a rising tide of Britishness was detected on every front: myriad native plant and animal species all seemed to give way before the familiar flora and fauna that the Britons had had transplanted from their north Atlantic home. So it was also with human beings. The Maori, Froude was convinced, would soon enough follow the Australian aborigines into extinction. Drunken, lazy, incapable of self-improvement, they reminded him of the Irish.

There were the same cabins, the same children running about barefoot and half-naked, the same pigs, the same savage taste for brilliant colours, the women wearing the madder coloured petticoats; the same distribution of employment between the sexes, the wife working in the fields, the man lying on his back and enjoying himself . . . Nature had created an identical organization on the opposite side of the planet. Even the children had learned to beg in the same note.[107]

More disturbing than the degradation of the Maori, however, were odd signs that New Zealand's and Australia's Anglo-Saxons might not share Froude's vision of an agrarian yeoman paradise. Too many of the colonists were drawn to mining camps and cities. Auckland, in particular, struck him as especially squalid and undistinguished. What if the British emigrants to Australasia were not interested in Froude's peasant arcadia? Too many had moved, not to escape urban industrialism, but to replicate it, albeit with improved living standards and higher wages. Their ties to the motherland seemed more instrumental than sentimental. They were using their vaunted political freedom to slap tariffs on metropolitan man-ufactures, balking at the prospect of exporting food and raw materials for all eternity. Here it is Froude, the disillusioned realist, who seems to have fallen victim to his counter-romance.[108]

It is telling to compare his essentialized account of British Australia with William Westgarth's *Colony of Victoria*, the first empirical Anglo-Australian history. Like Froude, Westgarth was an empire booster, an *aficionado* of Anglo-Saxonism, and a staunch advocate of federation

---

[107] Froude, *Oceana*, quote on 298.
[108] Froude, *Oceana*, 245–6; Derek Schreuder and Stuart Ward (eds.), *Australia's Empire* (Oxford, 2008).

with the mother country. But he was also a well-informed traveler who had lived in Melbourne during the 1840s and 1850s and traded with it ever since. He understood that if the British–Australian Union were to continue during the coming era, sentimental bonds would have to be reinforced by capitalist self-interest. Victoria, as Westgarth showed, had grown from nothing to a population of half a million in less than twenty-five years. The initial settlement had been based on sheep farming to meet the insatiable demands of British industry. Then, in the 1850s, the discovery of gold brought in thousands of prospectors, entrepreneurs, and adventurers of every race and nation, drawn in by the lure of lucre for a lucky few. In this dynamic melting-pot, Westgarth boasted, the Governor of the province was an Irish Catholic, and the Mayor of Melbourne was a Jew.[109]

Froude's *Oceana* cannot accommodate this aspect of the Australian experience, because it has abandoned the ground of eventful conjuncture for a vaguely indeterminate racial temporality. The terror that fuels his fantasy of Anglo-Saxon expansion is the nightmare that the global world of the twentieth century might turn out to be sixteenth-century Ireland writ large. Australasia would then become the modern Ulster, the land ordained for the revitalization of Anglo-Saxons. The West Indies, on the other side of the globe, would devolve as the habitat of the archetypal indegene. A year after returning from his antipodean voyage, Froude finally tacked westward across the Atlantic, this time to investigate race relations in the sugar colonies. In his published account, *The English in the West Indies*, Froude's frame of reference is partly set by the Carlylean image of *Quashee*. Yet Froude's West Indian Negro is a more interesting character, since he is – like Froude's Irishman – at once *both* the target for the author's animus *and* also the repository of his subliminal fantasies. Where Carlyle would use the whip to force Quashee back onto the plantation, Froude parodies him in place as a prelapsarian creature who has somehow escaped from "white" original sin. Where Carlyle excoriated him for living on pumpkins, the son and victim of Revd. Froude will not necessarily begrudge him the spontaneous fruits of his edenic Caribbean garden, "oranges and plantains, bread-fruit and cocoa-nuts, but not apples."

---

[109] Like Froude, however, Westgarth was a believer in race essentialism, at least to a degree. He regarded Australia's Chinese immigrants as dangerous, and the aborigines as doomed. See William Westgarth, *The Colony of Victoria: Its History, Commerce and Gold Mining; its Social and Political Institutions* (London, 1864); William Westgarth, *Half a Century of Australasian Progress: A Personal Retrospect* (London, 1889); *DNB*, XX: 1265–6; Edward Beasley, *Mid-Victorian Imperialists: British Gentlemen and the Empire of the Mind* (London, 2003), 53–63.

In their ordeal of slavery, Froude reluctantly allows, these African-Americans had to pass through "a brief purgatory." Now, however, in the era of emancipation, they had found an "eternity of blessedness [under] the English Crown."

Under the rule of England in these islands the two million of these poor brothers-in-law of ours are the most perfectly contented specimens of the human race to be found on the planet ... If happiness be the satisfaction of every conscious desire, theirs is a condition which admits of no improvement: Were they independent, they might quarrel among themselves, and the weaker become the bondmen of the stronger; under the benevolent despotism of the English Government, which knows no difference of colour, and permits no oppression, they can sleep, lounge, and laugh away their lives as they please.[110]

The one price which the Negro must pay for this edenic condition is to be stripped of the knowledge and self-consciousness of fallen humanity. Froude's Negro is alternately described as a "grinning monkey" and a "loyal spaniel," who (absent English mastery) will drift back into a mangy cur. "If for the sake of theory or to shirk responsibility, we force them to govern themselves, the state of Hayti stands as a ghastly example of the condition into which they will inevitably fall."[111]

In this grotesque self-projective fantasy of West Indian Negroes as a chosen non-people, the realities of imperial exploitation are figuratively reversed. Plantation slavery was actually the first installment of emancipation, since it took the Negro away from the cannibalistic bestiality of Africa and introduced him to the Adamic disciplines of productive work. Slavery was now unacceptable and outmoded, but the West Indian freedman (like the Irish peasant) still had to be subjected to English discipline. "Give them independence, and in a few generations they will peel off such civilization as they have learned as easily and willingly as their coats and trousers." The West Indies had fertile lands and "docile, good tempered workers." It need not degenerate into a moral and economic disaster. "But the future of the blacks and of our own influence over them for good depend on their being protected from themselves and from the schemers who would take advantage of them."[112]

It is instructive at this point to trace the language of "race" as it developed over the course of Froude's life's work – from its intermittent early appearance as a casual phrase in his Tudor *History*, through a core (but not colored) concept in his mid-career denunciations of the Irish, to

---

[110] Froude, *English in the West Indies*, 81; Carlyle, *On the Nigger Question*, 1–37.
[111] Froude, *English in the West Indies*, 50, 25, 81, 161.
[112] Froude, *English in the West Indies*, 287.

the central, all-encompassing explanatory category of his late tour of the Caribbean colonies. Froude certainly deserves his reputation, alongside Carlyle, as one of the most flamboyant race-mongers of an overtly racist century.[113] However, a close look at the way "race" works in both men's writings raises questions about Victorian understandings of the term. In particular, neither man was at all attracted by the "racial science" that current historiography holds responsible for converting white intellectuals to biological determinism during the second half of the nineteenth century.[114] On the contrary, both Froude and Carlyle were vehement opponents of biological determinism, as they were of all materialistic "pig philosophies." For both men, race was to a considerable extent a cultural or even a spiritual phenomenon that manifested itself superficially in the forms of color and physiognomy. Reflecting an implicit

---

[113] Froude's increasing propensity towards racial stereotyping can also be detected in his private correspondence, where he was more inclined to express his opinions candidly. He indicated that Anglo-Saxons were by nature freedom lovers, especially fit for the task of governing lesser peoples, but they would always choose death rather than slavery for themselves. The Irish (or "Paddies," as he privately called them) were thriftless and unruly, but might be improved by English Protestant dictatorship or a one-way ticket into the Australian bush. People of color were privately denominated as "niggers," and presented as wholly determined by their race, and therefore as scarcely capable of individual personality. This casual racism was not incompatible with a willingness to recognize merit in people of color, albeit only in the context of his racial and historical theories. "When I was travelling in South Africa," Froude recounted, "I had a black man and a white man with me, and the black was worth a dozen of the white. For all I know, the black race may be as good as the white when it has gone through the same training. Hitherto the Negro has had no chance: he has been a slave from the beginning of history" (quoted in DF, II: 613). On the other hand, racial equality in Froude's mental universe of competing peoples, struggling for survival in a world of scarcity, was not necessarily a pretty thing. Lord George Hamilton recalled a dinner party conversation in which Froude described "Zulus and Kaffirs" as "a virile and intelligent race, physically stronger than the average European, who were multiplying and increasing faster than white men ... [and would] ultimately demolish the white race." The only viable strategy was "to exterminate them." When Hamilton objected, Froude gloomily replied, "If you do not adopt that policy, they will exterminate you." Quoted in Michael Bentley, *Lord Salisbury's World: Conservative Environments in Late-Victorian Britain* (Cambridge, 2001), 225.

[114] The standard accounts are Christine Bolt, *Victorian Attitudes to Race* (London, 1971); Nancy Stepan, *The Idea of Race in Great Britain* (London, 1982); Douglas A. Lorimer, *Colour, Class, and the Victorians: English Attitudes to the Negro in the Mid-Nineteenth Century* (Leicester, 1978); Stephen Jay Gould, *The Mismeasure of Man* (New York, 1981); George Stocking, *Race, Culture, and Evolution: Essays in the History of Anthropology* (New York, 1968); George Stocking, *Victorian Anthropology* (London, 1987). My own contribution can be found in "Capitalism, Race and Evolution in Imperial Britain, 1850–1900," in Theodore Koditschek, Sundiata Cha-Jua, and Helen Neville (eds.), *Race Struggles* (Champaign-Urbana, 2009), 48–72. For stimulating treatments from a literary critical perspective see Robert J. C. Young, *Colonial Desire: Hybridity in Theory, Culture, and Race* (London, 1995); and H. L. Malchow, *Gothic Images of Race in Nineteenth Century Britain* (Palo Alto, 1996).

neo-Lamarckism that remained popular into the early twentieth century, Froude (like Carlyle) believed that racial essences were not eternally fixed, but could be slowly altered over multiple generations.[115]

For Froude, then, race was never a rigidly biological phenomenon, because it always remained fluid and *historical* in character. As such, its centrality in his later writings was a direct reflection of his changed understanding of history. During his early career as an empirical researcher into the sixteenth century, history was understood as a string of open conjunctures that were to be organized and related in a narrative frame. Deep structures such as "race" played little role in explanation, since the course of history was deemed to run on the surface of events. It was only later, when Froude grew more fatalistic, that he explained historical developments in racial terms. Even then, however, his "races" remained enmeshed in the flux of history. Though not susceptible to rapid improvement (or instant deterioration) they were seen as broadly mutable over the long run. In this manner, Froude could combine the most vicious disparagement of supposedly inferior races with an abstract endorsement of ultimate racial equality. "With the same chances and with the same treatment, I believe that distinguished men would be produced equally from both [white and black] races." "But it does not follow," he continues, "that what can be done eventually can be done immediately."

The gulf which divides the colours is no arbitrary prejudice, but has been opened by the centuries of training and discipline which have given us the start in the race. We set it down to slavery. It would be far truer to set it down to freedom. The African blacks have been free enough for thousands, perhaps tens of thousands of years, and it has been the absence of restraint which has prevented them from becoming civilized. Generation has followed generation, and the children are as like their fathers as the successive generations of apes. The whites, it is likely enough, succeeded one another with the same similarity.[116]

Some historical accident in the unrecorded past, however, had set the Anglo-Saxons on a long march of racial improvement. "Our own Anglo-Norman race has become capable of self-government only after a thousand years of civil and spiritual authority." In other words, Henry VIII had beaten sixteenth-century Englishmen into submission so that their nineteenth-century descendants could be free. Now, it was the duty of nineteenth-century Englishmen to beat Negroes into submission so that their descendants might someday be free. Racial others remained

---

[115] Conway Zirckle, "The Early Idea of the Inheritance of Acquired Characteristics and of Pangenesis," *Transactions of American Philosophical Society*, NS, 35.2 (Philadelphia, 1946). Discusses the long and venerable genealogy of such notions.
[116] Froude, *English in the West Indies*, 124–5.

intrinsically different, yet they were still distant members of the Greater British family.[117]

10   The race against *Froudacity*

Like his denunciations of the Irish over a decade earlier, Froude's infantalization of West Indian Negroes was predicated on the assumption that they were not part of his audience, would not read what he said about them, and could not write back. On the contrary, claimed the Revd. P. H. Doughlin, "here in the West Indies, and on the West Coast or Africa, are to be found Surgeons of the Negro Race, Solicitors, Barristers, Mayors, Councillors, Principals and founders of High Schools and Colleges, Editors and Proprietors of Newspapers, Archdeacons, Bishops, Judges, and Authors." Such men would not recognize themselves in Froude's simple savage, nor would they appreciate his rude jests and racist calumnies. In 1888, a Barbadian liberal, N. Darnell Davis, shot back with *Mr. Froude's Negrophobia*, which described *The English in the West Indies* as "a mere piece of Book-making, containing no real study of the past History, and still less of the real life, of the English and African Races in the West Indies. Of the actual condition of the British West Indies of today Mr. Froude knows as much, and as little, as a Cook's Tourist."[118] No less offended by this act of racial tourism was a retired colonial official, C. S. Salmon, who upbraided the famous English historian for his absolute ignorance of African-American history. Froude's failure to appreciate Africa's indigenous civilization had engendered a crude slander on West Indians' capabilities. Such people had not been savages before slavery degraded them. Since emancipation they had been reclaiming their heritage, and they were producing a Creole culture that was clearly beyond Froude's ken.[119]

Froude's inadequacies as an observer were most thoroughly exposed by the black Jamaican linguist J. J. Thomas, in his aptly titled *Froudacity*. The "Cook's Tourist," who professed to be trafficking in the exotic, was merely dispensing his familiar, garden-variety anglocentric bigotry. The relish with which Froude relayed tales of salted babies devoured by ravening black beasts, Thomas exposed as a malicious libel. The canard

---

[117] Froude, *English in the West Indies*, 125.

[118] N. Darnell Davis, *Mr. Froude's Negrophobia, or Don Quixote as a Cook's Tourist* (Demerara, 1888), quote on 3. See also Elsa V. Goveia, *A Study on the Historians of the West Indies* (Washington, DC, 1980), 152–7; and Eric Williams, *British Historians and the West Indies* (Brooklyn, 1994), 137–46.

[119] Davis, *Froude's Negrophobia*, 35; C. S. Salmon, *The Caribbean Confederation: A Plan for the Union of the Fifteen British West Indian Colonies* (London, 1888), 40–76.

of cannibalism was trotted out merely to frighten (or perhaps titillate) his English audience. Yet not a single piece of confirmed and authenticated evidence was offered in support of this central theme. In his travels Froude had never visited with a single Negro, but he had been wined and dined by wealthy planters who had shown him what they wanted him to see. All the manifest accomplishments of black West Indians had been ignored or dismissed. Only their failures and transgressions were loudly proclaimed. By such methods, Froude had placed the West Indian Negro in an inescapable trap. On the one hand, political enfranchisement was made contingent on acquiring a European education. Yet "when these qualifications are conspicuously mastered," imperialism "refuses [the Negro] the prize *because* he is a Negro."[120]

Davis, Salmon, and Thomas all insisted on the heterogeneity of West Indian society. Froude's efforts to fix it within his black-and-white racial polarity did violence to a more multi-shaded reality. The disappearance of most old-style white planters, the decline of sugar as a mainstay of the local economy, and the rise of a diverse and increasingly prosperous mulatto elite are all noted as central features of the West Indian experience, yet are completely absent from Froude's account. As a result, he had failed to grasp the central development of the post-emancipation period: the breakdown of the old plantation economy and the rise of a class of independent small-holding blacks. Here indeed, had he been so inclined, Froude might have found the stalwart yeoman farmers who were so conspicuously scarce among the Anglo-Saxons of Australasia.

It is the black men who pay taxes and support Her Majesty's Government. In the Islands, especially, it is the black men who are taking up the land and cultivating it. They are rapidly becoming peasant proprietors of the European type. It is the black men who do nearly all the labour. The West Indies are essentially agricultural, but the black men make very good mechanics, and skilful and bold sailors, and they do well mostly all the work that has to be done in this way. In times of trouble and difficulty they are found to be reliable soldiers, and a couple of these regiments of Mr Froude's black men help very materially to keep the flag of England from being thought too slightingly on the West Coast of Africa.[121]

Davis, Salmon, and Thomas were no less concerned about the place of the West Indies in Greater Britain than was Froude. However, they drew diametrically opposite conclusions about the best means to preserve Caribbean loyalties. Where Froude envisioned patriotism as exclusively

---

[120] J. J. Thomas, *Froudacity: West Indian Fables by James Anthony Froude* (London, 1888), 182; Salmon, *Caribbean Confederation*, 128–30.

[121] Davis, *Froude's Negrophobia*, 28–30; Salmon, *Caribbean Confederation*, 53; Thomas, *Froudacity*, 179–93.

white, Salmon and Thomas transposed it into a more living color, as the metropole became increasingly dependent on her multiracial colonies. As against Froude's insistence on central control and authoritarian government, his three critics argued that only the grant of representative institutions would preserve West Indians' sentiments of British affinity. "The demand for Reform in the Crown Colonies," according to Thomas,

A demand which our author deliberately misrepresents – is made neither by nor for the Negro, Mulatto, White, Chinese, nor East Indian. It is a petition put forward by prominent responsible colonists – the majority of whom are Whites, and mostly Britons besides. Their prayer, in which the whole population in these Colonies most heartily join in, is simply and most reasonably that we, the said Colonies, being an integral portion of the British Empire, and having, in intelligence and every form of civilized progress, outgrown the stage of political tutelage, should be accorded some measure of emancipation therefrom.[122]

Here again, the ironies abound. The colonial confederation that Froude would have foisted on unwilling South Africans was being eagerly sought by West Indians of all races, who argued that the best means of keeping them loyal to Greater Britain was to enable them to have a say in their own affairs. "Education," warned Davis, "has taught the West Indian African to think . . . He does not prove himself un-English by his desire to have some say in the election of those who are empowered to raise and spend his taxes, and to make laws for him." "The universal demand for more local self-government is not due to a want of loyalty to British rule," Salmon insisted, "but to a well-founded feeling that progress is hardly practicable without it." By thwarting this trans-racial progress and self-government in the West Indies Froude was (as he had earlier done in Ireland) actually undermining the very Greater British imperial union that he professed to advance.

A people can be made loyal, and they can be kept loyal, by granting to them their just demands. The withholding of these demands always endangers loyalty and sometimes destroys it . . . How a thing is given, and when, makes a great difference. Administrators who are unaware of this fact, or who under-estimate the sentiment that lies behind the facts of life are unworthy to have power in an empire, especially in one where the races differ from one another in their origin, their character, and their history.[123]

11   Conclusion

When Froude died in 1894, the eulogies rolled from the periodical press. Lion of the literary establishment, paragon of patriotic imperialism, he

[122] Thomas, *Froudacity*, 131; Salmon, *Caribbean Confederation*, 128–30.
[123] Salmon, *Caribbean Confederation*, 134.

was hailed as the Devonshire Englishman *par excellence*. Appointed Regius Professor of Modern History two years earlier, he had returned in triumph to the Oxford that had ignominiously expelled him as a youth.[124] Having prevailed over most of his rivals in the enterprise of history writing, he died with the laurels of Macaulay on his brow. True enough, a small group of academics sneered at his superficiality, his eclecticism, his indiscipline, and his romantic disillusionment with romance.[125] Froude had not cared, knowing that it was precisely these qualities that had gained him wide readership and had rendered his judgments a force to be reckoned with wherever the Union Jack flew. In fact, Froude's reputation as impressionistic, or incoherent, was largely undeserved. In this chapter, we have seen that a deep structure of thought and emotion loomed just below the textual surface of nearly all his writing, relentlessly imposing its fixed assumptions about the nature of mankind and society. Indeed, at some slight risk of oversimplification, we might suggest that Froude's writing – in all its baroque plenitude – is built around the architecture of four quite simple, overarching premises. (1) The world is a dark and dangerous place that is essentially divided between those who are being beaten and those who are doing the beating. (2) It is better to be among the latter than among the former group. (3) The beaters are to be celebrated for their success, and the beaten deserve contempt for their failure. (4) This ascendancy of the strong over the weak, which crude materialists might interpret as "might makes right," must be reinterpreted as a deeper spiritual unfolding of providential will.[126]

Introduced to these principles by his father's hand, Froude had been taught by Carlyle to put them into words. In the four decades after 1850, he emerged as an influential writer by applying them to three of the most burning preoccupations of his time: history, empire, and race. History, his first love, absorbed him throughout the 1850s and 1860s, teaching him to ground his personality in the life of his nation and to seek security in the image of an authoritarian but protective Tudor state. The history

---

[124] *London Times*, October 24, 1894; Burrow, *A Liberal Descent*, 234.

[125] In particular, E. A. Freeman mounted a vicious attack on Froude over a period of four decades, impugning his accuracy, integrity, intelligence, and style. This was particularly mystifying inasmuch as there were no deep differences between the two men in interpretation or ideology. Froude's revenge was to replace Freeman as Regius Professor of Modern History at Oxford when the younger man died in 1892. DF, II: 456–70.

[126] Consider, for example, the following passage: "As nature has constituted us that we must be ruled in some way ... the rule inevitably will be with the strongest, so nature has also allotted superiority of strength to superiority of intellect and character; and in deciding that the weak shall obey the more powerful, she is in reality saving them from themselves, and then she confers true liberty when she seems most to be taking it away" (*The English in Ireland*, I: 5).

of this state led him outward, to encompass an Empire that had been founded by the far-seeing inspiration of sixteenth-century statesmen, but was now offering a providential solution to many of the most perplexing social and political problems of the Victorian age. During the 1870s and 1880s, Froude's engagement with Empire brought him face to face with the phenomenon of race, a category of classification and explanation that virtually supplanted history in the books of his old age. Here, a host of complexities resolved themselves into a comforting dualism, in which stalwart Anglo-Saxons, heirs of the Protestant Reformation, could renew their hereditary vigor by emigrating to the colonies. There they would harness the labor of darker, lesser peoples to spread order and prosperity across the face of the earth.[127]

As the friend of leading politicians, as editor of *Fraser's*, and as author of many bestselling books, Froude was clearly one of the important "talking heads" of the later Victorian age. His exact significance, however, is not easy to pinpoint. Unlike Macaulay, who attracted a broad but diffuse audience, Froude was a more polarizing figure to whom reviewers responded with either strong hostility or vigorous praise. Since few were likely to look to him for expertise on specific subjects, it may be that his influence came from the sharpness with which he registered the mood-swings of middle-class propertied Victorian readers, who were exchanging the easy optimism of Macaulayite liberalism for the harsher, less confident spirit of a more straitened, neo-conservative age. Froude certainly did not cause these mood-swings, but he could be their beneficiary. When the progress narrative weakened, when it was temporarily superseded by xenophobia or by racial panic, those with a stake in the existing order might become attracted to Froudian thinking as they slipped from the buoyancy of hope into the shadow of fear. It was in this reflective and reactive sense that Froude contributed to changing the way in which Greater Britain was imagined during the second half of the nineteenth century. Once envisioned as a crusade to spread anglocentric values to the world's backward peoples, Greater Britain could then be reconceptualized as a necessary perimeter, sustaining Britain's economic expansion, absorbing the nation's surplus population, and providing a bulwark against foreign hostility.

Yet, as Froude was repeatedly at pains to demonstrate, this shift in attitudes toward race, nationality, and empire in his own era also required

---

[127] Froude himself acknowledged, late in life, "My character as a boy was a very miserable one – I don't know how I came by it. I have had hard work to mend it even a little, and I do not know that I have essentially succeeded, or whether characters as such admit of mending." Quoted in MJAF, 280–1.

corresponding changes in Britons' approach to history. His contribution here was to insist that history was not always and entirely a history of progress. Liberal individualism was not always a benefit. Authority was often needed, and freedom was frequently abused. Nations and peoples did not always advance, but sometimes deteriorated, falling short of the standard that their ancestors had set. Strong measures of self-defense were sometimes necessary, and sentimental devotion to the improvement of backward races was a luxury that the powerful could not always afford. Froude did not convince his readers to make these adjustments in their thinking so much as he resonated with the changes in the zeitgeist that they had made on their own. Here, paradoxically, we can perhaps see the limits of his influence. For if Froude helped his readers to think differently about history, race, and empire, *his* specific history of race and empire was not one that most of them could embrace wholeheartedly. His veneration of the Tudors, his glorification of authority, his celebration of preindustrial values, and his strange attraction to the moral climate of the sixteenth century were all deeply rooted in his own life-story. They were, however, quite idiosyncratic and of limited relevance to other members of his class and generation, especially those who were loath to make a clean break with the liberal allegiances into which they had been born. Such people were persuaded that the problems of race and of empire were indeed two of the most critical (and critically interconnected) dilemmas of the age. To resolve them, however, required a different kind of history – one far more radical and intellectually innovative – than the conventional narrative history that Froude offered up.

5 Greater Britain and the "lesser breeds": liberalism, race, and evolutionary history

The doctrine of evolution is nothing else than the historical method applied to the facts of nature; the historical method is nothing else than the doctrine of evolution applied to human societies and institutions.

F. Pollock, *Oxford Lectures* (Oxford, 1890), 41

We are now in a position to trace out all that the Comparative method of inquiry has to tell us of the earliest political state of that branch of mankind to which we ourselves belong. We are now ready to stand face to face with our kinsmen ... In this mighty drama of European and Aryan history, three lands, three races, stand before all others, as those to whom, each in its own day, the mission has been given to be the rulers and teachers of the world ... The Greek, the Roman, and the Teuton, each in his own turn stands above the other nations of the Aryan family. Each in his turn has reached the highest stage alike of power and civilization that was to be had in his own age, and each has handed on his own store to be further enriched by successors who were at once conquerors and disciples.

E. A. Freeman, *Comparative Politics* [1873] (London, 1896), 24–5

This would be a grand land if only every Irishman would kill a negro, and be hanged for it.

E. A. Freeman to F. H. Dickinson, New Haven, Connecticut, December 4, 1881, in W. R. Stephens, *The Life and Letters of Edward A. Freeman* (London, 1895), II: 242

In 1866–8, Charles Dilke, a young Londoner of independent means, took a tour of the English-speaking world. After returning home, he published his impressions in a book, which he entitled *Greater Britain*. Partly because of its catchy title, the book went quickly through four editions. In its pages, readers found a sober assessment of that progressive imperialism, which seemed no longer quite as simple and inexorable as it had in Macaulay's day. Elected to Parliament on the new reformed franchise, Dilke quickly rose to a leadership position on the Liberal left. In the House of Commons he articulated a radical version of Gladstonian Liberalism, and was mentioned as a possible successor to the Grand Old Man himself. With regard to the Empire, Dilke let his book do the speaking. Neo-conservatives like Froude accused Liberals of abandoning the Empire, but *Greater Britain* demonstrated that this need not be so. The triumph of federal government in post-bellum America showed that democracy and territorial expansion could be reconciled. "In America," Dilke avowed, "the peoples of the world are being fused together, but they are run into an English mold: Alfred's laws and Chaucer's tongue are theirs whether they would or no ... Through America, England is speaking to the world." Yet if the United States could ventriloquize in the voice of England, how much more effectively could England speak for herself, if only she learned how to devolve her overseas possessions and reunite them in a genuinely voluntary union that would radiate British liberalism through every continent on earth.[1]

Dilke's impact can be measured by the number of successor volumes that fleshed out his fragmentary argument: Frederick Young's *Imperial Federation*, F. P. Labilliere's *Federal Britain*, and H. M. Mortimer-Franklyn's *The Unit of Imperial Federation*, to name only a few. In 1884, these men founded a bipartisan Imperial Federation League, which drew in the leading Liberal politicians W. E. Forster, Lord Rosebery, James Bryce, and Joseph Chamberlain.[2] With the rise of a German as well as a North American federation, federalism was touted as the way of the future. In a world where states were metamorphosing into super-states, Britain's greatness was now, more than ever, contingent on her ever-increasing ability to become greater still. Surrounded to the east by Greater Russia and Greater Germany, to the south by Greater France, and to the west by the United States, Britain would have to break out of this enclosure. Leap-frogging oceans, her empire might be re-forged into a super-state that could encompass the globe. A century earlier, the thirteen North American colonies had been lost because such a trans-oceanic federation had been impossible under the conditions of that day. By 1884, however, all the white settler colonies – in Canada, Australasia, and the Cape – had acquired their own versions of "responsible" self-government. Moreover, with the advent of the railroad, telegraph,

---

[1] Charles Dilke, *Greater Britain: A Record of Travel in English Speaking Countries* (New York, 1869), quote on ix. On Dilke, see Stephen M. Gwynn and Gertrude Tuckwell, *Sir Charles W. Dilke*, 2 vols. (London, 1917); Roy Jenkins, *Victorian Scandal* (New York, 1965); Kali Israel, *Names and Stories: Emilia Dilke and Victorian Culture* (Oxford, 1999); David Nicholls, *The Lost Prime Minister: A Life of Sir Charles Dilke* (London, 1995).

[2] Frederick Young, *Imperial Federation of Great Britain and her Colonies* (London, 1876); F. P. de Labilliere, *Federal Britain; or, Unity and Federation of the Empire* (London, 1894); H. M. Mortimer-Franklyn, *The Unit of Imperial Federation: A Solution of the Problem* (London, 1887).

steamship, and global navy, it could be argued that distance had been "annihilated" and no longer posed a natural barrier to political unity. Through federation, British capitalism would gain a wider sphere of operation, British power would be configured for the coming era, and the world would be rendered safe for British democracy.[3]

Problems arose, however, when these general sentiments in favor of imperial federation were translated into definite constitutional schemes. Direct representation of the colonies in the existing Westminster Parliament was clearly impractical, while the creation of a non-binding executive advisory board giving advice to British ministers would hardly satisfy colonial aspirations. Yet to create a federal super-parliament *sui generis* would be tantamount to a constitutional revolution on which no consensus was possible. Given these practical impediments, it is not surprising that some of the greatest advocates of worldwide Anglo-Saxon union – E. A. Freeman, A. V. Dicey, Goldwin Smith, and even Dilke himself – concluded that formal federation of the Empire might never be achieved. As Freeman astutely pointed out, the two terms were inherently contradictory. "What is 'Imperial' cannot be 'Federal'" and *vice versa*, since federations were voluntary unions contracted between free peoples, while empires were political despotisms imposed by force. Those who imagined otherwise, Freeman indicated, "have forgotten the existence of India and the existence of the United States." In a true Greater British federation, he privately noted, "we all shall be outvoted by Hindus and Mahometans."[4]

Of course, the advocates of federation intended nothing of the sort. All the writers and politicians involved in this discussion – whether they favored a formal federation or preferred to muddle through with existing arrangements – agreed that democratic rights in the Greater Britain of the

---

[3] John Kemble, *Federal Britain: A History* (London, 1997), 1–78; Michael Burgess, *The British Tradition of Federalism* (Leicester, 1995), 1–79. These debates and discussions have been masterfully examined by Duncan Bell in *The Idea of Greater Britain: Empire and the Future of World Order, 1860–1900* (Princeton, 2007). Bell, however, has limited his focus to "the debate over the potential union of the United Kingdom with its so-called settler colonies" (1). These were indeed the terms in which the idea of Greater Britain was conceived by most late nineteenth-century British imperialists. But what of the relationship between the Anglo-Saxon would-be federators and Britain's vast "coloured" colonial dependencies? This chapter takes up where Bell left off, exploring the way in which history, race, and evolution were used, especially by liberals, to try to regulate the relationship between imperial Anglo-Saxons and the colonized "lesser breeds."

[4] W. R. Stephens, *The Life and Letters of Edward A. Freeman*, 2 vols. (London, 1895), 356–7; Burgess, *British Tradition*, 50–60; Bell, *Idea of Greater Britain*, 179–88; Ged Martin, "The Idea of Imperial Federation," in Ronald Hyam and Ged Martin (eds.), *Reappraisals in British Imperial History* (London, 1975), 121–39.

foreseeable future should be restricted to Anglo-Saxon males (or at least white males) alone. To be sure, Dilke had presented an attractive picture of the United States as a melting-pot in which immigrants were being anglicized, and even the freed Negro slaves were assimilating to the dominant culture. In the United States, however, Negroes comprised only about 13 percent of the population and white immigrants another 12 percent. In the British Empire, by contrast, only 12 percent of the population lived in autonomous (white) territories that remained in the Empire by choice. Even Dilke, who hoped for a more egalitarian future, was convinced that Greater Britain's 88 percent of colored subjects had to be governed by despotic means.[5]

These awkward facts were embarrassing to most Victorian Liberals, and it was only by ignoring them that they could persist in their quixotic federation schemes. Yet the question of how such dependencies should be governed could not be wished away. A generation earlier, it had posed no fundamental difficulty for James Mill or the Macaulays, since they were able to rationalize the despotism as a temporary condition that would lead to British acculturation and/or political independence in a matter of decades. By the late nineteenth century, however, it had become apparent that this was not happening, and that the road to postcoloniality would take a very long time. While most liberals continued to believe that all men should be protected in their property, active citizenship in governing the Empire would have to be restricted on racial grounds. Yet to articulate such racial restrictions too openly also caused discomfort because of cognitive dissonance with abstract liberal views. After all, the French Declaration of the Rights of Man and the fourteenth and fifteenth amendments to the United States Constitution, not to mention the Queen's India Proclamation within Greater Britain itself, all seemed to preclude legally enforceable civic discrimination based on race, religion, color, or creed. How then were such racial discriminations to be established and practically defended in liberal terms?[6]

In this chapter we will see how one part of the answer lay in the adoption of a new kind of evolutionary history. The need to rank the Empire's manifold ethnic groups hierarchically, along polarities of enfranchisement or dependence and inherently high or low wage capability, created the need for a new kind of racial theory that would naturalize these

---

[5] Population figures are from 1900. B. R. Mitchell, *Abstract of British Historical Statistics* (Cambridge, 1962), 12–13; J. A. Hobson, *Imperialism* (Ann Arbor, 1965), 20; Bureau of Census, *Historical Statistics of the United States, 1789–1945* (Washington, DC, 1949), 25.

[6] S. V. Desika Char, *Readings in the Constitutional History of India, 1757–1947* (Oxford, 1983), 299–300; C. A. and M. R. Beard, *A Basic History of the United States* (New York, 1944), 507–8.

distinctions in professedly objective ways.[7] Simultaneously, the appearance of new scientific theories of evolution enabled history to be re-written in the framework of an incremental *longue durée*. In Chapter 4, we saw Froude and Buckle groping for a way to incorporate a *longue durée* perspective into a traditional historiography that remained essentially conjunctural and narrative in form. The answers they came up with, vague notions of "race" and "environment," were becoming the coin of intellectual exchange in their time. In this chapter we will examine how these notions were elaborated between the 1860s and the 1880s, to forge a new kind of evolutionary history that seemed consistent with both the discoveries of science and the requirements of Empire.

The result of this new evolutionary history, as we shall see, was the bifurcation of historical writing along racialized lines. Those groups and peoples deemed capable of individual agency and political independence were to be chronicled through traditional methods of narrative exposition, albeit with one eye always trained on the distinctive qualities and features that had enabled them to preserve their racial superiority. By contrast, those groups and peoples deemed too backward to participate in politics were to be consigned to the long evolutionary timescale. Incorporation into the Empire had indeed brought such peoples within the ambit of recorded history; however, they could not properly become historical actors in their own right. Subordinated by their supposed civilizational deficiencies, they found that their place was to accept the tutelage of the white imperial masters, who deemed themselves to be more evolutionarily advanced. The task of liberal colonial administrators was no longer to force-march such backward peoples through the rapid paces of modernization, Christianization, or Anglicization, as had been the case in the Macaulays' day. On the contrary, by applying the new techniques of evolutionary and ethnological study, the liberal imperialist could discern the racial character of a given people, and thereby devise the precise regime of discipline and dependency by which they could be most efficaciously controlled.[8]

1   The advent of evolution and *longue durée* history

What did mid-Victorian liberals mean when they used the language of "race" and "evolution"? For older generations of liberals, from

---

[7] Nancy Stepan, *The Idea of Race in Science: Great Britain, 1800–1960* (London, 1982).

[8] Theodore Koditschek, "Narrative Time and Racial/Evolutionary Time in Nineteenth-Century British Liberal Imperial History," in Catherine Hall and Keith McClelland (eds.), *Race, Nation, and Empire: Making Histories, 1750 to the Present* (Manchester, 2010), 36–55.

J. F. Blumenbach to J. C. Prichard, race had been a patently visible but highly mutable feature. While it was closely associated with culture, morality, and intelligence, it was seen as alterable through racial mixing, environment, or the inheritance of acquired characteristics, within a relatively short period of time. For the defenders of slavery, by contrast, race was an indelible and immutable attribute. Over many generations the races had been preserved, virtually as separate species, and they were incapable of interbreeding for any length of time. All too conveniently, according to this view, some races (notably Anglo-Saxons) were destined by nature to be masters, while others (most notably black Africans) were preordained to be slaves. The abolition of slavery, first in the British colonies and later in the United States, tended to discredit these "polygenist" views. Nevertheless during the 1860s, 1870s, and 1880s there was no simple return to the Prichardian–Macaulayite position. On the contrary, the advent of evolution opened the way to a completely new approach to race, which more effectively addressed the needs of the late Victorian capitalist polity and society, and was neither strictly polygenist nor monogenist in the old racially absolutist terms.[9]

In the new framework, race was treated as neither immutable nor incidental, but as a *longue durée* historical phenomenon that developed (at least potentially) in progressive terms. While J. S. Mill, H. T. Buckle, and a few other students of progress steered clear of both "race" and "evolution," most others came to embrace the connection between them as foundational to a chastened liberalism, appropriate for an increasingly biologistic age. By making "race" progressive, evolution rendered it safe for liberalism. Yet by limiting "progress" to race, evolution tempered its velocity. There is a certain irony in the fact that, at the very moment when "progress" was disappearing from grand historical narratives, such as those of Froude, it was creeping into a new kind of bio-social evolutionary theory, where it could endorse the superiority of Anglo-Saxon civilization in a more formidable "scientific" manner and reaffirm the civilizing possibilities for lesser peoples, albeit in gradual, imperially directed ways.[10]

---

[9] For early nineteenth-century liberal approaches, see J. C. Prichard, *Researches in the Physical History of Man*, ed. and with introduction by George Stocking (Chicago, 1973); John C. Greene, *The Death of Adam: Evolution and its Impact on Western Thought* (Ames, 1959), 175–247; George Stocking, *Victorian Anthropology* (New York, 1987), 1–77. For polygenism, see Robert Knox, *The Races of Man* [1850] (London, 1862); Stepan, *The Idea of Race in Science*, 20–82; Christine Bolt, *Victorian Attitudes to Race* (London, 1971); and Stocking, *Victorian Anthropology*, 78–143.

[10] Stocking, *Victorian Anthropology*, 144–273; Theodore Koditschek, "Capitalism, Race and Evolution in Imperial Britain: 1850–1900," in Theodore Koditschek, Sundiata Cha-Jua, and Helen Neville (eds.), *Race Struggles* (Champaign-Urbana, 2009), 48–79.

In his 1844 *Vestiges of the Natural History of Creation*, Robert Chambers had asserted "Development" as the universal law of everything organic, in a manner that corresponded to the force of "gravitation" on inanimate objects. These ideas were taken up and further extended during the 1850s by Herbert Spencer, who claimed that "the evolution of the simple into the complex, through a process of differentiation," was "the law of all progress," in both biology and society. The most important contribution to this evolutionary discourse was, of course, Charles Darwin's *Origin of Species*, published in 1859. Just how far Darwin's theory of natural selection could be seen as progressive was heatedly debated at the time. Darwin's initial reluctance to discuss the human implications of his theory was not shared by many of his followers, who immediately began to speculate on the implications of applying "natural selection" to the origin and development of our species. The discovery of proto-human remains, mixed with the bones of extinct animals in Brixham Cave, greatly reinforced the belief that the 6,000-year chronology of the Bible would have to be abandoned as the timescale for human history, as it had been a generation earlier for the history of the earth. Charles Lyell's 1863 *The Antiquity of Man* laid out what had finally become the consensus position among scientists, that mankind was vastly older than Christian orthodoxy had allowed. Darwin, Sir Frederick Pollock concluded, was simply a historian who deployed the geological timescale to encompass organisms of every kind. Historians, he implied, might become Darwinians if they refigured human history on the timescale of race.[11]

Just how profoundly this new racial and evolutionary thinking impacted on Victorian intellectuals can be glimpsed by returning for a moment to the case of Froude. His sixteenth-century *History* had been conceived in the pre-Darwinian era, and displayed no inkling of evolutionary ideas. Although he never identified as a Darwinian, by 1875, when he made his trip to South Africa, a distinctively new layer in his thought had emerged. Profoundly shocked by the situation that he found in Natal, he warned Lord Carnarvon that a race war would soon be in the offing, and that only a well-designed policy of imperial discipline could prevent the

---

[11] Robert Chambers, *Vestiges of the Natural History of Creation* [1844] (Chicago, 1994); James A. Secord, *Victorian Sensation: The Extraordinary Publication, Reception and Secret Authorship of Vestiges of the Natural History of Creation* (Chicago, 2000); Herbert Spencer, "Progress: Its Law and Causes," *Westminster Review*, 67 (April, 1857), 445–7; Charles Darwin, *On the Origin of Species by Means of Natural Selection* [1859] (New York, 1963); Donald K. Grayson, *The Establishment of Human Antiquity* (New York, 1963); Peter Bowler, *Theories of Human Evolution: A Century of Debate, 1844–1944* (Baltimore, 1986), 25–35; Peter Bowler, *The Invention of Progress: The Victorians and the Past* (Oxford, 1989), 75–105; Charles Lyell, *The Geological Evidence of the Antiquity of Man* [1863] (London, 1914); Frederick Pollock, *Oxford Lectures* (Oxford, 1890), 41–2.

extermination of what he called the "Kaffir" race. The solution he proposed involved a controlled mixture of natural and artificial selection.

Break up the tribes at arms. Let each Kaffir family have its own adequate freehold.
Some will keep this land and cultivate it. They will learn industry. They will cease
to be dangerous, and it would be neither necessary nor just to interfere with them
or their children. But the few good will be rapidly sorted out from the many
worthless – In two or three years the majority, living in idleness and drunkenness,
will have sold their portions. They must become vagrants. They must not be
allowed to squat on the waste lands. They must work for wages until they have
earned their independence. Or they must leave the country and their children
under such circumstances may be equitably taken hold of and apprenticed.

Froude's proposal provides a good example of how "evolution" could
reconcile formal liberalism with *de facto* discriminatory policies. Allow
nature to run its course, and the optimal outcome will follow. "As it will
be with the Kaffirs, as with wild animals and with every inferior race of
man with whom a stronger race has come in contact." "They will become
domesticated and must conform to the usages of civilized society, or they
will cease to be," he portentously concluded. "This is a law of nature with
which it as idle to quarrel as with the law of gravity."[12]
    Froude had most of his substantive historical writing behind him when
he issued these pronouncements, but a new cohort of historians was
emerging, steeped from the very beginning in evolutionary thought.
Their histories would be conceived in two complementary registers.
Old-style narratives of the Macaulayite or Froudian type would continue
to be published, but they would be underpinned with a multi-millennial
logic of bio-social development. Contests of groups and individuals would
be amplified into struggles between races, while episodic conjunctures
would blend into an evolutionary *longue durée*. Where the older four-
stage models of social development had been essentially static, with no
clear mechanism of progression from one stage to the next, the new
evolutionism would at least purport to become dynamic (i.e. by assigning
the propensity to improvement as an essential racial trait). "Savagery,"
which had previously been a determinate stage of social development,
would now become something of a floating signifier – a term of anathema-
tization, applied to any group that was deemed to be developing improp-
erly or to be resisting British "improvement."[13]

---

[12] Froude to Carnarvon, January 12, 1875, British Library, London, Add. MSS, 60798.
[13] Koditschek, "Narrative Time." Since my concern here is with the uses of evolution in
    historical writing, I will not examine the phenomenon of "Social Darwinism" *per se*. The
    vast and often contentious literature on this subject is even-handedly reviewed by Mike
    Hawkins, *Social Darwinism in European and American Thought, 1860–1945* (Cambridge,
    1997).

As George Stocking and others have demonstrated, Darwinian descent, and the transposition of mankind's lifespan from a biblical onto a geological timeframe, had huge implications for the way in which race was conceptualized. Yet if the end of polygenism came conveniently in phase with the end of slavery, the "family of man" endorsed by evolution was something far more extended and distant than that which the old Prichardian monogenism had formerly proclaimed. Now that the common ancestor of the modern races was no longer the familiar patriarch, Adam, he had become a much more distant, brutish savage, who fell far short of the bourgeois individualism, intelligence, and respectability that modern liberalism valorized, and modern capitalism required.[14]

The new orthodoxy therefore allowed for a considerable residue of belief in the inequality of the races – not, to be sure, as absolutely permanent and indelible, but deeply enough rooted, at sufficient genealogical distance, as to make the progress and advancement of the "inferior" races no longer a project that could be completed in one or two generations. Rather, it was now reconceived as a protracted – even quasi-Darwinian – process that would have to extend (as Froude suggested) over several centuries. It was therefore extremely convenient that this new, incremental perspective on racial development came to fruition at the very moment when the colonial crises of 1857–86 were leading metropolitan liberals to doubt whether Greater Britain's racial others could easily be transformed into darker versions of themselves.[15] Through the new evolutionary histories, contemporary differences of culture and geography could be re-mapped as chronological distance on the scale of time. History and presumptive consanguinity were thereby turned into warrants for the way in which any particular dependency or people should be integrated economically and governed politically. National characters – fairly stable and predictable, but never entirely fixed – could now be juxtaposed in historical terms. Cultures and races differed, not in their essential humanity, but in the speed and success with which they had passed through a universal transformation from savagery to civilization. For those who were classified as savages, the progress narrative had become so prolonged and extended that the present generation ceased to experience it in narrative terms. No longer an arena in which they were allowed to act, it had become a colonized space in which they were properly managed and confined. The Empire had indeed

[14] George Stocking, *Race, Culture and Evolution* (New York, 1968), 42–68; Stocking, *Victorian Anthropology*, 96–104, 146–52.
[15] This new position on race was authoritatively articulated by Alfred Russel Wallace, "The Origin of Human Races and the Antiquity of Man," in Michael M. Biddis (ed.), *Images of Race* (New York, 1979), 37–54.

brought savagery and civilization face to face. But it was a mistake to think that the former could be transformed in a few lifetimes.

2   John Lubbock and the evolution of "savagery"

The liberal historian whose work earliest and most directly drew on the evolutionary revolution was John Lubbock. Scion of a wealthy London banking family, Lubbock became deeply interested in science as a child. Charles Darwin, who was a neighbor of the family, took the boy in hand and gave him a ringside seat at the re-conceptualization of evolutionary theory that was silently fructifying amid his Down House laboratories. Contributing his own slight experiments to supporting Darwin's theory, the twenty-five-year-old Lubbock had the privilege of helping to prepare the manuscript of *The Origin of Species* for the press. However, Lubbock understood (perhaps earlier than Darwin) the revolutionary implications of evolution for the history of mankind. By putting Brixham Cave together with *The Origin of Species*, he confirmed what some geologists had already suspected: Stone Age men had been walking the earth in the time of the mammoths, many millennia before Adam's day. In his own 1865 treatise, *Pre-Historic Times*, we can still savor a taste of Lubbock's excitement at the emergence of a new discipline, archaeology, that gave promise to throw an evidentiary bridge between the historian's era of written records and the geologist's mute fossil-attested eons of stone.[16]

Henceforth, human history and natural history would come together in a single scholarly endeavor that would trace the conjunctures and contingencies that buffeted human action, while simultaneously disclosing the hidden bio-social forces that shaped human capabilities over the long run. Lubbock's own contribution to this new history of the *longue durée* was his identification of the "neolithic" as a distinctive stage between the old stone age (paleolithic) and the bronze age fashioning of weapons and tools.[17] Yet the evidence for this and other eras of prehistory was fragmentary and ambiguous. To make the past come alive for the general reader, Lubbock drew on ethnological accounts of modern savages to flesh out the details of the European Stone Age that could not be discerned from excavations alone. Using illustrations, he showed how the implements of modern hunter-gatherers resembled the artifacts that

---

[16] Horace G. Hutchinson, *Life of Sir John Lubbock, Lord Avebury*, 2 vols. (London, 1914); J. W. Burrow, *Evolution and Society: A Study in Victorian Social Theory* (Cambridge, 1966), 228–34; Mark Patton, *Science, Politics and Business in the Work of Sir John Lubbock* (Aldershot, 2007); Adrian Desmond and James Moore, *Darwin: The Life of a Tormented Evolutionist* (New York, 1992), 302–3, 361.

[17] John Lubbock, *Pre-Historic Times* [1865] (London, 1869).

European archaeology had found. It seemed reasonable to infer that the "low mental culture" exhibited by these modern savages corresponded to an earlier stage of human evolution which white Europeans had left behind. At the same time, it was now clear that not all savages were equal. Some, like the Anglo-Saxons, passed quickly through the various stages of bio-social and technological development and became self-domesticated through their own efforts. Other peoples remained in a savage, mentally fossilized state.[18]

To address these more complex questions of development Lubbock published a follow-up study in 1869, entitled *The Origin of Civilization and the Primitive Condition of Man*. Probably influenced by E. B. Tylor's much more sophisticated *Researches into the Early History of Mankind* (1865), Lubbock now made a serious effort to examine not only the artifacts but also the marriage customs and religious beliefs of a wide range of savage and barbarian groups.[19] Like Tylor and Dilke, Lubbock acknowledged that race played a certain role in determining the behavior, habits, and civilizational aptitude of any given people. Yet he was struck by what he perceived as the similarities between groups which were widely separated by geography and ethnic origins, yet subsisted at the same civilizational stage. For Lubbock, as for Dilke, racial difference manifested itself primarily in the rate at which societies had passed through the same stadial sequence. The advanced races were those that passed quickly and successfully through an otherwise lengthy process that manifested itself in rising standards of morality. Thus marriage everywhere seemed to originate in naked lust, passing through successive stages of marriage by capture, by sale, and by treaty, before proceeding to increasingly complex forms of polygamous kinship exchange. Correspondingly, all religions had their roots in superstition. Those that were truly superior had advanced more quickly through the same forms of fetishism, animism, and idolatry before ascending to the heights of increasingly sophisticated monotheistic creeds. Certain vestiges of primitivism could always be found, even in the most advanced civilizations. The working classes often regressed to a lower form of culture when not under the proper guidance of elites. Conversely, primitive peoples usually exhibited some signs of spontaneous evolutionary progression, albeit at a rate that was so slow as to be almost undetectable.[20]

---

[18] Lubbock, *Pre-Historic Times*, 376–479.

[19] John Lubbock, *The Origin of Civilization and the Primitive Condition of Man* [1869] (London, 1882); E. B. Tylor, *Researches into the Early History of Mankind and the Development of Civilization* [1865] (London, 1870).

[20] Lubbock, *Origin of Civilization*, especially 72–387; Patton, *Sir John Lubbock*, 2–4, 23–52, 79–90.

Lubbock's archaeological and ethnological interests had to be squeezed into the odd hours when he could detach himself from his lucrative work at the bank. Yet he saw no contradiction between his weekday enterprise on the cutting edge of global capitalism and his weekend excavation of prehistoric caves. From Darwin, he had learned that even the most advanced forms of social organization and behavior had to be understood in the context of the origins from which they came. A close friend of Herbert Spencer, Thomas Huxley, and Joseph Hooker, Lubbock enjoyed a regular schedule of convivial dinners at which these four men traded ideas about an inevitable "law of progress" that each believed propelled the evolution of society. Lubbock's conviction that nineteenth-century Britain stood at the pinnacle of an evolution still in progress also fueled his decision to stand for Parliament. Here he focused his attention primarily on questions of education and the improvement of the British working and lower middle class. Between 1870 and 1874, he worked alongside Dilke to promote legislation for shorter hours and bank holidays, in the hopes that workingmen and clerks would use this leisure to take classes, attend lectures, and read (no doubt his) books.[21]

Unlike the savages that Lubbock analyzed in his scientific writings, these modern Anglo-Saxon artisans and clerks required only education and leisure to fit them for the world of capitalism and liberty. Since market competition had now replaced the competition of the cudgels, Lubbock looked forward to what was essentially a post-Darwinian future, in which life could be prolonged, the interdependence of nations could be fostered, and war would cease as a means of settling disputes. This visionary image of a nearly utopian liberal future clearly presupposed a process of mental and moral improvement that had rendered modern Britons biologically different creatures from the ancient (and modern) savages against whom they were juxtaposed. Where the former were adapted to a world of political campaigns, intellectual debates, and scientific innovations, the latter were relegated by Lubbock's gaze to a glacially moving landscape of primeval customs and irrational practices. Savage peoples never emerged as individuals in his books. They were wholly determined by their primitive character and encased in their low evolutionary stage. Yet, unlike Froude, who was inclined to "otherize" these delinquents, Lubbock (like many liberals) was inclined to naturalize them in the language of the family. Much like the European child, he observed, the adult savage tended to be moody, undisciplined, attracted to baubles, and addicted to dirty habits and superstitious beliefs.[22]

[21] Patton, *Sir John Lubbock*, 91–122.
[22] Lubbock, *Pre-Historic Times*, 121–4, 474–9, 502–4, 555–63.

Only in this context did the Empire enter Lubbock's thinking. As a young man he had felt no attraction to imperialism, associating it with the legacy of slavery, mercantilism, and a host of associated errors. These errors had led an earlier generation of (insufficiently liberal) Britons to degrade both themselves and their victims while impeding the forward march of progress. Lubbock's disposition was not improved by the colonial revolts that broke out in India in 1857, in New Zealand in 1861–3, and in Jamaica in 1865. Although he refused to join the Carlylean chorus of glee at their bloody suppression, his name was also conspicuously absent from the memorials and petitions circulated by his liberal friends (such as Darwin) in defense of native rights. By 1877, however, when Lubbock's ethnographic writings were largely complete, he changed his mind about the Empire and became an ardent imperialist, largely because he now saw British rule as just the right vehicle of supervisory benevolence that modern savages and other backward peoples required.[23]

In an article which he published in *The Nineteenth Century*, Lubbock depicted the British Empire of his day in a wholly positive light. The Americans, whom Dilke had perceived as successful assimilators, were now contrasted unfavorably with their British cousins, who recognized that primitive peoples had to be segregated and protected before they could function in the modern market world. Lubbock quoted with approval the words of an American bishop who complained of the way in which his supposedly liberty-loving republic "has spent five hundred million pounds in exterminating Indians," while

on the other side of the line are the same greedy, dominant Anglo-Saxon race, and the same heathen. They have not spent one dollar in Indian wars, and have had no Indian massacres. Why? In Canada the Indian treaties call these men "the Indian subjects of Her Majesty." When civilization approaches them they are placed on ample reservations, receive aid in civilization, have personal rights in property, are amenable to law, and protected by law, have schools, and Christian people send them the best teachers.[24]

3   Empire and the classification of racial and evolutionary others

Lubbock's conviction that savages had to be protected was widely shared by other Liberals. His belief that reservations provided them with secure

---

[23] Patton, *Sir John Lubbock*, 123–38; John Lubbock, "On the Imperial Policy of Great Britain," *The Nineteenth Century*, 1 (1877), 37–49.
[24] Lubbock, "Imperial Policy of Britain," 44.

enclaves in which they could be exposed to carefully calibrated doses of civilization, however, reflects his distance from the actual business of empire. Ironically, Froude had more empirical experience on this point. On the ground, in Asia, Africa, and America, the distinction between savagery and civilization was never so dualistically neat. The colonial dependencies, from Barbados to Assam, were not benevolent havens for the protection of savages. These environments contained a multitude of complexly interacting social groups: white planters, indentured laborers, and a host of diverse and often divergent indigenes, all at various stages in social development. Such environments were really more like quasi-Darwinian habitats in which various groups competed for resources and space. What rendered such conceptualizations compatible with eirenic Victorian notions of comity and progress was a neo-Lamarckian belief in the inheritance of acquired characteristics that was shared by nearly all lay and scientific Darwinians, not least by Darwin himself.[25]

In this view, British imperialism could be conceived as a kind of artificial selection that would guide development in the right direction and speed the process up in a manner that was still calibrated and controlled. Some indigenous groups, like the Native Americans, Tasmanians, Australian aborigines, and (possibly) New Zealand Maori, seemed destined for extinction, and metropolitans could bemoan but not alter their fate.[26] Others, notably those of African or Asian origin, were reclaimable, albeit only when they shed their debased indigenous folkways and allowed metropolitan imperialists to guide their evolutionary path. How long would this process of guided improvement last? "In the course of two or three centuries," Harry Johnston predicted, "the negroes of British Africa will only differ from their white fellow-subjects in the colour of their skins." But for some time to come, the forefathers of these ultimately civilized men of color "will require to submit themselves to our guidance and control." By contrast, Richard Burton, Edward Blyden, and Winwood Reade all regarded Christianity as too advanced for black Africans, who should be converted to Islam during this intermediate (imperial) phase. Even Samuel Baker, who regarded "African savages [as] quite on a level of that of the brute," reluctantly allowed that "perhaps

---

[25] Peter J. Bowler, *The Eclipse of Darwinism: Anti-Darwinian Evolution Theories in the Decades around 1900* (Baltimore, 1983), 58–106.

[26] A few Victorian histories, such as G. W. Rusden's *Auretanga: Groans of the Maories* (Christchurch, 1975), did take a more nuanced and sophisticated approach to the suffering of indigenous peoples and British injustice. However, the circulation of these books was restricted to small niche markets, and did not have much effect on the dominant discourse.

after some centuries, we may expect a certain class of civilization from the negroes."[27]

These assessments were a far cry from the blithe assumptions of David Livingstone, who, as recently as the mid-1850s, had envisioned that commerce and Christianity together might civilize Africa within a few decades. Yet the more the new evolutionists contemplated the stasis of "backward" peoples, the more they became convinced that the true regulator of the velocity of evolution lay in the bio-social (i.e. more or less Lamarckian) underpinnings of race. These conclusions were greatly reinforced by the colonial resistance movements of the post-1857 period.[28] The Indian Mutiny, the Maori King Movement, Irish Fenianism, and the Jamaica Revolt were all taken to indicate that even semi-civilized groups which had been under imperial tutelage for several generations could degenerate back to the savagery of their ancestors, if metropolitan controls on their improvement were prematurely relaxed. The West Indian freedman, warned Anthony Trollope, had become a race dangerously betwixt and between "No country of their own" and yet neither "any country of adoption." "No memory of Africa, but no approach to the civilization of his white fellow creature." Such people were "a servile race fitted by nature for the hardest physical work," in whom a little religion and a little education had become dangerous things. In the years that followed the Jamaica revolt, observers like Charles Kingsley and W. J. Gardner confirmed the prescience of Trollope's views.[29]

Not surprisingly, this changed orientation to colonial peoples was most clearly manifested in India after the 1857 Revolt. As Heather Streets has recently demonstrated, it became the basis for a complete reorganization of the Indian Army, as the relatively high-caste Bengali Sepoys were accused of being ringleaders of rebellion and were replaced by northern Sikhs and Gurkhas (often referred to as martial castes), who became the new Highlanders of the later nineteenth century. Here evolutionary backwardness was not necessarily deemed a disadvantage, if it was combined

---

[27] Johnston and Baker, quoted in H. A. C. Cairns, *Prelude to Imperialism: British Reactions to Central African Society, 1840–1890* (London, 1965), 90, 204–5, 207–14. For Winwood Reade, see *Savage Africa, Being the Narrative of a Tour in Equatorial, Southwestern and Northwestern Africa* (New York, 1864), 431–52.

[28] David Livingstone, *Missionary Travels in Africa* [1857], 2 vols. (Santa Barbara, 2001); Stocking, *Victorian Anthropology*, 78–109; Stocking, *Race, Culture and Evolution*, 110–32; Bolt, *Victorian Attitudes to Race*, 75–230.

[29] Charles Kingsley, *At Last: Christmas in the West Indies* [1871] (London, 1905), 16–28, 36–9, 51, 285–302; William James Gardner, *A History of Jamaica* (London, 1873), 461–3, 472–96; James Belich, *The Victorian Interpretation of Racial Conflict: The Maori, the British and the New Zealand Wars* (Montreal, 1986).

with the simple virtues of courage and loyalty.[30] W. W. Hunter, the most accomplished historian of the later Victorian Raj, was also fascinated by the virtues of evolutionary simplicity. His *Annals of Rural Bengal*, published in 1868, contained a penetrating ethnography of a cluster of hill tribes, the Santals, whom he deemed to be at the evolutionary stage of the Ancient Germans. They had "carried with them ... a certain degree of civilization and agricultural habits which hundreds, perhaps thousands of years of civilization have not been able to efface." In 1855, the Santals had rebelled, but Hunter saw that they had many legitimate grievances against usurious moneylenders and excessive taxation. Redressing these abuses would turn them into loyal workers, especially in railway construction and on tea plantations, where heavy labor was required. In later years Hunter was put in charge of a massive 128-volume statistical gazetteer of India, which combined geology, history, ethnology, anthropometry, philology, and mythology to map out the subcontinent's myriad social groups. To make sense of this mass of indigestible data, Hunter came to rely ever more completely on reified notions of caste and race.[31]

The most sweeping early practitioner of the new racial and evolutionary thinking was the Liberal Indian administrator and ethnologist Sir George Campbell. Sir George was the scion of a minor branch of the great clan Campbell, which had made so many contributions to the Scottish Whig aristocracy. Campbell's uncle had risen through the English bar to the positions of Chief Justice and Lord Chancellor, while his father had made a career in the EIC. Following in his father's footsteps, young George went to India in 1843 and steadily rose in the company hierarchy. Playing a significant role in the annexation of the Punjab, Campbell published a book, *Modern India*, a decade later, which surveyed the vast array of indigenous tribes and races in India while drawing heavily on Elphinstone's earlier account of the subcontinent's history. The only justification for British conquest had been the enforcement of peace, Campbell acknowledged, after centuries of internecine conflict between

---

[30] Heather Streets, *Martial Races: The Military Race and Masculinity in British Imperial Culture, 1857–1914* (Manchester, 2004), especially 52–115.

[31] W. W. Hunter, *Annals of Rural Bengal* [1868] (London, 1883), 14–260; W. W. Hunter, *A Brief History of the Indian People* (London, 1884). The application of a scientific culture to late Victorian India is examined in Gayan Prakash, *Another Reason: Science and the Imagination of Modern India* (Oxford, 1999). On the application of racial classifications see the following chapters in Peter Robb (ed.), *The Concept of Race in South Asia* (Oxford, 1995): Susan Bayly, "Caste and Race in the Colonial Ethnography of India," 165–218; Crispin Bates, "Race, Caste and Tribe in Central India: The Early Origins of Indian Anthropometry," 219–59; Lionel Caplin, "Martial Gurkhas: The Persistence of a British Military Discourse on 'Race,'" 260–81; and Indira Choudhury-Sengupta, "The Effeminate and the Masculine: Nationalism and Race in Colonial Bengal," 282–303.

different ethnic, religious, and caste groups. The continuation of Britain's rule, however, could be justified only by her role as a catalyst for modernization: building bridges, roads, railroads, telegraphs, harbors, and irrigation networks that would enable India's peoples to find their most advantageous niche in the burgeoning system of capitalist production and exchange.[32]

Campbell's thinking was greatly affected by the revolt of 1857, which he played a role in repressing. Henceforth, his primary goal for India would be political stability and the preservation of British geo-political supremacy. This change in his perspective manifested itself in a new-found emphasis on racial evolution and ethnology. Campbell believed that the Mutiny had been caused by lax administration in the army, and that the overwhelming bulk of India's peasants remained amenable to British rule. The fact that so few had risen up when British authority was in jeopardy could be taken as an indication of their satisfaction with the *status quo*. Nevertheless, he now worried that market forces were creating vulnerabilities for the peasant, demonstrated most notably by the Orissa famine of 1866, which he witnessed firsthand.[33] On the basis of his administrative experience, Campbell concluded that neither the zamindari nor the ryotwari land settlements had been entirely satisfactory, since the first had conjured up an artificial aristocracy, while the second had turned the peasant into an economic free agent before he had learned to think in utilitarian terms. Yet India was a very different place from Froude's savage Africa, since the vestiges of a once-vast civilization remained. Drawing on the ideas of the Irish tenant right movement, Campbell argued that similar notions of a traditional moral economy could be detected in India, where the state was all-powerful and a more even balance between landlord and peasant obtained. Through customary rents and partial peasant proprietorship, Campbell hoped, there could be a revival of traditional village institutions. Local self-government would provide an attractive alternative to anti-British sentiment on a national plane.[34]

Campbell believed that the stabilization of Victorian India depended on a proper understanding of race. To this end, in 1865 he published an *Ethnology of India*, which combined evidence from physiognomy,

---

[32] George Campbell, *Modern India* (London, 1852); George Campbell, *Memoirs of my Indian Career*, 2 vols. (London, 1893), I: 1–209; *DNB*, supplement XXI (New York, 1909), 383–5.

[33] Campbell, *Indian Career*, I: 210–305, II: 1–342.

[34] George Campbell, *India as it May Be: A Proposed Government and Policy* (London, 1853), 224–36, 394–438; George Campbell, *The Irish Land* (London, 1869); George Campbell, "The Tenure of Land in India," in J. W. Probyn (ed.), *Systems of Land Tenure in Various Countries* (London, 1881), 213–90.

language, religion, customs, and "mental characteristics" to divide Indians into three basic types. The people of the first were described as "fine Caucasian" Aryans, mostly in the north; the second as "Negrito types," mostly in the south; and the third as various shades of mixtures in between. According to Campbell, this pattern had been created by a *longue durée* historical process, in which several waves of Aryan invaders from central Asia had conquered the darker indigenous inhabitants of the subcontinent, creating the caste system to preserve their racial supremacy. A certain amount of interbreeding with their inferiors had occurred, and this had spawned the vast system of intermediate castes that occupied India by the Victorian epoch.[35]

Campbell was not much interested in the higher, more Aryan, castes, whose character was already well known. More in need of ethnological study were the tribes "in the lowest stage of barbarism," who were "modern representatives of one of the earliest phases in the history of mankind." Unlike Lubbock, who saw only their backwardness, Campbell hoped that these simple people might play a constructive imperial role. Such primitive races, he opined, might prove extremely malleable. If inculcated with "the art of agriculture and habits of industry," they might "make the best laborers and colonists in the country." Looking to the system of indentured service as a means of transferring low-caste or tribal Indians from the subcontinent, where they were superfluous, to the Caribbean, where their labor was required, Campbell used one of his furloughs to travel to the United States, where he conducted his own investigation of American reconstruction. Like Dilke, Campbell regarded the southern Negro as a very backward but eminently civilizable specimen. This lesson from across the Atlantic was definitely transferable to the British Empire. Throughout the African and South Asian world there were hardy, potentially industrious peoples whose labor could be harnessed for productive purposes, if only their true racial character could be understood.[36]

---

[35] George Campbell, *The Ethnology of India* [1865] (London, 1872), quote on 8–9. See also Susan Bayly, "Caste and Race in Colonial Ethnography," in Robb (ed.), *Race in South Asia*, 165–218, as well as her *Caste, Society and Politics in India: From the Eighteenth Century to the Modern Age* (Cambridge, 1999). Most recently, the Victorian construction of caste has been revisited by Nicholas Dirks, *Castes of Mind: Colonialism and the Making of Modern India* (Princeton, 2001), and Shruti Kapila, "Race Matters: Orientalism and Religion, India and Beyond, c.1770–1880," *Modern Asian Studies*, 41.3 (2007), 471–513, who examines the early history of race studies in Calcutta.

[36] Campbell, *Ethnology of India*; George Campbell, *White and Black: The Outcome of a Visit to the United States* (London, 1879), vi–xii, 111–99. See also his later *The British Empire* (London, 1887) and "On the Races of India, as Traced in Existing Tribes and Castes," *Journal of the Ethnological Society of London*, NS, 1 (1868–9), 128–40; and *Address to the Anthropology Section of the British Association* (London, 1886).

Toward the end of his life, Campbell surveyed the entire British Empire to underscore its contribution to British wealth and power. In a world where industrial capitalism was spreading to other western nations, and where market relations were penetrating everywhere around the globe, the Empire was no longer a luxury that liberals could dispense with. Like Froude and Dilke, Campbell understood that if Britain wanted to compete in this world of industrial giants, she would have to mobilize the resources of her global periphery more effectively. At the same time, he was highly skeptical of the plans for imperial federation that were being bruited about. The white settler colonies, which he deemed proper candidates for inclusion, were too prone to independence. Let them become autonomous, he argued, and they would remain culturally bound to their Anglo-Saxon cousins, even as they pursued their own (sometimes conflicting) geo-political and economic policies. Britain's own future, according to Campbell, lay in her relations with her tropical, racially mixed, colonies. These were lands for which white laborers were not fitted. As a result, imperial administrators had to be sent out to harness the labor of colored peoples, who would generate the raw materials that metropolitan industry required. Since such colonies easily degenerated into chaos, it was essential to understand how they should be administered and ruled.[37]

As in his earlier writings, Campbell emphasized the enormous possibilities for transferring colored labor from India, where it was superfluous, to Mauritius, the Caribbean, Burma, and other plantation colonies, where inexpensive workers were required. But now he was more attuned to the problems in the indenture system, and saw the need for firm metropolitan regulation and control. Rules were needed to protect these colored migrants, and this, paradoxically, required placing them in a special legal category that would not be defined by the rights of the freeborn Englishman, but by the disabilities and limitations of their race.[38] The biggest problem, according to Campbell, lay in the Crown colonies, such as South Africa and the Caribbean, where the population was racially mixed. Here the legacy of slavery had cast its long shadow far into the nineteenth century. Beset with racially exclusionary franchises, these colonies were dominated by white oligarchies of planters and adventurers who oppressed the colored majority. Pressed too hard, these colored laborers would become unproductive, or even revolt. Not surprisingly perhaps, Campbell's ideal model for the management of colored peoples was the Indian Raj in which he worked. Here the management of lesser peoples was entrusted to professional administrators, sent out from the

---

[37] Campbell, *British Empire*, 1–100.   [38] Campbell, *British Empire*, 31–9, 150–60.

metropolis, who ruled them paternalistically in their own interest, while also figuring out how to make imperialism pay. As a result there would be no need for dangerous instruments like colonial legislatures, through which whites oppressed the natives in the dysfunctional Crown colonies, while the latter nursed ambitions for self-government that could not be sustained.[39]

Given Campbell's general perspective on racial competence, the one type that had no place in his idealized imperial vision consisted of the English educated urban middle-class (bhadralok) liberals, whose development had been precipitated by Rammohun Roy, Elphinstone, and Macaulay, and whose rapid Victorian expansion far exceeded what any of these early nineteenth-century prognosticators dreamed. Not only had an extensive English-language education system been developed, but the prestigious Presidency College in Calcutta had been raised to full university status, garnering 1,300 entrants and graduating 250 annual BAs by the time Campbell wrote. Clearly different in color and physiognomy from Britons like Campbell, but even farther removed from the simple colonial peasant, these men were anomalies in Campbell's paternalist vision. Their articulate expressions of public opinion in magazines and newspapers, as well as their increasingly clamorous requests for participatory government, made Campbell extremely nervous. "The educated natives," he acknowledged, "are very nice people; one cannot but like them individually." He only objected when they pressed this individuality so far as to demand participation in the political sphere, either as elected office-holders or as administrative officials. "In mere intellectual capacity they are our equals," Campbell continued, "but I do not think they have the same energy and backbone of the European; if they had, we should not be where we are in India."[40]

Such people were fit for local government, but parliamentary institutions were beyond their ken. Their demand for access to leadership posts in the Indian Civil Service would destroy the impartiality of the governing body, empowering a new hothouse clique at the expense of traditional Muslim and Hindu elites. In a sharp post-Macaulay reversal, even the English-language proficiency of the bhadralok was now held against them. Campbell had grave doubts as to whether a young Hindu, who was brought up in the Presidency Colleges "and possibly has a year or two in England, and so acquires not only much European knowledge, but even a good deal of European feeling, is not at the same time cut off from the intimate native knowledge of former days." As he followed the careers of

---

[39] Campbell, *British Empire*, 101–49, 161–84.   [40] Campbell, *British Empire*, 75.

these men, Campbell saw them through the racial and evolutionary lens that he had honed during his years of working for the Raj. Viewed in this manner, they did not appear as like-minded fellow liberals, but as impertinent babus who had the temerity to believe that they were his equals, to question the wisdom and judgment of disinterested professionals like himself.[41]

Campbell's professed contempt for Calcutta's middle-class intellectuals is belied by his patent fear that their newspapers, speeches, and books might actually resonate with the masses, thereby dispensing with the need for outside race-managers like himself.[42] What made the bhadralok worrisome was the cognitive dissonance they created in the racial order. Because they did not fit into the "master-race" scenario of evolution, they could not be permitted the political empowerment that was appropriate for a fully modernized polity. Campbell's attitudes on this score are critical, since they help us to understand how good metropolitan Liberals could so sharply retreat from the aggressive reformism of the 1830s and reverse the Macaulayite vision of creating a collaborative bourgeoisie. A full exploration of the implications of these changes however was beyond Campbell's ken. To work out the finer points of this differential liberal vision – political freedom in the metropolis, enlightened despotism in the colonies – it is necessary to turn to Sir Henry Maine, who developed the same ideas on an altogether higher intellectual plane.[43]

4   The evolution of Aryanism: Henry Maine and imperial racial divergence

Though his ideas were developed by reflecting on the Empire, Maine's authority was derived from his precocious conquest of English scholarship. At Cambridge, he entered as a student in 1840, graduating to a fellowship in 1844 and rising to the Regius Professorship in Civil Law in 1847. Called to the Bar in 1850, he delivered a course of lectures at Middle Temple that became the basis for a boldly original treatise,

---

[41] Naoroji's critique of the "drain," which might have appealed to Campbell's liberalism, elicited only unctuous defensiveness: "Well, it is not tribute, but is paid for civil and military services, loans, railways, industrial investments and the rest" (Campbell, *British Empire*, 70, 82; Campbell, *Indian Career*, 314–15).

[42] Campbell, *British Empire*, 73–4.

[43] Alongside Maine, it is difficult not to give the top spot to John Stuart Mill. For recent examinations of Mill on India, "savagery," and race, see Lynn Zastoupil, *John Stuart Mill and India* (Stanford, 1994); Michael Levin, *J. S. Mill on Civilization and Barbarism* (London, 2004); Uday Singh Mehta, *Liberalism and Empire: A Study in Nineteenth-Century British Liberal Thought* (Chicago, 1999), 97–114; and Jennifer Pitts, *A Turn to Empire: The Rise of Imperial Liberalism in Britain and France* (Princeton, 2005), 123–62.

Ancient Law (1861). This seminal work presents a preliminary formulation of what has arguably become the central dichotomy of social science – the notion that traditional societies are initially bound together by bonds of *status* (e.g. kinship or hierarchy), while modernization entails their replacement by (impermanent, voluntaristic) relations of *contract*.[44]

Although Maine's treatise was published a mere two years after *The Origin of Species*, his central ideas pre-dated his acquaintance with Darwin's work. As J. W. Burrow has shown, the volume was intended as a corrective to Benthamite utilitarianism, and was inspired by the historicism of German philology. Nevertheless, Maine's book was read by a Darwin-primed audience, and he hoped it would become the cornerstone of a new evolutionary science. Like a fossil-hunting geologist, Maine showed his readers how to sift the surviving evidence from various textual strata. From such fragmentary materials, he contended, it was possible to reconstruct the fundamental structures of law, custom, and community in the past. Even more ambitiously, it was possible to infer the process by which these structures had changed (or failed to change) from one era to the next. In *Ancient Law*, Maine pioneered what he would later call "the comparative method." By juxtaposing the history of two or more societies at a considerable distance in time or space, the search for common features could provide a basis for inferring either a common genealogical origin and/or a comparable evolutionary stage.[45]

Indeed, Maine's book is not so much a conventional history as an archaeological excavation of Roman jurisprudence, designed to identify the moment when individuals and events broke out of their customary (status-bound) enclosures, and narratives worthy of (contract-making) record commenced. Maine seeks to explain why such narratives (and such contracts) had not arisen in places like India, and why history was the

---

[44] M. E. Grant Duff, *Sir Henry Maine: A Brief Memoir of his Life* (New York, 1892); George Feaver, *From Status to Contract: A Biography of Sir Henry Maine, 1822–1888* (London, 1969); as well as George Feaver, "The Victorian Values of Sir Henry Maine," in A. Diamond (ed.), *The Victorian Achievement of Sir Henry Maine: A Centennial Reappraisal* (Cambridge, 1991), 28–52; Henry Maine, *Ancient Law: Its Connection with the Early History of Society and its Relation to Modern Ideas* [1861] (n.p., 1986).

[45] Burrow, *Evolution and Society*, 139–40. In Victorian social science (as in Victorian biology) there was intense debate as to how far such common features should be interpreted as products of shared genealogies, or as indications of two unrelated societies following parallel evolutionary tracks. The distinction can be framed as one between "trees" and "ladders." Thomas Trautmann, *Aryans and British India* (Berkeley, 1997). On this point, Maine was ambiguous or, more likely, intent on having it both ways. The argument is that some branches of the tree rise up the ladder more quickly than others. In *Lewis Henry Morgan and the Invention of Kinship* (Berkeley, 1987), 179–86, Trautmann makes the case that Maine's thinking was explicitly evolutionary, although probably not Darwinian, at the time when he wrote *Ancient Law*.

product of men in the west: although there is no reason to think that they consciously influenced one another, Maine's "comparative method" is analogous to Lubbock's juxtaposition of archaeology with ethnology.[46] Where Lubbock compared prehistoric Europeans with modern savages, Maine compared ancient Rome with modern India to give his evolutionism an arrow of directionality. Of course, Maine's point was not to argue that either ancient Romans or modern Indians were savages. On the contrary, he saw both groups as a cut above savagery in evolutionary terms. Yet the same arguments that Lubbock was making about early human evolution could be applied to societies at the next evolutionary stage. To find the common ancestor of modern savages and Europeans it was necessary to go back to the dawning of mankind. The ancestors of modern Britons and Indians had diverged much more recently (c.1500 BC) with the separation of the western and eastern branches of the Aryan race. Yet where the first separation had enabled a few favored races (e.g. early Aryans and Semites) to rise from savagery to early civilization, the second separation had enabled even more favored races (e.g. Romans and Teutons) to rise to a higher level of civilization still.[47]

In Maine's deepest legal and philological layer, Roman history was lost in the preliterate mire of unrecorded custom that had entombed the early stages of every primordial human group. During this stage the individual was encased within the family, unable to act (or record) on his own. Bits and pieces of Roman customary law were gradually recovered, however, in surviving written documents or oral traditions. Here was the moment when Rome took the first decisive turn from a traditional community based on ascribed personal status to a proto-modern society, grounded in individuality and contract. Maine fastened on the codification of Rome's Twelve Tables (c.450 BC) as the event that precipitated the first transition from status to contract. Envisioned as a fossil remnant of an earlier era, this document was also identified as the key progressive instrument that succeeding generations re-sculpted in their societal advance.[48] Early codification of the law, at a time when it was still flexible, gave the Romans a competitive advantage over other traditional peoples. A simple code like the Twelve Tables was sufficiently prescriptive,

---

[46] Maine, *Ancient Law*, 1–36, 93–141.

[47] See Chapter 2 above for the early development of Aryanism. Trautmann, *Invention of Kinship*, 185–6, contends that Maine adhered to the biblical chronology in 1861 when he published *Ancient Law*, but was shortly thereafter impelled (like so many others) to accept the antiquity of man. This had little substantive impact on his work, since he chose to restrict future investigations to the Aryan societies where he could draw on the philological evidence with which he felt comfortable.

[48] Maine, *Ancient Law*, 1–60.

according to Maine, to provide for the protection of property and the stability of the family and to specify modes of inheritance, court procedures, legal punishments, and enforcement of contracts. At the same time, it was fluid enough to permit some adult men to break free from the collective power of the extended family. Patrilineal kinship groups thus evolved into self-governing confederations of male householders, with structures that were flexible and open to change. Religion was separated from law and politics, while law eventually gave birth to tripartite institutions of legislation, enforcement, and interpretation.[49]

In Republican Rome, this meant that the adult male patriarch, the *patria potestas*, forged a new realm of free association. Henceforth he could contract with those whom he chose and risk his person and his property in such ventures as the law no longer positively forbade. In this manner the free man entered the annals of recorded history as an epic hero, a Livian citizen, or a Tacitean patrician, looking outward to imperial enterprise. Women, children, slaves, and other dependents remained subsumed within the households of their lords and masters. Such was the liberating power of contract that eventually they too would gain some measure of legal protection, if not full opportunity to exercise public power.[50] By contrast, according to Maine, the Hindu Code of Manu (c.200 AD) was formalized at a much later point in India's Aryan civilization, and therefore came at a moment when this civilization had already begun to decay. As a result, the Brahman patriarch missed out on the political experience of republicanism. He became a slave to his religion, which turned him inward, unfitted him for citizenship, and rendered him effete. With its baroque excess of ritual and its exclusionary proscriptions, Manu's Code enfeebled the entire Indian population. Unable to rise to the individuality of historical action, Indian men remained immobilized in a frozen evolutionary state.[51]

With its catchy phrase "from status to contract," Maine's book brought him instant acclaim among British academics, and an offer to serve as Legal Member of the Viceroy's Council in India, the same post that Macaulay had occupied three decades earlier. Upon arrival in Calcutta in 1862, Maine initially saw his mandate as advancing the Macaulayite project of rapid modernization – dragooning India onto the world-historical stage. In the cautious climate of the post-Mutiny Raj, however, Maine saw that nervous officials – even Liberals like Campbell – had come

[49] Maine, *Ancient Law*, 12–17; Burrow, *Evolution and Society*, 137–78; Stefan Collini, Donald Winch, and John Burrow, *That Noble Science of Politics: A Study in Nineteenth-Century Intellectual History* (Cambridge, 1983), 209–46.
[50] Maine, *Ancient Law*, 139–41.   [51] Maine, *Ancient Law*, 5, 14–15.

to fear the destabilizing backlash that might follow from over-rapid change.[52] In the last analysis, the stability of India stood or fell on the welfare of her two hundred million peasants. Yet Maine could see that the peasants' sudden exposure to the icy blasts of contract was far more precipitous and destabilizing than what the natural course of evolution would have allowed. The railroads, ports, and administrative "improvements" that had been set in motion since the days of Elphinstone and Macaulay had indeed forced many Indian peasants into the maws of the world market so that they could provide raw materials (e.g. cotton and indigo) for Britain's factories. To a favored few, this had brought new-found prosperity. As the price of these primary products fluctuated, however, the subsistence of many peasants had become dangerously strained. The "Blue Mutiny" of 1860 and the Orissa famine of 1866 served as warnings of combustible materials even more volatile than those that had set 1857 aflame.[53]

Under these circumstances, Maine came to agree with many other post-1857 Anglo-Indian administrators that the modernization of rural India had been moving too fast. Unlike run-of-the-mill bureaucrats, however, he believed that his evolutionary theory – seemingly abstract – provided a practical remedy for slowing the pace of artificially induced social change. By his own account, modern India was a museum of collective, protective institutions that continued to function long after their analogues had disappeared in the west. In particular, the Indian peasant village possessed still-living traditions of collective property, joint inheritance, and local self-government that were capable of resisting the destabilizing impact of market forces, if only they were supported rather than undermined by the authority of the British government. In a series of powerfully argued minutes and speeches, Maine made the case that these institutions and traditions should be reinforced by officialdom because they were fitted to the Indian character at its current evolutionary stage.[54]

---

[52] Feaver, *From Status to Contract*, 65–109; Duff, *Henry Maine*, 1–84; Sandra den Otter, "Freedom of Contract, the Market and Imperial Law-Making," in Mark Bevir and Frank Trentmann (eds.), *Critiques of Capital in Modern Britain and America* (London, 2002), 49–72; Sandra den Otter, "The Political Economy of Empire: Freedom of Contract and 'Commercial Civilization' in Colonial India," in Martin Daunton and Frank Trentmann (eds.), *Worlds of Political Economy: Knowledge and Power in the Nineteenth and Twentieth Centuries* (London, 2004), 69–94; Karuna Mantena, "Law and 'Tradition': Henry Maine and the Theoretical Origins of Indirect Rule," in Andrew Lewis and Michael Lobban (eds.), *Law and History*, VI (Oxford, 2004), 159–88.

[53] Blair B. Kling, *The Blue Mutiny: The Indigo Disturbances in Bengal, 1859–1862* (Philadelphia, 1966). See also essays by G. Johnson and C. A. Bayly in Diamond (ed.), *Victorian Achievement of Sir Henry Maine*, 376–97.

[54] Reprinted in Duff, *Henry Maine*, 85–433.

When Maine returned to England, he published a new set of lectures, entitled *Village Communities in the East and West* (1871), which showed how his position had subtly changed. Modern India was once again presented as the past of Aryan Europe, but its law was no longer viewed through the dysfunctional lens of Manu. Rather, Indian law was apprehended directly and positively through the congeries of local village customs that Maine had encountered in his travels and through his extensive perusal of settlement reports.[55] So far from indicating decadence or senescence, these informal village codes were now deemed to be so brilliantly adaptive that they had survived virtually unchanged for over 2,000 years. Unlike western law, which had grown remote from the masses because it had risen to the level of abstract concepts, India's unwritten village law remained woven into the concrete fabric of popular life. Organically enveloping the peasant community, it organized villagers' labor in collective modes of production, enforced normative conceptions of justice, and preserved timeworn patriarchal family structures that remained impervious to outside influence.[56]

Paradoxically, it was English law and British capitalism that were now perceived as endangering this simple, idyllic life. Yet Maine could hardly indict his own regime for the evils of social destabilization that followed in its wake: "We do not innovate or destroy in mere ignorance. We rather change because we cannot help it. Whatever be the nature and value of that bundle of influences which we call Progress, nothing can be more certain than that, when a society is once touched by it, it spreads like Contagion."[57] Maine did not think it was possible or desirable for this progress to be arrested. But having set the forces of progress in motion, British administrators had a responsibility to regulate their velocity. Indian civilization was built on the circumscription of individual action, and this dictated a slow evolutionary pace. Since Indians were deemed to inhabit a world of communal property and inherited custom, it would be unwise to initiate precipitous innovations that might jeopardize their status within ascribed hereditary groups.[58]

In this picture – unconditionally bifurcated between modern west and backward east – there is no place for the spontaneously modernizing

---

[55] Sir Henry Sumner Maine, *Village Communities in the East and West* (New York, 1889), 7–25, 60–2, 76–8, 103–28. Karuna Mantena has suggested that this provided the fundamental intellectual underpinning for the entire system that came to be called "indirect rule" ("Law and 'Tradition,'" 170–88).

[56] Maine, *Village Communities*, 103–28, 175–201.

[57] Maine, "The Effects of Observation of India on Modern European Thought," in *Village Communities*, 205–39, quote on 237–8.

[58] Duff, *Henry Maine*, 59–60. "Each individual in India is a slave to the customs of the group to which he belongs" (Maine, *Village Communities*, 13–14).

Indian. Maine's ideal-type Indian was a Brahman traditionalist or a lore-laden peasant, deeply invested in the Raj's belated quest for stability. Of course, he was well aware of the existence of western-educated progressives, but they were restricted, he claimed, to a small Calcutta clique whose talent for self-promotion gave them a spurious appearance of accomplishment. Not one normally to trade in crude racial stereotypes, Maine let slip a few remarks about the "wily Bengali," a "calculating, astute and wide-a-wake character" who "knows his interests as well as the keenest Englishman, and is quite as hard a hand at a bargain."[59] The problem with such people was that their astuteness at contracts was a mark of inauthenticity. They had absorbed the visible trappings of an English education, but did not exhibit true English integrity. They professed cosmopolitan sentiments, but practiced these ideals only within their own group. They were, in short, superficial creations who could only mime a simulacrum of British modernity. By demanding individual rights that were beyond their evolutionary competence, they placed British officialdom in a quandary: "The Anglo-Indian Government is bound, by the moral conditions of its existence, to apply the modern principle of equality in all its various forms to the people of India ... but it has to make this application among a collection of men to whom the idea of equality is unknown or hateful." Maine did not object to a Bengal Legislative Council half-filled "with Bengal civilians and educated Bengal Natives," appointed by the British "to legislate for that ... wealthy and civilized province." Such people, however, were unfit to govern the vast expanse of rural India, which was still too deeply sunk in the anonymity of "status" to be represented by anyone but the British *ultra-patria potestas*, i.e. himself.[60]

Between Maine and the Bengali bhadralok one senses a connection missed. In 1862 he was appointed Vice-Chancellor of Calcutta University, and he marveled at the explosive growth of this institution of higher education, which modeled itself to a degree on his beloved Cambridge. Yet there was much about these students that Maine did not like: they were overly precocious, excessively imaginative, in some ways too imitative of English manners, in other ways not nearly British enough.[61] Most of all, they were too attached to their own history, which they interpreted in a way that offended Maine's evolutionary assumptions. "It is very difficult," he conceded, "for any people to feel self-respect, if they have no pride in their own annals." But some Indian students carried this romanticization of the Indian past "to

[59] Quoted in den Otter, "Freedom of Contract," 55.
[60] Quoted in Duff, *Henry Maine*, 40, 362–91.
[61] Maine, "Addresses to University of Calcutta," in *Village Communities*, 240–89.

extravagant length." When they vaunted Hinduism as the cradle of the world's first civilization or as the enduring font of elevated spirituality, these students were giving Maine back his orientalism, with the valences reversed. Some of them actually believed "that it was better to be a Brahmin or a scribe attached to some half-mythical Hindu king, than to follow one of the prosaic learned professions which the English have created." This Indian pride in being descended from the racially superior Aryans was a sentiment that Maine could hardly deny, since he had done so much to prove the point himself. But "depend upon it," he warned the students, "Very little is practically gained by the Native when it is proved, beyond contradiction, that he is of the same race with the Englishman ... Be sure that [this racial consanguinity] is a real equality. No man ever yet genuinely despised, however he might hate, his intellectual equal."[62]

This was odd, to close off the thought of equality with a *non sequitur* about hate. Maine invokes the equality of the Republic of Letters, yet he seems unnerved at the prospect that these students might really become his equals, and create their own national history and consciousness that were not a straightforward reflection of his own. "The British rulers of India," Maine once famously quipped, "are like men bound to make their watches keep true time in two longitudes at once." The reality perhaps was exactly the opposite: the longitudes were rapidly coming together, knit by British railroads, steamships, print, and telegraphy. Metropolitan-cum-historical time and colonial-cum-evolutionary time no longer beat to different rhythms, and were fusing together into a single chronometry. It was the specter of such a fully egalitarian future, in which racial, gender, or occupational status would no longer be constraining, that Maine envisioned in theory but found disconcerting in practice. It was this fear, perhaps, which led him to write *Village Communities*, and to re-figure all-too-rapidly modernizing Indians as the eternal child-Aryans who could not grow up.[63]

5   R. C. Dutt: evolution and the liberal middle-class other

Very likely in the audience at Maine's convocation speeches were two Presidency College students, Surendranath Banerjea and Romesh Chandra Dutt. Sons of long-anglicized Bengali Brahman families, they saw no contradiction in preparing for modern learned professions while

---

[62] Maine, "Addresses to University of Calcutta," quotes on 253, 289.
[63] Maine, "Observation of India," 237.

still venerating half-mythical Hindu kings. Within a few years (1868) they would travel to London together to study for, and pass, the Indian Civil Service (hereafter referred to as ICS) exam. Thus inducted into the covenanted service, they would become the first natives eligible for advancement into the high administrative elite. Although Banerjea was expelled from the service a few years later, Dutt spent the 1870s working his way slowly up the ICS promotion track. His time in London had corresponded with the 1868 election, and he had been struck by the way in which

Every Englishman takes a deep interest in politics and is either a conservative or a liberal ... Every man in this country considers himself as a constituent of a great nation, and prides himself on his nationality and the glory of the nation, and therefore keeps an eye on the welfare of his country ... Go and speak to the commonest tailor, the commonest greengrocer, the commonest bootmaker in London, and he will tell you the amount of the national debt ... your cabman will tell you that this bill will pass and t'other bill not, and your boatman will inform you that the conservatives are no good.[64]

Back in Bengal, Dutt could not but contrast this milieu, where all men regarded themselves as active citizens, with the stark class bifurcations of his own rural society, in which haughty zamindars, devoid of public spirit, exploited fatalistic peasants, hopelessly sunk in poverty. As he trudged his way through flooded and famine ravaged villages, filing reports, planning recovery, and organizing relief, Dutt acknowledged that the new policies of Campbell and Maine to educate and protect the ryot were important steps in the right direction. Delving deeply into Maine's theoretical writings, as well as those of Darwin, Lubbock, Tylor, and Spencer, the young civilian looked for a scientific basis from which to determine the optimal agrarian policy. As a leading metropolitan thinker who had spent some years in India, the recently departed Maine was beginning to enjoy immense prestige in policy-making circles. Nearly all the leading officials of the rising generation – Whitely Stopes, Denzil Ibbetson, Lewis Tupper, Harcourt Butler, Alfred Lyall, William Hunter, Raymond West, Septimus Thorburn, and James Wilson – were all making a fetish of Indian custom and tradition. In protecting the peasant from the harsh blasts of rapid modernization, these officials saw a program for stabilizing their authority. It was the "pregnant suggestions" of *Village Communities* that "constantly guided my work in India," claimed Tupper, while Lyall concurred that "Maine's remarkable insight into the real meaning and connections of archaic customs" had "greatly influenced local inquiries in India," and

---

[64] Surendranath Banerjea, *A Nation in Making* (Oxford, 1925), 1–36; GLD, 1–67; Romesh Chunder Dutt, *Three Years in Europe* (Lahiri, 1896), 13–14.

that these ethnological studies in turn provided recipes for changes in policy.[65]

Eager to join in these policy-making discussions, Dutt was dismayed by the subtle racism that not only blighted his own promotion chances, but also turned a laudable desire to protect the "backward" peasant into an excuse for treating all Indians as inferior beings. Like Lecky in Ireland, and for much the same reasons, Dutt grew skeptical of the racial determinism of the mainstream evolutionists, and fastened on H. T. Buckle's environmental approach as an alternative basis for understanding the *longue durée* of Indian history. In an 1874 study entitled *The Peasantry of Bengal*, Dutt charted their historical fortunes in environmentalist terms. In ancient times, "nature afforded us every facility for the advancement of our civilization," underwriting the glorious achievements of Indian antiquity. The heavy rains and fertile soil that guaranteed an easy bounty, however, also fostered a fatalistic spirit of passivity. Thanks to early marriage, population pressed hard upon resources, and periodic famines were necessary to restore demographic balance. Centuries of conquest and aristocratic oppression had reduced the peasant to "abject voiceless subjection." Finally, in the eighteenth century, this demoralizing pattern had been broken by the British, who brought "peace spreading from one end of the land to the other, commerce thriving, agriculture spreading, the resources of the country fast developing to a wonderful extent." Yet British rule had not been an unadulterated good. Steeped in their own aristocratic history and traditions, the British had empowered the zamindars with their Permanent Settlement, which destroyed the limited security that the ryot had formerly enjoyed. A new Permanent Settlement between landlords and tenants was needed to redress the imbalance.[66]

Following Buckle, Dutt believed that the inherent dynamism of modern progress had broken through the natural limits of environmental fatality. The railroads, telegraphs, and print media introduced by the British were bringing Indians from different backgrounds together, introducing them to new ways of thinking, and rendering them increasingly capable of managing their own affairs. This had been recognized in the

---

[65] C. Dewey, "The Influence of Henry Maine on Agrarian Policy in India," in Diamond (ed.), *Victorian Achievement of Sir Henry Maine*, 353–75; Collini, Winch, and Burrow, *Science of Politics*, 210.

[66] H. T. Buckle, *History of Civilization in England*, 2 vols. (New York, 1897), I: 29–66; Romesh Chunder Dutt, *The Peasantry of Bengal* [1874] (Calcutta, 1890), quotes on 33, 132, 135; R. C. Dutt, "Modern Researches into the Origin and Early Phases of Civilization," *Calcutta Review*, 75 (1882), 132–51; R. C. Dutt, "Progress in India," *Calcutta Review*, 199 (1895), 121–32; GLD, 78–114; Pauline Rule, *The Pursuit of Progress: A Study of the Intellectual Development of Romesh Chunder Dutt, 1848–1888* (Calcutta, 1977), 39–74.

1820s and 1830s by Munro, Elphinstone, and Bentinck, "whose names have lived ever enshrined in the affections of the people ... as the greatest and noblest Indian rulers." Unfortunately, just when the fruits of liberal imperialism were ripening, a new generation of British administrators was retreating from these goals, under cover of evolutionism. A year later, the leading EIC officials were all abuzz about H. S. Maine's latest book, *Lectures on the Early History of Institutions* (1875), which Dutt was "very anxious to read." Although he did not record his reaction to the volume, he must have sighed at this further effort to secure an English monopoly on modernity by figuring the colonial other as an evolutionary vestige from the past. Now the case of Ireland was added to the British–Indian comparative file. The Brehon Law was set alongside the ancient English Folk-Moot and the modern Indian village, all being deemed to be descended from the same Aryan root. Yet the English alone had trod the hard road of modernization and imperial expansion. They had allowed the Indians to slumber and stagnate, but were now forcing Ireland to join the onward and upward slog. English, Irish, and Indians could all feel a sense of common ancestry, yet citizenship accrued only to the English, who had scaled the heights of modern "contract." It had to be denied to Indians, consigned as they were to "status" dependency.[67]

Dutt pinpointed what he saw as the error in this thinking in a brief sketch of Sir Ashley Eden. He was "a good man" who "worked steadily for the good of my country," especially in "the battle he fought for the oppressed raiyats against the planters." Yet

He likes to see people come to him and *salâm* him; he likes to oblige them and to favor them with a benign smile, or with posts for their children ... Agitation for rights he hates; supplication for favors he understands and rewards. Representative institutions he hates of course, and his opposition to the Calcutta Municipality is one of his most frightful blunders.[68]

Just when members of Dutt's own liberal, urban bhadralok class were becoming effective Macaulayite mediators between British modernity and Indian tradition, the British concluded that India was unfit to be modern, and that these anglicized Indians were a dangerous mongrel breed. As an employee of the government, Dutt had to be careful about his public

---

[67] Henry Maine, *Lectures on the Early History of Institutions* [1875] (London, 1905), 9–23. For general discussions of Aryanism as a British imperial ideology in the nineteenth century, see Joan Leopold, "British Applications of the Aryan Theory of Race to India, 1850–1870," *English Historical Review*, 89.352 (July, 1974), 578–603; Trautmann, *Aryans and British India*; Tony Ballantyne, *Orientalism and Race: Aryanism and the British Empire* (New York, 2002).

[68] Quoted in GLD, 50–1.

statements, and he thought that his book on the peasantry had harmed his prospects for promotion.[69] When the ryots of Pabna organized a massive rent-strike to protest oppressive conditions, he published an anonymous article "confess[ing] we are pleased to find evidences that the millions of Bengal are at last awakening from their lethargy, and that, retaining the peaceful habits of their forefathers, they are yet in the present day capable of action in cases of emergency." When the protests petered out, Dutt was forced to recognize the limits of "action." Neither he nor the peasants had successfully broken out of their ascriptive enclosures or forced their way up onto the surface narrative of politically consequential events. When the new Viceroy, Lord Lytton, imposed his Vernacular Press Act of 1878, they were both forced to recognize their ineffectuality. According to Lytton, "the Baboodom of Lower Bengal" was unfit for most forms of administrative employment. "Though disloyal," this English poet-politician jeered, it "is fortunately cowardly and its only revolver is its ink bottle; which though dirty, is not dangerous."[70]

For a man like Dutt, who already had one foot in administrative employment and who hoped to use his ink bottle to join the theory-writing class, such words were not merely insults, but an existential threat. Was it merely a coincidence that, in the very year when Lytton shot forth these sallies, Dutt expressed frustration at his prospects for original intellectual work?

When I read the works of such great thinkers as Darwin, when I think of the great ferment of bold speculation and free thought now prevailing in the scientific circles of free England, how fervently do I wish to cut myself from society, and family, and service, and bury myself for years in the library of the British Museum and make at least one attempt to do something great and glorious.[71]

Yet four months later, on his thirtieth birthday, Dutt confessed,

Where are the great achievement and works, the European reputation, which were the dreams of younger years? . . . I have health, I have a good income, and I am not unknown to my countrymen. It would be ridiculous to compare this with what I once aspired to, but I have learned that it is still more ridiculous to make myself unhappy because I cannot do more than I can do.[72]

There was poignancy in Dutt's belief that distance from the "scientific circles of free England" had impeded his European reputation, or that access to the British Museum library might have broken his intellectual

---

[69] GLD, 56–60.
[70] Quoted in Anil Seal, *The Emergence of Indian Nationalism: Competition and Collaboration in the Later Nineteenth Century* (Cambridge, 1968), 141.
[71] Quoted in GLD, 203–4.   [72] Quoted in GLD, 204–5.

impasse. For the decade of the 1870s (when he was stuck in rural India) was the moment when metropolitan intellectuals consolidated the bulwarks of Eurocentrism, excluding men like Dutt from the possibility of full citizenship and empowering proconsuls like Lytton in their derisive mockery. On the face of it this new phase of evolutionary scholarship might seem unconnected to imperial questions, since its primary focus shifted to English medieval history. Nevertheless, by importing the evolutionary agenda into the historiography of England, three leading metropolitan historians, E. A. Freeman, J. R. Green, and William Stubbs, greatly reinforced the thrust of Anglo-Saxon exclusionism by asserting the unique character of English history.

In a manner that corresponded with Lubbock's "neolithic" a decade earlier, these scholars identified c.500–1500 as an intermediate period: a relatively neglected "missing link," when Europe broke away from the legacy of classical civilization and formed a bridge to modernity. Conventionally dismissed as a "dark" age of chaos and violence, this was now conceived to be a creative time, when Europe consolidated her superiority over Asia, and England acquired those distinctive national features that would secure her global dominance during the nineteenth century.[73] Never entirely breaking with the narrative mode of Froude and Macaulay (and wary of too direct an association with Darwin), these men nevertheless showed how historical analysis could be recast in evolutionary terms. The great Froudian or Macaulayite heroes (Henry and Cecil, or William and Clive) had no counterparts in their volumes, which were devoid of the outsize dramatic revolutionary moments in which entire eras were deemed to shift. By contrast, the more deeply buried monarchs of the middle ages – Alfred, Aethelred, William, John, the two Henrys, and the three Edwards – were presented as more shadowy, less fully limned, figures, whose capacity for consequential action had been shaped by the conditions of their time.

With the freedom-creating deeds of Macaulay's heroes now distributed over a wider cast of actors and conjunctures, it became easier to highlight the deeper racial and constitutional forces that operated only over the very long run. The task of history, in the eyes of these medieval historians, was not simply to celebrate the accomplishments of individual heroes, but also to map the deep structures of slow transmutation that were channeling the surface flow of events. To re-write medieval history in this incrementalist

---

[73] T. W. Heyck, *The Transformation of Intellectual Life in Victorian England* (London, 1982), 1–154; Reba N. Soffer, *Discipline and Power: The University, History and the Making of an English Elite, 1870–1930* (Stanford, 1994); Michael Bentley, *Modernizing England's Past: English History in the Age of Modernism: 1870–1970* (Cambridge, 2003), 1–91.

manner, Freeman, Green, and Stubbs had to find a new kind of inter-mediate chronometry. The *longue durée* of racial and constitutional evo-lution had to be reconciled with the surface narrative of actors and their deeds. In medieval England, as in Maineite Rome, free men were steadily departing from the enclosures of status. Kings, noblemen, and warriors were all being resurrected as Maine-like *patria potestas*. Momentarily escaping from the constraints of the collective (partly racial and partly constitutional), they slowly and incrementally transformed these struc-tures as they strove toward the future of modern contract.[74]

Since the focus of these three historians was relentlessly insular, it might seem odd to include them in an analysis of the role of history in recon-structing visions of Empire and race. In fact, the two tasks were intimately connected. By recasting their work in an evolutionary register, these English historians further refined the highly racialized "comparative method" which had been originally pioneered by Lubbock and Maine. Where Lubbock and Maine constructed imperial selves by evolutionizing about the colonial other, these three secured metropolitan dominance over this other by rewriting the history of England as the emergence of a master race. In the case of Stubbs and Green, this racializing agenda was implicit.[75] In the case of Freeman, however, the same move that privileged medieval Anglo-Saxons also demanded the abjection of racial others who, like Dutt, dared to contest their subalternity. To consign these abjects to the prehistorical prison of status, it was necessary to trumpet their incompetence, which correspondingly showcased the Englishman's inherent superiority. For Freeman, the essence of the "comparative method" lay in the elucidation of a natural racial hierarchy. Africans were dismissed as scarcely human, and Asians were only one step above. Irishmen and Indians were consigned to half-Aryan perdition, while generic European Aryans were inferior to Teutons, especially Anglo-Saxons, the *sine qua non* of the master race.[76]

In Freeman's hands, the progress narrative becomes a story of racial evolution that begins in Greece and Rome, jumps to Germany, migrates to England, and then finally spreads across the earth. It is a testament to his fixation with racial ordering that he encapsulated this evolutionary story in the two epigraphs at the head of this chapter. While the second

---

[74] SCH, III: 501–2.
[75] For an up-to-date discussion of Anglo-Saxonism, see Peter Mandler, *The English National Character: The History of an Idea from Edmund Burke to Tony Blair* (New Haven, 2006), 27–105, which synopsizes a wide range of Anglo-Saxonist discourse, even as it seeks to de-emphasize the theme of race.
[76] C. J. W. Parker, "The Failure of Liberal Racialism: The Racial Ideas of E. A. Freeman," *The Historical Journal*, 24.4 (1981), 825–46.

comment was reserved for his private correspondence, the first infused his published work. It condensed his vision of human development into a nutshell: from the Greek and the Roman we ascend Teutonic heights, with three successive branchings along the tree of English ancestors and three ascending rungs up the ladder of racial superiority. It was an unbroken evolutionary progression "which sets man before us in his highest form," a "long history of civilized man which stretches on in one unbroken tale from the union of the towns of Attica to the last measure of progress in England or in Germany."[77] To the history of "lesser breeds," by contrast, Freeman felt a visceral aversion. "I am yearning to make a speech, knock down a Jew, or anything that might be for the public good," he intimated to a friend in 1880. "I am fuming at this jew humbug," he announced eleven years later in reaction to British protests against the Russian pogroms. "Let every nation wallop its own Jews ... The best thing is to kick them out altogether, like Edward Longshanks of famous memory."[78]

6   E. A. Freeman: the rise of the Anglo-Saxon in racial and evolutionary history

Edward Augustus Freeman was born in 1823, the son of a prosperous Staffordshire coal owner, although he was raised by grandparents after both of his parents died. Like Froude, he came under the influence of the Tractarians while attending Oxford in the 1840s. Unlike Froude, however, Freeman gradually grew to identify as a Liberal, albeit one exceptionally conscious of race. Epiphany came in 1862, when he traveled to Switzerland and witnessed the *Landesgemeinden* or popular assemblies that ruled the free German-speaking cantons. "To stand with the clear heaven above, and the snowy mountains on either side," he enthused, "and see the descendants of the men of Sempach and Morganten discharge the immemorial rights of Teutonic free men is a sight which may well make us doubt whether we are in the common world, or in some historical paradise of our imagination."[79]

This would not be the last of Freeman's difficulties in distinguishing real consanguinity from ideological fantasy. The comparison of modern German-Swiss with the ancient Teutons is begun in the manner of Lubbock or Maine. Yet where Lubbock and Maine referenced the primitivism of ancient Europeans to underscore the backwardness of modern

[77] E. A. Freeman, *Comparative Politics* (London, 1873), 24.
[78] W. R. W. Stephens, *Life and Letters of E. A. Freeman*, 2 vols. (London, 1895), II: 173–4, 428.
[79] Stephens, *Life and Letters*, I: 1–174, 296.

savages or Indians, Freeman referenced the civic virtue of modern Swiss citizens as a way of demonstrating the political precocity of the prehistoric Teutons. "Not in fancy, but in reality," Freeman concluded, these popular assemblies of the Aryan present and past represented "the eternal democracy, well nigh as eternal as the hills that guard the constitution which was of immemorial antiquity in the days of Tacitus, and which since the days of Tacitus, has suffered no interruption save during the momentary havoc of the hordes of revolutionary France."[80]

Freeman spent the rest of his life thinking about how this Teutonic *racial* democracy could be fitted for the modern epoch, and how it could serve as an antidote to the soulless, pseudo-democracy that was being peddled by the radical and socialist heirs of revolutionary France. His first impulse was to focus on the Swiss Confederation, treating it as a modern-day analogue to the ancient federation of Greek city-states. The federal idea appealed to Freeman because he envisioned it as a way to create moderately sized political units such as were necessary to survive as independent polities in the modern era of sovereign states. Voluntary union in external relations combined with autonomy in internal affairs might redirect (without destroying) the intense local solidarities that he saw as a necessary feature of racial democracy. Yet after publishing the first volume of a *History of Federal Government* (1863), Freeman concluded that the Greek and Swiss models were un-adaptive dead ends. Even at their most expansive, they would constitute only micro-polities, which could hardly stand up to the super-states of the emerging industrial world. The collapse of American federalism during the early 1860s – and its multiracial reconstruction after 1865 – convinced him that true (ethnically homogeneous) federalism was not possible on the scale of a super-state.[81]

By the mid-1860s, Freeman had come to see that the evolution of successful polities was a complex historical problem that had to be traced out in detail over many centuries. It was this realization that drew him to the history of medieval England, which he now saw as the crucial moment when an already superior Anglo-Saxon race adapted to the requirements of political centralization without sacrificing that scope for individual (male) initiative that had made their ancestors great. Centuries of preparation in this new political structure, combining freedom with authority, finally enabled the post-medieval Englishman to perform the great deeds of the Reformation, Glorious Revolution, and

[80] Freeman, "The Landesgemeinden of Uri," *Saturday Review*, 18 (May 21, 1864), 622.
[81] Freeman, *The History of Federal Government* (London, 1863); Freeman, *Comparative Politics*, 65, 81.

imperial expansion that had been chronicled (however badly) in the annals of Macaulay and Froude.[82]

Since Freeman believed that the Anglo-Saxons were predestined to become the ruling race, he had to find a version of prehistory that spun the story in this way. Though personally uninvolved in archaeological excavation, he became close friends with Boyd Dawkins, an Oxford geologist, who had the necessary expertise. In his popular book *Cave Hunting*, Dawkins presented a vision of European prehistory that differed significantly from the irenic progressivism of Lubbock. Western Europe in general, and Britain in particular, had been the site of constant struggles between ever more superior races, as brow-ridged Neanderthals (using Mousterian tools) gave way to Ice Age Eskimo hunters (using Magdalenian tools), who were replaced by a "dark haired, swarthy" (Bronze Age) race of people whom Dawkins identified as the ancestors of the Basques. During the Iron Age, these primitive peoples were replaced by the Celts and the Belgae, and then finally by the Germans, whose conquests ushered in the age of written historical records. It was left for the reader to draw the implication that Britain's global and imperial ascendancy was deeply encoded in her racialized past. In Asia, Africa, and indigenous America, primitive dark men still subsisted in a Stone Age or Bronze Age mentality. By contrast, British history had become a Darwinian proving ground where, again and again, the weaker race (dark and low-tech) had perished and only the strongest race (light and high-tech) had survived.[83]

For Freeman, this premise – that the Anglo-Saxon conquest had resulted in the near extermination of the indigenous inhabitants – became the starting point, at which a distinctively English evolution commenced.[84] Of course, much had happened since the days of these bloody race struggles, and it was only because Anglo-Saxons had successfully adapted to further challenges that they remained the top branch of the modern evolutionary tree. To understand this more nuanced process, Freeman decided to write a detailed history of the Norman Conquest. Although this topic had already been extensively researched, he considered the existing works to be inadequate. For far too long, the "Norman Yoke" had been invoked by English radicals as a badge of class oppression. Although this myth had been partly dismantled by Sir Francis Palgrave, Freeman wanted to refigure it as a catalyst for a new consensus

[82] FNC, I: xii–xx.
[83] Boyd Dawkins, *Cave Hunting: Researches on the Evidence of Caves Respecting the Early Inhabitants of Europe* (London, 1874).
[84] FNC, I: 14, 17–18, 20–1.

around an alternative ideal of national unity. Conquered and defeated in 1066, the Anglo-Saxons momentarily stood in danger of becoming a lesser breed. But disaster was transformed into an adaptive opportunity. The foreign strain was successfully absorbed, laying the foundation for a stronger, more formidable English nationality.[85]

Freeman began by pointing out that long before their appearance in the historical record, the primordial Teutonic ancestors of the Anglo-Saxons had already developed most of the features that facilitated their survival in the turbulent struggles of antiquity. In particular, their love of freedom, their warlike demeanor, their egalitarian social structure, and their democratic system of direct self-rule all worked together to make these barbarians formidable fighters, who could utterly crush the more sophisticated (but also effete) Latin and Celtic inhabitants of the lands that they coveted. Drawing on the work of German historians, as well as the Englishman John Kemble, Freeman argued that Anglo-Saxon economic and political structure was based on an institution known as the Mark. Like Maine's village community, the Mark was depicted as a voluntary association of free warriors, who united to defend (and where possible extend) their landholdings. Although some social distinctions developed within these communities, leaders were chosen by assemblies of freedmen, which regularly met (on the Swiss model) to renew the hallowed traditions of patriarchal democracy.[86]

Once they had wiped out the indigenous Britons, Freeman's Anglo-Saxons settled down on their new island, exhibiting adaptations that fitted them for the future. Christian conversion tempered their blood-letting and enabled them to co-exist with the surviving Celtic communities to the north and west. At the same time, constant pressure from the Danes compelled them to refine their military organization and to coalesce in ever larger political units for self-defence.[87] The Mark, with its folkland, began to exhibit a new set of individuated variations as portions of the common fields were converted into allodial property, which could be handed down from generation to generation. Correspondingly, the comitatus (band of male warriors), with its elective chief, became integrated with other bands under a co-ordinating aristocracy. Chiefly alliances were further integrated into petty kingdoms, which were patched together into

[85] FNC, I: 2–4; Christopher Hill, "The Norman Yoke," in Puritanism and Revolution: Studies in the Interpretation of the English Revolution of the Seventeenth Century (New York, 1964), 50–122; Augustin Thierry, History of the Conquest of the Normans, 2 vols. (London, 1907).
[86] Stephens, Life and Letters, I: 114–20; John Kemble, The Saxons in England: A History of the English Commonwealth till the Period of the Norman Conquest, 2 vols. (London, 1849), I: 35–71; FNC, I: 83–90.
[87] FNC, I: 22–71.

an overarching heptarchy. This process finally culminated in the achievement of King Alfred of Wessex, whose unified monarchy turned Anglo-Saxon tribalism into an English national identity.[88]

While these changes facilitated greater political and military organization, Freeman indicates that they had their costs. Inequalities began to harden in both political and economic terms. A feudal hierarchy gradually developed as landholding became private and hereditary. Poorer sectors of the ceorl (warrior) community sank into serfdom, which undermined national solidarity. But there were compensating features that preserved the libertarian heritage: the hundred and shire emerged as new foci for local and regional self-government, while the Witangemot provided guarantees, at the highest level, against the danger of royal tyranny.[89] Freeman's *idée fixe* is that the Norman Conquest preserved much that was authentically English, including elements that would have disappeared had the Anglo-Saxon polity survived. A weak monarchy, such as developed under Edward the Confessor, might have split the kingdom up into a handful of magnate fiefdoms, with consequences resembling those that decimated medieval France. Key to this argument was the premise that the Normans were actually Teutonic cousins, who had left their Nordic home a few generations earlier. Conquering France, they had become dangerously Frenchified. Their northern turn to England therefore represented a return to their original Teutonic roots.[90]

As Europe became ever more densely interconnected during the twelfth and thirteenth centuries, the bridge that the Angevin Empire threw outward to the continent worked to preserve England's insular autonomy.[91] Over this period there was a gradual fusion of the two languages, legal systems, and aristocratic elites. In each case, the Norman infusion served to quicken a Teutonic heritage that might otherwise have grown inbred. Most importantly, this Norman infusion enabled the Anglo-Saxon tradition of self-government to evolve, after the Magna Carta, into forms of representative government that were better suited to the emerging conditions of proto-modernity. Such were the effects of incremental evolution that "time did its work without any formal enactment, without any change of established custom, the Assembly of foreigners changed back into an assembly of Englishmen."[92] The Anglo-Saxon courts, institutionally reconstructed by despotism, were transformed by the jury into popular

---

[88] FNC, I: 83–97.

[89] FNC, I: 97–147, especially 110–11, 112. Freeman contrasts Anglo-Saxon paradigms of nation formation through hierarchy and loyalty with the Swiss and Scottish Federal model (FNC, I: 129–47).

[90] FNC, I: 149–50, V: 53–68, 333–9.   [91] FNC, V: 340–64.

[92] FNC, V: 364–458, quote on 415.

institutions. "The Parish and the Manor are in truth the ancient Mark, changed into new shapes according to ecclesiastical, and according to territorial ideas." Even villeinage and the spread of servile tenures were compensated by the rise of the borough, with its system of urban chartered liberty.[93]

Gradually, by a silent change, freedom learned to turn despotism itself to its own purpose. We see, at every turn in our story, how foreign tyranny worked in the end for the establishment of native freedom ... Step by step we have thrown off the yoke only because the yoke was there to be thrown off. And it is the process of throwing off a yoke which ever makes freedom sweet. Had there never been a time of foreign tyranny, our liberties might have crumbled away without our knowing it.[94]

Feudal Europe had become a quasi-Darwinian arena, in which only the fittest survived. Unlike other subject peoples, then and later, the English had proven that they were worthy of autonomy. Their agency and their evolution had become one and the same.

It was because our old institutions were for a moment perverted rather than abolished, that we have been able to win them back under new shapes ... Had the shock of foreign conquest never come upon us, we might have slumbered on till we woke up to find ourselves under a despotism like that of France, or an oligarchy like that of Denmark ... We have kept our freedom because we had to win it; had it never been wrested from us by force, it might have slipped away from us by force.[95]

7   **E. A. Freeman: the triumph of Anglo-Saxonism
        in the nineteenth century**

After the last volume of Freeman's *History* had been published (1879), he grew despondent at the sluggish sales of his book. He had hoped for a reception that would rival Macaulay's. In the event, his book attracted a smaller audience than that of the man whom he most detested, J. A. Froude.[96] Friends and reviewers complained that his five volumes were too long and tedious to hold the interest of the general public. Part of the problem lay in the fact that Freeman was trying to combine narrative exposition with evolutionary explanation in a medium that really only sanctioned the first. In contrast to Macaulay, who could

---

[93] FNC, V: 459–81, quote on 462.   [94] FNC, V: 458–9.   [95] FNC, V: 504–5.
[96] In spite of the fact that their positions on race, nationalism, and history were remarkably similar, Freeman took a violent aversion to Froude, tormenting him on the appearance of every new volume with a vituperative notice in the *Saturday Review*. Over many years Freeman was relentless, disputing Froude's accuracy and impugning his integrity. W. H. Dunn, *James Anthony Froude: A Biography* (Oxford, 1963), 456–70.

play out his glorious revolutionary transformation directly in the chronicle of great events, Freeman's narrative is compromised by its dependence on a subterranean evolution that must be registered on the deeper chronometry of the *longue durée*. Since Freeman's men could never be crushed as individual agents, the narrative had always to be kept open and crowded with their deeds: Normans busily returning to their ur-Teutonic essence, or Englishmen frantically renewing their racial advantage by adapting to the innovations that the Normans have introduced.[97]

Because Froude and Macaulay were able to weave transformative processes directly into narrative action, they could provide their readers with a satisfying story that played out over the scale of a human lifetime: decades, years, or even days. In Freeman, by contrast, the narrative could not be so readily tethered to a transformative process that was now measured in multi-century increments. On this scale, even the most dramatic episodes appear as minute accretions, less important for themselves than as periodic soundings of the profounder racial or constitutional changes underneath. The Norman Conquest seemed remote to Victorian readers, in a way that the Reformation or Glorious Revolution did not. Freeman's famous quip that "history is past politics, and politics present history" was perhaps less anachronistic than it sounded, since his continuum between past and present stretched almost to infinity.[98]

So what were the implications of the Norman Conquest for the nineteenth century? Though Freeman was uncharacteristically reticent in laying out lessons, an agenda can be discerned in his subsequent work. In 1877, he published an article entitled "Race and Language," in which his conclusions on the subject were duly laid out. To a degree that may have surprised his earlier readers, the doctrines of absolute racial fixity and purity were now denied. Those who wished to equate race with skin and skulls were being myopic in Freeman's view. Race always involved a cultural element, which interacted with the physical and hereditary components in complex and often mysterious ways. For this reason, purist efforts to separate discussion of "race" from the study of language were missing the boat. Races did slowly evolve, albeit at different rates, and cultural or linguistic changes both reflected and sometimes precipitated

---

[97] As he approached the critical year of 1066, Freeman also drastically slowed his narrative down, perhaps too slowly. Whereas he covers the entire period up to 975 in 147 pages, the period between 975 and 1087 requires 2,186 pages to traverse.

[98] John Burrow, *A Liberal Descent: Victorian Historians and the English Past* (Cambridge, 1981), 164, 178–87.

this evolution. In some obvious cases – he cited Africans in America and Jews in Europe – inferior races might adopt the language of their masters, without any corresponding racial improvement. In other cases, he acknowledged, "language is not a test of race [but] it is, in the absence of evidence to the contrary, a presumption of race."[99]

Another source of incremental racial change was the slow influx of foreign influences into every ethnic group. "Every nation will have some adopted children of this kind," and "as soon as we allow the exercise of the law of adoption, physical purity of race is at an end." Some nations, such as the French, were created entirely out of racial mixtures. In England, the reintegration of racial cousins kept the nation more ethnically homogeneous. Freeman would not even rule out some mysterious Lamarckian mechanism whereby cultural advance or degradation could work its way back into the bloodlines. Indeed, he went so far as to acknowledge that race might even seem an "artificial" construct, since the national solidarities on which modern people acted did not always correspond to racial lines. Who could determine with certainty the racial provenance of any individual or group? Even the original Aryans might not have been consanguineous. "They might have been more like an accidental party of fellow-travelers."[100]

When Freeman wrote about the European continent these strictures about racial mixing were generally kept in mind.[101] When it came to Anglo-Saxons, however, he expressed his recessive penchant for racial purity. Here race was reinforced by geography, as the English people's island existence isolated them from continental currents and – over many generations – made them unique. "It is the insular character of Britain which has, beyond anything else, made the inhabitants of Britain what they are, and the history of Britain what it has been." Island life made the English people into seafarers, and, after the discovery of America, seafaring drove them to replicate the great colonizing deeds of their Saxon forebears, this time on a truly global scale. In the thirteen North American colonies of the eighteenth century, and in the Canada and Australasia of the nineteenth, the English used their mastery of the most advanced technologies – sail, steam, rail, telegraph, and firepower – to spread their superior seed around the world.[102]

---

[99] E. A. Freeman, "Race and Language," in *Historical Essays*, 4 vols. (London, 1892), I: 191–2.
[100] Freeman, "Race and Language," 191, 193, 199.
[101] Stephens, *Life and Letters*, II: 101–70; Burrow, *Liberal Descent*, 166, 188–92.
[102] E. A. Freeman, *Greater Greece and Greater Britain, and George Washington the Expander of England* (London, 1886); E. A. Freeman, "Alter Orbis," *Contemporary Review*, 41 (1882), 1041.

In this most glorious chapter in the history of the race, evolution was amplified by expansion. George Washington turned out to be the greatest "expander of England" in spite of himself. His good Saxon name, taken from an aboriginal settlement, had given title to the capital of the ultimate "English" polity. Of course, being good, freedom-loving Saxons, these American colonists would inevitably revolt against excessive control from the metropolitan center. No matter. Blessed with the prospect of a vast open continent, the independent-minded Americans were becoming the greatest Englishmen the world had ever known. Surely the Canadians and Australasians would follow the example of the thirteen colonies, and just as surely this was not a bad thing.[103] "The tie of national brotherhood, the abiding feeling of the oneness of the folk lives through physical distance, through political separation, through political rivalry and [even] through wasting war." Formal empire for Freeman is but one intermediate stage in a longer-term process of racial imperialism, in which Anglo-Saxons spread out to dominate the earth. But what of the colored dependencies, in which small numbers of Englishmen are set out to rule over millions and millions of "lesser breeds"?

Without any personal stake in the bureaucracy of empire management, Freeman holds fast to his racial exclusionary dream. Unlike Lubbock, Campbell, or Maine, he takes no pleasure in the prospect of improving "lesser breeds." England's conquest of India was a fact of history, incurring obligations that could not be gainsaid. Yet the colored dependencies were a "burthen" rather than a benefit in Freeman's view. Their main function was to illustrate the impossibility of any formal permanent imperial federation, since such a polity would have to include "millions on millions of dark skinned Mussulmans and Hindoos" while leaving out the American brethren across the seas.[104] Had Freeman been able to view India as he viewed continental Europe, he might have deemed these millions to be Aryan second cousins, and therefore people with sufficient racial connection for political Union to work. Indeed by subordinating commonalities of language and culture to differences in skins and skulls, he was violating his own racial rules. But this was not the way he viewed the matter. A vague Aryan cousinship might be sufficient for Asians or European continentals, but Anglo-Saxons were the *über*-Aryans of the modern era who had the obligation to stand watch at the gates of racial nirvana. Just how far Freeman feared the dangers of race-mixing and race dilution became clear in 1881, when he visited the United States. "My chief feeling," he wrote of an environment that reminded him of

[103] Freeman, *George Washington*, 64–102.   [104] Freeman, *Greater Britain*, 38–49.

home, "is the strangeness of the lack of strangeness." One discordant feature, however, could not be ignored. "The really queer thing is the niggers who swarm here," he wrote to his friend Dawkins,

My Aryan prejudices go against them, specially when they rebuke one, and order one about. And the women and children are yet stranger than the men. Are you sure that they are men? I find it hard to feel that they are men acting seriously: 'tis easier to believe that they are big monkeys dressed up for a game.[105]

In St. Louis, he acknowledged that "some of them are fairly human and speak decent English," while in others he heard only "the grunt of these hideous Apes whom Darwin has clearly left unfinished." In fact, however, it was the respectable well-dressed Negroes that elicited Freeman's sharpest sarcasm. "At Baltimore we tried the black Methodists till their temple grew too hot, and then adjourned to black Episcopals," he recounted to a friend. "If these half-men, and still more half-women, would instead of a Frank dress wear something of shawls and turbans they would look one degree less grotesque." The problem, then, was not so much the presence of Negroes, but their presumption in adopting the manners of civilized Englishmen, in stepping above their properly subhuman state. "The freed nigger," he complained, after taking a trip on the railway, "seems to have a fancy generally for making us feel our Aryan inferiority – I am sure 'twas a mistake making them citizens. I feel a creep when I think that one of these great black apes may (in theory) be President. Surely treat your horse kindly; but don't make him Consul."[106]

It would be easy to dismiss these twisted words as the ravings of a sick humor, utterly uncharacteristic of other liberal intellectuals of the day. Yet closer examination shows that they provide a particularly crude exemplification of a pattern that we have already seen in the more presentable responses of Lubbock, Campbell, and Maine. In each case, it is not the pure savage, the wild tribesman, or the traditionalist peasant who elicits metropolitan unease. Such backward specimens might prove compliant or incorrigible, but they did not disrupt the liberal evolutionist's conceptual categories. They might exemplify the possibilities of gradual progress or the impediments that hindered such advance. Either way, they offer no cognitive challenge to the ideal of gradual improvement under the umbrella of a benevolent Empire. By contrast, it is the colonial hybrid – the civilized Tahitian, the educated Negro, or the anglicized Bengali – who disturbs the liberal imperialist's equanimity. In his or her very existence, he or she suggests that improvement may be possible without compulsory outside intervention, that progress may be achievable

---

[105] Stephens, *Life and Letters*, II: 234–5.   [106] Stephens, *Life and Letters*, II: 242, 236–7.

by indigenous means. In the case of Freeman, it is worth noting that he voiced no objection to blacks serving as field-hands or coal-haulers. His ire was raised by the railroad-conductor in smart uniform inspecting the tickets of white passengers, and by the Baltimore congregants dressed in their Sunday finest, with their own adaptations of the Englishman's Protestant Creed. From there it was but a short step in Freeman's imagination to the freedman's induction into Anglo-Saxon citizenship, and even to "a great black ape" in the White House.

Of course, it would be a mistake to make too much of Freeman's gross invective, since most other liberals wore their prejudices – and their notions of civilizational hierarchy – more lightly. Yet it may be here, rather than at the level of overt racism, that Anglo-Saxon exclusionism stigmatized most effectively. This can be seen in the work of the two other main Anglo-Saxonist historians of the 1870s, J. R. Green and William Stubbs. Close friends of Freeman, these two scholars eschewed his overt obsession with race. Yet their more complex vision of Anglo-Saxon history may have contributed more than Freeman's tirades to excluding racial others from constitutional rights in the late Victorian Empire.

8   The failure of hybrid evolutionism: a tale of two Greens

Although J. R. Green found a mentor in Freeman, his experience led him to see the world more in class than in racial terms. As a poorly paid curate in an east London slum, Green saw that his parishioners' struggles for survival could not be understood through the lens of Darwin. Poverty, unemployment, pollution, and low wages were the primary causes of their high mortality. Working people responded with makeshift expedients – scrimping, saving, searching for bargains, collective organization, and informal reciprocity. Drawing his vision of the past from the contemporary world around him, Green allowed his historical eye to rove more freely over everyday medieval scenes. "We see the mills grinding along the burns, the hammer rings in the village smithy, the thegn's hall rises out of its demesne, the parish priest is at his mass-book in the little church that forms the center of every township."[107]

Here was a vision of the old English peasantry that not only conjured up a merrier England, but also bore comparison with R. C. Dutt's nineteenth-century ryot. Yet where Dutt labored unsung in remote

---

[107] Anthony Brundage, *The People's Historian: John Richard Green and the Writing of History in Victorian England* (Westport, 1994); and *Letters of John Richard Green*, ed. Leslie Stephen (London, 1901), 1–206; J. R. Green, *The Conquest of England* (London, 1884), 8; Rosemary Jann, *The Art and Science of Victorian History* (Columbus, 1985), 141–69.

outposts of the Empire, Green distilled his vision into a *Short History of the English People* that sold half a million copies over the next few decades. Not only was this popular history *à la* Macaulay, but it was also a populist revision *of* Macaulay, adapting his Whiggism to the democratic liberalism of the Gladstonian age. "It is a history," Green announces in his opening sentence, "not of English kings or English conquests, but of the English people." "In England more than elsewhere," he continues, "constitutional progress has been the result of social development." What he aims for is an embryonic social history.[108] Where Freeman's narrative was driven by the political relations between Normans and Saxons, Green's is driven by class relations between a freedom-seeking people and the feudal lords who try to keep this people yoked and constrained. Driven into serfdom by political centralization, a section of the people found a new basis for freedom in the burgeoning towns. Capitalizing on conflicts between kings and barons, they were able to play one off against the other and to lay a new foundation for popular liberty. In many ways, the Peasants' Revolt of 1381 is the pivot of Green's social history, much as the Norman Conquest was at the center of Freeman's account. In the short term, the peasants were defeated, but their descendants obtained almost everything that the rebels had sought. "During the century and a half after the Peasant Revolt, villeinage became a rare and antiquated thing. A hundred years after the Black Death, the wages of an English labourer could purchase twice the amount of necessaries of life which could have been obtained for the wages paid under Edward the Third."[109]

Such was the popularity of Green's attractive volume that it sold well, not only in Anglo-Saxon colonies, but also in India. Incorporated into the curriculum of the universities of Calcutta, Bombay, and Punjab (and probably others), it was read by many undergraduates as *the* set text in English history.[110] Of course, we do not know what these students made of Green's *Short History*, but if they applied it to their own situation they might have drawn a number of controversial conclusions: that national liberation is an arduous process, that it is achieved only through organization and struggle, and that *panchayats* or other officially sanctioned institutions are unlikely alone to bring it within reach. These inferences, however, would have to be made by the reader, since Green is exclusively focused on the Englishness of his story and has nothing to say about its relevance to other parts of the globe. Even Freeman, with his interests in

---

[108] J. R. Green, *A Short History of the English People* (New York, 1912), xvii; Stephen, *Life and Letters*, 209–383.
[109] Green, *Short History*, 1–303, quote on 257.
[110] *Report of the Indian Education Commission* (Calcutta, 1883), 270–2.

continental Europe and his fear of inferior races, was not so parochial in his conception of history.

Indeed, it is hard to shake the feeling that there may be a connection between the generosity of Green's democratic sentiments and the insularity of his anglocentricity. Is the exclusion of others no more than an oversight, or is it necessary for his saga of English liberty? Since his story begins with the Anglo-Saxon invasions there is some cognitive dissonance between the violence exhibited by these barbarians and their oppressed descendants' quest for justice. Had Green confronted this contradiction between external violence and internal democracy, he might have actually strengthened his argument. The rise of feudalism could then have been depicted as the price of England's foreign aggressions, and English serfdom as the final fruit of reducing the indigenous Britons to slavery.[111]

Green's failure here to radicalize the comparative method rendered his work less innovative than it might have been. Green himself was a radical in the context of the 1870s, expressing his distaste for British aggression and his support for the fledgling cause of Irish Home Rule. His premature death in 1883, however, made it impossible to know how he would have responded to the political challenges of the 1880s and 1890s. Would the enthusiasm of his Indian readers have drawn him into support for their national aspirations, or would the vehemence of the Irish Home Rulers have tested the limits of his genial inclusivity? Green's wife, Alice Stopford, whom he married in 1877, was certain that she knew her husband's mind. "No one could come in contact with Mr. Green," she observed, "without a deepened sense of how free peoples should rightly live." Alice Stopford herself was the daughter of an Anglo-Irish Protestant family, and was moved by the first stirrings of the Celtic revival that was just beginning in her youth. During her marriage to Green, she set these interests aside to serve as his assistant. After his death, however, she became absorbed in the Irish Question, and the experience she gained in revising her husband's manuscripts led her to apply the same methods to Irish history.[112]

Before the advent of the Tudors, Alice argued, in a book that she finally published in 1908, the Anglo-Irish relationship had been fundamentally healthy. Like England, Ireland had been subject to a long string of invasions, from the Belgae to the Celts, the Danes, and finally the Anglo-Normans. In each case, however, the invaders assimilated to the existing culture, always adding a new racial element into what became an ever

---

[111] Green, *Short History*, 2–16; see also his *Conquest of England*.
[112] Brundage, *Green*, 157; Stephen, *Life and Letters*, 390–2.

richer ethnic mix. In contrast to her husband's Anglo-Saxonist account, she laid great stress on the hybrid character of the Irish people, attributing their high civilization in the middle ages to the many diverse influences they received.[113] It was only during the Tudor period, according to Green, that the English destroyed this rich cultural mixture and imposed an imperial mono-culture of their own: Irish schools were shut down, Irish customs were proscribed, attacks were launched on the Irish language, culture, and poetry. Irish trade was cut off for the benefit of English merchants, and English monopolies were allowed to crush the most lucrative Irish industries. Worst of all, the land was stolen from the traditional Irish and Anglo-Irish chieftains. When it was handed over to a new breed of greedy English proprietors, the life of the ancestral peasantry collapsed.[114]

By setting the work of the two Greens side by side, we might show how their arguments can be brought into alignment: true Englishness was created not by imperial elites, but by the people who have struggled through the centuries to regain the freedoms that their ancestors lost. This struggle must be fused with the efforts of colonial peoples to recover their own national cultures and identities, which have been suppressed by the same English ruling oligarchy. In short, genuine movements for national liberation do not conflict with one another, and must join together against the common enemy in creating new forms of subaltern hybridity. Had any such Greater British history been written at the time, it would have been of enormous relevance to India, as well as Ireland. Yet neither the Greens nor anyone else in the metropolis succeeded in crafting such a comparative method from below. Whatever the quality of their marriage, the historiographical union between the Greens was never consummated.[115]

Of course it would be anachronistic to fault the Greens for their failure to write a social history of subalterns such as became historiographically possible only at the end of the twentieth century. Yet the insistence of the franchise question in their lifetimes did raise more limited questions of civic agency. Were English workingmen to be inducted into the full rights of citizenship? Was the vote to be extended to women? Should anglicized Indians be granted real representative institutions? How far were the Irish to be allowed to manage their own affairs? The force of these contemporary questions required a fundamental re-examination of British constitutional evolution and a

[113] Alice Stopford Green, *The Making of Ireland and its Undoing* (London, 1909), 1–122.
[114] Green, *Making of Ireland*, 123–324.
[115] Brundage, *Green*, 136–59; Stephen, *Life and Letters*, 396.

consideration of the extent to which hitherto subordinated groups now displayed a fitness for political agency.[116]

9   William Stubbs and the evolution of the English Constitution

From this perspective, the most notable achievement of the 1870s was neither the completion of Freeman's *Norman Conquest*, nor the appearance of Green's *Short History*, but the publication of a new *Constitutional History of England*, in three volumes, by William Stubbs. Born in 1825, two years after Freeman, Stubbs became acquainted with Freeman at Oxford, and mutual interest in medieval sources deepened this friendship over the next twenty years. Yet differences in orientation and personality gradually appeared, for while Freeman dashed off his fiery screeds, Stubbs worked quietly in a rural Essex vicarage, editing and annotating medieval charters and other documents. On the strength of this painstaking scholarship, Stubbs was appointed Regius Professor of Modern History at Oxford in 1866, over the candidacies of Freeman and Froude.[117]

It was his new duties as a university professor that turned Stubbs's mind to the relationship between history and citizenship. In his audience, after all, the future rulers of Britain were likely to be found. What might a historian teach them to enhance the quality of their future work? Though a moderate Tory himself, Stubbs insisted that it was a historian's duty to show that the politics of the past could be examined with relative dispassion, in a manner that enabled the student to broaden his understanding of the contemporary world. Froude and Macaulay, for all their talents, had failed in this task, and it had to be re-engaged on a more neutral historiographical ground. According to Stubbs, the medieval period was well suited to this pedagogical mandate, since it was "sufficiently akin to modern life to engage lively feeling and yet sufficiently apart from it to prevent party views from being predominant." Let the students "learn the history of early England and early France before they are called on to exert their tender judgments on the Great Rebellion, or the French Revolution."[118]

The job of the history professor was to dampen adolescent enthusiasms by showing the complexity of life and the merits of those who took a

---

[116] Catherine Hall, Keith McClelland, and Jane Rendall, *Defining the Victorian Nation: Class, Race, Gender, and the Reform Act of 1867* (Cambridge, 2000).

[117] Heyck, *The Transformation of Intellectual Life*, 120–54; Soffer, *Discipline and Power*, 78–127; Bentley, *Modernizing England's Past*, 23–32.

[118] William Stubbs, *Seventeen Lectures on the Study of Medieval and Modern History* (Oxford, 1887), 254.

different side.[119] But how far did this ecumenicism extend beyond British male elites, to those myriads among Greater Britain's masses of a different class, race, gender, religion, and creed? As a Christian, Stubbs believed that "every soul has an equal value," but as a historian, he was convinced that "every national history does not contribute equally valuable results towards the general progress of mankind." English history was privileged because it was "the history of [one of] those nations and institutions in which the real growth of humanity is to be traced, in which we can follow the developments, the retardations and perturbations, the ebb and flow of human progress, the education of the world, the leading on by the divine light." But was this history the exclusive possession of a single race, or could it be exported, to raise up the "lesser breeds"? In his academic lectures, Stubbs seemed to follow the line of Freeman, simply assuming that the legacy of English freedom and the English Constitution were inextricably connected with the history of the Anglo-Saxons as a master race.[120] However, when he came to publish his grand synoptic *Constitutional History of England* between 1874 and 1878, Stubbs adopted a different tone. Here race consciousness was considerably muted. "The growth of the English Constitution" was now attributed to "the reciprocal interaction of national character, the external history and institutions of the people." Where race was virtually fixed, the "national character" developed in interplay with the nation's history. It is the history of institutions, created and slowly changed by a developing constitution, that stands at the center of Stubbs's account. If this is not the predestined rise of a chosen people, it is also not – he warns the reader – a colorful narrative of deeds by great heroes. It is rather a slow accretion of gradual changes, which have shaped constitutional and institutional development in a particularly fortunate way.[121]

Of all the historians we have so far considered, Stubbs was most conscious of working in an evolutionary framework, and yet this realization also made him nervous, since he feared that any explicit theoretical allegiance might compromise his commitment to empirical impartiality. "I am no believer in the philosophy of history," he complained, after reading Buckle. "I am opposed to the school of thinkers which exalts the generalization of partially informed men into laws and attempts out of those laws to create a science of history."[122] At one point, he compared the English Constitution to many old country houses which have a grand history, having been "now castles, now abbeys, now manor houses."

---

[119] Stubbs, *Seventeen Lectures*, 20.
[120] William Stubbs, *Lectures on Early English History* (London, 1906); Stubbs, *Seventeen Lectures*, 96.
[121] SCH, I: 1–3; Burrow, *Liberal Descent*, 97–151.   [122] Stubbs, *Early English History*, 194.

Having begun "with a little farmhold in the Teutonic clearing," the Constitution "grows up and becomes a feudal manor; it builds a national church and a court of justice," always retaining "much that it could do without" and doing without "much that might well have been added, if it were not that the addition would stop the working of some more important part." As this simile demonstrated, Stubbs's method was essentially adaptationist, since he sought to show how the Constitution changed in response to its socio-political environment, while also stabilizing the environment in which it thrived.[123]

Like Freeman, Stubbs emphasized the freedom-loving and self-governing character of the Anglo-Saxons, but he doubted whether that made them unique. Like many semi-civilized peoples throughout Europe and Asia, the early English were content to stagnate for centuries, and advanced only under pressure from within and without. From the outside, it was the exigencies of war and military organization that acted as the primary impetus toward political growth and centralization. Exposed to invasion and internecine strife, local chieftains consolidated under regional kings, who eventually united under a national monarch. Continual war enhanced the power of elective kings, who were culled by a "process of natural selection." As a national monarchy arose above the regional level, it evolved into a hereditary institution, accumulating an apparatus of central control and administration that enabled kings to transmute charismatic leadership into structural sovereignty over people and land.[124]

In the primitive German constitution the free man of pure blood is the fully qualified political unit; the king is the king of the race, the host is the people in arms ... In the next stage the possession of the land has become the badge of freedom; the freeman is fully free because he possesses land, he does not possess land because he is free; the host is the body of landowners in arms; the courts are the courts of the landowners ... The king still calls himself the king of the nation, but he has added to his old title new [powers and obligations] as supreme landowner, the representative of all original, and the fountain of all derived, political right.[125]

Against the hereditary rule of territorial monarchs, with their institutions of central administration, Stubbs set the countervailing power of hereditary feudal landholders with their own manorial courts, vassals, retainers, and serfs. Replacing the old free warriors (and absorbing their military functions), these new aristocratic landholders (both Norman and Saxon after 1066) turned out to be the fittest agents of freedom in a complex society that had evolved both central government and landed property. The greatest originality of Stubbs's approach to English

---

[123] Stubbs, *Early English History*, 332–3.   [124] SCH, I: 74, 170.   [125] SCH, I: 166–7.

constitutional history lay in his recognition that it consisted of two partly related levels of development – the local and the national – that were evolving at different rates. Local government, which could be traced back to the Germanic Mark, was the slow-evolving organism, as it passed almost imperceptibly through the vill, the township, the tithing, the manor, and the parish, even into the modern era, with little fundamental change. By contrast, the process of centralization, which began in the late Anglo-Saxon period, picked up speed under the rule of the Norman and Plantagenet kings. The freedom which arose spontaneously on the local level of the warrior community had now to be laboriously reconstructed on the national level by institutions which formed around a sequence of negotiations and renegotiations between feudal lords and centralizing kings. These negotiations culminated in the Magna Carta, which "although drawn up in the form of a royal grant was really a treaty between the king and his subjects."[126]

To put it in the language of Maine, the Anglo-Saxon freedman's (original, local) ascent from status to contract was confirmed at a higher (feudal, national) level by a comprehensive written covenant that recapitulated all the customary rights and liberties of the ancient constitution while laying the foundation for their elaboration and extension in the coming institutional age. Consciously or unconsciously the feudal nobility was acting to construct a new kind of liberty that would eventually apply to the nation as a whole. Representative institutions (i.e. the embryonic Parliament) were providing new sites for the exercise of male agency to replace the primordial freedom of the forest. During the thirteenth and fourteenth centuries, with the emergence of chartered towns, lesser landholders, and an embryonic House of Commons, government will be delegated to representatives who would articulate the freedman's interest on an increasingly crowded national and international stage.

The great characteristic of the English constitutional system ... the principle of its growth, the secret of its construction – is the continuous development of representative institutions from the first elementary stage in which they are employed for local purposes and in the simplest form, to that in which the national parliament appears as the concentration of all local and provincial machinery, the depository of the collective powers of the three estates of the realm.[127]

Yet it is only because freedom is preserved at the enduring local level that "the administrative order is worked into the common law of the people and the common institutions of the people are admitted to a share in the administration of the state." The central government limits the tyranny of serfdom, while Parliament checks the tyranny of kings.

[126] SCH, I: 530.   [127] SCH, I: 544.

Even during the civil wars of the fifteenth century the evolution of institutions proceeds. Constitutional adaptation and refinement continue "to emerge from a confused mass of unconscious agencies, rather than from the direct action of a great lawgiver, or from the victory of acknowledged principles." Yet amid all the "superficial refinement, heartless selfishness and moral degradation" the late middle ages are an age of "great constitutional results."[128] By the Tudor period, when Stubbs closed his account, it has already been reshaped to meet the requirements of the era to come.

> Here as everywhere the dawn is approaching. Here as everywhere the evil is destroying itself, and the remaining good, lying deep down and having yet to wait long before it reaches the surface, is already striving toward the sunlight that is to come. The good is to come out of the evil … The thread of national life is not to be broken, but the earlier strands are to be sought out and bound together with threefold union for the new work. But it will be a work of time … Much will be destroyed that might well have been conserved, and some new growths will be encouraged that ought to have been checked. In the destruction and in the growth alike will be seen the great features of difference between the old and the new.[129]

10   The English Constitution and Anglo-Indian history

The publication of the final volume of Stubbs's *Constitutional History* marked a significant watershed. For the first time history had been written by an English academic fully up to the highest standards of German scholarship. Of course, the book would never be popular, and even students might consult it primarily as a reference work.[130] Nevertheless Stubbs had breathed new life into medieval constitutional history, and his book was followed by the (sometimes revisionist) work of Maitland, Pollock, and Vinogradoff, as well as others who further transformed the historiography of medieval England. Stubbs himself resisted appeals to shorten and simplify his study for the textbook market. His book had stimulated others to take up this task, and he recommended D. J. Medley's *A Student's Manual of English Constitutional History* in particular.[131] Like Stubbs, Medley viewed the English Constitution as an

---

[128] SCH, I: 545, II: 317.   [129] SCH, III: 614–15.

[130] Burrow, *Liberal Descent*, 119–25, 129–31. James Vernon notes the way in which the professionalism of Stubbs was used to attack the amateur impressionism of Macaulay, while the more rigorous professionalism of Maitland was used to sideline the professionalism of Stubbs. "Narrating the Constitution: The Discourse of the 'Real' and the Fantasies of Nineteenth Century Constitutional History," in James Vernon (ed.), *Re-Reading the Constitution: New Narratives in the Political History of England's Long Nineteenth Century* (Cambridge, 1996), 204–38.

[131] D. J. Medley, *A Student's Manual of English Constitutional History* (Oxford, 1894); *Letters of William Stubbs*, ed. W. H. Hutton (London, 1904), 366.

evolutionary product, "the result of a practically unbroken development of thirteen hundred years." Yet, like Stubbs, he had little to say about how it was adapting to an imperial polity that was global in scale. Could the democratic installments of the nineteenth century – which were turning more and more British men from subjects into citizens – be extended to the mixed and "coloured" colonies? Conversely, could the British parliamentary electors in the Home Island be regarded as trustees for the welfare and liberties of colonial dependents, in much the same way as Stubbs and Medley made medieval aristocrats into the agents of freedom for all Englishmen? As Antoinette Burton has demonstrated, English feminists were staking their own claims to the franchise, in part, on their role as protectors of even more subjugated women in the colonies. Could the rights of women be traced back to the Anglo-Saxon forests, or the Magna Carta? If so, was this to be taken as a mark of Englishwomen's racial superiority?[132]

Stubbs had nothing to say about this fast-moving modern constitution, but his whole approach conduced to viewing it as a continuum, in which enfranchisement and subordination were interconnected categories. The Saxons had not remained colonial subjects of their Norman masters. Rather, the two groups had assimilated and their institutions had fused in a particularly fruitful way. "The ancient system of the [Saxon] Shire rises to the highest functions of government; the authority of royal justice permeates the lowest regions of the popular organization." But how far could this sleek Darwinian organism of the English Constitution – the product of many centuries of societal selection – be further adapted to incorporate the local institutions and traditions of the many racially diverse subjects of Victoria's Crown? The Oxford historian E. S. Creasy was wary of over-rapid change. He noted that there were "many great differences and variations" between different colonies and dependencies "with regard to the amount of local self-government as to legislation, as to taxation and other matters." These differences were partly the result of historical accident, but more broadly they were reflective of the level of evolutionary development which any given colonial people had achieved. While favorably disposed to the semi-civilized Negroes of the West Indies, who were absorbing much of Anglo-Saxon culture, Creasy regarded "a very large portion of the natives ... the Hottentots and Kaffirs of the Cape, the Aborigines of Australia, the Eskimaux and Red Indians of the Hudson Bay territories," to be "unfit for the constitutional franchise."[133]

---

[132] Medley, *Constitutional History*, 197–207, 227–30; Antoinette Burton, *Burdens of History: British Feminists, Indian Women, and Imperial Culture, 1865–1915* (Chapel Hill, 1994), 10–11, 171–205.

[133] SCH, I: 551; E. S. Creasy, *The Imperial and Colonial Constitutions of the Britannic Empire* (London, 1872), 3, 36–7.

In the colonies of Anglo-Saxon settlement, by contrast, "men of European race form a majority; men whose education and property are at least on a level with the bulk of the electors in the home country." Like their predecessors who had settled American shores, these Anglo-Saxon colonists were fit for self-government because they demonstrated an innate "constitutional morality," without which "no democratic community can long exist." Predisposed to independence under the rule of law, these heirs of the Magna Carta exhibited a spontaneous order. They had succeeded in taming the wilderness because they had carried their civilization with them into the bush. Such a people could not be taxed by an Empire in which they were not represented. Only responsible government and political autonomy within a globe-spanning Anglo-Saxon federation could keep their allegiance to Greater Britain alive.[134] Given his equation of colonial autonomy with historical civilization, Creasy found the case of India perplexing. Here it was not savagery but "over-civilization" that unfitted Indians for self-government. "It was a country where (with some few local exceptions) there was no idea of internal liberty, and there was in the mass of the population no pride as to national independence." India had been repeatedly conquered, and these conquests produced "a false and cowardly people" who were "abject, degraded, false to the very core." The trouble with the anglicized bhadralok was that their acquisition of an English education had not been accompanied by the backbone, initiative, and character exhibited by Anglo-Saxons everywhere around the globe.[135]

Of course, not all metropolitan liberals agreed with Creasy. Charles Dilke, in *Greater Britain*, argued that "India [under British rule] is being made a country, is being created under the name where none has yet existed." He saw no reason why this incipient Indian nationalism should be incompatible with his Greater British imperial allegiance. "Whether the India which is being thus rapidly built up by our own hands will be friendly to us, or the reverse, depends upon ourselves." Offering an overture to men like Dutt, he opposed racial restrictions in the ICS and advocated the very gradual introduction of representative institutions. Yet Dilke mused about whether some Anglo-Saxon racial atavism might not preclude this peaceful transfer of power. Interviewing officers in their barracks about their experience during the Mutiny, he came to realize that many had welcomed what they saw as a golden opportunity to run amuck.

It is in India, when listening to a mess-table conversation on the subject of looting that we begin to remember our descent from Scandinavian sea-robbers. Centuries

---

[134] Creasy, *Imperial and Colonial Constitutions*, 37, 108, 154–6.
[135] Creasy, *Imperial and Colonial Constitutions*, 174–89, 193–4, 211.

of education have not purified the blood; our men in India can hardly set eyes on a native prince or a Hindoo palace before they cry, "What a place to *break up!*" "What a fellow to *loot!*"[136]

Duly appalled by such attitudes in the military, Dilke worried that these martinets might bring their acquired taste for despotism back home. Nevertheless, pride of race left him with some vestige of that adventuring spirit that had enabled his ancestors to conquer an empire. "Love of race among the English rests upon a firmer base than either love of mankind or love of Britain, for it reposes upon a subsoil of things known." These "race distinctions will long continue," for "miscegenation will go but little way towards blending races." Yet Dilke had not given up the traditional liberal dicta "to act justly towards Ireland" and "to govern India aright," nor even had he given up the long-term "possibility of planting free institutions among the dark-skinned races of the world."[137]

Nevertheless, by the 1890s, British politics was falling into the hands of a new generation that now took evolutionism for granted, and was casually familiar with the tomes of Maine, Freeman, Green, and Stubbs. In 1892, a review of Indian administration called upon Parliament to consider whether the traditions of representative government that had been won by their forebears had any relevance for the inhabitants of the Indian subcontinent. Speaking on behalf of Lord Salisbury's Tory government, the young under-secretary G. N. Curzon was prepared to enlarge the existing (appointive) legislative councils, to allow members to criticize the budget, and to authorize the Viceroy to introduce a few elective seats, at his discretion. When a few radical MPs proposed to incorporate the elective element directly into the Bill, Curzon demurred, complaining about liberals "whose ideas of political progress have been formed in the breathless atmosphere of the West, and who are perhaps unable to accommodate their pace to the slower movement of life in the East." "The idea of representation is alien to the Indian mind," he continued, "we have only arrived at it by slow degrees ourselves, through centuries of conflict and storm ... How can you predicate political equality of a community that is sundered into irreconcilable camps?"[138]

From this point onward, the debate became a referendum on the perceived ability of Indians to represent themselves on the imperial stage. According to the Manchester radical Charles Schwann, "the Indian people" had "now attained to a clear idea of nationality" through exposure to the English language and the English institutions of

---

[136] Dilke, *Greater Britain*, 423.
[137] Dilke, *Greater Britain*, 423–546, quotes on 544 and 546.
[138] *Parliamentary Debates*, 4th ser., III (London, 1892), 53–68, March 28, 1892.

commerce, free assembly, and a free press. This national voice was embodied in the recently formed Congress movement, where "you will find representatives of all the races of India acting together for political ends." By contrast, sneered James MacLean, "no amount of English education could change the character [of the Indian people] or give them that sobriety and robustness of disposition which is essential to the smooth and even working of representative institutions." Free institutions were the birthright of English Teutons, "a race that has love of freedom instinctively in its life-blood." "You are running a great risk," he warned, "in proposing to transfer a large portion of the administration of India to men like the Bengalees, who have been slaves, nay, the bondsmen of slaves, for fifty generations."[139]

Having survived the condescension of Maine and the jests of Lytton, anglicized bhadralok like Dutt were not inclined to lose sleep over such crude reactionary jeers. More alarming was the indifference of Liberal leaders who, like W. E. Gladstone, made it clear that he was satisfied with Curzon's moderate Tory measure, regarding it as suited to the condition of the Indian people.[140] With both parties eager to move on to other subjects, the bhadralok intellectuals saw that they were on their own. The idea that Saxon freedoms might now evolve in an Indian context was a conceit that they had to nurse secretly, among themselves. In the metropolis, they now heard only a handful of sympathetic voices, such as that of Charles Dilke – now discredited by a divorce scandal, expunged from the Liberal leadership, and representing no one but himself.

As has been well shown, men who speak better English than most Englishmen; who conduct able newspapers in our tongue; who form the majority on town councils which admirably supervise the affairs of great cities; who, as native judges, have reached the highest judicial posts; who occupy seats on the Provincial, the Presidency, and the Viceregal Councils, or, as powerful ministers, excellently rule vast native states, – can no longer be treated as hopelessly inferior to ourselves in governmental power.[141]

---

[139] *Parliamentary Debates*, 4th ser., III: 68–78, 83–95.
[140] *Parliamentary Debates*, 4th ser., III: 78–84.
[141] Charles Dilke, *The Problems of Greater Britain* (London, 1890), 433.

6   Indian liberals and Greater Britain: the
     search for union through history

> The mutual intercourse of England and India, political as well as social,
> is destined to promote the true interests and glory of both nations . . . For
> greater will be our rejoicing when all the chiefs and people of India shall
> be united with the English nation in a vast International assemblage,
> before the throne of the King of Kings, and the Lord of Lords.
>
> Keshub Chandra Sen, Delhi, 1877, quoted in MLS, 284

> Rightly or wrongly, for good or evil, Englishmen and Indians have been
> knit together, and it behooves both races so to mould themselves as to
> leave a splendid legacy to generations yet to be born, and to show that
> though Empires have gone and fallen this Empire may perhaps be an
> exception and that this Empire is not founded on material but spiritual
> foundations.
>
> M. K. Gandhi, Cape Town, 1914, in *The Collected Works of Mahatma Gandhi*,
> XII (New Delhi, 1964), 505

On the evening of February 13, 1866, the President of the London
Ethnological Society, John Crawfurd, addressed its assembled members,
arguing that European races were superior to those of Asia in almost every
respect. Exactly five weeks later, Dadabhai Naoroji, a Parsi merchant
from Bombay, stood before the same body to deliver a paper refuting
Crawfurd's claims. Unintimidated by the glittering array of brilliant
scientific minds in front of him – probably including Thomas Huxley,
Francis Galton, Sir John Lubbock, Sir Roderick Murchison, and many
others – Naoroji ripped Crawfurd's tendentious confection into hopeless
shreds. Crawfurd was guilty of "superficial observations and hasty conclusions," Naoroji complained.[1] The notion that Europeans were more
intelligent than Asians was no more than a shallow prejudice. Asian
students performed at parity with their European counterparts whenever

---

[1] John Crawfurd, "On the Physical and Mental Characteristics of European and Asiatic
Races of Man," *Transactions of the Ethnological Society of London*, NS, 5 (1867), 58–81.
Dadabhai Naoroji, "Observations on Mr. John Crawfurd's Paper," *Transactions of the
Ethnological Society of London*, NS, 5 (1867), 127–49, quote on 133; names are taken from the
list of officers published therein.

open examinations were held. The masterpieces of Asian literature were in no wise inferior to those of Europe, according to objective judges who were equally familiar with both. Instances of perjury in Indian courts were hardly the basis for impugning the integrity of an entire nation. How would Englishmen like to be evaluated by rigged, defamatory standards of this kind? Naoroji related the story of an Indian acquaintance, who had privately complained:

Look at the mass of untruths in the [London] daily advertisements; in the daily language of the shopkeepers; how much swindling there is in the concoction of companies for the benefit of the promoters only; see what the book on facts, failures and frauds discloses; what extremely watchful care one is obliged to have in his dealings in the city, when every kind of scoundrelism is so rife . . . As long as an Englishman wanted anything he was the model of politeness, but the object gained, he was no more the same person.

On the basis of such observations, the Indian had concluded "that the English were the most selfish and unprincipled people." If this was a rash and unjust conclusion, how was it any different from those that Crawfurd had pseudo-scientifically made?[2]

1   The Calcutta bhadralok and British racial ideology

In Chapter 5, we have seen how Crawfurd's sloppy retreat into racist assumptions was fueled by the new evolutionary approach to history. Yet Naoroji's bold invocation of a better cross-cultural science was also the product of changes that had occurred during the previous thirty years. By the 1860s, his native Bombay had become a thriving international commercial center, while Calcutta could now boast a large English-educated bhadralok. On one level, these facts reflected the triumph of Macaulay's program of anglicization. Yet on another level, they revealed the complications and contradictions that Macaulay had failed to grasp. Of the 1,300 English-educated students who were enrolled in Calcutta University, very few would enjoy Rammohun Roy's economic independence, and even fewer could aspire to the high-level governmental employment first achieved, in 1868, by R. C. Dutt. To be sure, these Bengalis streamed into lower levels of the civil service, but the poor salaries and limited promotions to which such positions confined them precluded the role of *patria potestas*, which Maine had identified as the precondition for autonomous masculinity. Even the fortunate few with economic resources tended to retreat from economically innovative entrepreneurship,

---

[2] Naoroji, "Observations on Mr. John Crawfurd's Paper," 141–2.

which still seemed viable in Rammohun Roy's day. After the commercial crisis of 1848, when native elites lost a great deal of money to what they perceived as European swindling, most withdrew their remaining capital into the safety of landholding. As a result, large-scale business became an increasingly British affair. The leading families, the Roys, the Tagores, the Sens, and many others, had now been collaborating with the British for two or three generations, and yet felt, if anything, more uncertain about their place. After Rammohun's death, Brahmo Samaj fell into abeyance, largely because of the indifference of his friend Dwarkanath Tagore, a thoroughgoing secularist, who became wealthy and traveled to Europe, where he died in 1846. Thereafter, the organization was revived by his son, Debendranath, who cultivated a more austere and contemplative lifestyle.[3]

Nevertheless, the Brahmo Samaj of the late 1840s and 1850s turned into a far more modest undertaking than what Rammohun Roy had originally envisaged. Gone was that bold reformer's highly visible persona of the 1820s, as his ambitious syncretic claims to having reconciled Hinduism with the teachings of Moses, Mohammed, Buddha, and Christ were allowed to lapse. The more pragmatic Tagore was content to remain a practicing Brahman, continuing most of the familiar Hindu rituals and ceremonies but giving them a more rationalistic and mono-theistic gloss. There were several good reasons for Debendranath's caution. In the first place, the Christian missionaries were growing steadily more ubiquitous and aggressive under the leadership of the pugnacious Presbyterian Alexander Duff. Although few scions of the Bengali Brahman elite were likely to become Christians, a significant number were becoming radical secularists, or even atheists, under the inspiration of Henry Derozio and David Hare. These devotees of "Young Bengal" seemed to be aping the worst habits of Englishmen. Spouting Tom Paine and flouting Brahman customs, they turned to beefeating and indulged in strong drink. A return to Hindu traditions was necessary, Debendranath concluded, if Bengalis were to preserve their cultural identity and retain their self-respect.[4]

[3] R. P. Masani, *Dadabhai Naoroji: The Grand Old Man of India* (Mysore, Kavyalaya, 1957); Narendra Krishna Sinha, "Indian Business Enterprise: Its Failure in Calcutta," in Rajat Ray (ed.), *Entrepreneurship and Industry in India* (Oxford, 1984), 70–82; Amiya Bagchi, *Private Investment in India, 1900–1939* (Cambridge, 1972), 165–81. For the social history of the bhadralok community, see John McGuire, *The Making of a Colonial Mind: A Quantitative Study of the Bhadralok of Calcutta, 1857–1885* (Canberra, 1985); J. H. Broomfield, *Elite Conflict in a Plural Society* (Berkeley, 1968), 1–41.
[4] David Kopf, *The Brahmo Samaj and the Shaping of the Indian Mind* (Princeton, 1979), especially 42–6; Amiya Kumar Sen, *Tattwabodhini Patrika and the Bengal Renaissance* (Calcutta, 1979); Devendranath Tagore, *Autobiography of Maharisi Devendranath Tagore*

It is in this context that we must assess the consequences of the increasing racism of the Victorian Raj. In the age of Malcolm and Elphinstone, the bhadralok had friends in high places, but this was no longer the case. Even the most broad-minded and intellectually sophisticated policy-makers, such as Campbell or Maine, had grown wary of the Bengali babus, since the very existence of these cultural hybrids raised the disturbing prospect that India might be able to modernize without British control. For the less discriminating and more arrogant of the new sahibs, all Indians were lumped together as inconsequential "niggers" who needed to be kept in submissive obloquy. This put anglicized bhadralok like Debendranath in a bind. To follow blindly along Macaulay's path of anglicization was to risk humiliation and rejection, and yet repudiation of the British connection would be tantamount to squandering their economic position and denying their own identity.[5]

Matters came to a head in 1849, when Macaulay's friend (and successor as Law Member of Council) J. D. Bethune proposed a sweeping overhaul of India's judicial system that would extend the principle of legal race equality from civil to criminal jurisdictions. To the surprise of liberals in both countries, this proposal precipitated a shockwave of fury and vituperation from the European community in Calcutta, which fixated on the prospect that white men (or, even worse, white women) might find themselves subject to the mercies of a native magistrate. When asked how he could possibly justify the existence of a separate and unequal legal system for each race, the leader of this agitation had the temerity (and the candor) to proclaim,

Considered politically, my sable friend, our right to be well-governed does not rest on the same basis. You are one of a conquered race, who have no original and strictly political right to be well-governed. You are at the mercy of your conquerors. But I am one of a nation who have their right guaranteed by such things as Magna Carta, the Bill of Rights, the Act of Settlement, and a few other conditions.[6]

For Indian liberals, it was a shock to be told in such blunt and unequivocal language that the Magna Carta and the Bill of Rights did not apply

(Calcutta, 1909); David Kopf, *British Orientalism and the Bengal Renaissance: The Dynamics of Indian Modernization, 1773–1835* (Berkeley, 1969), 215–94; M. K. Haldar, "Introduction," in Haldar (ed. and trans.), *Renaissance and Reaction in Nineteenth Century Bengal* (Calcutta, 1977), 1–145, especially 6–23, 54–72, 79–82; E. W. Madge, *Henry Derozio, the Eurasian Poet and Reformer* [1904] (Calcutta, 1982).

[5] Nemai Sudhan Bose, *Racism, Struggle for Equality, and Indian Nationalism* (Calcutta, 1981); Haldar, "Introduction," 53. See also Anil Seal, *The Emergence of Indian Nationalism: Competition and Collaboration in the Later Nineteenth Century* (Cambridge, 1968), 1–130.

[6] Bose, *Racism, Struggle*, 1–129, quote on 101.

to people like themselves. When the government withdrew Bethune's bill, when even Macaulay remained silent about this repudiation of his principles, Young Bengal (now aging) had to face the prospect that anglicization might be a dangerous and untenable ruse. The problem was not that British liberals had completely disappeared from India, for there were still a minority, like Macaulay's nephew G. O. Trevelyan, who protested the racist belittlement of "niggers," who denounced planter exploitation of peasants, and who exposed British atrocities in the repression of mutiny. Yet Trevelyan's writings also reveal the subtle influence of the new evolutionary thinking, in a manner that led him to caricature the anglicized native in whom his uncle had placed high hopes. The Bengali babu was not "like the north American Indian, a barbarian" or "like the European of the middle ages, the member of a community rude ... but replete with germs of vigorous civilization." He was a man whose evolutionary development had been arrested, whose "fundamental characteristic is want of stamina," and who "is perfectly contented to glisten and bask in the sun for days and weeks." Trevelyan might well endorse such a man's legal rights, but could never regard him as an equal. If nature, not discrimination, had excluded such men from attaining the Bill of Rights or the Magna Carta, there was nothing the English liberal could do. Such attitudes help to explain why the members of Brahmo (and the bhadralok in general) felt impelled to embrace their "oriental" difference, and to hope that they might find a metropolitan interlocutor who could authorize their efforts to turn it from a disability into an advantage, underwriting an alternative evolutionary path into consequential history.[7]

Although British orientalism was effectively dead by the 1840s and 1850s, its death paradoxically opened the way for Indians to take possession of it, and for such an interlocutor to appear. For the center of indological studies had passed during this period to Germany and France, where it acquired a more detached ideological character that was no longer implicated in the daily management of the British Empire. Thus when a young German philologist named Friedrich Max Müller made his way to Oxford in 1848, key members of the English intelligentsia were intrigued. Somewhat embarrassed by the breakthroughs of their European competitors in setting comparative philology on a scientific footing, they were prepared to support the young German to stay among them. Encouraged by these supporters (including his future brother-in-law, Froude), Max Müller gained a reputation as a dynamic and engaging lecturer. Great advances, he explained to his audiences, had been made since the days

[7] G. O. Trevelyan, *The Competition Wallah* [1864] (New Delhi, 1992), quotes on 141–2.

of Sir William Jones. The connection between Sanskrit and classical European languages that Jones had been the first to point out was not merely one of grammar, mythology, or culture. It had to represent a deeper consanguinity of heredity and race. Müller invited his audiences "to imagine that there was a time when the ancestors of the Celts, the Germans, the Romans, the Slavs, the Greeks, and the Italians, and the Hindus were living together beneath the same roof." From this perspective, Britain's Indian Empire was itself a reunion of long-lost cousins, returning "to their primordial soil, to accomplish the glorious work of civilization, which had been left unfinished by their Aryan brethren." To justify his many years of preparing the first truly accurate, scholarly edition of the *Rig Veda*, Müller encouraged his listeners to read this ancient, seemingly alien document, in which they might discover "the childhood of the Aryan mind."[8]

As they followed Max Müller's work from the distance of Calcutta, the bhadralok intelligentsia were delighted to find a metropolitan interlocutor who would publicly articulate a respect for their history.[9] Not directly implicated in the machinery of government, and something of an alien himself, Max Müller gave hope of a new kind of bordering, in which educated Indians might find their own unique road to modern accomplishment through a reinterpretation of their ancient history. It might be that Indians had no Bill of Rights and no Magna Carta, but they had documents that were much older, profounder, and therefore closer to the moral foundations of humanity. The western Aryans (culminating with the British) had indeed evolved sophisticated forms of political organization that combined representative government with geo-political power. However, the eastern Aryans had perfected those spiritual resources, whose germ could be detected in the three-thousand-year-old *Veda*, but which the occident had abandoned in its quest for worldly might. Like the English imperialists, then, the Bengali bhadralok could regard itself as a people of world-historical significance. No longer need they remain pathetic suppliants at the hands of the foreign master. From the

[8] Nirad Chaudhuri, *Scholar Extraordinary: The Life of Professor the Rt. Hon. Friedrich Max Müller P.C.* (London, 1974), 311–16, who tends to be too forgiving of Max Müller's many sins. See also Thomas Trautmann, *Aryans and British India* (Berkeley, 1997), 172–83 and *passim*, for a full discussion of the relationship between Aryanism as a philological category and as a racial concept, as well as Tony Ballantyne, *Orientalism and Race: Aryanism in the British Empire* (London, 2002), 38–55, 169–87.

[9] "What a sublime spectacle," proclaimed Krishna Bihari Sen (Keshub's brother). "The Hindu and Englishman are brothers! ... Do not jealousies, struggles and bloodshed appear contemptible where every brother man is learning to recognize in the face of his fellow-creature the image of his first forefathers?" Quoted in Joan Leopold, "British Applications of the Aryan Theory of Race to India," *English Historical Review*, 89.352 (July, 1974), 578–603.

spiritual and historiographical riches at their disposal, they might craft an alternative "moral" road to modernization, providing – from their oriental vantage – a lesson of hope and faith for all humanity. During the 1820s, of course, Rammohun had tried to forge such a synthesis, but the times had been unpropitious, and his message proved premature. Now, however, in the 1850s, his Brahmo descendants looked for another spokesman who might repackage spiritual syncretism into a form that would be appropriate for the Victorian age. Debendranath could not provide the requisite charismatic leadership, but when he found these skills in a younger disciple, Keshub Chandra Sen, he was happy to raise the young man up.[10]

2   Keshub Chandra Sen and the quest for spiritual history

Like the Roys and the Tagores, the Sens were an old Bengali zamindar family that had gained wealth and power from collaboration with the British over many years. However, unlike his counterparts in the other leading families, Ram Camul Sen (Keshub's grandfather) remained faithful to the most traditional Hindu religious practices, even as he participated in Calcutta's modern capitalist economy. The result was a contradiction between the tenor of commercialism in the office and the traditionalism that reigned at home. Like Rammohun two generations earlier, the young Keshub interpreted this cognitive dissonance as a mark of hypocrisy. Turning to Debendranath as an alternative mentor, Keshub disdained what he regarded as his uncles' empty agnatic rituals, removed his child bride from his aunts' zenana, and educated her in the principles of rational religion. Finding a family substitute in Brahmo Samaj, Keshub got swept up in its associational activities, taking a leadership role in outreach efforts to the younger (his own) generation. With a powerful voice and a theatrical manner, he quickly developed a reputation as a dynamic, inspirational speaker. "Those who desire to reform their country must first reform themselves," he admonished the devotees of Young Bengal. "I am extremely happy to learn that you have recently abandoned those skeptical notions which you hitherto so obstinately cherished." Although skepticism had weaned them from idolatry and superstition, it offered only "a spurious liberalism" in their place.[11]

[10] Tapan Raychaudhuri, *Europe Reconsidered: Perceptions of the West in Nineteenth Century Bengal* (Oxford, 2002); Indira Chowdhuri, *The Frail Hero and Virile History: Gender and the Politics of Culture in Colonial Bengal* (Oxford, 1998), 40–65.
[11] BKCS, 1–16; MLS, 44–59, 60–72.

Keshub sympathized completely with his compatriots' desire to become modern, but he insisted that for Indians, modernization had to take the form of new and experimental modes of spirituality. Boldly taking a leaf from the Christian proselytizers, he opened a Brahmo school, established a newspaper, and created a Brahmo missionary agency that sent evangelists out to Madras, Bombay, and the Bengali countryside. As new recruits streamed into the Calcutta Samaj, membership rose to over 6,000. Somewhat astonished at Keshub's accomplishment, Debendranath acknowledged him as co-leader of the congregation. Yet amid all this bustle of fresh activity, many of the older Brahmos began to murmur complaints: Keshub was moving too fast and trying too much. In particular, he was pushing radical ideas about gender and the family that threatened to strike at the very heart of Hindu patriarchy. Indeed, to Keshub, it simply followed from the logic of Brahmo rationalism that men and women of every caste ought to be encouraged to participate equally in the same religious fellowship. Caste differences should be ignored, caste intermarriage and widow re-marriage should be encouraged, child marriage should be abolished, and wives should have independent legal rights.[12]

To the conservative faction, with which Debendranath was increasingly sympathetic, such radical innovations were tantamount to a social revolution. They would represent a humiliating concession to alien British customs and a complete betrayal of all Hindu tradition. Somewhat reluctant to fall back to the stance of absolute Hindu traditionalism, the Brahmo conservatives sought to justify their resistance to Keshub by wrapping it in the mantle of cultural-nationalist history. "Under present conditions," warned Debendranath's son Dwijendranath, "an adoption of European habits would be like wearing a badge of slavery."

With our present inferiority and infirmities we are little better than the Christian Negro of North America, who speaks English, dresses himself with the jacket and pantaloon, and whose habits of life and fact are mostly borrowed from the European settlers there. And why so? Simply because his civilization is nothing more than an image of European manners and habits ... By means of mere imitation we can be just so much like the Europeans as slaves are like their masters.[13]

The Tagores recognized, as well as anyone, that if Indian men were to escape from their "slavery," they would have to become masters of modern technology and political organization. However, such modernization

[12] BKCS, 1–46; MLS, 73–109. See also Sen's "Autobiography," reprinted in MLS, 325–56.
[13] Quoted in Kopf, *Brahmo Samaj*, 183.

would only lead to further dependence and disaster if it were achieved at the expense of India's long, honorable tradition of spiritual superiority. Contra Macaulay, they insisted that modernization had to be translated into a Hindu idiom and synchronized with the rhythms of Indian history. "Each nation holds a distinct nationality," Dwijendranath argued, "and for so holding it, is entitled to the appellation of a civilized nation." The trouble with Indians was that they "rush madly to their own degradation by acting under the supposition that to imitate English civilization ... is synonymous with making progress ... instead of making national institutions the basis of all progress."[14]

To Keshub and his followers, these arguments were unpersuasive, not because they were content to become second-rate English imitators, but because they believed that Brahmo Samaj – while certainly modeled on British prototypes – represented a considerable advance over the British in creating genuinely cosmopolitan spiritual and organizational forms. If the Hindu bhadralok was willing to give up his retrograde caste and patriarchal privileges, according to Keshub, he would be able to access Rammohun Roy's syncretist principles, around which Brahmoism had originally crystallized. Only if Brahmo Samaj detached itself from its objectionable entanglements, and accessed the deeper channels of its indigenous traditions, could it hope to play a catalytic role in forging the nineteenth century's new chapter in universal history. The bhadralok had the chance to create a new spiritualized progress narrative, if it avoided the errors of dogmatic anglicization and dogmatic Brahmanism alike. By returning to the purity of his original pre-caste religion, the "effeminate Bengali" so despised by English racists could re-make himself into the agent of a future human fraternity.[15]

3   Brahmo Samaj and the evolution of spirituality

To understand the logic of Keshub's position it is necessary to grasp the dangerously exposed situation in which the bhadralok community found itself after the 1857 Revolt. Rejected by the rebels as an alien excrescence, the bhadralok were yet dismissed by the British as ineffectual prattlers, openly compliant, but secretly disloyal. Caught in the maws of this double rejection, the more perspicacious among them saw that they could afford neither to blindly imitate the British nor to reject the urban anglocentric culture from which they themselves came. Here again, Max Müller, now well ensconced in Oxford, appeared as the rare

---

[14] Quoted in Kopf, *Brahmo Samaj*, 183; Haldar, "Introduction," 84–9.
[15] Kopf, *Brahmo Samaj*, 3–156; MLS, 73–133; BKCS, 38–65.

metropolitan interlocutor who both appreciated their predicament and served as a catalyst in their search for a solution. Müller's own reaction to the Mutiny was to blame it on EIC officials' ignorance of Indian languages and cultures, which blinded the Raj to such symptoms of impending disaster as any competent ruler ought to have perceived. The British were fixated on the loyalty of traditional elites and the passivity of the peasants, forgetting that they "must please and conciliate the educated classes of the native community," so that these Indian opinion-makers might be "charmed out of their prejudices or the errors of their preconceived opinions." Two years later, in 1859, he published *A History of Ancient Sanskrit Literature*, in which he indicated some of the ways in which his type of scholarship might provide a ground on which educated Britons and Indians could meet.[16]

The first gift of Sanskrit scholarship to the Indians was the evidence it provided of their racial quality. "What authority," he asks, "would have been strong enough to persuade ... the English soldier that the same blood was running in his veins and in the veins of the dark Bengalese?" "There is not," he concludes, "an English jury now a days, which after examining the hoary documents of language, would reject the claim of a common descent ... between Hindu, Greek and Teuton." Late in life, Müller became persuaded of the toxicity of "race" as a category in historical science. With some annoyance, he complained that "to speak of an Aryan race, would be akin to speaking of a dolichocephalic grammar." The "confusion in the popular mind," he insisted in a letter to E. A. Freeman, "arises chiefly from a confusion of terminology which was meant for linguistic purposes" being applied inappropriately as a measure of consanguinity. "Let people classify blood as much as they like," he concluded, "only let them use their own bottles for that." The problem was that Müller himself often used his own "linguistic bottles" to make claims about racial kinship in his published writings, so determined was he to convince Britons that "there *was* a time when the ancestors of the Celts, the Germans, the Slavonians, the Greeks, and the Italians, Persians, and Hindus were living together within the same fences."[17]

Of course, the western and eastern Aryans had eventually separated, and their divergent experiences underwrote two different evolutionary histories that shaped them on their way to modernity. Where the western

---

[16] John Rosselli, "The Self-Image of Effeteness: Physical Education and Nationalism in Nineteenth Century Bengal," *Past and Present*, 86 (1980), 121–48; Friedrich Max Müller, *A History of Ancient Sanskrit Literature* (London, 1859).

[17] Müller, *Sanskrit Literature*, 13; Georgina Max Müller, *The Life and Letters of the Rt. Hon. Friedrich Max Müller* (London, 1902), I: 396; Chaudhuri, *Scholar Extraordinary*, quote on 312.

Aryans had to fight their way through a Darwinian proving ground of struggling peoples, all contending for a limited European space, the eastern Aryans endured only a brief initial contest against primitive indigenes before they settled down to a contemplative life in the "rich plains and beautiful groves" of their fertile new country.

Greece and India are, indeed, the two opposite poles in the historical development of the Aryan man. To the Greek, existence is full of life and reality ... The Hindu enters this world as a stranger; all his thoughts are directed to another world ... The highest object of their religion was to restore the bond by which their own self (âtman) was linked to the eternal Self (paramâtman); to recover that unity which had been clouded and obscured by the magical illusions of reality.

"It might," Müller acknowledged, "be justly said that India has no place in the political history of the world," but "it certainly has a right to claim its place in the intellectual history of mankind."[18]

When Keshub and his Brahmo associates read these words, they took them as an invitation to offer their own vision of a modern Greater British imperial union, which would neither make unwanted demands for political inclusion nor compromise their sense of inner integrity. The union that Keshub now proposed was built on the notion of a reciprocal division of labor, in which Britain would provide the political infrastructure and administration for Empire, while India (i.e. Keshub) would provide the spiritual resources necessary to infuse these structures with moral vitality. Fired with a new-found sense of confidence, Keshub strove to pick up Rammohun's syncretism where that prophet had left it off. Having freed Brahmoism from the fetters of caste and male privilege, he re-established lines of communication with a new generation of British and American Unitarians with a view to creating a worldwide federation of rational theism, in which Indians would be equals or even take the spiritual lead. In correspondence with James Martineau, Frances Power Cobbe, Mary Carpenter, and S. D. Collet, he came to see the striking parallels between the associational culture long practiced by Nonconformist liberals in Britain and the program of social reform and rational religion that he was determined to inject into the Indian scene. From this perspective, the historical vicissitudes that had linked Britain and India together appeared to be providential. In the past the relationship might have been predatory and unequal. With the triumph of nineteenth-century liberalism, however, this was no longer the case. Now Britain and India were able to work together. They could help one another in a

---

[18] Müller, *Sanskrit Literature*, 18, 19, 25, 31–2.

manner that was no longer exploitative, because their union presaged a global future of universal harmony.[19]

Of course, Keshub's reluctance to characterize the nineteenth-century Anglo-Indian relationship as exploitative flew in the face of the obvious power imbalance between them. Where Britons claimed the big benefits of political power and representative government, what could Indians throw into the scales to assert their equality? Keshub found his answer in 1866 while reading J. R. Seeley's recently published *Ecce Homo*. This English academic backhandedly acknowledged what Rammohun had proven fifty years earlier: Jesus was no divinity, but an inspired human prophet who stood in a long line of moral reformers stretching from Moses to the nineteenth century. But if Jesus had been a human prophet, what kind of person had he been? Again picking up an idea that Roy had thrown out in passing, Keshub pointed out that "Jesus was an Asiatic." "Christianity," he now claimed, "was founded by Asiatics in Asia ... In Christ we see not only the exaltedness of humanity, but also the grandeur of which the Asiatic nature is capable." Here was yet more proof that the eastern races (including the Semites in this case) had a special vocation for spirituality that the occidental races lacked. For two millennia, European Christians had lost sight of the fundamental message of Jesus, degrading it into arid theological dogmas, which diminished Christ to a pallid occidental like themselves. Since the time of the *Vedas*, Asia in general, and India in particular, had been the incubating ground of human spirituality. Christ had been but one episode in a line of prophetic succession that had stretched through Moses, Buddha, and Mohammed, finally returning to the Indian subcontinent in the modern epoch. Whenever north Europeans had transported Asian spiritual goods into their frigid climate, they had spoiled the merchandise by turning its message of universal communion into bloodcurdling battle-cries of warring creeds.[20]

Willing to grant the superiority of British goods in government, technology, trade, and administration, Keshub proposed that India exercise its comparative advantage by exporting its natural resources of "Asiatic" spirituality. Brahmos like himself would be essential in this operation, since they alone could refine India's indigenous spiritualism, ridding it of its retrograde idolatrous accretions, rendering it compatible with modern social organization, and honing its competitive advantage over

[19] Kopf, *Brahmo Samaj*, 4–41; MLS, 73–133; BKCS, 38–65.
[20] Kopf, *Brahmo Samaj*, 18–21, 112–18, 177–9, 268–9, quote on 113; BKCS, 66–73. Keshub's biographer, P. C. Mazoomdar, elaborated on these ideas of his master in his book *The Oriental Christ* (Boston, 1883). For a sophisticated analysis of the development of these tropes – eastern (spiritual) *contra* western (political) Aryans – see Raychaudhuri, *Europe Reconsidered*.

dogmatic Christianity. As an anglicized Bengali who spoke perfect English, Keshub made a plausible claim for the export license in Indian spirituality. He saw himself as uniquely qualified to translate (both literally and figuratively) India's message to Britain, while reconciling Indians to the material benefits that the union with Britain opened up. The logical conclusion of this line of thinking was to resolve that he should actually go to Britain to confer with European theists, and to preach his Brahmo ecumenicism in the imperial metropolis.[21]

When Keshub arrived in London, in March, 1870, he was not entirely certain of his reception. Unlike the small handful of Indian students or merchants then residing in Britain, he arrived as a public figure, with a busy schedule of addresses and meetings and considerable media interest in reporting his activities. Over the next seven months he delivered thirty-six speeches and twenty-four sermons to an audience of over 40,000 in fourteen different towns. Staying in the homes of many of the leading British Unitarians, he was wined and dined by Max Müller, Dean Stanley of Westminster, the philosopher John Stuart Mill, most of the leading Indian officials and politicians, and even the Prime Minister, W. E. Gladstone. The high point of his visit came on August 13, when he was granted an audience with the Queen. As Keshub himself put it, "they lionized me, and made too much of me ... they put me on platforms and carried me from town to town ... and thousands upon thousands came to hear me."[22]

When he returned home, Keshub assured his Indian audience that the results of his mission were "cheering and encouraging in the extreme." He brought with him "the genuine sympathy that thousands of Englishmen and Englishwomen" had expressed for his work. This was not to say that everything was perfect in England. "Destitution, poverty in its worst and most frightful phases is to be found on the streets of London – ignorance, frightful and appalling, pervade the masses of the people." Even more shocking to a spiritual man like himself were the "bigotry and superstition" of many of those who professed religion. "There are sects far more numerous in England than I ever thought. Two hundred and fifty small narrow sects into which Christendom in England has been split up! Oh a lamentable spectacle indeed." Clearly, the English had

---

[21] Keshub Chunder Sen, "Asia's Message to Europe," in *Lectures in India* (New York, 1904), 49–119; and his "Philosophy and Madness in Religion," in William Theodore de Barry (ed.), *Sources of Indian Tradition*, 2 vols. (Columbia, 1964), II: 67; MLS, 134–7.

[22] MLS, 134–52; BKCS, 100–34. Quote from Keshub Chunder Sen, "General Impressions of England and the English," in *Lectures in India*, 287–8. For a general analysis of nineteenth-century London see Antoinette Burton, *At the Heart of Empire: India and the Colonial Encounter in Late Victorian Britain* (Berkeley, 1998), especially 37–44.

much to learn from Indians about purity of devotion and ecumenical harmony.[23]

What Indian reformers like the Brahmos had to learn from the British was the power of voluntary associations to channel philanthropic resources and to effect social change. Many of these organizations were staffed and even managed by women. As a result of his extensive dealings with Francis Power Cobbe and Mary Carpenter, Keshub was profoundly impressed by their ability to improve the lot of women through education and political lobbying, as well as by criminalizing male domestic violence and regulating drink. Though he shared the sensitivity of all Bengali men to taunts of "effeminacy," Keshub had the self-confidence, during the early 1870s, to appreciate the ways in which British feminists' claim to a separate sphere of "moral" regeneration paralleled the "spiritual" claims for Indian men that he was asserting.[24] Let British men keep the spheres of militarism, business, and politics, he avowed. Bhadralok men and British women would share the moral and spiritual spheres among themselves. In this way they would make themselves indispensable to a complex modern society which could not live by guns, butter, or power alone.

Let the millions of my countrymen, Hindus, Parsees, Mahomedans, all races and sects and denominations of India, believe that Providence has, for noble benevolent and wise purposes, entrusted their destinies to England, and that good will eventually come out of such political connection. Those days are gone by never to return when men thought of holding India at the point of a bayonet ... Men [in England] are beginning to feel that India is a solemn trust ... God will not tolerate a Government at this time of the day based on principles other than those which we recognize as the principles of justice and benevolence.[25]

In the age of liberal imperialism, according to Keshub, Indian men no longer had to fear the threat of British brutality. If Indians wanted to be

---

[23] Sen, "General Impressions," 274, 285–6, 293–4.
[24] For a rich and comprehensive analysis of Indians' encounter with Britain during the late Victorian period, see Burton, *At the Heart of Empire*, which briefly touches on Dutt and Keshub and considers the case of several others in greater detail.
[25] Sen, "General Impressions," 275–6, 283–4, 286. Freemasonry, as Vahid Fozdar has shown, provided another arena in which Indian bourgeois men could seek equality with their Anglo-Saxon counterparts, although the strength of this movement lay not in Calcutta but in Bombay, where a somewhat less imbalanced relationship existed between capitalist elites of both races. Vahid Fozdar, "Imperial Brothers, Imperial Partners: Indian Freemasons, Race, Kinship, and Networking in the British Empire, and Beyond," in Durba Ghosh and Dane Kennedy (eds.), *Decentering Empire: Britain, India and the Transcolonial World* (Hyderabad, 2006), 104–29. In Bengal, Keshub's strategy was more circuitous but more aspirationally ambitious. Rather than claim a direct "brotherhood" with British men (which would almost certainly have been refused), he offered himself and the Brahmo bhadralok as partners in a trans-imperial endeavor in which Indian men would play a spiritually indispensable, but politically subordinate, role.

confirmed in their special spiritual vocation, they had only to "be loyal to the Queen and to the British Government," and to forgive past grievances in the manner of (orientalized) Christ. "Let not our enemies, let not our friends say that we are wanting in gratitude." Through a new rebalancing of the realms of matter and spirit Indians and Britons would learn from one another: "Let then India learn from England practical righteousness; let England learn from India, devotion, faith, and prayer . . . If we enter into a sort of moral and spiritual covenant with each other, mutually and independently resolving to supplement our respective deficiencies by receiving and accepting from one another . . . then I say a glorious result will accrue to both."[26]

For a few years, Keshub's vision of a Brahmo–British union seemed to be working as he created a Bengali culture filled with voluntary associations, temperance societies, Bands of Hope, industrial schools, and even ladies' normal schools, specially designed with the aid of Mary Carpenter, who traveled to India to lend a hand. Invited to the Viceroy's summer residence in Simla, Keshub was able to consolidate the legal status of Brahmo Hinduism by negotiating a special Brahmo Marriage Act.[27] Nevertheless, forces were gathering during the late 1870s that would show just how vulnerable Brahmo reformism really was. In the first place, Keshub's meteoric rise and his celebrity status in London generated a strong backlash of envy, both within the Calcutta bhadralok and among Anglo-Indian administrative elites. The Tory triumph of 1874 in the metropolis left a belated echo in India with the advent of Lord Lytton's Viceroyalty in 1876. Lytton's flagrant disregard for Bengali babus like Keshub released the hostility of many lesser EIC officials, who had long waited to cut such garrulous malcontents down to size.[28] Keshub's response to the petty harassment that ensued was to retreat into the company of those close disciples who accepted his authority. Brahmos who stood outside the charmed circle, however, now began to cavil and complain: Keshub preached Brahmo liberalism and democracy, yet he acted like an autocrat within the organization. He favored his relatives in important positions, and was trying to turn the Samaj into a family principality. Most alarmingly, for all his lofty talk about female emancipation, he ran his household according to the utmost standard of Hindu patriarchy.[29] Matters came to a head in 1878, when Keshub

---

[26] Sen, "General Impressions," 283, 291–2, 297; BKCS, 135–6.
[27] MLS, 153–70. See also Rachel Sturman, "Marriage and the Morality of Exchange: Defining the Terrain of Law in Late-Nineteenth Century Western India," in Ghosh and Kennedy (eds.), *Decentering Empire*, 51–75.
[28] Bose, *Racism, Struggle*, 85–151.
[29] MLS, especially 167–70; and F. Max Müller, *Biographical Essays* (New York, 1884); BKCS, 174–201; Seal, *Emergence of Indian Nationalism*, 140–1.

married his own fourteen-year-old daughter to the Maharajah of Couch Behar, in a ceremony where all the old objectionable Hindu rituals returned. To Keshub, this was a strategic concession designed to enhance his influence in India's more backward, less westernized, native states. To more consistent liberals, such as Sivanath Sastri or Ananda Mohun Bose, however, it was rank hypocrisy.

In 1865, Debendranath and the Brahmo conservatives had broken away in fear of the consequences of Keshub's reforms. Now, in 1878, the Samaj suffered another schism, this time with the rebels carrying away the lion's share of young energy and talent into campaigns to end child marriage and to achieve political reform.[30] Since Keshub professed to support these goals in principle, his tactical opposition left him open to criticism as a renegade, or as an apologist for British despotism. After this rift within the Samaj, Keshub fell into a deep depression. When he finally emerged, after a long meditative retreat, he announced the advent of a "New Dispensation." Abandoning the austere monotheism that had hitherto been Brahmoism's *sine qua non*, his new cult incorporated many of the symbolic and ritual elements of popular Hinduism into an ersatz worship service. Dressed now in colorful robes and surrounded by music, Keshub reinvented himself as a maharishi who embodied the accumulated wisdom of the east. His household was transformed into an ashram, with a new crop of dutiful acolytes coming and going. The old Hindu gods returned, no longer as idols, but as "avatars" of the different elements of a once and future cosmic unity. The original Brahmoism had been a relatively cerebral affair that sought the true path of spiritual communion in India's and other nations' actual religious history. By contrast, the New Dispensation was organized around Keshub's charismatic lectures, in which the trinity of Moses, Jesus, and Chaitnya was transubstantiated into a reified pantheon of human spirituality.[31]

It would be easy to dismiss Keshub's New Dispensation as a prefiguring of the twentieth-century guru who sells eastern enlightenment to the pocketbooks of the west.[32] The very longevity of this phenomenon, however, indicates the durability of the dichotomy on which it rests. It was

---

[30] MLS, 204–15; BKCS, 174–202. See also Keshub's correspondence with Max Müller in Müller, *Biographical Essays*, 84–124. Unlike Keshub, some of these radicals, such as Bose, did involve themselves in the proto-nationalist political movements of the 1880s. Kopf, *Brahmo Samaj*, 26–41, 93–4, 38, 145–7; Sen, "Autobiography," in MLS, 334.

[31] Sen, "Autobiography," in MLS, 331–3.

[32] MLS, 216–324; BKCS, 202–35. Central to the change in Keshub's thinking, which eventually led him to undertake the New Dispensation, was his encounter with the mystic Ramakrishna in 1876.

very difficult to dislodge the notion that India might find its future place in Greater Britain, not by demanding the representative government of a Dominion but by offering the spiritual specialty of an oriental race. Just how deeply rooted this dichotomization was can be seen by turning to Bankimchandra Chattopadhyay, another bhadralok figure who was not initially inclined to see himself, India, or the Empire in this way.

4 Bankimchandra Chattopadhyay and the contradictions of imperial history

Born in the same year as Keshub (1838), Bankim came from a similarly privileged background, although the spendthrift ways of his father and brother reduced his own generation of the family to genteel poverty. Educated alongside Keshub at Presidency College, the slight, sickly Bankim cut a poor figure beside the dynamic charismatic future leader of Brahmo Samaj. Yet where Keshub was captivated by the high ideals and finely turned phrases of others, Bankim preferred to cultivate formidable skills of logical reasoning and argumentation on his own. As he proceeded in his studies, Bankim steeped himself in the Histories of Lecky and Buckle and eagerly devoured the philosophical works of Auguste Comte and J. S. Mill. Most of all, however, he fell in love with English literature. The universality that Keshub was later to seek on a spiritual level, Bankim found already embodied in Shakespeare and Walter Scott.[33] As he grew to maturity, he diverged even more markedly from Keshub's personality type. Where Keshub deflected effeminacy by becoming a charismatic preacher, Bankim took a more literal view of his predicament, adopting a daily diet of eight eggs and four chickens to fortify his blood. Temperamentally fastidious and introspective, he revealed himself not through lectures but indirectly, with his pen. Since Bankim was compelled by family circumstances to earn a living, and was averse to a career in either business or law, he took a lowly job in the uncovenanted civil service, to which all who could not travel to London were consigned. Starting at the bottom, he was appreciated for his competence, but the racial ceiling kept him permanently in subordinate positions. Mortified by this and other perceived racial slights, Bankim came to hate his job, repeatedly deriding it as "the curse of my life."[34]

---

[33] Sisir Kumar Das, *The Artist in Chains: The Life of Bankimchandra Chatterji* (New Delhi, 1984), ix–xii, 1–64; Raychaudhuri, *Europe Reconsidered*, 105–18, 171–6; Haldar, "Introduction," 1–4.

[34] Das, *Artist in Chains*, 11–15, 51–4; Raychaudhuri, *Europe Reconsidered*, 108–9, 115–18.

What saved the sensitive bureaucrat from a life of resentment and bitterness was his literary avocation, which quickly became the absorbing center of his energies. His first three novels, published during the 1860s, were fairly transparent efforts to transpose Sir Walter Scott into a Bengali idiom. Yet raking over the coals of India's history was a tricky business. The *Waverley* formula could be applied to Hindu struggles against the Muslims, but not without reinforcing sectarian divisions, while the British conquest was still too raw for the reconciliatory ending that the formula required. In fact, Bankim was ambivalent about the British conquest, which he saw as a necessary evil, interrupting the romance of India's history but enabling the nation to modernize.[35] He himself was forced to develop a bi-cultural persona, writing most of his romantic novels in Bengali while using English to address the complex social problems of modernization in a backward world.

Bankim's initial thinking about these problems was encapsulated in a series of essays on "Equality," published together in 1874. Grounding his analysis in the ideas of leading European theorists and developing his own thinking along logical lines, Bankim tried to understand the great disparities between wealth and poverty in the India of his time. Like R. C. Dutt, he initially drew on the climatological determinism of Buckle, but he decided (much earlier than Dutt) that inequality was a social phenomenon and that it had to be explained in sociological terms. Here the primary culprit was the caste system, which imposed a built-in tendency towards torpor. By establishing themselves as an artificial elite, with a monopoly of leisure and knowledge, the Brahmans not only kept the lower castes in poverty and ignorance, but also ended up deluding and emasculating themselves. Enslaved to a corrupt and bigoted philosophy of privilege, they became ineffectual and lost touch with reality.[36]

Built on top of this age-old status inequality, however, new forms of economic inequality were driving a wedge between landlords and peasants. Bankim paints a vivid picture of the latter, "bare-footed and bare-headed, driving two emaciated bullocks to pull a blunt plow through knee deep mud, in the scorching noon-day sun." Unable to acquire land of his own or to afford instruments of production, the peasant remained chronically undercapitalized and in debt to moneylenders, who were happy to keep him dependent and impoverished. India was not unique in bearing

---

[35] Das, *Artist in Chains*, 24–5, 51; Raychaudhuri, *Europe Reconsidered*, 183–4. As Bankim put it in another context, "we are a dependent nation – we shall remain dependent for a long time." Quoted in Haldar, "Introduction," 137.

[36] Bankimchandra Chattopadhyay, "Equality," in Haldar (ed. and trans.), *Renaissance and Reaction*, 149–203.

the onus of dysfunctional landlordism, and Bankim drew on Rousseau and J. S. Mill to show how similar inequalities plagued even the most advanced European countries. Europe, however, had begun to address the problem by enlightened policies of emigration and delayed marriage, which enabled it to keep its population in check. Following Mill, Bankim regarded the inequality of women as key to the problem of socio-economic development. While women were "slaves to men" in every country, this was one hundred times truer in India than in Europe. India would have no chance of advancing until this problem was addressed. Women should be educated like men, they should move freely in public, they should pursue careers, and they should have control over their own property. Widows should be allowed to re-marry, child marriage should be abolished, and the government should raise the age of consent.[37]

By resolutely nailing his colors to the mast of women's emancipation, Bankim, like Keshub, signaled his alignment with the most progressive bhadralok forces of his day. Even more than with Keshub, however, his public position – pro-progress, pro-British, and pro-equality – masked a cluster of private anxieties that made these public commitments extremely brittle. As a subaltern employee of the Raj, daily subject to humiliating disempowerment, Bankim was acutely conscious of the insults to his masculine pride that drew him back toward patriarchal privilege when the pressures mounted. Indeed, at the very moment when he was celebrating the benefits of British progress, he was silently seething over the new caste inequalities that the Raj had imposed on educated Indians like himself. These feelings surfaced in a set of satirical sketches, *The Journals of Kamalakanta*, that Bankim published alongside his other works.[38]

Kamalakanta Chakraborty, the fictional author, is presented as an archetypal babu, redolent with self-regard and universal aspirations yet sadly condemned by a heedless world to insignificance and poverty. English-educated, Kamalakanta once served as clerk to a powerful British sahib, but he was fired from his job when he wrote poems and quotations from Shakespeare on official documents. Since then, he has lived entirely on handouts from his spiritual admirers, and has so far freed himself from worldly attachments that he needs only the opium that fuels his reveries, and thinks only of Prasanna, the milkmaid, who is so mercenary as to expect payment for her goods. Written under the influence of opium, Kamalakanta's *Journals* are filled with thinly veiled allegories of the relation between the sovereign Englishman and the dependent babu.

---

[37] Chattopadhyay, "Equality," 188–203, quotes on 167, 189.
[38] Bankimchandra Chattopadhyay, *Kamalakanta*, trans. Monish Ranjan Chatterjee [1815] (New Delhi, 1992).

As fruits, the sahibs are mangoes, "plump, pink but deadly sour when raw," while Bengali babus are "juicy kernels, some are rather sticky, some are rotten and useless, fit only for cattle."[39]

Kamalakanta may be Keshub Chandra Sen, or one of his even less consequential theological hairsplitters. On a deeper level, he is the damaged alter ego of Bankim himself. Having been branded a garrulous and effeminate babu by the colonial master, the Bengali man has begun to resemble this creature in his own eyes. Keshub might seek the acclaim of English crowds as antidote to this psychic wound. Bankim knows that the ultimate power of colonial hegemony lies in the way it makes the subaltern carry the marks of inferiority and ineffectuality within. This searing truth can be seen with even starker clarity in a parodic *Hymn to the Englishman*, in which Bankim wrote:

O Englishman I salute thee. Thou art resplendent with virtues, adorned with beauty and endowed with wealth. Therefore I salute thee. Thou art the destroyer of enemies, thou art the protector of law and thou art the dispenser of employment. Therefore I salute thee. O knower of all minds! Thou knowest that whatever I do is only to propitiate thee. I donate because thou callest me generous. I help others because thou callest me benevolent. I learn because thou callest me learned. O Lord, I am a beggar waiting at thy door. Be propitiated. I offer thee gifts. Be propitiated, O Englishman. I salute thee again and again.[40]

Brutally encapsulated in this caricature is the central dilemma of the anglicized Victorian bhadralok. They have sought advancement through a system that exacts their abasement. They have hinged their identity on recognition by superiors who dismiss them with contempt. They have wagered their masculinity on an imperialist patriarchy that condemns them to a netherworld of eternal effeminacy. While this predicament might not conduce to open resistance, it insured deep wellsprings of resentment and hostility, such as were incompatible with whole-hearted investment in the liberal imperial project. What this incarnation of Bankim really thought of the British (and of himself) is probably best captured by another satire on the victory of the chattering monkeys over the long-tailed tigers. When the latter appear, the monkeys run for cover; but then they return to abuse their predators once these dangerous

---

[39] Chattopadhyay, *Kamalakanta*, especially 9–12.

[40] Quoted in Das, *Artist in Chains*, 53. *Kamalakanta* is a perfect example of Homi Bhabha's syndrome of colonial mimicry; see Homi K. Bhabha, *The Location of Culture* (London, 1994), especially 85–92, 119–21. But does this mean that its author Bankim was critiquing or satirizing this phenomenon, or exemplifying it himself? Kamalakanta's *Journals* have been disparaged as Bengali imitations of De Quincy's *Confessions of an English Opium Eater* (see M. R. Chatterjee's preface to *Kamalakanta*, xv, xvi). The question is complicated.

creatures are no longer in the neighborhood. After many hours of deeply satisfying invective, the monkeys return home, convinced that the tigers must surely be dead from these shafts of verbal abuse.[41]

Did this mean that Bankim's collaboration with the British was inauthentic, that he secretly waited for the day when the monkeys would no longer chatter, but would acquire sharper weapons and throw the tigers out? Certainly, Bankim resisted the Keshubite delusion of a separate spiritual sphere, but this obliged him to acknowledge the contradictory position in which he and the rest of the bhadralok were placed: on the one hand, a genuine belief in Greater British liberal imperialism, lofted by the vague promise of future improvement; on the other hand, a cynical disillusionment with these broken promises, fueled by the arrogant condescension of racist sahibs. Unlike Keshub, Bankim recognized that there could be no New Dispensation, that is, no merely verbal resolution of the contradictions that came to a head during the 1876–84 period. The anglicized bhadralok had to keep all options open. Collaboration if possible, resistance if not. Yet if logic did not permit a clear response to this dilemma, history, particularly historical fiction, provided a fluid medium in which tensions between them could be explored.[42]

In Bankim's opus, the novel *Anandamath*, published in 1882, was the most important fruit of this period. With its stirring anthem, "Bande Mataram" ("Hail to the Motherland"), it became a founding text of twentieth-century Indian nationalism, and survives as Bankim's most enduring popular work. Yet *Anandamath* is deeply ambiguous and enigmatic, offering a tenebrous portent for India's future independence by invoking an oracular reading of her subservient past. Set amid the famine of 1770, during the early period of British rule, the narrative tells the story of the Sanyasa revolt, a shadowy cult of Hindu mystics who briefly led a movement of social bandits and guerilla fighters, dedicated to uprooting British rule.[43]

On one level, Bankim's Sanyasi might have come straight from the pages of Walter Scott: a romantic, swashbuckling band of holy martyrs, who are nevertheless doomed by the march of Greater British progress to be crushed underfoot. Yet this is very far from the tone with which the novel engages the reader, or in which the public responded to the book.

---

[41] Das, *Artist in Chains*, 52
[42] Haldar, "Introduction," 101–6. See also Andrew Sartori, *Bengal in Global Concept History: Culturalism in the Age of Capital* (Chicago, 2008), 95–108.
[43] Das, *Artist in Chains*, 129–48; Raychaudhuri, *Europe Reconsidered*, 119–21, 133–5; Sudipta Kaviraj, *The Unhappy Consciousness: Bankimchandra Chattopadhyay and the Formation of Nationalist Discourse in India* (Oxford, 1995), 107–57; Bankimchandra Chatterji (Chattopadhyay), *Anandamath*, trans. Basanta Koomar Roy (Delhi, 1992).

For the Sanyasi are presented (and were certainly received) as portents of a brighter national future. Spiritual to a fault, they are also armed to the teeth, and they invoke the millennial dream of Indians uniting together to liberate their motherland from foreign rule. This determination to write what Sudipta Kaviraj calls "an alternative history of India" begins in the very first chapter, when the reader (personified in the protagonist Mahendra) is enlisted into the refrains of "Bande Mataram," and inducted into the ruined abbey Anandamath, where the rebels have established their secret redoubt.[44]

Where Keshub's ashram of the New Dispensation translates political disappointment into the coin of spiritual exaltation, Bankim's fictional ashram converts Hindu traditions for spiritual exaltation into the coin of (imaginary) political revolt. Bankim might well deride Benagli spiritualists for their ineffectual castle-building, but his own novel simply revels in an even more delusory fantasy, in which the effeminate Bengali has been magically converted into an ascetic warrior, proudly obsessed with displaying his masculinity. Having renounced all contact with their wives and children until the glory-day of national independence, Bankim's warriors exorcise their shameful legacy of servile impotence by devotion to the abstract symbol of the Motherland, which they invent (under the guise of historically resuscitating her) through their deeds of derring-do. Although the female fighter Shanti is allowed a few comic moments of cross-dressing, we are now in a very different atmosphere than that depicted less than a decade earlier by the younger Bankim's tract *Equality*.[45]

Of course, Bankim had not dropped all his opinions, and at the very end of his novel he finally reasserts all the liberal imperial maxims that his fevered narrative has just decried: British rule was only beginning in 1770, and the violent conquistadors would soon give way to the enlightened modernizers who would follow in their wake. This protracted process would be a necessary precondition for the emergence of a new kind of post-liberal nationalism capable of assuming the mantle of capitalist modernity.

There is no hope of a true revival of the true faith, if the English do not become rulers of the country ... True Hinduism is based on knowledge and not action ... To revive Hinduism to its purity, it is necessary to propagate external knowledge. There is no one in the country capable of doing that. The English are well-versed

---

[44] Chattopadhyay, *Anandamath*, 23–64; Kaviraj, *Unhappy Consciousness*, 123. It is almost as though Waverley's wild encounter with clan Fergus had the effect of turning him into a manifesto-writing Scottish nationalist ideologue. See Chapter 1 above.

[45] Chattopadhyay, *Anandamath*, especially 33–70; Tanika Sarkar, *Hindu Wife, Hindu Nation* (Bloomington, 2001), 135–62.

in external knowledge and they are expert teachers too. Therefore, we shall make them kings. English education will impart external knowledge to the people of this country and thus enable them to understand spiritual knowledge.[46]

As this conclusion demonstrates, for all his greater intellectual sophistication, Bankim could not escape the same dreary dualism between spiritualism (Indian) and materialism (English) that had animated (and imprisoned) Keshub's life and work. In Bankim's last major book, *Dharmatattva* (1888), he comes closest to the message of Keshub, offering the inward spiritual turn as an antidote to worldly disempowerment. Yet where Keshub's Hinduism evaporates into a "higher" universalist synthesis, Bankim's retains its Indian character. Here the essence of Hinduism is located in dharma – the sense of duty and devotion that facilitates a good life of spiritual welfare and mental prosperity. By casting his book in the form of a dialogue between a guru and his somewhat skeptical disciple, Bankim appeals to the bhadralok, which needs to be convinced that Hindu dharma still has meaning in the modern world. English education is acknowledged as a medium for scientific training, but is criticized for its soullessness and amorality. The equality that Bankim once preached is not entirely repudiated, but respect is demanded for natural authority. The superiority of leaders over followers, of teachers over students, and of men over women is now asserted as the natural order of things. Love is offered as the highest good, but love for self and even love for family are deemed to be inferior to a selfless love for the motherland. To bear arms for one's country is dharma in its highest form.[47]

Like *Anandamath*, *Dharmatattva* is notable for its disconnection from real-world history. The Indian "spiritual" progress narrative has lost its connection with reality. Both books oscillate between dreams of revolt and nightmares of humiliation. They offer paeans to national unity that are couched in language that can only inflame sectarian division. Convinced of his own moral superiority, Bankim is a man who is determined to make a difference, and yet he can find no point of entry into the current of actual events. Bankim's history, as Kaviraj perceptively argues, is an "imaginary history": the history of what did not happen, but which he hoped to convert, through his writings, into a history of what might yet become. "Bengal has no history," Bankim lamented, and "Bengal must have her own history, or else there is no hope."[48] Yet instead of buckling

---

[46] Quoted in Das, *Artist in Chains*, 136.

[47] Bankimchandra Chattopadhyay, *Dharmatattva*, trans. Apratim Ray (Oxford, 2003).

[48] Kaviraj, *Unhappy Consciousness*, especially 123. Perhaps this is what Bankim meant when he cryptically avowed that "there is not a single work in English that is a true history of Bengal ... A Bengali who accepts this kind of writing as the history of

down to forge this genre, he had to opt for the fictional safety of his compensatory masculinist fantasies. Yet for bhadralok men, even a decade younger than Keshub and Bankim, new realms of possibility were opening up. R. C. Dutt was able to work his way into the covenanted civil service, while Surendranath Banerjea, who also passed the civil service exam, found himself catapulted onto a career-path more momentous still.

5   Surendranath Banerjea and the Indianization of Macaulay's constitutional romance

It is perhaps fitting that Banerjea got into trouble with the British authorities for so perfectly following the Macaulay strategy. Having educated himself to become an Englishman in taste and opinions, and having qualified through the test that Macaulay helped set up, he found his ICS appointment quashed on a technicality. Drawing on his rights as a British subject, he used the judicial system to get the decision reversed. Foisted on a bureaucracy that did not want him, he was posted to a remote district, in a hostile work environment, where, once again, a technicality tripped him up. Expelled from the ICS, he returned to London and retrained as a barrister, only to discover that his expulsion disqualified him from practicing in the courts. At this point, young Banerjea might have been defeated or crushed. Fortunately, he had read his Macaulay, and understood that corrupt establishments never concede without a struggle and that the triumph of liberty over tyranny is always hard-won. "In the Iron grip of ruin I had already formed some forecast of the work that was awaiting me in life. I felt that I had suffered because I was an Indian, a member of a community that lay disorganized, had no public opinion, and no voice in the counsels of their Government."[49]

And so Banerjea built his own career as a teacher, started a newspaper, and commenced an agitation to gain the rights of a freeborn Briton for Indians like himself. On April 2, 1883, his paper *The Bengalee* published a biting editorial, comparing a High Court Justice to the seventeenth-century English Judge Jeffreys. Although official censorship had recently been lifted, Banerjea was cited for contempt of court and sentenced to four months in prison. This time, the authorities discovered that their persecution of Banerjea was a serious mistake. Three years earlier the

Bengal, is not a true Bengali." Quotes in Ranajit Guha, *An Indian Historiography of India: A Nineteenth Century Agenda and its Implications* (Calcutta, 1988), 1, 56, and Haldar, "Introduction," 104.
[49] Surendranath Banerjea, *A Nation in Making* [1925] (Oxford, 1963), 1–90, quote on 30. For background on Indian students in London, see Burton, *At the Heart of Empire*, 1–71. On the covenanted ICS more generally, see David Gilmour, *The Ruling Caste: Imperial Lives in the Victorian Raj* (New York, 2006).

Tory Lytton had been replaced by Lord Ripon, a Viceroy who came to India under the mantle of Gladstonian liberalism, with a mandate to restore Macaulayite policies, to conciliate the bhadralok, and to move in the direction of juridical equality. Upon arrival, Ripon found himself confronted on the one side with the fervid hopes of anglicized natives, on the other with the fevered hostility of the white community. When his Legal Member, Ilbert, tried once again to extend the authority of native judges to jurisdiction over Europeans, Ripon received a reaction even more furious than that which had greeted Macaulay in 1836, and Bethune in 1849.[50]

Coming at the height of the Ilbert Bill controversy, Banerjea's conviction and imprisonment reinforced the message that the Raj had classified all Indian natives as hereditary inferiors, unfit for the rights of freeborn Britons. The educated babu in particular was charged with being incompetent and inauthentic, as the old trope of the "effeminate Bengali" was unleashed from the Anglo-Indian press. In this perhaps there was nothing new. But Banerjea's determination to fight this derogation by invoking the historical struggles of British history was, in fact, a novel development, since it reflected the determination of men like himself to refuse inferior status as objects of evolution, and to transform themselves into subjects who could act in history. For this reason the case electrified the bhadralok community. By the time Banerjea was released, he had become a celebrity: a symbol of resistance, and a leading figure in a fledgling movement that sought to force colonial administrators to live up to the promises of the EIC Charter of 1833 and the Queen's India Proclamation of 1858.[51]

As they formulated their goals in the course of agitation, Banerjea and his associates drew again and again on the themes of Macaulay's English constitutional history. Representative government, individual rights, the right to bear arms, "no taxation without representation," institutional checks and balances: these had all been won by seventeenth-century Britons, and it was only logical that they should be claimed by Indians in the nineteenth century. Since British officials were hard pressed to deny the force of these arguments, they resorted to *ad hominem* attacks

---

[50] S. Gopal, *British Policy in India, 1858–1905* (Cambridge, 1965), 64–179; Seal, *Emergence of Indian Nationalism*, 131–93; R. J. Moore, *Liberalism and India Politics* (London, 1966), 1–62. For a fuller discussion of this shift, see Thomas R. Metcalf, *Ideologies of the Raj* (Cambridge, 1994), 28–159; Wilfred Scawen Blunt, *Indian under Ripon* (London, 1909); Bose, *Racism, Struggle*, 152–239.

[51] Banerjea, *Nation in Making*, 37–90; Mrinalini Sinha, *Colonial Masculinity: The "Manly Englishman" and the "Effeminate Bengali" in the Late Nineteenth Century* (Manchester, 1995), especially 1–99; Heather Streets, *Martial Races: The Military, Race and Masculinity in British Imperial Culture, 1857–1914* (Manchester, 2004), 158–68.

on the agitators, reinforced by the observation that they represented only a minuscule portion of the Indian population. Constitutional agitation was disparaged as the crotchet of Bengali intellectuals, for which the mass of India's struggling illiterate peasants and "martial races" of the north cared not a whit. Calls for "representative government" and "careers open to talent" were dismissed as the ruses of covetous Brahmans.[52]

Stirred by these criticisms from the imperial masters, Banerjea and his colleagues understood that they would have to demonstrate their untruth. To mount an effective political movement, they would have to encompass every region of India and gain support from at least the majority of all middle-class social groups. Banerjea, who would entitle his autobiography *A Nation in Making*, understood the importance of achieving this goal. He knew that if India were ever to take her proper place as a self-governing dominion in the British Empire, she would have to develop a distinctively *political* identity. The Hindu-inflected spiritualism of Keshub, Debendranath, and Bankim would have to be replaced with something more open and secular. Indian nationality would have to encompass all the many diverse castes, regions, cultures, and religions that had hitherto merely co-existed on the subcontinent.[53]

To this end, in 1883, Surendranath organized an all-India national conference in Calcutta that drew delegates from all the leading cities and towns. The following year, he went on a speaking tour of northern India to spread the gospel of national organization and unity. In 1884, a second annual conference was planned for December. These plans, however, were complicated by the perception that the Bengali bhadralok leadership was too dominant within the movement, and that the second conference should be held in the west. In the event, meetings were held simultaneously in both Bombay and Calcutta. In the aftermath of these stirring and inspiring occasions, the two groups coalesced, agreeing to rotate their officers and meeting venues on an annual basis. In this manner, the Indian National Congress was born.[54]

In retrospect, we see the creation of Congress as an awesome milestone in India's history. At the time, however, its leaders knew that it was fragile

---

[52] "It was constantly dinned into our ears that our political demands, whatever they were, came from people of the deltaic Ganges, who did not contribute a single soldier to the army, and who were separated from the North by a wide gulf of isolation, if not of alienation." Banerjea, *Nation in Making*, 81; Seal, *Emergence of Indian Nationalism*, 131–340.

[53] Banerjea, *Nation in Making*, 79–90.

[54] Banerjea, *Nation in Making*, 90–113; S. R. Mehrotra, *A History of the Indian National Congress* (New Delhi, 1995), I: 1–46.

and weak. The ICS was dead-set against it, and the new Viceroy, Lord Dufferin, was wary.[55] The sectarian divisions among the Indian groups were not so much resolved as suspended, and the participation of Muslims was spotty at best. For all these reasons, the movement resolved to steer clear of both religion and the social issues (i.e. those connected with women's emancipation) that had caused so much trouble even within the Hindu community. Patriarchal assumptions, which Keshub and Bankim had at least momentarily questioned, were taken for granted in the Congress program, which was couched entirely in masculinist constitutional terms. In 1891, when the government tried to raise the age of sexual consent from ten to twelve, a storm of protest arose in many traditional Hindu circles. Liberals who, like Banerjea, opposed child marriage in principle were placed in a bind. Patriotic considerations obliged them to join in opposition to reforms that they would have supported under other circumstances. What would Englishmen think if Indians interfered with their divorce laws? "Any interference from outside is the officious impertinence of strangers, and it can do no good, but may do a great deal of harm."[56]

Yet when male nationalists united around the defense of Hindu (or Muslim) patriarchy, this did not really strengthen the movement, as Mrinalini Sinha has pointed out. It merely insured that the early Congress would be de-legitimized in the metropolis, and would pose no fundamental threat to British imperial autocracy. As we have seen over the course of this volume, the one thing on which the Edgeworths, Walter Scott, the Macaulays, Froude, and the evolutionary historians all agreed was the normativity of separate-spheres domesticity, on which the foundation of true Britishness was deemed to rest. This gender norm was important, not merely as the basis for a modern bourgeois family, but because it underwrote a new kind of centrist politics that eschewed the reactionary or impotent (effeminate) and radical (hyper-masculine) extremes. By failing to place the rights of women at core of their program, the early Congress leaders lost a certain amount of potential metropolitan sympathy. As Sinha shows, this played into the hands of Maineite policymakers, who rationalized their refusal to grant political rights by declaring child marriage to be an inviolable custom, thereby compensating these men with their own separate "traditional" uncolonized space.[57]

---

[55] Howard Brasted, "Indian Nationalist Development and the Influence of Irish Home Rule, 1870–1886," *Modern Asian Studies*, 14.1 (1980), 44–5.

[56] Sinha, *Colonial Masculinity*, 138–80, quote on 142.

[57] Sinha, *Colonial Masculinity*, especially 108–9, 130–1, 140–2, 150–1, 180–5; Sarkar, *Hindu Wife*, 191–249.

Trapped yet again in the maws of a contradiction, the Congress leaders tried to prove the *bona fides* of their liberalism by emphasizing the moderation of their political demands. All they wanted was (1) the expansion of Indian legislative councils to include a minority of elective members, (2) the separation of judicial from executive functions in government, (3) the raising of the age of Civil Service eligibility, and (4) for exams to be added in Calcutta, simultaneous with those in London.[58] Because they knew that the entire force of the ICS was against them, the Congress leaders understood that they had to seek support among English liberals, who were likely to view them skeptically on both race and gender grounds. This desire to appeal to wary metropolitan liberals probably explains the prominent role played by the retired ICS officer A. O. Hume in the early years of Congress. It also explains why the movement put a premium on the skills of men like Naoroji and Banerjea, who had lived in England and who embodied British manners and respectability to a fault.[59] Eager to transcend the internal divisions that kept Indians from uniting, Banerjea turned to the history of Europe to make his case that such differences could be overcome. "Let us take the example of Switzerland," he would say, or "of Belgium," or "the case of Germany" or "Italy." In each of these instances, peoples who had been divided by language, religion, customs, and manners had recognized that their future depended on the ability to set aside these differences and create powerful nation-states in the political realm. In India, this task of creating political union was being signally advanced by the British Empire itself.

> It is England's mission in the East to save, regenerate, emancipate from the chains of ignorance, error and superstition, 150 millions of human beings, to heal the wounds that have been inflicted on them by the rapacity of their former rulers ... to reconcile the jarring conflicts of the diverse Indian nationalities, to ... make them feel that they have to make common cause for the redress of common grievances.[60]

Through the spread of the railroad, through the development of the economy, through English education, through the unifying force of the English language, Indians were being brought together. Through England's own history of representative government – the long struggles of its people for freedom against tyrants – India would learn the value of her own national liberty. That this English-inspired freedom had to be wrested from the tyranny of Britain was simply one of history's ironies. "We shall

---

[58] Sinha, *Colonial Masculinity*, 138–80; Mehrotra, *Indian National Congress*, I: 22–30.
[59] Mehrotra, *Indian National Congress*, I: 1–46; Seal, *Emergence of Indian Nationalism*, 245–97; Banerjea, *Nation in Making*, 104; Briton Martin, *New India, 1885: British Official Policy and the Emergence of the Indian National Congress* (Berkeley, 1969), 53–78.
[60] Surendranath Banerjea, *Speeches* (Calcutta, 1970), I: 36.

borrow that page from England's history, fasten it on our own banner, and unfurl that banner before the gaze of our own countrymen."[61]

Some years later, in a speech before the Oxford Union, Banerjea developed this line of analysis further, in a direction that aimed to please, but also to challenge, his hosts.

Representative institutions are a consecrated possession, which in the counsels of Providence have been entrusted to the English people, to guard that possession, to spread it, and not to make it the property of this people or that people, but the heritage of mankind at large. England is the home of representative institutions; from England as the center, representative institutions have spread far and wide until this country has justly been called the august mother of free nations. The people of India are children of that mother, and they claim their birthright, they claim to be admitted into the rights of British citizens and British fellow-subjects.[62]

With this clever presentation of Indian nationalism as a distinctively *British* (even English) creation, Banerjea believed he had resolved the contradiction that had undermined his predecessors. They had tried to circumvent British colonial subordination by escaping into a separate sphere of Indian spirituality (or patriarchy), only to find that, even here, imperial domination thwarted their agency. By boldly appropriating Britain's liberal history for his own Indian emancipatory project, Banerjea turned the tables on the colonial master: Britain was in danger of betraying her own best traditions, which had now been taken over by Indian patriots such as he.

Because Indian nationalists of later generations would seek a political rupture with Britain, it is important to emphasize just how far this first generation envisioned their own nationalism in distinctively British terms. This position was not unique to Banerjea, but was also articulated by many of the other early Congress leaders. In 1887, B. C. Pal acknowledged that he was "loyal to the British Government, because with me loyalty to the British Government is identical to loyalty to my own country." "It should not be forgotten for a moment," avowed C. S. Nair, "that the real link that binds us to England is the hope and the belief that we shall, under her guidance alone, attain national unity and national freedom." According to M. M. Ghose, "our allegiance to the British Government is based, not only on the feeling of gratitude ... but also on the highest grounds of expediency."[63]

These statements should not be read as the servile submissions of colonial dependents. They were intended as clear-sighted calculations by trailblazing nationalists who recognized that the highest hope for Indian unity and independence lay in cultivating the British connection.

---

[61] Banerjea, *Speeches*, I: 44.   [62] Banerjea, *Nation in Making*, 108.
[63] Quoted in Mehrotra, *Indian National Congress*, I: 118. See also Kopf, *Brahmo Samaj*, 131.

In an era when Canada, Australia, and New Zealand were becoming self-governing British dominions, it was not absurd to suppose that the Indian government might be reorganized along comparable lines. With London and Manchester as the centers of global capitalism, the British connection had obvious potential advantages, particularly if India could (like the white dominions) obtain some leeway in formulating her own economic and tariff policies. Last, but not least, the huge challenges of creating unity among the subcontinent's vast array of castes, regions, religions, and cultures might be easier if it were cast in a Greater British mold. Just as England, Scotland, and (it was hoped) Ireland were resolving their own inner class, ethnic, and religious divisions within the British framework, the same process might work for India too.[64]

Of course, all this assumed that the Anglo-Saxons of the British metropolis could be recalled to their libertarian historical traditions and brought to see the virtue (as well as the self-interest) in Indian political unity and autonomy. For Banerjea's generation of early nationalists, this was not an unreasonable assumption. True enough, they could see the racism, brutality, and contempt of the British planters and civil servants who had descended on their homeland like a plague. They could also see how this public disempowerment had sent many Indian men on quixotic spiritual quests, or into exaggerated forms of domestic patriarchy. Yet they could console themselves with the hope that these attitudes, on both sides, were the pathological products of arbitrary power. The problem, they believed, was that ordinary decent-minded Britons had no cognizance of the corrupt and oppressive policies that were perpetrated in their name.[65]

Such rhetoric, it must be said, came more easily to men like Banerjea, who spent only a few years in the metropolis. To Dadabhai Naoroji, who spent most of his time in London, such happy illusions were more difficult to sustain. He understood how little most Britons either knew or cared about India. Worst of all, he saw how the pseudo-scientific racism of ethnologists like Crawfurd, or historians like Froude, was making it difficult for Britons of any political stripe to see Indians as their equals and fellow citizens. Yet in spite of these difficulties, Naoroji persevered in the hope of obtaining justice to India through the medium of Greater British politics. The result was not only a more consequential political

---

[64] Charles Dilke, *The Problems of Greater Britain* (London, 1890), 349–698; see J. E. Taylor, *The Struggle for Imperial Unity, 1869–1895* (London, 1938); and Ged Martin, "The Idea of Imperial Federation," in *Reappraisals in British Imperial History* (London, 1975), 121–38.

[65] Banerjea, *Nation in Making*, 103–13.

program, but also a more profound and original contribution to historiography.[66]

6   Dadabhai Naoroji: imperial mis-government and the history of the "drain"

Born a full generation before Banerjea, in 1825, Dadabhai Naoroji first traveled to London in 1855, at the age of thirty. Over many years, as a merchant, a teacher of Gujerati, a public speaker, a father substitute for Indian students, and a parliamentary lobbyist for Indian interests, he came to know the imperial metropolis very well. Emerging as a key figure in the British India Association, he served as intermediary between its London and Indian branches. Working closely with a handful of sympathetic British politicians like William Wedderburn, Henry Fawcett, and John Bright, he anticipated what would become the leading demands of Congress long before there was any real organization in India to back them up. Tirelessly, he canvassed metropolitan politicians to open up the civil service to qualified natives, to create meaningful institutions of representative government, and to force the government to become accountable to the people whom it taxed.[67] Yet Naoroji also understood that the problem was structural. The reason why the Irish Question was constantly before the metropolitan Parliament and public was that Irish nationalists had a phalanx of MPs in Westminster, and were able to use this political clout to keep Home Rule on the political agenda. Given the dearth of sympathetic parliamentary spokesmen, Naoroji realized that what India needed was at least a few MPs. To this end, during the 1880s he began focusing his work on trying to build an alliance with English trade unionists and Irish Home Rulers to seek a seat in the House of Commons for himself. In 1886, at the height of the Home Rule crisis, he stood for Holborn, and appealed to English electors' own historical self-narratives as grounds for supporting Irish and Indian emancipation. "What is the proudest chapter in British history?" he asked. "That of the Stuarts. You did not tolerate the laws of your own sovereign, because you thought they were not your laws, (cheers). You waged civil war, regardless of consequences, and fought till you established the principle that the English will be their own sovereign."[68]

[66] Masani, *Dadabhai Naoroji*, 1–47.
[67] Masani, *Dadabhai Naoroji*, 1–80; Mary Cumpston, "Some Early Indian Nationalists and their Allies in the British Parliament, 1851–1906," *English Historical Review*, 76.299 (April, 1961), 279–97.
[68] Dadabhai Naoroji, *Speeches and Writings* (Madras, 1917), 206; Brasted, "Indian Nationalist Development," 37–63.

In this speech, Naoroji went on in the same vein of radicalized Macaulayism. So far from jeopardizing the Empire, Home Rule for Ireland and justice for India were the only means for preserving it over the long run. Irishmen and Indians were not separatists. They wanted to join the glorious stream of British history, albeit as fellow citizens rather than as racialized menials. When Naoroji was defeated in the general election, he refused to be disheartened and simply relocated his efforts elsewhere. In 1892, he stood for Finsbury Central. This time the Prime Minister, Lord Salisbury, himself drew attention to the contest, when he "doubt[ed] if we have yet got to the point where a British constituency would elect a [*sic*] black man." The Finsbury electors, however, proved Salisbury wrong. When Naoroji was returned by the narrowest of margins, Indians were exultant. Many hoped that a new day had dawned.[69]

Naoroji's parliamentary career, however, proved to be disappointing and brief. As a lowly backbencher in support of Gladstone's fourth government, he found the political agenda crowded with other issues. He was naturally frustrated by his inability to direct attention to Indian concerns. While his fellow legislators were indifferent to his invocations of Elphinstone, Bentinck, or Macaulay, they did agree to create a Royal Commission on Indian Expenditures. Shortly before his defeat in the general election of 1895, Naoroji was appointed to the commission. Here, amid expert testimony, piles of returns, and masses of statistics, Naoroji – both as historian and as politician – was finally able to come into his own.[70]

Because of his background as a Bombay merchant (and as a former mathematics professor), Naoroji had always been more attuned to the economic dimension of India's condition than the purely literary Calcutta bhadralok had been. For many years he had been collecting information about the economic consequences of British rule. Here he had encountered a paradox: from the very moment when the principles of liberal imperialism had been proclaimed, the Indian population had been getting poorer. The spread of western education and creation of a capitalist economy had brought no benefits to the mass of the people. On the contrary, from the 1770s onward, a series of devastating famines had led to hunger, epidemics, and millions of deaths. How was this paradox to be explained? Naoroji was extremely critical of the statistics that the Indian government made available, but through a series of ingenious calculations he had already discerned, by the 1870s, that whereas the per

[69] Masani, *Dadabhai Naoroji*, 81–117; Jonathan Schneer, *London, 1900: The Imperial Metropolis* (New Haven, 1999), 184–202.

[70] Naoroji, *Speeches and Writings*, 121–4; Schneer, *London, 1900*, 184–202.

capita income of Britain was approximately £30, that of India was a mere
£2. Yet where Britons were taxed at a rate of 8 percent, the far poorer
Indians were taxed at a rate of 15 percent. Such figures put the relationship between taxation and representation in a novel light. They called
into question the central British claim that theirs was a benevolent
dictatorship, and that they were providing the Indians with good,
cheap government that was of far higher quality than anything the
Indians had hitherto provided for themselves.[71]

What did India really obtain from the British government, in return for
the £50,000,000 that was annually collected in taxes? A system of rule that
was overly expensive and ill suited to Indian needs and conditions.
A system that was tailored to the desires of British aristocrats, who looked
to India to pay for Britain's global political and military ambitions.
A system which transferred huge sums of money into the pockets of
British officials, investors, and entrepreneurs, who would spend it in the
metropole. Adding up all the figures that he obtained from a multitude of
sources, Naoroji calculated that every year some £30,000,000 to
£40,000,000 was drained away from India. Both Naoroji's numbers
and his logic were questioned by Raj apologists, but it was difficult
to dispute either the originality or the analytical force of his research.
His theory of the "drain" blasted a huge hole in the rhetoric of liberal
imperialism. By casting doubt on the vaunted benevolence of
British rule, it raised fundamental doubts about the progressive character of the entire Anglo-Indian epoch. To be sure, Naoroji did not
dispute the benevolent *intentions* of Britain's liberal imperialists, and he
repeatedly acknowledged that India had gained important benefits
from her rule. Indeed, it was the very promises made that had raised
expectations, and insured that British performance would be rigorously
judged.

It is useless for the British to compare themselves with the past native rulers. If the
British do not show themselves to be vastly superior in proportion to their enlightenment and civilization, if India does not prosper and progress under them far
more largely, there will be no justification for their existence in India ... It is
useless and absurd to remind us constantly that once the British fiat brought order
out of chaos ... The natives of the present day have not seen that chaos, and do
not feel it.[72]

What they had seen, and did feel, according to Naoroji, was the experience of political disenfranchisement combined with economic drain.
Precisely because this drain *was* a genuine product of wealth-enhancing

---

[71] NUBR, 60.   [72] NUBR, 218, 222; see also 381, 458–61.

economic development, Indians would become all the more resentful as they saw the benefits diverted into England's purse.

In the case of former conquests, the invaders either retired with their plunder and booty, or became the rulers of the country. When they only plundered and went back, they made no doubt, great wounds: but India, with her industry, revived and healed the wounds. When the invaders became the rulers of the country, they settled down in it ... Whatever the country produced remained within the country ... With the English the case is peculiar ... those wounds are kept perpetually open and widening, by draining away the life-blood in a continuous stream. The former rulers were like butchers hacking here and there, but the English with their scientific scalpel cut to the very heart, and yet, lo! There is no wound to be seen, and soon the plaster of the high talk of civilization, progress and what not, covers up the wound![73]

The problem for Naoroji (as for all the figures treated in this chapter) was that they genuinely believed the high talk of civilization and progress. They were themselves the products of this talk, and could not exist in its absence. Yet the wounds hurt all the more for this being so. Naoroji had discovered something profoundly important about the progress narrative: it suffered from internal contradictions. The very forces that propelled it forward also undermined it, at least in the form in which it was experienced by imperial capitalism's subaltern groups. Initially at a loss to know what to do with this discovery, Naoroji convinced himself that it was a correctable error. The contradiction was not inherent in British imperialism. It was the result of bad policies by ill-informed policy-makers, who needed to be convinced that they were besmirching the true British traditions of progress and liberty. For this reason, he entitled the collection of papers in which he developed the drain theory *Poverty and Un-British Rule in India*, with its implication that true British rule *was* bringing progress and plenty, whereas poverty eventuated only because of the drain.

True British rule will vastly benefit both Britain and India. My whole object in all my writings is to impress upon the British People, that instead of a disastrous explosion of the British Indian Empire, as must be the result of the present dishonourable un-British system of government, there is to be a great and glorious future for Britain and India to an extent unconceivable at present, if the British people will awaken to their duty, and will be true to their British instincts of fair play and justice.[74]

This belief that the vast majority of the British people were losers by the drain was key to Naoroji's political calculations, if not to his

[73] NUBR, 211.   [74] NUBR, xii, xiii.

historiographical claims. Again and again, he argued that a prosperous India would provide markets for more British products, repeatedly quoting Macaulay on the absurdity of the policies that "would keep a hundred millions of men [now more than 200] from being our customers in order that they might continue to be our slaves." The enslavement of Indians, he implied, might be inconsistent with the long-term survival of liberty in Britain. Leaving aside a small sector of aristocratic elites, he did not believe that the vast bulk of Englishmen, Scotsmen, and Irishmen really benefited from the drain. They had an interest in resolving the contradiction, since allowing it to fester would prevent their own progress narrative from proceeding.[75]

While Naoroji hoped to make his drain theory an effective bargaining card with the British, he also recognized its effectiveness in promoting Indian unity. Unlike the versions of nationalism purveyed by Keshub and Bankim, it promised to draw Indians of every caste and religion away from their differences, and toward the common grievances against Britain that they shared. It appealed to the educated urban middle classes, while focusing on the plight of the lower classes, and the poverty of the rural peasantry. Yet in appropriating the drain theory to their critique of the British Raj, the overwhelming majority of these men continued to insist that their criticisms were meant to be constructive. It aimed to strengthen rather than to destroy the British–Indian union, by negotiating an end to political misgovernment and fiscal inequity.[76]

7   R. C. Dutt and the riches of ancient Hindu civilization

When Naoroji published his first paper on the drain, he was already fifty-three years old. When *Poverty and Un-British Rule* was fully compiled, he was seventy-six. Under these circumstances, a major focus from the 1860s onward was to mentor new generations of Indian students who came to London to study for government or legal careers. Indeed, Banerjea and Dutt were only the first in a long line of young men who had open access to Naoroji's larder, company, and sage advice.[77] Clearly, Naoroji hoped that the younger generation would be able to achieve many of the goals that had eluded him, and that as Indians such as Dutt moved into positions of

---

[75] "After having a glorious history of heroic struggles for constitutional government, England is now rearing up a body of Englishmen trained up and accustomed to despotism – Is it possible that such habits of despotism, with which Indian officials return from India, should not, in the course of time, influence the English character and institutions?" (NUBR, 214). MMW, 571.

[76] Mehrotra, *Indian National Congress*, I: 28–30.

[77] GLD, 1–38; R. C. Dutt, *Romesh Chunder Dutt* (New Delhi, 1968), 1–19.

authority, they would be able to reverse the bad policies that were responsible for the drain. During his early years in the ICS, as we have seen, Dutt also hoped that this would be the case. When he ran into resistance as a bureaucrat and as a thinker, he began to see that the problem ran deeper than mere differences over policy. Britons and Indians viewed the world differently, and needed an intermediary – someone with a foot in both camps – who could interpret the one group to the other. Given the vast economic, cultural, and physical distances between the two societies, much translational work (both literal and figurative) would be required. Before any headway could be made on the question of the drain, cultural communication had to be substantially improved.

Even after he resigned himself to the likelihood that he would never gain a "European reputation," Dutt recognized that there was much intellectual work that he could usefully do. As the product of both a London and a Bengali education, invested with official status and indigenous authority, he was perhaps the one man who might bring imperial masters, English readers, and Bengali babus (literally) together on the same page. Thus, in 1877, he published *The Literature of Bengal*, the first historical survey of its kind to be written in English. Locating the origin of Bengali literature in Kasiram Das's fifteenth-century translation of the *Mahabharata*, Dutt was inspired to re-translate it into English. So impressed was Bankim with these efforts that he persuaded Dutt to write four Bankim-style historical novellas, published together in 1879.[78] In all this shuttling back and forth between English, Bengali, and Sanskrit, Dutt was groping his way toward a new kind of intellectual bordering that would simultaneously contribute a peripheral perspective to European social science, help develop modern Bengali as a literary language, and recover ancient Sanskrit texts for an English reading audience, while bringing British socio-economic knowledge to the people of his native land. Although Dutt did not belabor the difference, the whole point of this effort was to demonstrate (contra Keshub) that the Indian and British progress narratives ran together, rather than in separate spiritual and material tracks. To draw out these connections, Dutt entangled himself in thickening webs of intertextuality, as ancient epics were interleaved with modern manifestoes, and adventureful historical romances were converted into the coin of analytical history.

Belatedly promoted to District Officer in 1883, Dutt became the first Indian to have full executive charge of an entire province. Yet officialdom

[78] I have been unable to obtain this edition. Instead I have used a later edition, which was titled *Cultural Heritage of Bengal* (Calcutta, 1962); GLD, 40–4, 51–77; Dutt, *Dutt*, 20–34.

was not without its frustrations, since he could not intervene in the Ilbert crisis, nor could he do anything openly to help his friend Banerjea. Scholarship was the one thing that Dutt could always contribute, and, in 1885, he risked the ire of Brahman fundamentalists by translating the *Rig Veda* into Bengali. It was left to Banerjea, now back at the helm of *The Bengalee*, to draw out the connections between Dutt's translation and the imperial politics of the late Victorian age. "We have fallen very far from the high ideal," the paper acknowledged, referring to the Hindu Aryans of the Vedic Age. In the *Veda*, the paper continued, "our Indian patriots are straining every nerve, and are preparing themselves to make every sacrifice to further the interests of Indian unity."

Only in December last, all India met . . . in solemn Congress assembled. They met in response to their own patriotic aspirations, and to the great lesson that the west has taught them; but they also met in obedience to a still higher call – that which comes to them from their sires of olden times . . . The translator of the *Vedas* has rendered a public service by calling attention to this passage, and we join with him [Dutt] in the appeal which he makes that these slokas should be graven on the heart of our people.[79]

While this engraving on the national body politic was being etched, Dutt was on his way to a furlough year in the imperial metropolis, where he hoped to recharge his intellectual batteries. It had been eighteen years since he had first come to London, as a brash young aspirant on the seemingly impossible mission of breaking the racial barrier of the Raj. Now he returned as an established civil servant, with a wife, four children, and a brother in tow. Happy to be back, he took his family on the round of tourist sites, marveling at, among much else, the "small and obscure corner of [Westminster] Abbey" where "the House of Commons held its sittings for three hundred years up to the time of the Tudors and the first foundations of the free and noble English constitution were laid."[80]

Yet Dutt had to acknowledge that England had changed. In 1868, he had witnessed "an election in which the Liberal party triumphantly came into office, beating the Conservatives on an Irish Question." In 1886, to his regret, the Liberals were "signally beaten" on the even more divisive question of Irish Home Rule. When the Indian candidate Lal Mohan Ghose was defeated by the defection of Unionist voters, Dutt noted the connection between Ireland and India, whose fortunes he now saw as intertwined. In the end, Dutt believed, Home Rule would triumph in both places, and politicians of all stripes would learn that they could not

[79] GLD, 78–112, quotes on 117–18.
[80] Romesh Chunder Dutt, *Three Years in Europe* (Calcutta, 1986), 97–113.

"govern any people ... without some kind of representative institutions."
"The divine right of conquerors will be as obsolete a phrase in the political
dictionary of the twentieth century, as the divine right of kings is in the
nineteenth, and the people of India will be proud of their connection with
England as the sons of Englishmen in Australia or Canada." Yet, as he
attended a Colonial Institute dinner, Dutt could see that the Australians
were using their Home Rule to erect restrictive tariffs, protecting their
nascent industries and keeping out cheap British goods. In truth, British
industry was suffering, and two million workers were unemployed. In
the new climate of cut-throat international competition even the safety-
valve of emigration was in danger of being closed.[81] Asked to participate in
the work of the Colonial Reception Committee, Dutt was struck by all the
talk about imperial federation, and saw it as a potential solution to
England's woes.

> The idea of a sort of federation of all these colonies and dependencies with
> England was in the heart of hosts and guests alike, and was expressed forcibly in
> many an eloquent speech ... Of course there are practical difficulties in the way of
> such a federation, for free nations will not tax themselves to help England in a
> European war in which they have no interest – and a federation which does not
> mean co-operation in war and peace, is scarcely worthy of the name.

The inclusion of India, as a constituent in this federation, was seen by
Dutt as the precondition for making such a project work: "Every true
Indian hopes and trusts that India too will be admitted into this noble
federation with England on the same terms, or as nearly the same terms as
the other colonies as possible, and that the day is not far distant when she
too will have a voice and a hand in the management of her own affairs."[82]
    With his mind perhaps focused on India's relation to such a federal
imperial union, Dutt paid a visit to the aging Max Müller in Oxford. A few
years earlier, Müller had published his most extensive excursus on the
political value of oriental studies to Britain, in a series of lectures entitled
India: What can it Teach Us? Here he railed against the pernicious influence of Mill (still assigned to ICS applicants) and made an eloquent plea
that the study of Sanskrit afforded a better window into the origins of
British civilization than the study of either Latin, Hebrew, or Greek.
Sanskrit scholarship, he contended, "has imparted to the whole ancient
history of man a reality which it never possessed before." Even more
importantly, perhaps, it had "taught us to embrace millions of strangers
and barbarians as members of one family."[83] As so often in the past with

---

[81] Dutt, *Three Years*, 131, 134–6; GLD, 464.   [82] Dutt, *Three Years*, 127–9, 145–60.
[83] Friedrich Max Müller, *India: What can it Teach Us?* (London, 1883), 1–113, quote on 30.

Indians, Müller's words had an authorizing and empowering effect on Dutt. He had long made an avocation out of following oriental scholarship, and had admired the original monographs of Müller, Monier Williams, Bernouf, and many others. If there had remained any doubt, the research of these men proved conclusively that the most objectionable practices of nineteenth-century Hindus – caste oppression and the subjugation of women – had not been part of the original Hinduism of the Vedic Age. Unfortunately this gold-mine of erudition was scattered in recondite scholarly journals to which the British and Indian reading publics had no access. There was need for "a clear historical account of the civilization of Ancient India, based on ancient Sanskrit literature, and written in a sufficiently popular manner to be acceptable to the general reader," Dutt mused. If such a work were driven by a strong, connected narrative, it might convince metropolitan readers that the ancestors of the Indians were people of consequence: a progressive people who had pioneered civilization and were worthy of descendants who could also act in history. On the Indian side, the need was even more imperative since most Indian students knew nothing of the pre-Muslim period of their peoples' history. "Such things," Dutt thought, "should not be."

For the Hindu student the history of the Hindu Period should not be a blank, nor a confused jumble of historic and legendary names, religious parables, and Epic and Puranic myths. No study has so potent an influence in forming a nation's mind and a nation's character as a critical and careful study of its past history. And it is by such a study alone that an unreasoning and superstitious worship of the past is replaced by a legitimate and manly admiration.[84]

So during the period 1887 to 1890, after he returned to India, Dutt worked feverishly to produce a massive 240,000-word *History of Civilization in Ancient India*. The book begins with an aphorism, taken from Max Müller, invoking the Anglo-Indian union at the deepest stratum, rooted in the equation of the Aryan tongues: *Dyaush Pitar* (Sanskrit) = *Zeus Pater* (Greek) = *Jupiter* (Latin) = *Tyr* (Old Norse). The *Rig Veda*, where these names originated, is no mere relic of Indian history, for it is the joint possession of all Indo-European peoples, "the oldest work in the Aryan world," a window into that primal aboriginal culture from which *both* Hindu and Anglo-Saxon civilizations had sprung.[85] Long before there were Greeks, Romans, Hindus, or Teutons, the ur-Aryans began to compile the oldest elements of a common culture, and it was the barbarians who gathered four thousand years ago on the plains of Punjab and who left such traces of ur-Aryanism as had survived into the modern world.

[84] DHAI, I: vi–xix, quotes on xiii–xiv, xv.   [85] DHAI, I: vii.

As one might expect, Dutt's Indo-Aryans are bold, manly warriors, worthy cousins to the blond-haired, blue-eyed devotees of Zeus. Conquering, courageous, meat-eating horsemen, these freedmen-farmers were as yet untainted by effeminizing vices or Brahminical obsessions with ritual purity. Caste was an open, flexible classification without restrictions on occupation or access to spirituality. Child marriage was rare, widow re-marriage was common, and the seclusion of women was unknown. Yet from an early point, Dutt acknowledges a subtle difference between the Aryans of the east and west. While the latter may have remained obsessed with racial purity, the former mixed with the darker-skinned aborigines whom they conquered as they pressed southeastward down the Gangeatic plain. As Hindu civilization advanced from the Vedic Age (2000–1400 BC) to the Epic Age (1400–1000 BC), the Aryans did try to herd the races they subordinated into an inferior Sudra caste. However, Hindu history was "not just a story of conquests," but also "of the spread of Hindu civilization among hitherto unknown countries and aboriginal nations ... The Gift was accepted and cherished, and henceforth the Dravidian and other tribes of southern and eastern India bore the livery of Aryan religion, Aryan language and Aryan civilization" through the end of the "Rationalistic Period" (1000–320 BC).[86]

As Dutt's narrative proceeds through the first millennium BC, he periodically renews his juxtaposition of the Aryans, east and west. Although he never explicitly links Hindu achievements to their propensity for race-mixing, he repeatedly demonstrates that the precocity of Hindu civilization was connected to the eastern Aryans' ability to achieve higher levels of social organization and their more robust capacity for cultural hybridity. The *Mahabharata* and the *Ramayana* bore many resemblances to the *Iliad* and the *Odyssey*. Yet where Bankim would simply ransack the former for tales of manly valor, Dutt emphasized their multilayered character. Suffused with sentiments of a higher ethic, they caught a moment in a complex civilization that was rapidly evolving beyond the primitive warrior stage.[87] So long as ancient Hinduism did not degenerate into an exclusive Brahman caste possession, it was able to ward off the danger of effeminacy. In particular, the active participation of Kshatriyas in framing practices of worship and devotion kept religion firmly tethered to reality. Where Hinduism had been a narrowly spiritual creation for Keshub, Dutt depicted it as the foundation of an entire civilization. As the formulaic Brahmanas gave way to the philosophical sublimity of the Upanishads, Dutt's Hindus opened up a new epoch in human history.

---

[86] DHAI, I: 1–390, quotes on 212–13, 127.   [87] DHAI, I: 120–43.

Pioneers of monotheism, pantheism, and reincarnation, they were also the inventors of astronomy, mathematics, decimal notation, and geometry. Indian imports were the basis of the Chinese zodiac, Dutt contends, while Pythagoras transmitted metempsychosis and triangular calculation to the west.[88]

The ultimate triumph of early Hindu civilization, according to Dutt, came with the metamorphosis of this esoteric elite culture into a more open, democratic, and ecumenical form. The motive force in this great transformation was Gautama Buddha, who preached the most comprehensive gospel of universal love and salvation, a full five centuries before the appearance of Christ. Two centuries later, the great Emperor Asoka renounced the use of violence, embraced the path of Buddhism, and spread the gospel of peace and justice throughout the Asian world. Although Dutt depicts Buddhism as the world's first experiment in egalitarianism, after the third century BC he feels compelled to hand the baton of human progress on to the west.[89] Plato and Aristotle broke new ground in philosophy, while the armies of Alexander left India suddenly exposed to the encroachments of the Bactrian Greeks. Since the immediate threat was successfully resisted for several more centuries Hindu civilization seemed, on the surface, to retain its vitality. Dutt sees many parallels between the slow erosion of ancient Hinduism and the protracted decline and fall of the Roman Empire. The difference, of course, was that where Europe eventually recovered from its dark ages, in India, the first wave of barbarian invasions was but a prelude to the bondage of a more enduring foreign rule. Dutt does not attribute this outcome to any inherent inferiority in Hindu culture but, rather, to the slow strangulation of caste privilege and prejudice.[90]

"The caste system in India has much to answer for," Dutt concludes, but its "worst and most lamentable result" was to separate Indians from one another and to create "this permanent breach and disunion where there should have been fusion and union." Gradually, but inexorably, it strangled one vital dimension of national life after another. The exaggeration of Brahman patriarchy eventuated in the degradation of Hindu women, child marriage, and private seclusion, finally issuing in the ultimate horror of sati. Radiating outward from the family, infecting every aspect of public life, caste gained a hereditary stranglehold on trades and occupations, undermining national prosperity and impeding economic

---

[88] DHAI, I: 136, 180–98, 269–404. In making the argument that ancient Indian civilization was more advanced than that of the Greeks, Dutt is careful to cite the evidence of the Greek traveler Megasthenes. DHAI, I: 210–30, 250–3.

[89] DHAI, I: 305–90.   [90] DHAI, II: 1–123.

advance. Yet if all these late developments represented the antithesis of Hindu civilization at its peak, then the British efforts to extirpate them need not be represented as attacks on true Hinduism. The progress that the British connection brings is not a separate western tradition for Dutt, but an opportunity for India to reconnect with its own past, to restore all that was best in ancient Hinduism, now adapted to modern political and technological realities. "It may be England's high privilege," Dutt proclaims at the end of his book, "to restore to an ancient nation a new and healthy life." But "If the science and learning, the sympathy and example of modern Europe help us to regain in some measure a national consciousness and life, Europe will have rendered back to modern India that kindly help and brotherly service which India rendered to Europe in ancient days – in religion, science and civilization."[91]

8   R. C. Dutt and the history of modern Indian poverty

Dutt's assault on caste and patriarchy as inauthentic un-Hindu institutions was of course nothing new. Rammohun, Keshub, and even Bankim, in certain moods, had already made similar points. In its erudition and sophistication, however, Dutt's *magnum opus* was unmatched. Even more novel was his belief that the British connection might bring not only the benefits of modern progress, but also a reawakening of the true Hindu traditions, painstakingly discovered through orientalist research. Indians – both Hindu and Muslim – could exalt in their aboriginal Aryan status, while also recognizing that the high civilization of their ancestors had been the product of racial mixing and the repudiation of an arrogant racial exclusivity.

Given the enormous effort that Dutt had put into this scholarly undertaking, he could not but be somewhat disappointed at the lukewarm and uneven reception of his book. Among Hindus it was, as he hoped, appreciatively acknowledged, becoming something of an instant classic and an enduring reference work. Yet Dutt's attacks on the authenticity of patriarchy and the evils of caste were bitterly resented by the Hindu fundamentalists. To envision the road back to original Hinduism as running through the detour of British modernity was widely doubted. It was even dismissed as the idiosyncratic crotchet of one who had a strong personal need to reconcile the patriotic sentiments of his leisure with the imperial obeisance required at work. In Britain, the book was tepidly praised, but broadly ignored. It was reviewed in none of the leading monthlies or quarterlies,

[91] DHAI, II: 124–334, quote on 334.

and was only cursorily noted in *The Glasgow Herald*, the *Athenaeum*, and the *Morning Post*. With orientalism no longer in vogue, and racial purity in the ascendant, it was seen as primarily of antiquarian and local interest. No awareness was evinced of Dutt's powerful message that the road to future imperial union and liberal progress lay through racial hybridization, the recognition of cultural differences, and the cultivation of distinct (albeit genealogically related) national histories.[92]

If Dutt was disappointed with the neglect of his writings, he was becoming even more frustrated with the failure of his employers to reward his administrative work. Having attained the rank of Divisional Commissioner, he found that he had hit the glass ceiling of race. "They have treated me on the whole fairly," he reported to his brother, "but without special favor." As he watched juniors being appointed over his head, he complained, "the doors of the secretariat [i.e. high-level, policy-making positions] have been closed to me." If "Government is not disposed to repose any real trust and confidence in me," he continued, he would "feel free to utilize my powers and abilities" to advance the interests of his country in other ways. Thus in 1897, Dutt took another leave of absence and traveled to England to restore his health. After some thought, he decided to take early retirement and devote his remaining years to serving India and the Empire through scholarly and political work.[93]

Appointed as Lecturer in Indian History at University College, London, he was able to expand on the themes of his published writings and to reach a wider metropolitan audience. A series of English abridgements and translations of the *Mahabharata* and the *Ramayana* became brisk sellers, and probably contributed more than any of his other writings to raise the status of Indian civilization in British eyes.[94] At the same time, Dutt now felt free to speak his mind openly about contemporary politics and modern history. To this end, he published a short book entitled *England and India*, in which he explored the various ways in which the histories of the two nations had become inextricably intertwined. In the preface, he proclaims the goal of demonstrating "how the history of progress in England and in India have flowed in parallel streams. Indian history, or rather the progress of India under British rule is unintelligible, without reference to the history of progress in England."[95]

---

[92] GLD, 125–35.   [93] Dutt, *Dutt*, 52–4; GLD, 124–216, quote on 206.
[94] See R. C. Dutt (ed.), *Mahabharata* (London, 1899). See also GLD, 256–69, for letters and reviews in the English press praising Dutt's translations and abridgements.
[95] GLD, 217–28; Romesh Chunder Dutt, *England and India: A Record of Progress during a Hundred Years, 1785–1885* (London, 1897), xi.

This premise, however, is problematized in the first chapter, where Dutt juxtaposes the pomp and circumstance of the Queen's 1897 Diamond Jubilee with contemporaneous scenes of Indian desolation and poverty. How then had British progress resulted in Indian retrogression? The triumph of British liberalism, it turned out, was a necessary but not a sufficient condition for Indian advance. Between 1825 and 1848, the same movement that produced legal and political reform in the metropolis and the abolition of slavery in the colonies also underwrote the Indian reforms of Munro, Elphinstone, Bentinck, and Macaulay. Then again, the advent of Gladstone (1865–74) had opened promising vistas of democratic change in British Ireland and India alike. But British liberalism failed to take root in the motherland. Consequently, between the repression of Chartism and the death of Palmerston, progressive imperial initiatives had stopped. Aggressive policies of expansion had crushed the independence of subaltern peoples on every continent. Moreover, this adventurism had been financed out of Indian revenues, thereby imposing ruinous taxation on the peasantry and exacerbating Naoroji's drain. This toxic mix had been repeated on a larger scale during the administrations of Disraeli in London and Lytton in Calcutta. The same policies that checked British radicalism and treated the Bengali bhadralok with racist contempt also underwrote aggressive expansionism in Africa and Afghanistan, which further weakened the Indian peasant taxpayer and culminated in the devastating famine of 1877, in which five million Indians died.[96]

The return of Gladstonian Liberalism in 1880 is depicted by Dutt as a great missed opportunity. Gladstone's Midlothian speeches, which thrilled newspaper readers in both Britain and the colonies, promised to replace imperial arrogance with aid to oppressed subaltern peoples. Yet the government he formed after winning the election delivered only a small portion of what it had promised. As a consequence, its achievements were spotty and its influence did not last. Here Dutt almost unconsciously reverses his formula, when he shows how the Liberals' acquiescence in reactionary treatment of the colonies fatally weakened their progressive agenda at home. When the Cabinet intervened militarily in South Africa, Burma, Egypt, and Sudan, and when it failed to conciliate Ireland with Home Rule, this violation of its own principles only guaranteed its demise. In India of course the New Liberalism had been embodied in Lord Ripon, who delivered so little after promising so much. In his book, Dutt drew a veil of silence on the post-1885 Salisbury era, but in other writings he made clear how much he despised the jingoistic Toryism of the later Victorian age.

---

[96] Dutt, *England and India*, 1–112; Mike Davis, *Late Victorian Holocausts: El Niño Famines and the Making of the Third World* (London, 2001), 25–60.

Never since the Crimean War has imperialism been so rampant in England; never have the purely animal instincts of self-love and self-aggrandizement been stronger or more violent ... Do you now understand why the Indian Government has, in recent years, turned to methods of coercion and repressive legislation? Talk to the serried ranks of Tory members in the House, and to high Indian officials about reposing trust and confidence in the people of India ... you may as well speak Chinese to them.[97]

Dutt himself could survive personal snubs in London and racist jibes in Calcutta. He could retire from the ICS and immerse himself in his books. He was staggered, however, when he thought of the poor peasant, living at the margins of subsistence and now compelled to finance reckless British expansionism at various points around the globe. Then, between 1898 and 1902, came the devastating famine in which another six million Indians died. Was it still possible to celebrate the progressive character of the British Empire under these circumstances? As he frankly acknowledged in a speech to Congress, educated Indians had little choice. As the products of anglicization they could scarcely repudiate the system that had produced them. Their lives (including his own) had been dedicated in service to the Empire, and they really had no alternative but to stand as loyal Anglo-Indians, seeking to strengthen the Empire by constructive criticism from within. In this spirit, he published five open letters to the new Viceroy, Lord Curzon, that drew attention to the connection between famine and overtaxation. The only remedy was the Congress program of gradual self-government, which would enable India to abandon confiscatory policies and provide herself with relief.

Like Naoroji a generation earlier, but with a force and urgency heightened by the intervening years, Dutt came up against the contradictions in the imperial progress narrative. Did British capitalism and British prosperity necessarily spell Indian underdevelopment and poverty? To find the answer, Dutt realized that he had to redirect his historians' skills from the study of ancient civilization to modern economic history.[98] Dutt's decision to turn his hand in this new direction was a measure of

---

[97] Dutt, *England and India*, 112–60. Quote in GLD, 240. "I am proud as anyone can be of England's glory, England's triumph, and England's world-wide Empire," Dutt avowed, but reports of the Battle of Omdurman "make me sick." He adds, "There was no real battle but slaughter only ... The barbarians had no chance against the maxim guns of our troops, and they hurled themselves against our arms of precision with a bravery and reckless valor, which has never been excelled in the history of the world, only to be mowed down and exterminated!" GLD, 240–1.

[98] For the later period in Dutt's life see GLD, 229–504, and Dutt, *Dutt*, 68–194. On famine, see Romesh Chunder Dutt, *Open Letters to Lord Curzon on Famines in India* (London, 1900); Dutt's 1899 presidential address to Congress is reprinted in Dutt, *Dutt*, 197–234. Davis, *Late Victorian Holocausts*, 119–76.

both his courage and his self-confidence. At the time, economic history was still in its infancy as a genre. Even in the west, there was no consensus about how such a history should be written, what topics should be covered, or what evidence used. Yet for Dutt, such a study was simply a logical outgrowth of the paradox he had uncovered in his earlier book: in what sense could British rule be regarded as progressive for India, when its result had been the pauperization of the vast bulk of the population? In the preface to the first volume of the *Economic History of India*, Dutt posed the paradox this way: "Englishmen can look back on their work in India, if not with unalloyed satisfaction, at least with some legitimate pride." They had brought peace, western education, and modern institutions. "On the other hand," he continued, "No open-minded Englishman contemplates the material condition of the people of India under British rule with equal satisfaction." Poverty was ubiquitous and famines were endemic. In the last quarter of the century, the two together had "carried off fifteen million people," a number equal to half of the population of England itself. Dutt considered and rejected the operation of extraneous and indigenous factors, such as (1) overpopulation, (2) the fecklessness and improvidence of Indian peasants, (3) the debilitating effect of usury and moneylenders, and (4) the effects of climate and drought. The impoverishment of India, he concluded, was substantially the result of British policy itself. Here Dutt issued an indictment that goes beyond Naoroji's preoccupation with fiscal drain. "India, in the eighteenth century, was a great manufacturing as well as a great agricultural country," he noted, "and the products of the Indian loom supplied the markets of Asia and Europe."[99]

From the moment of British hegemony, however, she was determined to put an end to this state of affairs. Indian weavers were corralled into EIC workshops. Indian silks and muslins were excluded from British markets, while Lancashire goods were admitted into India duty-free. The result was to destroy Indian manufacturing, first in textiles, then in a host of other trades and crafts. British policy decided that India was to be transformed into a producer of raw materials, such as cotton, indigo, tea, and opium for British industry and re-export. At the same time, it would become a consumer of Britain's cheapest, lowest-grade manufactured goods. The primary products that India exported were to be produced either by an impoverished, economically dependent peasantry or by large plantations financed by British capital, with profits expatriated to the mother country. As these enterprises proliferated, it became evident that they contributed little to the healthy development of the Indian economy.

[99] DEHI, I: v, II: vi, vii, viii. For a further analysis of these volumes, see Gayan Prakash, *Another Reason: Science and the Imagination of Modern India* (Princeton, 1999), 181–7.

Even the railroads – invariably vaunted as shining examples of Anglo-Indian modernization – were largely built for the benefit of foreign enterprise and the military. Financed by foreign capital, they offered guaranteed returns to attract investors, and these were financed out of the Indian state treasury. All the while, irrigation works, which might have saved lives and increased agricultural output, were left to languish for lack of government support.[100]

It was thus, with the economic dice already loaded heavily against them, that the Indian population – especially the mass of impoverished peasants – were exposed to further bleeding from Naoroji's drain. To remove £30 million every year from a country so poor and deindustrialized was a recipe for periodic famine, epidemic, and mass mortality. Yet the late Victorian Raj was so shameless in its rapacity that

Coarse Indian goods, which did not in any way compete with Lancashire goods, were taxed, as well as finer fabrics. The miserable clothing of the miserable Indian laborer, earning less than 2½ d. a day, was taxed by a jealous Government. The infant mill industry of Bombay, instead of receiving help and encouragement, was repressed by an excise duty unknown in any other part of the civilised world.[101]

In the pages of his *Economic History*, Dutt was quick to discount any deliberate plan or conscious design on the part of the British to weaken India. Privately, he was more scathing, and the tone of bitterness occasionally made its way into print. The original conquistadors of the Clive and Hastings era had been little better than pirates. These had been replaced during the early nineteenth century by men like Elphinstone, Munro, Bentinck, and Macaulay, who genuinely worked to bring India into the modern age. While the British officials and civil servants of the post-Mutiny period had fallen off from this elevated standard, the ICS had its fair share of hard-working, well-intentioned functionaries, who were dedicated to the welfare of the populations that they ruled.[102]

What then had gone wrong? The real problem, according to Dutt, was that major policy decisions were rarely made in India by people attentive to Indian needs. These decisions were imposed from the outside by narrowly constituted English interests. Before 1857, policy-making had been hostage to EIC directors and shareholders, who were interested only in maximizing their dividends. After 1857, policies were made by narrow-minded English politicians interested only in protecting English industries, or in advancing an ambitious imperial agenda on the cheap. Given that real power was always concentrated in London, the best-laid

[100] DEHI, I: v–xii, II: 168–96.   [101] Quoted in GLD, 362.   [102] DEHI, I: 1–80, 326–97.

plans of enlightened administrators were repeatedly undone. Tariff policy reflected the interests of Lancashire, not those of Bombay or Calcutta. Meanwhile, the unrelenting imperative to maximize revenue had led to insatiable tax demands that had undermined traditional village communities. It had simultaneously eroded the position of the pre-existing landlord classes and driven the peasant masses into the ground. Wherever "permanent settlements" were established, they turned out to be only as permanent as was convenient for British imperialism.[103]

What then was Dutt's solution to this dilemma? Like all the other figures treated in this chapter, Dutt was always at great pains to proclaim his loyalty to the Empire. How could it be otherwise for a man who had dedicated his life to serving the Raj? "The Indian Empire will be judged by History as the most superb of institutions in modern times." The problem did not lie in the *ideal* of liberal imperialism, but in its implementation. Bad decisions were repeatedly made, simply because all the power was held by the British, and Indians were never consulted about the policies by which they were governed. "History does not record a single instance of one people ruling another in the interest of the subject nation," he concluded. "Mankind has not yet discovered any method for safeguarding the interest of a subject nation without conceding to that nation some voice in controlling the administration of their concerns."[104]

Following the position adopted by Congress, Dutt insisted that he advocated only gradual constitutional change. "The people of India are not fond of sudden changes and revolutions ... They prefer to work on lines that have already been laid down." Indeed, Dutt believed that, of all the Empire's peoples, Indians were the most intrinsically loyal to the British Empire ideal. While Canadians, Australians, and New Zealanders might choose to pursue their separate interests, leaving their Anglo-Saxon kin behind, Indians knew that the common good could best be advanced by building on what history had ratified over an extended period.

It may be a heresy to say it in these days that the Empire of India will last after the British colonies [e.g. the white settler colonies of Canada and Australasia] have ceased to owe allegiance to the British Crown ... In India, the people honestly desire a longer connection with Great Britain, not through sentimental loyalty, but, as Lord Dufferin once said, through a sense of self-interest. They still believe that they have much to gain by being in close touch with the West, through the rule of a Western Power. They have cast their lot with Great Britain; they have identified with British rule; they honestly desire that rule to last. But they do not desire the administration to last in its present absolute and exclusive form.[105]

---

[103] DEHI, I: 398–432, II: 3–617.   [104] DEHI, I: xvi, II: xviii.   [105] DEHI, I: xvii.

9 Conclusion: liberal imperialism's reappearance on the periphery

The individuals treated in this chapter have not fared well at the hands of posterity. Subsequent generations of British imperialists saw in them merely embarrassing reminders of promises unmet. Indian nationalists have viewed them, at best, as transitional, equivocal figures: men who sometimes pointed the way toward the separatist patriotism of the future, but who were too blind – or too craven – to make a clean break with the humiliating posture of empire loyalty. Even today's postcolonial scholars do not quite know where to place these hybrid creatures: embodiments of the colonial other, who refused the refusal of metropolitan hegemony.[106] And yet, despite their failure to fit the received historiographical categories, these men demand to be given their due. Their impact was felt far beyond the borders of the subcontinent, and they were the main shapers of Indian public opinion during the second half of the nineteenth century. If we approach them from the standpoint of this book, however, their significance becomes more comprehensible, for they were liberal imperialists, situated in late Victorian India, who adapted for their own purposes the universalistic vision of a progressive Empire that had been first formulated by metropolitan liberals during the early nineteenth century. The irony of course is that by the time these children and grandchildren of Macaulay took up the imperial progress narrative, it had been abandoned by most London-based policy-making elites.

From one perspective it is certainly possible to dismiss these men as engaged in a hopeless mimicry of the master, trapped in the confines of a derivative discourse. No one would dispute that liberalism first began in Britain, and was only later translated and transposed to the colonies. Yet, as this chapter has sought to demonstrate, this work of translation and transposition turned it into something different from what it had originally been. The celebration of universal imperial progress that flowed so fluently from metropolitan pens was, on the periphery, a more complicated, contradictory, and hard-bought accomplishment. Well aware that their liberal imperial embrace might turn into slavish imitation, these men were at pains to demonstrate that their liberal imperialism had taken root on a soil of cultural difference, that it was not incompatible with national aspirations, and that it had registered the contradictions of capitalist

---

[106] Bhabha, *The Location of Culture*, 85–92; and Partha Chatterjee's superb *Nationalist Thought in the Colonial World: A Derivative Discourse?* (Minneapolis, 1986), which – its subtitle notwithstanding – recognizes that the discourse of a man like Bankim was not entirely derivative; see 36–83.

modernity.[107] In the cases of Keshub and Bankim, this emphasis on cultural difference took the form of insisting that India had its own distinctively spiritual version of the progress narrative that either ran in parallel track (Keshub) or represented a superior version (Bankim) that the future would empower. Unable to revel in the romantic nostalgia of Walter Scott, these men focused their romances on the future, purporting to ground them in the foundations of India's unique history of spirituality.

When the limits of these formulations became evident, a younger cohort – represented here by Banerjea and Dutt – returned to the political arena and the original British progress narrative, to demand that Macaulay's romance of representative government be extended to people like themselves. To press this demand they quickly discovered that it was not sufficient to become "English in taste and opinion." Denigrated as backward, inauthentic objects of evolutionary incompletion, they were forced to re-interrogate their own national history to prove their own fitness for capitalist modernity. By demonstrating that India had once been the source of progress and civilization, they asserted that this legacy entitled them to enter the modern political arena as historical subjects capable of consequence and agency. Only through such exercises in historical re-interrogation and reflexive self-transcendence would Indians be able to overcome their cultural, linguistic, and religious divisions and take control of their destiny as a modern nation. Finally, for Naoroji and the later Dutt, this re-interrogation of history took them in completely original directions as they confronted the contradictions of the progress narrative and strove to understand the causes of modern Indian poverty. Here, ironically, it was their very desire to save the Empire that led them to grasp the sources of capitalist underdevelopment, which they saw were driving India and Britain in opposite directions, and which (because they genuinely believed in British liberalism) they associated with illiberal and un-British rule.

Notions of imperial citizenship that they saw emerging in the white settler colonies inspired each of these men to novel critiques of the racial and evolutionary exclusions that, in keeping them out of the imperial federation of the future, prevented that federation from coming to be. And yet these men also realized that the capacity to create the future was not really within their power. For the most part, the metropole had rejected their efforts to broaden the progress narrative. The chance of

---

[107] Another way to put this would be to say that they sought to improve the existing version of liberalism by translating it into a Hindu idiom. Only in this way, they avowed, could liberalism become truly *liberal* – a dialectic negotiated between two mutually respecting partners, rather than a patronizing concession handed down from above.

achieving a genuinely inclusive liberal Empire would henceforth depend on Britons' willingness to expand and ability to complicate their own metropolitan understandings of history.

Much remains to be done, and the impetus must come from England. To England we look for inspiration and guidance. To England we look for sympathy in the struggle. From England must come the crowning mandate which will enfranchise our peoples . . . English history has taught us those principles of freedom which we cherish with our life-blood. We have been fed upon the strong food of English constitutional freedom . . . We have been brought face to face with the struggles and the triumphs of the English people in their stately march towards constitutional freedom. Where will you find better models of courage, devotion and sacrifice? . . . Never in the history of the world have the inheritors of an ancient civilization been so profoundly influenced by the influx of modern ideas . . . The course of civilization following the path of the sun has travelled from East to West. The West owes a heavy debt to the East. We look forward to the day when that debt will be repaid.[108]

[108] Banerjea, *Speeches*, I: 143–4.

Epilogue: From liberal imperialism to Conservative Unionism: losing the thread of progress in history

> The sentiment of empire may be called innate in every Briton. If there are exceptions, they are like those of men blind or lame among us. It is part of our patrimony ... a portion of our national stock, which has never been deficient, but which has more than once run to rank excess, and brought us to mischief ... What we want from the Colonies is something better than "food for powder." To give birth and existence to these States, which are to form so large a portion of the New World, is a noble feature of the work and mission of this nation, as it was of old in the mission of Greece [but] the prospective multiplication of possessions oversea is, to say the least, far from desirable ... England, which has grown so great, may easily become little; through the effeminate selfishness of luxurious living; through neglecting realities at home to amuse herself everywhere else in stalking phantoms; through putting again on her resources a strain like that of the great French war, which brought her people to misery and her Throne to peril; through that denial of equal rights to others.
>
> W. E. Gladstone, "England's Mission," *The Nineteenth Century*, IV (1878), 560–8

With these words, W. E. Gladstone signaled his return to the political arena, at the head of a campaign against the "New" Tory imperialism of the 1870s. Roused from retirement by Disraeli's appeasement of Ottoman genocide in the Balkans, Gladstone demanded a morally defensible Christian foreign policy that would end bellicose posturing and work to advance human rights. He embraced the British Empire as an essential instrument for spreading civilizational values, but he rejected the Tories' bombastic and aggressive "imperialism," which racked up costly debts, inflated unaccountable military establishments, inflicted violence on indigenous peoples, and grasped at the acquisition of ever more distant lands. As this logic of aggressive imperialism continued to take more brutal turns throughout 1878–9, Gladstone focused his anger ever more sharply against the Disraeli administration, which threatened Russia, annexed the Transvaal, made war on the Zulus, and invaded Afghanistan. Sensing the approach of a general election, Gladstone addressed a series of mass meetings among his Midlothian constituents that electrified Liberals everywhere when they were published the next day in the press.[1] "If we cast our eye to South Africa," he thundered, "what do we behold?"

That a nation whom we term savages have in defense of their own land offered their naked bodies to the terribly improved artillery and arms of modern European science, and have been mowed down by hundreds and by thousands, having committed no offence, but having, with rude and ignorant courage, done what were for them ... the duties of patriotism.

"Go from South Africa to the mountains of central Asia," he continued. In the hills of Afghanistan, British troops had been ordered to attack uncooperative tribesmen and to burn their villages when they dared to resist.

Those Hill Tribes had committed no real offence against us. We, in the pursuit of our political objects, chose to establish military positions in their country. If they resisted, would not you have done the same? ... The meaning of the burning of the village is, that the women and the children were driven forth to perish in the snows of winter. [Does that not rouse in British women] a sentiment of horror and grief, to think that the name of England, under no political necessity, but for a war as frivolous as ever was waged in the history of man, should be associated with consequences such as these?[2]

Gladstone's eloquent indictment of the Tory government's imperial policy certainly demonstrated that he hoped to replace it with a more humane alternative, but how far did he really believe that people like the Zulus or Afghanis had "equal rights" or should be allowed to manage their own affairs? Was the liberal imperial spirit, marginalized in the metropole since the 1840s, about to be revived by the leader of the British left? Was the progress narrative to be reasserted in a form that endorsed the right of Greater Britons of other colors and creeds?

1   Gladstone's progress: from youthful reactionary to aging radical

These questions are complicated, since the leader in question, Gladstone, had begun his political life as a Tory, and his circuitous odyssey from High Church theocrat to the "People's William" only gradually brought him to accept democracy as a viable form of government, even in Anglo-Saxon

[1] John Morley, *The Life of William Ewart Gladstone*, 2 vols. (London, 1908), II: 117–79; Richard Shannon, *Gladstone*, 2 vols., II, *1865–1898* (Chapel Hill, 1999), 157–247; Richard Shannon, *Gladstone and the Bulgarian Agitation* (London, 1963).
[2] W. E. Gladstone, *Midlothian Speeches* (Leicester, 1971), quotes on 90–1, 91–2.

lands. As a firm believer in established institutions and authorities, the young Tory orator had shown scant belief in progress during the 1830s, when conventional wisdom held it high. At a time when T. B. Macaulay was anticipating Indian self-government as "the proudest day in English history," Gladstone spoke from the opposite Commons bench to excuse his father's mistreatment of West Indian slaves. As an able, precocious advocate for the planters, this young man maneuvered to delay slave emancipation, schemed to augment financial compensation for the owners, set "apprenticeship" controls on black labor, and sought to promote the immigration of Indian indentured servants so that plantation labor would remain docile and cheap. It was difficult in all this to see the Christian conscience that, even then, the young Gladstone sententiously claimed.[3] It was only during the 1840s, when he attained high office in Peel's administration, that Gladstone sloughed off the coercive mercantilist imperialism he had learned from his father and embraced free labor, free trade, and free immigration. During a brief stint as Colonial Secretary, in 1845–6, he went further, tentatively experimenting with the distinctively liberal approach to the Empire that he would forcefully articulate three decades hence: the colonies were to be conceived as maturing children of the motherland. They were to be endowed with institutions of responsible self-government at the earliest opportunity. They should be weaned from their dependence and made responsible for their own defense.[4]

Yet throughout the 1850s and 1860s, Gladstone gave scant evidence that he believed these institutions of "responsible government" could (or should) be applied beyond the "white settler" colonies of Canada, Australia, and New Zealand.[5] As a Philo-Hellene, with somewhat idiosyncratic notions of ancient history, Gladstone viewed Anglo-Saxon colonization of these distant lands as a reprise of the great diaspora that had been spread across the Mediterranean by the ancient Greeks. Like the

[3] Morley, *Gladstone*, I: 1–85; Shannon, *Gladstone*, I, *1809–65* (London, 1984), 1–43; H. C. G. Matthew, *Gladstone*, 2 vols., I, *1809–1874* (Oxford, 1986), 1–58; Peter Stansky, *Gladstone: A Progress in Politics* (New York, 1981); S. G. Checkland, *The Gladstones: A Family Biography, 1764–1851* (Cambridge, 1971), 3–262. When Gladstone re-read his maiden speech many years later, he was duly chagrined.

[4] Morley, *Gladstone*, I: 86–241; Shannon, *Gladstone*, I: 44–196; Matthew, *Gladstone*, I: 59–102; Checkland, *Gladstones*, 263–406; Madhavi Kale, *Fragments of Empire: Capital, Slavery and Indian Indentured Labor in the British Caribbean* (Philadelphia, 1998), 1–87; Paul Knaplund, *Gladstone and Britain's Imperial Policy* (Hamden, Connecticut, 1966), 5–63, 167–85.

[5] Although Gladstone was closely involved with questions of native policy during the 1830s and 1840s, he left only a few anodyne public statements on these matters. Canny politician that he was already becoming, he probably saw that fully articulating his increasingly "humanitarian" views would probably lose him old friends, without making him many new ones. Knaplund, *Imperial Policy*, 34–7.

Hellenes of the post-Homeric era, modern Britons should not be interested in territorial acquisition, but rather in spawning daughter polities on
other continents that would become self-governing and capable of spreading British values and institutions around the world. In this manner, the
same dispersive energies that had originally created European civilization
could now be extended outward, on a global scale. Convinced that imperial federation was neither practical nor desirable, Gladstone (by blood,
himself a Scot) was persuaded by E. A. Freeman that Greater Britain
could still hang together as a loose coalition of quasi-autonomous states,
choosing freely to bind together in alliance on the basis of mutual interest,
a shared anglocentric culture, and the legacy of a common history.[6]

It was only when Gladstone became Prime Minister, in 1868, that he was
forced to confront the fact that the overwhelming majority of British subjects were not white Anglo-Saxons, but racially alien dependents in the
"colored" colonies. Ironically, it was in Ireland, ostensibly an integral part
of the United Kingdom, that Gladstone was first obliged to come to terms
with this reality. Having vowed "to do justice to Ireland," he discovered that
Ireland required different laws, policies, and institutions to become equal
with the other constituent nations in the Union. Having entered politics to
protect the State Church and landlord property, he now discovered that in
Ireland, the Church had to be disestablished, and the sanctity of landlord
property had to be breached. The common history and culture that he once
assumed to underpin the constituent parts of Greater Britain now reap-
peared in a fractured and contradictory form: the triumphs of British
liberalism were disasters for Ireland, and the hopes for liberalism in
Ireland entailed recasting Britishness in an altered frame.[7] Never entirely
comfortable as an icon of the left, Gladstone hoped to hand these conundrums on to the next generation when his government was defeated in the
1874 election. But then came the unexpected departures of the 1876–80
period, when the Grand Old Man returned to the platform, rejuvenated, for
his Midlothian crusade. When the landslide electoral victory of 1880 put
him back in Downing Street, Gladstone was again forced to wrestle with
the contradictions of liberal imperialism, no longer only in Ireland, but
also in the Mediterranean, the Balkans, Egypt, South Africa, Afghanistan,
India, Burma, and other global hotspots.[8]

---

[6] Knaplund, *Imperial Policy*, 65–139, 185–246; Morley, *Gladstone*, I: 242–666; Shannon,
    Gladstone, I: 197–556; Matthew, *Gladstone*, I: 103–67.
[7] Knaplund, *Imperial Policy*, 15–139; Morley, *Gladstone*, I: 667–771, II: 1–77; Shannon,
    Gladstone, II, *1865–1898* (Chapel Hill, 1999), 1–156; Matthew, *Gladstone*, I: 168–255.
[8] Morley, *Gladstone*, II: 78–179; Matthew, *Gladstone*, II, *1875–1898* (Oxford, 1995), 1–98;
    Shannon, *Gladstone*, II: 157–247; Paul Knaplund, *Gladstone's Foreign Policy* (Hamden,
    Connecticut, 1970), 1–65.

It is easy to dismiss Gladstone's second administration as a failure. In fact, it was a profoundly consequential failure that produced many occasions for puzzlement and paradox. The Midlothian rhetoric that lofted the Liberals into office also imposed upon them a series of mandates that they simply could not fulfill. Thus the government that vaunted its belief in national self-determination ended up fighting nationalist movements on three continents. Professing its commitment to protect indigenous peoples, this government stood by as indigenous peoples were slaughtered in areas under British suzerainty, and even within the Empire itself. Finally, the government that opposed further territorial acquisition ended up conquering Egypt, annexing Upper Burma, and precipitating the scrambles for Africa and southeast Asia that drove all of Europe into the empire-madness of the high imperial age.[9]

Nevertheless, such justly harsh assessments must not be allowed to obscure what Gladstone and the Liberals did accomplish during the 1880s. In Ireland and India, in particular, where restive natives were demanding their rights, more significant experiments in liberal imperialism were attempted. Here, the progress narrative was taken seriously, and the goal of turning the Empire's racial others into Greater British citizens was resumed. If these efforts also ultimately failed, they left the faint trace of an alterative Greater Britain – politically decentralized, culturally diverse, and ethnically polyglot – a liberal Empire that might have been. In both cases, it was quickly discovered that the road to a more inclusive constitutional future had to be wrested through battles over the understanding of history. To a considerable extent, it was the Liberals' failure to win these battles for control of the historical narrative that insured that their liberal imperial initiatives would collapse.

2   Midlothianizing India: evolutionary objects or historical agents?

Gladstone's policy in India was initially motivated by his determination to reverse what he regarded as the outrages and falsifications of the previous Disraeli regime. The failure of the Tories' Afghan War virtually guaranteed a fundamental policy reversal, but Gladstone was determined to expose the "lies" on which this disastrous policy had been

---

[9] Morley, *Gladstone*, II: 180–330; Shannon, *Gladstone*, II: 248–364; Matthew, *Gladstone*, II: 99–210; C. J. Lowe, *The Reluctant Imperialists: British Foreign Policy, 1876–1902* (New York, 1967), 1–120; D. M. Schreuder, *Gladstone and Kruger: Liberal Government and Colonial "Home Rule", 1880–85* (London, 1969); Ronald Robinson and John Gallagher, with Alice Denny, *Africa and the Victorians: The Climax of Empire* (New York, 1961), 1–26, 53–159.

based. Indeed, over the previous five years, Disraeli and his Viceroy, Lytton, had combined to cook up a new conservative image of British India, in which the progress narrative would be replaced by a very different image of oriental immutability. Cleverly combining several of the strands that we have examined in the last few chapters – evolutionism, racial differentiation, peasant stabilization, and indirect rule – this mix was given a powerful new ideological impetus by the Disraeli–Lytton team. In a manner not seen since the days of Scott, these two writer-politicians were able to concoct a new, hierarchical vision of trans-imperial union, by refiguring the relationship between metropole and the "orient" around an imaginary pseudo-history.[10]

As an ethnic Jew who had risen to the Prime Ministership by hiding his alien persona behind an enigmatic mask, Disraeli had long been fascinated by the mystique of race. In his novel *Tancred* (1847), he had the sagacious Jew, Sidonia, enigmatically intone, "All is race; there is no other truth." To prove the point, an impressionable young English aristocrat is then sent on a pilgrimage to Jerusalem, where he learns that Jews should not be persecuted, but rather venerated, because in killing Christ, they saved the world. Armed with this knowledge, the novel's hero prepares to conquer all of Europe and Asia, assisted by the races of Syria and Arabia. At this point, the novel dissipates into incoherence, but not before Disraeli gets in a dig at "some flat-nosed Frank, full of bustle and self-conceit (a race spawned perhaps in the morasses of some northern forest hardly yet cleared) talks of progress! Progress to what, and from where?"[11]

No doubt Disraeli recalled these passages nearly thirty years later when Queen Victoria implored him to make her Empress of India. Here was a brilliant real-life oriental adventure that might attach India's teeming millions to the Raj in a simple symbolic language that everyone could understand. To those who had second thoughts about modernization on the subcontinent, the British monarch could now be presented as the dynastic successor of the Mughals – time-hallowed overlord of the princes and maharajahs who, in their turn, held sway over jagirdars, talukdars, and zamindars, in storied principalities.[12] To

---

[10] Knaplund, *Imperial Policy*, 203–4; Benjamin Disraeli, *Selected Speeches of Lord Beaconsfield* (London, 1882), II: 523–35; R. Koebner and D. Schmidt, *Imperialism: The Story and Significance of a Political Word: 1840–1960* (Cambridge, 1964), 27–165.

[11] Benjamin Disraeli, *Coningsby* [1844] (London, 1983); Benjamin Disraeli, *Tancred* [1847] (Teddington, Middlesex, 2007); Todd M. Endelman, "Disraeli's Jewishness Reconsidered," *Modern Judaism*, 5.2 (1985), 109–23; Robert Blake, *Disraeli* (New York, 1967), 55–70, 190–220.

[12] Blake, *Disraeli*, 534–628; L. A. Knight, "The Royal Titles Act and India," *The Historical Journal*, 11.3 (1968), 488–507.

Disraeli and Lytton this invention of tradition offered a way of diverting attention away from the realities of war, taxation, famine, and unrepresentative government, by enlisting Indians in a romance of pseudo-medieval pageantry. A year after the proclamation of Victoria's new title (underscored by an Indian visit by the Prince of Wales), Lytton organized a vast durbar in Delhi, attended by eighty-four thousand, including most of India's potentates and nobles, who pledged their fealty to the great British Mother amid impressive displays and lavish festivities. This pioneering venture into what David Cannadine has labeled "ornamentalism" was designed to bring British and Indian hierarchies into alignment with one another. The myriad caste, race, religious, status, and linguistic distinctions of "traditional" India could thus be harnessed to buttress British authority, and *vice versa*, so that British aristocrats could obtain appropriate colonial employment, while India was endowed with a new super-aristocracy.[13]

To Gladstone and his Liberal followers, no part of Disraelian Conservatism seemed more menacing than this effort to supplant constitutional rights with propagandistic trumpery. Turning Victoria into an Indian Empress was disputed as a violation of the English Constitution, which set an alarming Napoleonic precedent for the mother country. Lytton's pseudo-feudal Indian extravaganza seemed scarcely less problematic, since it dovetailed so well with other hierarchy-making projects, such as W. W. Hunter's statistical gazetteer, which sought to count and classify the entire subcontinental population into an elaborate array of caste, race, and tribal categories. Hunter's work was by no means incompatible with liberalism, but to categorize Indians entirely on the basis of ascriptive group status – to render them exclusively as evolutionary objects – went against the grain of liberal agendas in the metropolis, which invested emerging groups (i.e. respectable male workers) as historical agents with the rights of franchised individuality.[14]

Unfortunately, India was a distant problem for which Gladstone himself had little time and even less expertise. Neither he nor anyone else in his Cabinet knew much about India's actual past or had any more authentic alternative to substitute for Tory pseudo-history. Thus when Lord Ripon replaced Lytton as Viceroy, he was sent out with no very precise instructions beyond a tentative mandate to restore the

[13] Bernard S. Cohn, "Representing Authority in Victorian India," in E. Hobsbawm and T. Ranger (eds.), *The Invention of Tradition* (Cambridge, 1983); David Cannadine, *Ornamentalism* (Oxford, 2001).

[14] Nicholas B. Dirks, *Castes of Mind: Colonialism and the Making of Modern India* (Princeton, 2001); Susan Bayly, *Caste, Society and Politics in India* (Cambridge, 1999), 97–143.

Macaulayite program of increasing the rights and roles of the westernized urban middle class. At first, these efforts seemed to go uncontested, as when Ripon repealed Lytton's Vernacular Press Censorship
Law, proposed opening volunteer militias to native enlistment, and
sought to create new elected local councils that could manage their
own municipal affairs. Yet with the Ilbert Bill, he passed the limit of
white, Anglo-Indian tolerance, as we have seen. By attempting to give
Indian judges potential jurisdiction over Europeans, Ripon found – like
Macaulay and Dalhousie before him – that the British community in
India, both official and unofficial, would not tolerate a serious move
toward racial equality.[15]

In a sense, Ripon's error had been a mistake of historical interpretation.
Reading the history of Anglo-India through the lens of Macaulay, he
envisioned its future as a land of freeborn Britons, whose union with the
United Kingdom would transcend racial difference, since it would rest on
common notions of democratic citizenship. By contrast, the ICS was able
to demonstrate that India about 1884 still remained a caste-ridden, race-
divided society, in which covenanted civil servants and their allies were
able to consolidate their incipient status as the new master caste. To put it
bluntly, they were demonstrating their ability to render India ungovernable, by threatening to veto Ripon's policies with a "white mutiny." All the
old arguments were trotted out to explain why it was really in the interest
of Indians that the covenanted civil service remain a racially closed, self-
perpetuating power monopoly: loosening the reins and opening the gates
to Bengali babus would put decision-making in the hands of a "micro-
scopic minority" that was entirely unrepresentative of the larger Indian
population, narrowly self-interested in its own avaricious careerism, and
fundamentally unfitted to the manly responsibilities of political work.
"How can 180 millions of souls govern themselves?" the aged Henry
Maine asked in the London India Council, where he now held a seat.
"Responsible and representative government are terms without meaning
when they are applied to such a multitude." It was "ethnologically impossible and historically improbable that any human effort or will could ever
weld these [India's castes, religions, and races] into one nation," echoed
Augustus Rivers Thompson, the Lieutenant Governor of Bengal.[16]

---

[15] Sarvepalli Gopal, *The Viceroyalty of Lord Ripon, 1880–1884* (London, 1953); Sarvepalli
Gopal, *British Policy in India, 1858–1905* (Madras, 1965), 64–179; Anil Seal, *The
Emergence of Indian Nationalism: Competition and Collaboration in the Late Nineteenth
Century* (Cambridge, 1968), 131–93.
[16] Gopal, *British Policy*, 166; Nemai Sudhan Bose, *Racism: The Struggle for Equality and
Indian Nationalism* (Calcutta, 1981), 152–239; Briton Martin, *New India, 1885: British
Official Policy and the Emergence of the Indian National Congress* (Berkeley, 1969), 26–9.

As we have seen, the historiographical basis for questioning these official assumptions scarcely existed in 1884. Banerjea's campaigns had not yet culminated in Congress, Dutt's major historical writings still lay before him, and Naoroji was still beginning to formulate his theory of the drain. Only the most astute among the Raj authorities sensed the first stirrings of change. When Ripon was banqueted by the bhadralok on the eve of his departure, Sir Auckland Colvin anxiously marveled at the novelty of the spectacle: in this ancient land of oriental quiescence, a genuinely modern, national political movement was "at length awakening to the consciousness of its own powers and the assurance of its own success."[17]

If Colvin was expert in detecting such symptoms, it was because he had just arrived from a previous posting in Egypt, where he had witnessed (indeed he had largely precipitated) the British military suppression of an incipient nationalist movement, led by patriotic officers in the Egyptian army. The leader, Colonel Ahmed Arabi, made it clear that he and his colleagues were liberal constitutionalists who had embraced a European model of historical development. They merely wanted the Khedive (Egypt's ruler) to hold elections and accept the limitations of parliamentary control. As representative of the European bondholders in Egyptian state debt, however, Colvin was determined that Egypt should not default on its obligations, or even fall into the hands of people whose European pretensions might lead to awkward expectations, such as "no taxation without representation." Colvin's hostility toward the Arabi movement was precisely a function of its liberal character, since he believed that parliamentary institutions were unsuited to a non-European race. "The Egyptian," he contended, was "incapable of conducting the administration of affairs," and "we are rapidly approaching a state of affairs which differs little, if at all, from anarchy."[18]

By sending a naval squadron to bombard Alexandria, the Gladstone government turned this prognosis into a self-fulfilling prophecy. When the local residents rioted, killing fifty Europeans, the Cabinet voted to send in an army of occupation that remained, in effect, for the next seventy years. The decision to intervene did cause some hand-wringing among the ministers. "The Government of England would run counter to its most cherished traditions of national history," warned the Foreign Secretary, Lord Granville, "were it to entertain a desire to diminish that liberty, or to tamper with institutions to which it has given birth." Such strictures were swept aside, however. The Egyptian government

---

[17] Martin, *New India*, 22; S. R. Mehrotra, *A History of the Indian National Congress*, I, *1885–1918* (New Delhi, 1995), 1–113.
[18] Robert T. Harrison, *Gladstone's Imperialism in Egypt* (Westport, 1995), quote on 91.

owed £90 million to European investors, much at exorbitant interest rates. No less significant were control of the Suez Canal and the route to India. Granville and Gladstone were not about to let these assets fall into independent hands.[19]

Colvin showed the face of Gladstonian imperialism that gave the lie to the lofty rhetoric of Midlothian. On his transit from Egypt to India, however, he was shadowed by a very different character, Wilfrid Scawen Blunt, who showed why the promises of Midlothian could not entirely be disowned. Blunt was a colorful figure – eccentric, romantic, independently wealthy, and well connected – who chose the life of a trans-Asiatic borderer two generations after conventional wisdom had deemed this role to be obsolete. An accomplished horse-breeder who was fluent in Arabic, he befriended desert Bedouins and haunted Cairo bazaars, witnessing the Egyptian Revolution first-hand. Outraged by Britain's unprovoked military assault, Blunt undertook to organize and finance Colonel Arabi's defense, insuring that this "rebel" was not summarily hanged, tortured, or shot. Following his convicted client to exile in Ceylon, Blunt took the opportunity to travel to India, intent on making contact with her nascent nationalist leaders and on offering unsolicited advice to the beleaguered Viceroy Ripon.[20]

Blunt's personal charm earned him the trust of many Hindu and Muslim community leaders, most of whom were already aware of his work in saving Arabi. Remarkably free of the blinders of race stereotyping, he approached his interlocutors as individuals in communities, rather than as specimens of a given caste or race. The Hindu notables, in particular, struck him as extraordinarily competent spokesmen for a public that was intellectually advanced. Fully acculturated to the western model of representative institutions, they chafed at the limits of a political system that treated them with contempt. The newspaper editors in Madras were "intelligent, clear headed men, contrasting by no means unfavorably with men of their profession in London." They showered him with data showing that the ryots of the Deccan were grossly underpaid and overtaxed. Raganath Rao, a deposed Maratha minister, was "a man of the highest distinction, much wit, and the widest possible intelligence. There are not a dozen men in the House of Commons who could hold their own in talk with him." In Calcutta, Surendranath Banerjea's speech for civil

---

[19] Harrison, *Imperialism in Egypt*, quote on 59; D. K. Fieldhouse, *Economics and Empire, 1830–1914* (Ithaca, 1973), 119. Alone among the Liberal ministers, only John Bright was sufficiently troubled by the decision to occupy Egypt to resign from office.

[20] Elizabeth Longford, *A Pilgrimage of Passion: The Life of Wilfrid Scawen Blunt* [1979] (London, 2007), 1–92; W. S. Blunt, *Secret History of the English Occupation of Egypt* [1907] (New York, 1922).

service reform was "quite as good as I have ever heard in my life." The point was reinforced by a highly cultured millowner who told Blunt that Ripon "was an honest man" who meant well, but "who had been able to do nothing for them" so long as the ICS stood in his way.[21]

These Indians, Blunt emphasized, were remarkably loyal, and he was struck that "there should be so few agitators of Indian opinion who speak even in secret of any real rupture with England." Yet the "race hatred" of the English was doing much to squander this devotion. Fueled by pseudo-scientific theories of race and evolution, British disdain had increased with each successive generation, and "if it be not allayed by a more generous treatment [it] will in a few years make the continued connection between England and India altogether impossible." At a time when English fiscal extractions were increasing, the poverty of the Indian masses was deepening, and the natives were demonstrating their capacity for better and cheaper government, it was only by establishing representative government that Britain could preserve a more limited, conditional version of imperial rule.[22]

Since Blunt had gone out to India with a special interest in her Muslims, he was disconcerted to find them in a more perilous condition than the Hindus. Where the Hindu leaders looked self-confidently toward the future, the Muslim leaders remained anxiously fixated on the past. Hearkening back to the glory days of the Mughal Empire and acutely conscious of what they had lost, they were often embittered toward the British, who had stripped them of their authority, and envious of the Hindus, who were outpacing them in the battle of ideas and the competition for jobs. According to Blunt, Muslim life was most vital in princely states, such as Hyderabad, where the courtly culture of old India had been preserved. Unfortunately, such living museums were out of step with the needs of modernity. He accused the British of actively conspiring to keep princes like the Nizam ignorant and infantilized, out of fear that competence would offer a credible model of native self-rule. Blunt's solution to all these problems was to promote Islamic education, which he found inadequate, and much of his time in India was spent in a frustrating and abortive attempt to establish a Muslim university.[23]

Blunt urged Muslims to shelve their resentments and to learn to work alongside the enlightened Hindus as Indian patriots. However, he

---

[21] Longford, *Blunt*, 180–206; W. S. Blunt, *India under Ripon* (London, 1909), quotes on 36–7, 43, 52, 55, 114, 255.
[22] Blunt, *India under Ripon*, 233–58.
[23] Blunt, *India under Ripon*, 57–138, especially 110, 278–98; W. S. Blunt, *The Future of Islam* (London, 1882).

recognized the potential danger of sectarian divisions and the threat they posed to Indian hopes for unity. Lord Dufferin, the new Viceroy (replacing Ripon, in 1885), was no less attentive to these fissures in Indian society. As an Anglo-Protestant landlord from County Down, he tended to look at India through Irish eyes. Deeply familiar with the significance of sectarian divisions in quasi-colonial settings, he immediately saw that the historic antagonism between Hindus and Muslims (as between Protestants and Catholics) did more than anything else to keep both groups dependent on external British rule. "It would," he conceded, "be a diabolical policy on the part of any Government to emphasize or exacerbate race hatreds among the Queen's Indian subjects." However, since the antagonisms between Hindus and Muslims had pre-dated the appearance of the British, he was not culpable in adopting a strategy of "divide and rule."[24]

In fact, Dufferin found Indians as difficult to govern as his Irish neighbors. He had been sent out with explicit instructions to slow the pace of Ripon's innovations and to stop "Midlothianizing India," to use his own words. He had no intention of going back to the frauds and fictions of the Disraeli–Lytton era, but he shared their dislike of the anglicized bhadralok, who thought that British constitutional history applied to people like themselves. "I have discovered," Dufferin complained, "that the Bengalee Baboo is a most irritating and troublesome gentleman ... He has a great deal of Celtic perverseness, vivacity and cunning, and seems to be now employed in setting up the machinery for a repeal agitation." To Indians, the appointment of Lord Dufferin was a great disappointment. Once again, they were being demoted from contract-makers to status-objects. It seemed that Gladstone and the metropolitan Liberals did not take them seriously. Yet if Gladstone had decided to sacrifice liberal imperialism in India, as he had in Egypt, it was not because he had forgotten the rhetoric of Midlothian. Rather, it was because he had made a tactical decision that all his Midlothianizing had to be focused on Ireland. Here too, he ultimately failed, but not before offering one comprehensive vision of how the Greater British future might be democratically and progressively reorganized.[25]

3   Midlothianizing Ireland: conquered colony or Celtic "Home Rule"?

There were of course many good objective reasons why Gladstone had to focus his energies on the Irish Question from the moment he took

[24] Blunt, *India under Ripon*, 299–326; Seal, *Indian Nationalism*, quote on 189.
[25] Martin, *New India*, 79–133; Gopal, *British Policy*, 144–76, quote on 153.

office in 1880. India and Egypt were far away, whereas Ireland was ominously close at hand. The agricultural depression of the late 1870s had hit Ireland exceptionally hard. Low crop yields and plummeting prices raised the specter of another famine as a wave of evictions swept the land. This time, however, the peasants were not quiescent in the face of disaster. With the creation of Michael Davitt's Land League in 1879, a tide of resistance suddenly surged: through boycotts, rent strikes, and exclusive dealing, the community responded, cajoling and, where necessary, compelling the landlord class to delay evictions and accept a "just" rent. As intimidation spilled over into agrarian violence, the authorities began to act as though public order was on the verge of collapse. Meanwhile, in the House of Commons, a party of about sixty Home Rulers now formed a tight-knit voting bloc under the radical leadership of C. S. Parnell. Having gained the entree to parliamentary institutions (from which Indians were still excluded), these Home Rulers saw that they could gain a hearing for their demands only by approaching the British Parliament in adversarial tones. Engaging in filibusters, angry speeches, and other tactics of obstruction, they showed their ability to bring public business to a halt.[26]

While Irish nationalists thrilled at their new-found ability to challenge the system, most Tories and many Liberals saw this as yet another violent effort to bring the system down. The Irish were again proving themselves to be a breed of brawling wreckers. Unfit for representative institutions, they had to be ruled with an iron fist. The standard remedy for such spasms of disorder consisted of the Coercive Acts, in which civil liberties were limited and police powers were augmented, either for specific counties or for Ireland as a whole. Because Pitt's Union had supposedly made Ireland an integral part of the United Kingdom, this withdrawal of the rights of freeborn Britons posed a much more serious ideological sticking point than when such recisions were imposed on the streets of Calcutta. This recision of constitutional rights implied that Ireland was not really a part of Britain but, in essence, still a conquered colony.[27]

As in other colonial settings that we have considered (e.g. India, South Africa, the West Indies) this gap between the principle of freedom and reality of coercion was bridged by a racial-cum-evolutionary theory.

---

[26] F. S. Lyons, *Ireland since the Famine* (London, 1973), 141–76; R. F. Foster, *Modern Ireland* (London, 1988), 373–428; D. George Boyce, *Nationalism in Ireland* (London, 1991), 192–227; Conor Cruise O'Brien, *Parnell and his Party* (Oxford, 1957), 1–72.

[27] Oliver MacDonagh, *Ireland* (Engelwood, 1968), 1–62; Patrick O'Farrell, *Ireland's English Question* (New York, 1971), 1–160.

Indeed, from the 1840s onward, public discourse about the Irish had become increasingly inflected with the language of race. As Celts, the Irish were acknowledged to be members of the Aryan family, but they were often classed, with Indians, as belonging to the eastern branch. Intemperate, emotional, sentimental, predisposed toward violence, but capable of loyalty, the Irish were deemed (e.g. by writers like Froude) a race inferior to the Anglo-Saxon, but fit for effective service when closely controlled.[28] During the 1850s, 1860s, and 1870s, this racialization of the Irish was buttressed by the work of John Beddoe and others on the geographic distribution of British physiognomies. Analyzing a mass of data on skin, hair, and eye color (what he called his "Index of Nigrescence"), Beddoe showed that western and southern Ireland and parts of northern Ireland had a proportionally darker population than in other parts of the British Archipelago. From this, he inferred that many Irish people were racial hybrids, in whom the Aryan element was outweighed by a more primitive and backward stock that was Basque, Mediterranean, or even African in origin. Like Indians of the lower castes, these "black Irish" were deemed to be inherently uncivilized and disorderly when they were not restrained by a firm paternal hand. Taken from the pages of esoteric treatises on racial science, these ideas were given widespread circulation, as we have seen, through the simianized caricatures of Irishness that were frequently published in popular magazines like *Punch*. In these cartoons, the violence of the bomb-thrower is graphically fused with the lecherous leer of a rapist, the fisticuffs of a street brawler, the indolence of a wastrel, and/or the incontinence of a drunk. All together are given form through the delineation of ape-like or prognathic facial features that signify the marks of a primitive, inferior breed.[29]

Of course, these were not the only ways in which the Irish were represented. The degree of evolutionary backwardness depicted tended to increase during episodes of Fenian terrorism or agrarian violence,

---

[28] Joseph Lennon, *Irish Orientalism: A Literary and Intellectual History* (Syracuse, 2004), 1–199; L. P. Curtis, *Anglo-Saxons and Celts: A Study of Anti-Irish Prejudice in Victorian England* (Bridgeport, 1968).

[29] L. P. Curtis, *Apes and Angels: The Irishman in Victorian Caricature* (Washington, DC, 1997); R. F. Foster, *Paddy and Mr. Punch: Connections in Irish and English History* (London, 1993), 171–94; Richard Ned Lebow, *White Britain and Black Ireland: The Influence of Stereotypes on Colonial Policy* (Institute for the Study of Human Issues, Philadelphia, 1976); Thomas Huxley, "The Forefathers and Forerunners of the English People," in Michael Biddis (ed.), *Images of Race* (New York, 1979), 157–70; John Beddoe, *On the Stature and Bulk of Man in the British Isles* (London, 1870); John Beddoe, *The Races of Britain: A Contribution to the Anthropology of Western Europe* (London, 1885); H. L. Malchow, *Gothic Images of Race in Nineteenth Century Britain* (Stanford, 1996), 121–7.

while diminishing during periods of relative calm. The key point, however, is that here, in contrast to India, indigenous authors had been writing their own histories for at least a generation, and had therefore been able to contest racist or derogatory depictions of their culture and character. Throughout the 1860s and 1870s, as we saw in Chapter 4, Irish writers as diverse as the Catholic Burke, the Fenian Mitchel, and (most influentially) the scholar Lecky had been taking the Irish story out of the museum of racial object-hood and restoring it to the manly domain of consequential history. Nor did the racialization of the Irish depict them in all cases as inconsequential or derogatory. As with Indians, the racial quality of the Irish could be magnified by stressing their Aryan character, and by asserting the complementarity of both Celt and Saxon to the evolving civilization of Greater Britain. Thus where Keshub Chandra Sen had extolled the uniquely spiritual quality of Indians, Ernest Renan, at about the same time (1859), posited a uniquely Celtic genius for language and poetry. As in India, this involved an effort to rescue the native peoples from racial and evolutionary abjection, not by deconstructing theories of racial hierarchy but by assigning them a separate (feminized) civilizational sphere. Defeated by the stolid, pragmatic Saxon in the prosaic arenas of government and war, the Celtic bards were deemed to have won their own compensatory triumphs in the field of literature. Forging great epics of resignation and redemption, they left a haunting (but not threatening) series of oral traditions (eventually written) that extolled the romantic qualities of their race.[30]

Taken up in much more sophisticated fashion by Matthew Arnold, this notion of a special Celtic genius for literature was advanced as the basis for valorizing the distinctive contribution of Ireland to British culture in the arena of creativity and imagination without threatening the Saxons' dominant power. In 1879, when the Land War broke, Arnold published a series of essays in which he worked out the political consequences of this cultural complementarity. His "great contention" was "that in order to attach Ireland to us solidly, English people have not only to *do* something different from what they have done hitherto, they also have to *be* something different from what they have been hitherto." As Arnold made clear, this "being something different" was closely tied up with ethnic differences in approaches to history. To the busy, practical Saxon, eager to get on with his improvements, the nightmares of Irish history might be best forgotten. But to the Celt, endlessly narrativizing and re-narrativizing his

[30] Ernest Renan, in his "Poetry of the Celtic Races," in Charles Eliot (ed.), *Literary and Philosophical Essays* (New York, 1910), 143–94.

disabilities and defeats, this dark history remained an omnipresent reality. If the English really wanted the Irish to join them in the march of progress, they had to take responsibility for the evils of their ancestors' retrogressive deeds. "The truth is," Arnold concluded, "what is most needed with the land in Ireland, is to redress our injustice, and to make the Irish see that we are doing so."[31]

It is not surprising that Gladstone incorporated similar arguments into his major speeches on the Irish Question, since his journal notes that he was reading Arnold's book at key moments in 1882 and 1886, in preparation for debate. Like every other British politician of the period, Gladstone regarded the Land War as unacceptable, and when intimidation turned acute in 1881, he sponsored yet another Irish Coercion Act. Nevertheless, coercion, for him, was a regrettable necessity, and it had to be accompanied by conciliation, in the form of meliorative measures sufficiently comprehensive so that the era of coercion would be permanently closed. To sell conciliation to his parliamentary colleagues and the British electorate, he insisted that Irish violence be placed in the seven-century-long record of English conquest and re-conquest. It was "a broad and black blot on the pages of [our] history," which "are a sad exception to the glory of our country." The repeated dispossessions from the land, the refusals of self-government, and the "poison of religious ascendancy" all explained – if they did not justify – Irish bitterness and militancy. "Ireland has great wrongs, and those wrongs will be redressed by the generous wisdom of England, if the English people accepts its responsibility, or righted by the desperate violence of the Irish if England waits for retribution."[32]

Of course, Gladstone was aware that many of his British auditors bridled at such stark formulations, which were reminiscent of Sydney

---

[31] Matthew Arnold, *On the Study of Celtic Literature and On Translating Homer* [1867] (London, 1913), vii–xix, 1–137; Matthew Arnold, *Mixed Essays* [1879]; *Irish Essays and Others* [1882] (New York, 1924), 1–133, 263–353, quotes on 264 and 289. Concerned as he was with the philistinism of English middle-class culture, Arnold thought that the Celtic poetic sensibility made an important contribution to British political culture. In 1886, however, he opposed Gladstone's Home Rule proposal and made it clear that he regarded the Irish as unfit for self-government in their own land.

[32] Morley, *Gladstone*, II: 215–442; Shannon, *Gladstone*, II: 406–44; Matthew, *Gladstone*, II: 183–249. The classic work here is J. L. Hammond, *Gladstone and the Irish Nation* [1938] (Hamden, Connecticut, 1964), quote on 324; W. E. Gladstone, *Speeches and Public Addresses*, IX, *1886–88*, ed. A. W. Hutton and H. J. Cohen (London, 1894), 75, 117, quotes on 127, 172, 194. In his diary for April 5, 1882, Gladstone thanked Arnold for receipt of his book, began reading the volume, and tried to get Arnold to come to one of his Thursday breakfasts. Then, in January 1886, while preparing his first Home Rule Bill, Gladstone again noted reading Arnold on Ireland. *The Gladstone Diaries*, ed. H. C. G. Matthews (Oxford, 1990), X: 231 (April 5, 1882), XI: 481 (January 19, 1886).

Owenson's admonitions, eight decades earlier, that English elites had to atone for the crimes of their ancestors as a precondition for reconciliation and trans-national unity. That message had not been popular in 1806, and it was no more popular in the 1880s. "I am all against sitting in perpetual sack cloth and ashes," grumbled Gladstone's friend the Duke of Argyll, "because the Irish are violent and disaffected." No doubt, Ireland was once "ill used and ill governed," but "for the last two generations at least, there has been a general disposition to deal justly with Ireland." Gladstone's task in the 1880s was to convince skeptics like Argyll (who surely spoke for many other upper-middle-class and aristocratic Britons) that this was a mistake. To implement his four major pieces of Irish legislation – land reform in 1881 and 1886, and Home Rule in 1886 and 1892 – it was necessary to show that Ireland had never truly yet been a part of the United Kingdom. If, historically, its people had been fundamentally oppressed and mis-governed, then it would require these anomalous (and seemingly un-British) pieces of legislation in order to bring them truly into the Union.[33]

Gladstone's ability to assume this rhetorical challenge was enhanced by the fact that, in 1870, he had already wrestled with the contradictions of Anglo-Ireland in a more limited way. At that time, he had been persuaded of the need to legislate tenant right, thereby violating the principles of political economy, strictly construed. As a strong believer in freedom of contract, Gladstone had been uneasy about this measure, and justified it with the supposition that "tenant right" had been the traditional custom of Ireland until the penal laws destroyed it during the first imperial age. By 1881, however, it was clear that stronger, more intrusive legislation was necessary. When he proposed the second Land Act, with special courts to regulate eviction and to adjudicate rents, Gladstone knew that this would be a tough sell. Five years later, another scheme to use taxpayer loans to finance tenants in buying out their landlords proved to be an even tougher (and initially unsuccessful) sell.[34]

To justify these measures, Gladstone invoked "a careful study of the whole history of Ireland." "We cannot wash ourselves clean and clear of the responsibility," he argued, "the deeds of the Irish landlords are to a great extent our deeds." In a propaganda coup, he read quotes from Froude's *English in Ireland* to show that even this hostile witness had

---

[33] Quoted in Hammond, *Gladstone*, 109.

[34] Hammond, *Gladstone*, 67–531; W. E. Gladstone, *Speeches*, ed. H. W. Lucy (London, 1885), 15, 23, 48–50.

been forced to acknowledge the facts of landlord oppression. The land-lords had been the "garrison of England," the means of forcing English interests down Irish throats. "We used the whole Civil Government of Ireland as an engine of wholesale corruption. We did everything in our power to irritate and exasperate the Irish people." When Lord Fitzwilliam proposed a juster policy, he was recalled. Because of this ruthless, tyrannical history, special remedial measures were required. Tainted by the past, Irish landlordism had a doubtful future. If Ireland was destined to become a country of peasant proprietors, Britain had an interest in facilitating this process. Given the Irish tenants' dearth of resources, the British state would have to intervene to help them attain independence and a stake in private property.[35]

Gladstone made much the same argument in 1886 in his efforts to explain why it was in the interests of Britain to support Irish Home Rule. Home Rule did not mean separation or break-up of the Empire, he insisted again and again. His proposed Bill specified that matters of war and peace, the military, and colonial and foreign policy, as well as customs and excise, would continue to be handled in the Westminster Parliament, in which Irish MPs might, or might not, participate. Most of all, however, Home Rule would strengthen the Union, since it would turn the Irish from disaffected subjects into loyal and law-abiding citizens. Once again, to explain this, Gladstone turned to history. Bad as were the penal laws and the seventeenth-century invasions, they were not as pernicious as Pitt's efforts to "solve" the Irish Question against the wishes of the Irish people. "I know of no blacker or fouler transaction in the history of man than making of the Union." Once the Act was railroaded onto the statute book, six consequences ensued: "First, broken promises: secondly, the passing of bad laws; thirdly, the putting down of liberty; fourthly, the withholding from Ireland benefits that we took to ourselves; fifthly, giving to force and to force only what we should have given to honour and justice; and sixthly, the shameful postponement of relief to the most crying grievances."[36]

The "terrible stains" which Gladstone wanted to efface from the fame of England required that the British Parliament restore to the Irish that national Parliament that had been wantonly stolen from them at the beginning of the nineteenth century. "The impression I derive from

---

[35] Gladstone, *Speeches*, ed. Hutton and Cohen, IX: 59; *Parliamentary Debates*, 3rd ser., CCCIV (London, 1886), 1780–3, 1787–8, 1791, 1810, April 16, 1886.

[36] Gladstone, *Speeches*, ed. Lucy, 169, 172; Gladstone, *Speeches*, ed. Hutton and Cohen, IX, especially 6, 10, 14, 72–4, 116, 165–8, quote on 170.

anything I know about the history of Ireland is that the Irishman feels and suffers more profoundly in his nationality than in any other thing." This was not a matter of race but of political justice. While Gladstone had always been a friend of Irish self-determination, he had held off advocating the specific remedy of Home Rule until the 1885 election, when Ireland returned 86 Home Rulers out of 105 seats. This was a verdict that no honest person could misconstrue. To refuse to honor this mandate would be an insult to the Irish, and a message to all of Britain's subject peoples that they were to remain more or less permanently disenfranchised, without the right to any national political institutions of their own. It was never sufficient just to give a people good laws. It was necessary "that they [laws] should proceed from a native and congenial source, and besides being good laws, should be their own laws." It was because Home Rule conferred legitimacy on government, which it could not otherwise acquire, that it would not "mean disunion from England."

It is the recognition of the distinctive qualities and separate parts of great countries and empires which constitutes the true basis of union, and to attempt to centralise them by destroying those local peculiarities is the shallowest philosophy and the worst possible of all practical blunders. It is a mode at once to destroy strength and impair and break up union.[37]

In light of these high stakes, the Prime Minister was unapologetic about having made his third administration stand or fall on Irish Home Rule. The principles of the Magna Carta were the great English inheritance. But their continued vitality required extending them to all British subjects. "We have before us," he urged, "a great opportunity of putting an end to the controversy of seven hundred years – aye, and of kitting together by bonds firmer and higher in their character than those which we have mainly used." This moment was "a golden opportunity" to set the British Empire on a more democratic, a more multi-national, and therefore a more viable long-term footing by granting to Ireland (and, by precedent, to dependencies in other places) the same institutions of "responsible government" that had already been established in the white settler colonies. But "if this golden opportunity be lost, we know not when it will return." "Lost opportunities," Gladstone warned, "do not return, or they return only after long intervals, and after heavy damages have been paid." Britain and her Empire stood at a crossroads. One road

[37] Gladstone, *Speeches*, ed. Hutton and Cohen, IX, especially 14, 17–18, 46–8, 50, 126, 192, 226.

led to good government, while the other "un-constitutional" road meant "repressing the liberties of the people," thus inviting the violence and disorder likely to follow such a course.[38]

Gladstone's prophetic acuity was put to the test when his Home Rule and Land Purchase Bills of 1886 went down to defeat. Annoyed with his barrage of dark history and dire exhortations, a majority of the British electorate soundly repudiated the Gladstonian message. The result was two decades of Tory rule, interrupted only briefly, in 1892–3, when Gladstone, now aged eighty-four, took a final stint in office to introduce a second Home Rule Bill, which was quickly thrown out by the House of Lords. For a long time, most historians followed Gladstone's junior colleagues in blaming the Grand Old Man for his Irish obsessions, which allegedly drove the Liberal Party into the wilderness. The presumed result was to delay the party's ability to adapt to the changing political landscape within Britain, in which the crying issue now was the need for domestic social reform.[39] More recently, studies of liberal activists at the grassroots level have suggested that Gladstone was right: Home Rule drew on the idealism of young political operatives. It kept British radicalism in tune with Irish nationalism and the Indian Congress. It helped pave the way for post-laissez-faire versions of liberalism, and it formed a bridge to the labor-centered politics of the coming age. For a time, the Tories did seem to make the problem of Ireland go away. Yet their quick fix of "Constructive Unionism" could not address the underlying issue, since it was premised on a continued denial of the right of self-government and the assumption that the Irish were inherently fractious and politically incompetent. It was entirely unacceptable, the Tory leader Lord Salisbury insisted, for the Irish to engage in illegality and violence because their distant ancestors had been misgoverned and dispossessed. They were unfit for self-government, which worked only "when it is confined to peoples who are of the Teutonic race." "Rightly or wrongly," he privately wrote to

[38] Gladstone, *Speeches*, ed. Hutton and Cohen, IX: 24, 101, 125, 251, 341. Gladstone argued that Irish Home Rule was not a radical but a conservative measure, since it was simply restoring the Irish Parliament that had been taken away illegitimately in 1800. It was a renegotiation rather than a repeal of the Union that was designed to turn Irish disaffection into British loyalty. It would simply grant to Ireland the "responsible government" that had already been achieved by the settler colonies. Gladstone, *Speeches*, ed. Hutton and Cohen, IX: 14, 27, 75, 83, 173, 194, 198, 226, 327, 288–9.
[39] H. C. G. Matthews, *The Liberal Imperialists: The Ideas and Politics of a Post-Gladstonian Elite* (Oxford, 1973), 265–86; Eugenio Biagini, *British Democracy and Irish Nationalism, 1876–1906* (Cambridge, 2007).

Lord Carnarvon, "I have not the slightest desire to satisfy the national aspirations of Ireland."[40]

4   Chamberlain and Seeley: Unionism, history, and progress in the high imperial age

Much more damaging than the views of an arch-Tory like Salisbury was the defection of large numbers of Liberal Unionists from the ranks of the Gladstonian Party in response to its advocacy of Home Rule. Largely urban, educated, and situated at various strata within the middle class, such people had hitherto been mainstays of mid-Victorian liberalism. Their gradual fusion with the Tories over the next two decades, under the "Unionist" label, was one of the momentous political realignments of the modern era.[41] No one articulated the concerns – and reflected the characteristics – of the Liberal Unionists better than Joseph Chamberlain, the universally acknowledged leader – and exemplar – of the type. Because he had risen alongside Gladstone, and his friend Charles Dilke, among the leaders of British radicalism during the early 1880s, Chamberlain's *volte-face* was particularly shocking. Indeed, the break ultimately sabotaged the career of this ambitious politician, since it subverted every plank in his "Radical Programme" and deprived him of the chance to succeed Gladstone as Liberal chief, while rendering him dependent on the Tories, who never really trusted him. Not surprisingly, historians have long debated Chamberlain's motives in sustaining this political re-alignment, particularly during the 1890s and early twentieth century, when the bad blood of 1886 had passed. The fact that Chamberlain had his own devolution scheme, involving Irish, Scottish, and Welsh national councils ("Home Rule All Around"), only deepens the mystery.[42]

To understand Chamberlain's motives, however, we need only take him at his word. Gladstone's version of Home Rule, he insisted, *would* break up the Empire. An Irish Parliament would soon vote to separate from Britain, and this would inspire the South African Boers, disgruntled

[40] Andrew Roberts, *Salisbury: Victorian Titan* (London, 2000), 387; Hammond, *Gladstone*, 730; Michael Bentley, *Lord Salisbury's World: Conservative Worlds in Late-Victorian Britain* (Cambridge, 2001), quote on 235.

[41] Henry Pelling, *Social Geography of British Elections, 1885–1910* (London, 1967), 414–20; E. Spencer Wellhofer, *Democracy, Capitalism and Empire in Late Victorian Britain, 1885–1900* (London, 1996), 82–90; James Cornford, "The Transformation of Conservatism in the Late Nineteenth Century," in Peter Stansky (ed.), *The Victorian Revolution* (New York, 1973), 287–318.

[42] Peter Marsh, *Joseph Chamberlain: Entrepreneur in Politics* (New Haven, 1994); J. L. Garvin, *The Life of Joseph Chamberlain*, I (London, 1932), 3–284.

Indians, and other subaltern colonial groups to follow suit. Steadily, separatist fever would spread, until the Empire was dismantled. In the end, even Anglo-Saxon settler colonies would defect, either casting their lot with the USA or setting up white republics of their own. From this perspective, the danger of Irish Home Rule was substantive but, even more, symbolic. It would start a cascade of departing dominoes, which would ultimately leave Britain naked, alone, and reduced to a second-rate power.[43]

Chamberlain's mounting concern over the fate of the Empire represented itself as a major re-orientation in his (and many other entrepreneurs') thought. Hitherto, the Empire had mainly served as a playground for aristocrats and Evangelicals. Chamberlain himself had initially risen to wealth and power by focusing his energies on the manufacturing center of Birmingham: in his twenties, he had become rich as a leading screw manufacturer. Then, in his thirties, he had taken local politics by storm, pressing schemes for the municipalization of gas and water provision that improved the urban environment, while simultaneously raising revenue to support other local government activities. In 1880, when Chamberlain shifted his attention from local to national politics, he mused that the change of venue would be justified only if he could accomplish, on an imperial scale, the sort of transformative reforms that he had already effected in his home town. Like many entrepreneurs, he was worried about mounting competition in foreign markets, and he envisioned a solution in the cultivation of inter-imperial trade. Inspired by his friend Dilke's synoptic sketch *Greater Britain* he accepted Gladstone's offer of a seat in the Cabinet as President of the Board of Trade.[44]

Yet as Chamberlain wrestled with the complex cross-currents of imperial politics during the 1880s, he tried to understand what reform on this scale might mean. To some extent, he seemed to embrace the racial-cum-evolutionary vision, which bifurcated the Empire into (active) Anglo-Saxon agents and (passive) evolutionary objects. Greater Britain was the in-gathering of "kindred races with similar objects," who would draw on their shared Anglo-Saxon heritage to join together in a "true democracy," spanning their dispersed homelands around the globe. By contrast, the colored dependencies were peopled by races that were as yet incapable of self-government, according to Chamberlain. Such races should be ruled paternalistically and

---

[43] Marsh, *Chamberlain*, 233.
[44] Marsh, *Chamberlain*, 1–131, especially 128–9; J. L. Garvin, *The Life of Joseph Chamberlain* (London, 1932), I: 3–284.

protected from extreme exploitation, but their lands should be managed from London, as "undeveloped estates" that could be turned into profitable concerns through a judicious mixture of private investment and central government control. In places like the Caribbean, affairs were being mismanaged by "half-breeds," whom Chamberlain dismissed with contempt. When the Irish engaged in intimidation or demanded Home Rule, they revealed the underlying fracture of two unequal races cohabiting on a single unhappy isle. "To put a race which has shown all the qualities of a dominant people under the other, which has always failed in the qualities which compel success," he contended, "is an attempt against nature [which] can only lead to disaster."[45]

Nevertheless, it would be a mistake to make too much of comments like these. Race was a casual rather than an essential element in Chamberlain's thinking. It did not provide him with his core vision of how Greater Britain should be governed and organized. This came, by his own admission, from a book by the Cambridge historian J. R. Seeley. No longer preoccupied with the life of Jesus, Seeley was ready, by 1883, to weigh in on more worldly themes. The result was *The Expansion of England*, a tome that elaborated a series of university lectures that the author had delivered over the previous two years. Chamberlain, so it turned out, was not alone in admiring this volume, which sold a remarkable 80,000 copies in the first two years. As late as 1919, 11,000 copies were still being sold. The success of Seeley's volume is all the more impressive inasmuch as the author made no efforts to court popularity, openly proclaiming his contempt for romantic, narrative histories in the style of Macaulay that sacrificed intellectual substance for gratification of form. *The Expansion of England*, he bracingly warned, was intended to be analytical and scientific, rather than attractive and picturesque. History, according to Seeley, should study problems rather than periods, and it should seek to discover law-like regularities in its data, rather than simply amassing a plenitude of undigested facts.[46]

When the data of modern English history were approached in this manner, according to Seeley, one over-mastering pattern presented itself: the steady expansion of the English/British state, as Wales was absorbed in the sixteenth century, and Scotland, Ireland, Virginia, and Barbados were added in the seventeenth. During the eighteenth century other parts of America and India were conquered, which paved the way for the

---

[45] Marsh, *Chamberlain*, 132–481, quotes on 285, 294, 219, 411, 546–7.
[46] Marsh, *Chamberlain*, 176–8; Garvin, *Chamberlain*, I: 494; SEE; Deborah Wormell, *Sir John Seeley and the Uses of History* (Cambridge, 1980), 48–109, 154; C. A. Rein, *Sir John Robert Seeley: A Study of the Historian* (Wolfeboro, 1987), i–xxix, 1–48.

annexation of the rest of India, Australasia, Canada, South Africa, and other parts of Africa and Asia during the nineteenth.[47] In sharp contrast to many of the other writers whom we have recently considered, Seeley denied that this expansion of England was the result of any inherent superiority of the Anglo-Saxon race. On the contrary, it was contingent and largely circumstantial, the product of England/Britain's success in a competition with four other potentially expansive states – Portugal, Spain, the Netherlands, and France – each of which was trying to gain control of the system of trans-oceanic trade and colonialism that was crystallizing between the sixteenth and nineteenth centuries. In an underhanded swipe at Froude, Seeley stressed the paltry performance of the Tudors during the early stages of this global contest. England (bulked up as Britain) emerged as a real player only during the seventeenth century, when the small size of the Netherlands placed it at a disadvantage, while Portugal and Spain went into irreversible declines. The result was to leave only two viable eighteenth-century contenders: Greater Britain and Greater France.[48] Between 1689 and 1815, the decisive struggle between these two global rivals played itself out, and Seeley's account of their contest is his book's *tour de force*. He begins by pointing out the obvious (but strangely neglected) fact that France and Britain were at war for more than half of this period (sixty-four years). While each of the seven wars encompassed during this time had its own unique set of issues, disputes, and protagonists, they were all part of a larger conflict for dominance of the world-spanning trading and imperial system that was just then taking shape. Britain's sustained victory in this early modern "Hundred Years War," he contends, laid the foundations for the *Pax Britannica* of the nineteenth century.[49]

"History," according to Seeley, "should not merely gratify the reader's curiosity about the past"; it should also "modify his view of the present and his forecast of the future." Not only had the British state steadily expanded over the course of three centuries; it had undergone a series of structural reorganizations, which enabled it to adapt to the changing conditions of several successive epochs. Now again, at the time of writing, Seeley saw the need to take advantage of modern transport and communication technology, to weld Greater Britain into a unified super-state that would be able to hold its own with Greater Russia and the United States during the coming twentieth century. The distinction between the first (mercantilist) and second (liberal) empires is implicitly played down in Seeley's account. The *Pax Britannica* of the

[47] SEE, 43, 106–60.   [48] SEE, 98–140.   [49] SEE, 20–6.

1815–75 period, grounded in open competition and the spread of free trade, did not turn out to be the opening of a new eirenic era as early Victorian liberals had hoped. Rather, it had been a temporary interlude in which Britain preached laissez-faire because it served her interest, and no other power was in a position to insist otherwise. But in the late nineteenth century all this was changing. The great powers were all protecting their fledgling industries with tariffs, and Britain might soon feel the necessity of following suit. Empire could no longer be based on a liberal philanthropic mission. It was coming to constitute the most promising framework around which the commerce of the future might crystallize.[50]

This synoptic vision of an economically and politically integrated Empire was clearly compelling to Chamberlain and to Seeley's many other readers, who spanned the political spectrum, from Liberals to Unionists and to traditional Tories. No utopian, Seeley understood the difficulties that impeded federation and that would prevent even a successful federation from evolving into an integrated super-state. The strength of his argument lay in its appeal to history, which could be read as a trajectory that was headed in the direction of competing world empires. In the eighteenth century, Seeley pointed out, the thirteen North American colonies had been lost to Greater Britain because neither the technological, political, nor ideological conditions for such an entity existed at that time. Yet, once freed, these colonies had embarked on their own project of super-state creation on a continental scale. Now that the Americans had proven such an entity to be possible the British had another chance to replicate the same feat. Having learned how to mollify her Anglo-Saxon colonists with grants of self-government, she had now to gather them in through the railroad, telegraph, and steamship, and rally them round the Union Jack. Once Chamberlain resurfaced as Colonial Secretary during the 1890s, he gave considerable thought as to how this goal might gradually be accomplished. In the end, he concluded that success would require abandoning the entire free trade system, either turning the Empire into one vast customs union, or embarking on even more drastic tariff reforms.[51]

But why was it necessary to limit self-government within this imagined super-state of the future to the Anglo-Saxons? In fact, there was no inherent reason for such a limitation, even though both Seeley and Chamberlain took it for granted. In their minds, "Greater Britain" was equated with Anglo-Saxon democracy, while compulsory Unionism was

---

[50] SEE, 1, 74–5, 161–78; Wormell, *Seeley*, 75–133; Rein, *Seeley*, 49–84.
[51] SEE, 64–5, 147, 158; Marsh, *Chamberlain*, 299–405.

deemed essential for Ireland and the "colored colonies." To appreciate
how this inference was accomplished, it is necessary to focus on some of
the deficiencies of Seeley's account. His entire argument rested on the
assumption that the nation-state was the only meaningful actor on the
stage of geo-politics, and that this state could be reified as a single
unified collective agent, which completely reflected the interests of its
constituent individuals, classes, and groups. For this reason, Seeley
believed that viable states had to maintain a broad official religion, and
had to be limited, for the most part, to a single ethnicity. With the
exception of the slave plantations, which he denounced, and Ireland,
which he flagrantly ignored, Britain's eighteenth-century Empire came
sufficiently close to meeting these conditions that his account can be
made to seem generally plausible, without running afoul of fundamental
facts. By Seeley's own time, however, this ethnic homogeneity no longer
prevailed, although the "predictive" part of his book never registers the
change. Thus, with the exception of India, the entire Empire is identified as essentially Anglo-Saxon. In passing, Seeley does acknowledge
that the Empire contains, in addition to many Celts, "a good many
French and Dutch and a good many Caffres and Maories," but these
are brushed off as of no great ethnological consequence, "and may be
admitted without marring the ethnological unity of the whole."[52]

Given the thoroughly multi-ethnic character of South Africa, the West
Indies, West Africa, Canada, and even New Zealand, this is a remarkable evasion. Either ethnic cohesion is not really necessary for a viable
polity, or none of these colonies should be allowed self-government
by Seeley's own rule. Here Seeley's lapses are particularly instructive,
since they probably reflected the attitudes of his many middle- and
upper-class Victorian readers, who were neither virulent racists nor
adherents of multi-ethnic democracy. Like Seeley, such people found
it easy just to ignore the whole question, to equate Greater Britain with
ethnic Anglo-Saxons, and to dismiss serious demands for self-rule by
subject peoples either as dangerous experiments likely to lead to disorder
or as naive utopian philanthropic delusions that a beleaguered Empire
could not afford.

This characteristically Seeleyan perspective comes out even more
clearly in his handling of India, a subcontinent with a population
nearly three times the size of all other parts of the Empire combined.
Seeley certainly cannot be accused of ignoring India, which occupies
32 percent of his text. Moreover, much of what he has to say about the

---

[52] SEE, 46–50, quote on 50; Wormell, *Seeley*, 36–8, 77–9, 129–30, 140.

place is sensible, if unoriginal. He denies that the fact of English conquest reflected any racial superiority, since he shows that the English came in under conditions of crisis (resembling the European Dark Ages), when Indians welcomed any force that could maintain public order. Moreover, the arms with which Englishmen triumphed were largely Indian, so that "India can hardly be said to have been conquered at all by foreigners; she has rather conquered herself." Seeley believed that British rule was essentially benevolent and was, in any case, accepted by the Indians, since they did not act when the 1857 Rebellion gave them the chance to kick the British out. Here Seeley's evasions become the most telling feature of his account. He is too astute to deny categorically that modernization *might* produce an Indian national identity, and he even hints that this would not be an improbable outcome. But instead of following the lead of the bhadralok liberals, taking responsibility for such a future and making plans for reforming the Empire to accommodate this change, he throws up his hands and declares ignorance of what is to come.

The wisest men may easily be mistaken when they speculate on such a subject. The end of our Indian Empire is perhaps almost as much beyond calculation as the beginning of it ... A time may conceivably come when it may be practicable to leave India to herself, but for the present it is necessary to govern her as if we were to govern her for ever.[53]

For a historian as sharp and intellectually curious as Seeley, this is a remarkable attitude to take. India might someday become independent, but instead of starting to think about how to keep her in the Empire, we must continue to rule her despotically and arbitrarily, thereby ensuring her departure when independence takes place. The *non sequitur* is even more remarkable when we remember that Seeley's whole aim in writing was to *save* the Empire, and that little as he may have known about Banerjea, Dutt, and Naoroji, he surely knew that they too shared the same aim. Why then were leading British leaders like Chamberlain, and opinion-makers like Seeley, so preoccupied with the twentieth-century Empire of the future and yet so oblivious of the multi-national resources that it would require? Well aware of the growing presence of nascent colonial nationalism, they did absolutely nothing to foster the inter-racial imperial citizenship that would be needed in a democratic multi-national Empire. No doubt, part of the answer lies in a kind of unconscious racism, a visceral distaste for men of a different color, who could not be relegated to the status of evolutionary objects, but whom

[53] SEE, quotes on 193–4, 202.

they did not like to recognize as fellow citizens similar to themselves. Yet closely connected with this unconscious racism (and perhaps subsisting at its very core) was a refusal to recognize the historical narrative of this other. If Seeley, for example, in subsequent editions of *Expansion*, had taken account of the work of Banerjea, Naoroji, or Dutt, he would have been obliged to transform his book. With his triumphant narrative of the rise of Greater Britain, he would have had to juxtapose less happy recitals of dispossession and oppression, in Ireland, India, and many other places as well. Instead of simply equating the imperial common-wealth with the expansion of England, he would have had to consider the contribution of other national stories, from medieval Ireland, Ancient India, and other times and places too. Finally, he would have been obliged to complicate his analysis of imperial capitalism with Naoroji's disturbing evidence of the drain.

Here indeed, we encounter a remarkable irony, since men like Seeley and Chamberlain prided themselves on being consummate realists, in contrast to what they saw as the irresolute idealism of the Gladstonian mentality. Yet from our perspective, more than a century later, it is Gladstone and the Liberals who followed him into the multi-national wilderness who seem the better realists, more accurately grasping the imperial challenges that lay ahead. Gladstone was neither a great histor-ian nor a philosopher, but he had the sense to see that the progress narrative had encountered complications and contradictions. This did not necessarily mean that it was finished, but did indicate that it could no longer be dictated from the metropole alone. Other voices were now audible, from Ireland and from India, and liberalism needed to incor-porate the stories that they told. The commanding imperial histories of a Seeley (and the policies of a Chamberlain), which subordinated all other progress to England's advance, were, for all their seeming sophis-tication, pre-emptive strikes that did not so much silence the voice of colonial others as deafen British ears to the amplifying colonial sounds.[54]

5   **The strange death of liberal imperialism**

While J. R. Seeley never registered the work of R. C. Dutt or any other Indian historian, Dutt carefully read and considered Seeley's book. Praising Seeley as "one of the most thoughtful writers of the Victorian age," he demurred at the Englishman's claim that Indians required English

---

[54] Wormell, *Seeley*, 167–75; Rein, *Seeley*, 70–1.

domination to bring them the benefits of national unity. In particular, he caviled when Seeley condoned the feverish annexations of Lord Dalhousie, who seized eight large Indian kingdoms during a viceroyalty of as many years. "Lord Dalhousie was the last of the Old Imperial School of rulers who believed that the salvation and progress of the Indian people were possible only by the destruction of their autonomy and self-government... He lived to see the East India Company abolished, and the Doctrine of Lapse disavowed by his sovereign and Queen."[55]

In 1905, when Dutt composed this hopeful passage, he was actually writing under the shadow of another authoritarian Viceroy, G. N. (now Lord) Curzon, who had ignored his open letters on the cause of Indian famines, and seemed determined to undermine whatever limited autonomy and self-government Indians had left. Most egregious among Curzon's despotic moves was his plan to defy a vast outpouring of Calcutta public opinion by partitioning Bengal at least partially along sectarian lines. Although the Indian Secretary, John Morley, made a show of consulting him in London, Dutt could see that Curzon's cynical maneuver to separate Hindus from Muslims represented the real thrust of British policy. Hell-bent on disenfranchising and marginalizing bhadralok liberals, Curzon was prepared to play with fire in hopes of turning his vision of a religiously fractured subcontinent into a self-fulfilling prophecy. As he contemplated this scheme to polarize Indian opinion, Dutt had to wonder whether his own lifelong commitment to Greater British imperialism had been a mistake.[56] Following Scott and Macaulay, he had embraced the centrist notion that moderation is the handmaiden of progress, that the manly course requires the repudiation of extremes. Yet where had this moderation gotten him in the end? As a harder-edged generation of younger nationalists grew up around him, Dutt found it ever more difficult to counter their anti-British attitudes, or even to explain why their campaigns for *swadeshi* (economic self-reliance) were anything but the logical consequence of his own books. For these young men, Curzon's partition plan was really the last straw – proof positive that the strategy of moderation had failed. Yet Dutt could not help but be alarmed at their "extremist" responses – organizing angry mass meetings, and mounting a boycott of British

[55] DEHI, II: 31–2. See also R. C. Dutt, "Presidential Address," in R. C. Dutt, *Romesh Chunder Dutt* (New Delhi, 1968), 197–234.
[56] GLD, 297–374, 456–85; Anthony Read and David Fisher, *The Proudest Day: India's Long Road to Independence* (New York, 1997), 83–101; David Gilmour, *Curzon: Imperial Statesman* [1994] (New York, 2003), 271–361.

goods. Taken aback by these militant measures, Dutt could see that they were likely to backfire and play into reactionary British hands.

> I am not aware that the extremists have any definite aims and aspirations, which they themselves can, or do, believe in. I do not know of any men of real influence, resource, or substantial stake in the country who have ever joined the so-called extremist leaders ... The movement has no foundation in the hearts of the educated people. It was born of that feeling of bitterness and despair, that unreasoning hostility against the British, which seven years of retrograde and unsympathetic and ungenerous administration generated in the country ... The movement will die a natural death with the return of a sympathetic administration, and substantial concessions to a loyal nation.[57]

These words might be dismissed as the dying gasps of a superannuated leader, unable to adapt to Young India's post-imperial turn. But Dutt was not entirely mistaken in his belief that India's youth remained attached to the English Constitution. Even in the face of Curzon's hostility, the generation born at the turn of the century still looked to a future of imperial federation, in which India would join the Dominions, with Home Rule and a Parliament of her own. In the classrooms of Calcutta University, the histories of Green and Stubbs remained on the syllabus and – for all their anglocentrism – could still be read as silent reproaches to the expansionary bombast of Seeley. "Educated Indians with their newly acquired sense of politics took to these subjects as ducks take to water," reported the student Nirad Chaudhuri. "The craze for constitutional history and law which prevailed in our midst" led many of his classmates to fancy themselves as, "if not Jeffersons, at least Sieyeses." Individualistically roused by this aspiration from their ascriptive status, these Bengali students were driven by the refusal of British imperial citizenship to a new-found collective sense of Indian national autonomy.[58]

In the end, most of these patriots settled down, becoming lawyers, small businessmen, or minor officials and pinning their fading hopes for a constitutional future to the rising stars of Nehru, Jinnah, or the charismatic Gandhi. For Chaudhuri himself, the road to citizenship was paved by a continued attachment to Stubbs and Green. Green's appeal lay in his "literary quality." That of Stubbs struck a deeper nerve. "A combination of technical power with an historical mind" drew the young Indian into a lifelong engagement with the history of medieval

---

[57] GLD, 399–438, quote on 464.
[58] Nirad Chaudhuri, *The Autobiography of an Unknown Indian* [1951] (New York, 1989), 324, 327.
[59] Chaudhuri, *Autobiography*, 344.

England, and fostered "reverence to the great medievalists, Stubbs, Round, Vinogradoff, Maitland."[59]

Had Chaudhuri grown up in Britain he would likely have settled down as a history professor, with a specialized field, a steady job, and a stable identity. In the highly politicized atmosphere of interwar India, his fate was more problematic. Brought up in a reformed Brahmo family and steeped in English literature as a child, he had been nourished on the heady mix of Shakespeare and Bengali poetry that had fueled so many syncretisms during the nineteenth century. No longer quite able to believe that such histories could save the British Empire, Chaudhuri opted for the Rankean ideal of absolute objectivity. Utterly voracious in his quest for positive knowledge, the young man "swallowed complete sets of the *English Historical Review* and of the *Revue Critique* as others swallow light novels." Annoyed by the one-sided nationalism of so many of his compatriots, he touted the equal significance of all times and all places, setting his hand to the study of ancient Greece, Rome, and Islam as well as modern German, Italian, and French history. By no means immune from masculinist fantasies of revolutionary self-assertion, and eager to give the lie to racist taunts of effeminacy, Chaudhuri took up the history of war and armaments, which he pursued in great detail and with avid expertise. Not even content with the confines of the human experience, he set himself a course of private reading in chemistry, geology, and evolutionary biology.[60]

Conducive as they may have been to a rich inner life, these heroic bouts of autodidactic profusion did little to advance Chaudhuri's worldly prospects. After winning first place in Calcutta University's BA Honors List, he was mentally exhausted by his study for the MA and, to the surprise of everyone, failed his exam. Although he could easily have retaken the test, Chaudhuri refused to avail himself of so philistine an option, permanently blighting his employment prospects and foreclosing academic work. It was almost as though his eclecticism was too precious and too personal to sully with the taint of careerist ambition. His history had become a kind of private universe: a solipsistic sphere of compensatory achievement, where encyclopedic feats of recollection and reconstruction could substitute for the bold strokes of purposive action that were still denied to Indian men in the public, political realm.[61]

As he pursued this idiosyncratic path of self-realization through self-narration, Chaudhuri's *History* crystallized into the form of an autobiography. As the last chapter to this *Apologia pro vita sua*, he appended "An Essay on the Course of Indian History." In this sketch, the history of

---

[60] Chaudhuri, *Autobiography*, 3–353, 434–56, quote on 325.
[61] Chaudhuri, *Autobiography*, 46–390.

India is presented as evolution writ small. In the advance and recession of biological genera and species, the author portentously detects the same cycles of descent with modification that he perceives in India's civilizational rises and falls. Yet where was this evolution tending? The commonwealth ideal that inspired so many other Greater British historians of Chaudhuri's generation – W. K. Hancock in Australia, Nicholas Mansergh in Ireland, or Reginald Coupland in Britain itself – held no attraction for the isolated Indian scholar, who not only saw that his compatriots remained second-class citizens, but also doubted whether a federation of free and equal dominions would even be capable of resuscitating the liberal imperialist project. "An Empire is hierarchical," Chaudhuri insisted, and it cannot exist "without a conglomeration of linguistically, racially and culturally different nationalities, and the hegemony of one of them over the rest." Yet to survive, any Empire "had to be justified morally," by its mission in "tak[ing] over the keepership of civilizations when its creators [as in India] had become incapable of maintaining them." By the 1920s, however, Chaudhuri saw that the British too were rapidly degenerating, and he was "driven back on the conclusion ... that the greatness of the British people has passed away for ever."[62]

On all levels, then, Chaudhuri's account is a tale of disillusionment, in which the thread of the progress narrative has been irrevocably lost. Twentieth-century India and contemporary Britain are both depicted as societies sunk in mutual retrogression, in which the latter is doomed to a premature senescence, while the former bears the weight of its unredeemed antiquity. An atavistic throwback, by his own admission, Chaudhuri saw no personal alternative but to continue his private veneration of the English Constitution, even though this worship was devoid of actual British interlocutors, and was in danger of devolving into an internal monologue. Through satyagraha, sectarian slaughter, and the final partition of the subcontinent he continued to hold these conversations with himself. In 1951, his *Autobiography* was finally published, four years after India had achieved her independence as a sovereign democratic nation-state. Chaudhuri chose to dedicate his book "To the memory of the British Empire in India which conferred subjecthood on us but withheld citizenship; to which yet every one of us threw out the challenge: '*Civis Britannicus Sum*' because all that was good and living within us was made, shaped, and quickened by the same British Rule."[63]

[62] Chaudhuri, *Autobiography*, 456–506; Nirad Chaudhuri, *Thy Hand, Great Anarch! India 1921–1952* (New York, 1987), 773–80, quotes on 776–8; W. R. Louis, "Introduction," in Robin Winks (ed.), *Oxford History of the British Empire*, V, *Historiography* (Oxford, 1999), 1–34.
[63] Chaudhuri, *Autobiography*, vi.

Index

Act of Union of 1800, 9, 21, 141,
    180, 187
Acts of Union of 1707, 8, 38
Adam, William, 94
American Revolution, 104
Anderson, Benedict, 21
Anglo-Saxon, 14, 15, 104, 140, 158, 208,
    209, 217, 224, 238, 255, 260, 292,
    301, 310, 315, 327, 335, 337, 338
Anglo-Saxonism, 160
Arabi, Colonel Ahmed, 322
Arnold, Matthew, 328–9
Aryan and Aryanism, 14, 60, 61, 70, 206,
    223, 228, 231, 236, 239, 241, 247,
    248, 268, 272, 327, 328
    and R. C. Dutt, 301–3

Babington, Thomas, 100, 102
Baghavad Gita, 60
Baillie, Joanna, 34
Baji Rao II, 74, 79, 80
Baker, Samuel, 219
Ballantyne, John, 36
Banerjea, Surendranath, 15, 233, 286–92,
    323
    The Bengalee, 286, 299
    A Nation in Making, 288
barbarism, 11, 37, 83, 85, 129, 132, 150,
    183, 223
Bayley, W. B., 56
Beddoe, John, 327
Bentham, Jeremy, 5, 80
Bentinck, William, 81, 236, 306
Bethune, J. D., 266
bhadralok, 97, 225–6, 232, 236, 260, 262,
    264–9, 271–2, 276–9, 282, 283–8,
    294, 306, 322, 325, 340, 342
Blanc, Louis, 155
Blumenbach, J. F., 210
Blunt, Wilfrid Scawen, 323–5
Blyden, Edward, 219

borderer, 39, 120
    John Malcolm, 57, 77
    Walter Scott, 31
        Guy Mannering, 41
        The Heart of Mid-Lothian, 45
    Wilfrid Scawen Blunt, 323
Bose, Rajnarian, 146
Boyne, Battle of the, 31
Brahmans, 62, 64, 66, 83, 84, 88, 92, 96, 97,
    229, 232, 233, 265, 280, 288, 302
Brahmo Samaj, 15, 96, 97, 265, 271–9
Bright, John, 164, 293
Britishness, 8, 21, 28, 40, 48, 50, 52, 54, 90,
    134, 195, 289, 317
Brougham, Henry, 113
Bryce, James, 207
Buckle, H. T., 15, 210, 211, 235, 255, 280
    History of Civilization, 183, 279
Bulwer-Lytton, Edward Robert Lytton
    (Lord Lytton), 237, 319, 320, 321
Burke, Edmund, 125, 127
Burke, T. N., 181–2, 328
Burton, Richard, 219
Butler, Harcourt, 234

Calcutta Unitarian Committee, 97
Campbell, George, 221–6, 229, 234, 248,
    266
    The Ethnology of India, 222
    Modern India, 221
Cannadine, David, 320
Carlyle, Thomas, 157, 175, 198, 203
    French Revolution, 157
    Heroes, Past and Present, 157
    Latter-Day Pamphlets, 158
    *An Occasional Discourse on the Nigger
        Question*, 158
    Quashee, 196
Carpenter, Mary, 273, 276, 277
Catholic Emancipation, 20, 115, 141
Cecil, Robert (Lord Salisbury), 294

Chamberlain, Joseph, 207, 334–6, 341
Chambers, Robert
  Vestiges of the Natural History of Creation,
    154, 212
Chander, Bholananath, 147
Channing, E. T., 49
Chapman, John, 156
Chattopadhyay, Bankimchandra, 15, 146,
    279–86, 304
  Anandamath, 283–4
  Dharmatattva, 285
  essays on "Equality," 280
  Hymn to the Englishman, 282
  The Journals of Kamalakanta, 281–2
  masculinity, 282
Chaudhuri, Nirad, 147, 343–5
  The Autobiography of an Unknown Indian,
    345
Clive, Robert, 136
Clydeside, 43, 46
Cobbe, Frances Power, 273, 276
Cobden, Richard, 3, 164
Colebrooke, H. T., 63–4, 66, 82
Coleridge, S. T., 50
Collet, S. D., 273
Colvin, Auckland, 322–3
Communist Manifesto. See Marx, Karl
Comte, Auguste, 279
Cooper, James Fenimore, 53
Coupland, Reginald, 345
Crawfurd, John, 263
Creasy, E. S., 259
Crimean War, 13, 164
Culloden, Battle of, 31
Curzon, G. N., 261, 342

Dalberg-Acton, John, 143
Darwin, Charles, 14, 215, 219, 234,
    238
  The Origin of Species, 14, 212, 227
Davis, N. Darnell
  Mr. Froude's Negrophobia, 200
Davitt, Michael
  creation of Land League, 326
Dawkins, Boyd, 242
  Cave Hunting, 242
Dean Stanley. *See* Stanley, Arthur Penrhyn
Derozio, Henry, 265
Dickens, Charles, 146, 166
Dilke, Charles, 206, 260–1, 262, 334
  Greater Britain, 206, 207, 260, 335
  Problems of Greater Britain, 262
Disraeli, Benjamin, 189, 314, 318–20
  Tancred, 319
Doré, Gustave, 112

Doughlin, P. H., 200
Duff, Alexander, 94, 265
Dundas, Henry, 66
Dutt, R. C., 15, 233, 250, 260, 262, 280,
    297–310, 341–3
  The Economic History of India, 307–10
  England and India, 305–7
  History of Civilization in Ancient India,
    301–4
  The Literature of Bengal, 298
  The Peasantry of Bengal, 235
  Rig Veda, translation of the, 299

East India Company (EIC), 11, 58, 59, 61,
    62, 63, 65, 66, 70, 74, 77, 86, 97,
    118, 136, 221, 236, 272, 277, 309
  Charter of 1833, 118, 135, 287
  and H. T. Colebrooke, 63, 64
  and James Mill, 86, 87
  and James Mill's *History of British India*,
    82
  and John Malcolm, 58, 71, 72
  and Rammohun Roy, 91, 94
  and T. B. Macaulay, 119
  and Vans Kennedy, 87
Eden, George (Lord Auckland), 143
Edgeworth, Maria, 37, 38, 52, 54, 106, 143
  on Daniel O'Connell, 29
  on education, 122
  novels, 9, 107
    The Absentee, 28
    Castle Rackrent, 21, 22–4
    Ennui, 24–6
    Ormond, 28
Edgeworth, Richard, 17, 19–21, 29, 106, 184
  on education, 122
Eliot, George. *See* Evans, Mary Ann
Elphinstone, Mountstuart, 11, 59, 77–82,
    88, 105, 119, 120, 221, 225, 230,
    236, 306
  The History of India, 88–9
Engels, Friedrich
  Communist Manifesto, 117
English Constitution, 15, 128, 129, 255,
    258, 299, 320, 343, 345
English Revolution of 1688, 148
enlightenment, 9, 19, 24, 92, 278
  four-stage model, 3, 67, 108, 213
Erskine, William, 68
Evans, Mary Ann (George Eliot), 143, 156
Exclusion Crisis, 132
Eyre, Edward, 175, 190

Fawcett, Henry, 293
femininity, 10

Ferguson, Adam, 37, 67
feudalism, 37, 38, 39, 70, 252
Forster, W. E., 207
Freeman, E. A., 15, 206, 208, 238, 239–50,
    261, 317
  and Anglo-Saxonism, 241–5, 247–50
  The History of Federal Government, 241
  *The History of the Norman Conquest of
    England*, 241–5
  and *longue durée*, 246
  and Max Müller, 272
  "Race and Language," 246–7
French Revolution, 3, 94, 101, 115, 254
Froude, Hurrell, 152
Froude, J. A., 13, 15, 151–82, 210, 212–13,
    219, 238, 245, 267, 327
  and Anglo-Saxonism, 189–200
  "England and her Colonies," 175–7
  "England's Forgotten Worthies," 159, 168
  *The English in Ireland in the Eighteenth
    Century*, 13, 178–82, 330
  The English in the West Indies, 196–7
  History of England, 13, 159–64, 169–74, 212
  masculinity, 13, 153, 157, 164, 193
  The Nemesis of Faith, 155–6
  Oceana, 194–6
  and race, 197–200
  relationship with Thomas Carlyle, 157–9
  response to Goldwin Smith, 167
  and South Africa, 189–92

Galton, Francis, 263
Gandhi, M. K., 263, 343
Gardner, W. J., 220
Gentoo Code, 60
George IV, 48, 49
Ghose, Lal Mohan, 299
Ghose, M. M., 291
Gibbon, Edward, 108, 112
Gladstone, William, 16, 177, 185, 189, 262,
    275, 294, 306, 314–34
  and Irish Home Rule, 331–4
Glorious Revolution of 1688, 140, 145,
    241, 246
Goethe, J. W., 34
Grant, Charles, 105
Granville, 177
Grattan, Henry, 20, 186
Greater Britain, 8, 13, 14, 15, 97, 145, 172,
    173, 175, 201, 204, 208, 214, 255,
    260, 279, 317, 318, 328, 335, 337, 341
Great Famine, Ireland, 141
Green, Alice Stopford, 252
  The Making of Ireland and its Undoing,
    252–3

Green, J. R., 15, 238, 239, 250–4, 261
  A Short History of the English People,
    250–2, 343

Halhead, Nathaniel, 60
Hall, Catherine
  Civilising Subjects, 5–6
Hamilton, Elizabeth, 34
Hamilton-Temple-Blackwood, Frederick
    (Lord Dufferin), 325
Hancock, W. K., 345
Hare, David, 94, 265
Hartley, David, 20
Hastings, Warren, 59, 136
Hazlitt, William, 50
Highlanders, Scottish, 8, 43, 46, 69, 70, 75,
    85, 220
Hollwell, John, 60
Home, Henry (Lord Kames), 67
Hooker, Joseph, 217
Hume, A. O., 290
Hume, David, 67
  History of England, 114
Hunt, James, 14
Hunter, William, 234, 320
  Annals of Rural Bengal, 221
Huxley, Thomas, 217, 263

Ibbetson, Denzil, 234
Ilbert Bill, 321
imagined community, 35, 69
Imperial Federation League, 207
Indian National Congress, 288–91
Indian Revolt (Mutiny) of 1857, 165–6,
    271, 340
Irish Home Rule, 16, 299, 306, 330, 331,
    334, 336
Irish Parliament, 20, 21, 186, 334
Irish Rebellion, 18
Irishness, 21, 327

Jeffrey, Francis, 50
Jewsbury, Geraldine, 156
Johnston, Harry, 219
Jones, William, 11, 60, 62, 63, 82, 268

Keble, John, 153
Kemble, John, 243
Kennedy, Vans, 87
Kingsley, Charles, 157, 220
  Westward Ho!, 169
Knox, Robert, 14

Labilliere, F. B. de
  Federal Britain, 207

Lecky, W. E. H., 183–9, 235, 279, 328
  History of European Morals from Augustus to Charlemagne, 184
  A History of Ireland in the Eighteenth Century, 13, 185–8
  Leaders of Public Opinion in Ireland, 184, 186
  The Rise and Influence of the Spirit of Rationalism in Europe, 184
Leveson-Gower, Granville (Lord Granville), 322
Lewes, G. H., 156
Leyden, John, 58, 62
liberal imperialism, 4–9
Liberal Unionists, 16
liberalism
  definition of, 1
Lives of the English Saints, 153
Livingstone, David, 220
Locke, John, 5, 20
Longford Town, 17
longue durée, 14, 67, 126, 210–15, 223, 235, 239
Lord Acton. *See* Dalberg-Acton, John
Lord Auckland. *See* Eden, George
Lord Dufferin. *See* Hamilton-Temple-Blackwood, Frederick
Lord Granville. *See* Leveson-Gower, Granville
Lord Kames. *See* Home, Henry
Lord Lytton. *See* Bulwer-Lytton, Edward Robert Lytton
Lord Ripon. *See* Robinson, George
Lord Salisbury. *See* Cecil, Robert
Lubbock, John, 215–18, 228, 234, 238, 239, 240, 248, 263
  The Origin of Civilization, and the Primitive Condition of Man, 216
  Pre-Historic Times, 215–16
Lyall, Alfred, 234
Lyell, Charles
  The Antiquity of Man, 212
Lytton, Charles, 262

Macaulay, T. B., 12, 14, 15, 99, 106–50, 151, 161, 166, 209, 225, 230, 238, 245, 251, 306, 316
  "Chatham," 135
  "Clive," 136–9
  Collected Essays and Speeches, 143
  and constitutional reform, 116–18
  femininity, 108
  and gender, 111–12
  "Hastings," 136–9
  "History," 109

History of England, 12, 110, 129–36, 139–40, 152
  gender, 131
History of the French Revolution, 125
"Horace Walpole," 135
on Indian education, 121–3
and Ireland, 140–3
masculinity, 120, 131, 134
"Milton," 113, 124
Minute on Education, 121, 138, 147
"The War of Spanish Succession," 135
"The Wellingtonian," 124
"William Pitt," 135
Macaulay, Zachary, 12, 101–6, 119, 209
  The Christian Observer, 104
  and Christianity, 103–6
  Governor of Sierra Leone, 101–2
  and Jamaica, 100
  masculinity, 101
Mackenzie, Colin, 67, 68
MacLean, James, 262
Magna Carta, 244, 257, 259, 260, 266, 267, 268, 332
Maine, Henry, 15, 226–33, 234, 239, 240, 248, 261, 262, 266, 321
  Ancient Law, 227–9
  and Aryanism, 226–33
  Lectures on the Early History of Institutions, 236
  Village Communities in the East and West, 231
Malcolm, John, 11, 59, 71–7, 99, 105, 120
  Memoir of Central India, 74–6
  Political History of India, 73
  A Sketch of the Sikhs, 73
  and Walter Scott, 57
Mansergh, Nicholas, 345
Maratha or Marathas, 11, 65, 68, 70, 72, 74–5, 78–80, 323
Martineau, Harriet, 51
Martineau, James, 273
Marx, Karl
  Communist Manifesto, 117
Medley, D. J.
  A Student's Manual of English Constitutional History, 258
Mehta, Uday Singh
  Liberalism and Empire, 5
Mill, James, 5, 12, 14, 82–90, 105, 119, 128, 209
  The History of British India, 11, 56, 59, 82–5, 121
  and Walter Scott, 85
Mill, John Stuart, 5, 211, 275, 279, 281
  England and Ireland, 56

Millar, John, 67
Mitchel, John, 181, 328
Mongols, 68
Monmouth, Duke of, 132
Morley, John, 144, 342
Mortimer-Franklyn, H. M.
    The Unit of Imperial Federation, 207
Mughals, 65, 68, 73, 79, 137, 319, 324
Müller, Friedrich Max, 267–9, 271
    A History of Ancient Sanskrit Literature,
        272–3
    India: What can it Teach Us?, 300
    scholarly edition of *Rig Veda*, 268
Munro, Thomas, 67, 236, 306
Murchison, Roderick, 263

Nair, C. S., 291
Naoroji, Dadabhai, 15, 263, 293–7
    drain theory, 294–7
    Poverty and Un-British Rule in India,
        296, 297
neo-Lamarckism, 14, 198
Newman, J. H., 153
Nonconformist, 273
novel, rise of the, 109

O'Connell, Daniel, 29, 141, 180, 187
orientalism, 11, 59, 61, 62, 65, 66, 82, 98,
    233, 267, 305
Owenson, Sydney (Lady Morgan), 9, 16,
    25, 29, 37, 54, 329
    The Wild Irish Girl, 26–7

Pal, B. C., 291
Palgrave, Francis, 242
Parkes, Henry, 146
Parnell, C. S., 326
Pax Britannica, 50, 55, 61, 337
Permanent Settlement of 1793, 61, 64,
    86, 235
Peterloo, 113
Pitt, William, 9, 18, 66, 187
Pitts, Jennifer, 5
Pollock, F., 206
Porter, Jane, 34
Prendergast, J. P., 181
Prichard, J. C., 211
print capitalism, 35
progress narrative, 4, 7, 10, 12, 16, 30, 54,
    55, 108, 151
    and Anglo-India, 11, 59
    and Dadabhai Naoroji, 296
    and E. A. Freeman, 239
    and evolutionary theory, 14,
    and H. T. Buckle, 183

and India, 15
and Ireland, 24
and J. A. Froude, 13, 160
and James Mill, 11, 59, 84, 87
and Maria Edgeworth, 9
and R. C. Dutt, 307
and Rammohun Roy, 59, 96
and Sir John Seeley, 16
and T. B. Macaulay, 12, 15, 112, 125,
    128, 144, 149
and the bhadralok, 271
and the Macaulays, 100
and W. E. H. Lecky, 192
and Walter Scott, 37, 40, 44, 51
and William Gladstone, 341
Punch, 327
Pusey, E. B., 153

Radcliffe, Ann, 34
Rajput *or* Rajputs, 11, 69–71, 75
Rao, Raganath, 323
Reade, Winwood, 219
Reform Act, 117, 118
Reform Bill, 95, 116
Regulating Act of 1773, 86
Renan, Ernest, 328
Revolutionary Settlement, 42
Robertson, William, 67
Robinson, George (Lord Ripon), 287,
    320–1
Robinson, Henry Crabb, 49
Rossa, O'Donovan, 178
Rousseau, Jean-Jacques, 281
Roy, Rammohun, 11, 15, 59, 90–7, 105,
    122, 225, 264, 269, 271, 273, 304
    *An Appeal to the Christian Public in Defense
        of "The Precepts of Jesus,"* 91
    *Precepts of Jesus, the Guide to Peace and
        Happiness*, 91
Ruskin, John, 158, 175
Russell, Lord John, 116
ryot *or* ryots, 86, 234, 235, 237, 250, 323
ryotwari, 67, 80, 86, 222

Said, Edward, 61
Sakuntala, 60
Salmon, C. S., 200
Sand, George, 155
Sanial, S. C., 147
Sanskrit, 58, 59–66, 82, 95, 96, 268, 272,
    298, 300
sati, 96
savagery, 37, 134, 142, 165, 213, 214,
    215–18, 220, 228, 260
Schwann, Charles, 261

Scott, Walter, 17, 54, 67, 68, 70, 99, 100,
    106, 107, 111, 149, 279
  Abbotsford, 35
  Bridal of Triermain, 36
  History of Napoleon, 48
  History of Scotland, 48
  and John Malcolm, 57, 73
  The Lady of the Lake, 33
  The Lay of the Last Minstrel, 33, 57
  Malachi Malagrowther, 48
  on Maria Edgeworth, 30
  Marmion, 33
  masculinity, 34, 48, 50, 55
  Minstrelsy of the Scottish Border, 32
  novels, 11
    The Abbot, 48
    The Antiquary, 41
    Guy Mannering, 40–1, 53
    The Heart of Mid-Lothian, 44–8
    Ivanhoe, 48
    Kenilworth, 48
    Old Mortality, 41–2
    Rob Roy, 42–4, 53
    St. Ronan's Well, 53
    Waverley, 9, 11, 12, 17, 36, 38–40,
      43, 48, 49, 50, 51, 53, 54, 57, 74,
      76, 280
  partnership with John Ballantyne, 36
  Rokeby, 36
  "The Surgeon's Daughter," 53
Second Maratha War of 1803, 77
Seeley, J. R., 16
  Ecce Homo, 274
  The Expansion of England, 336–41
Sen, Keshub Chandra, 15, 263, 269–79,
    304, 328
Seward, Anna, 34
Shakespeare, William, 279
Shore, Sir John, 73
Sikhs, 72, 75, 92, 220
Sindia, Mahadji, 74–5
Sinha, Mrinalini, 289
Smith, Adam, 3, 5, 67, 177
  Wealth of Nations, 1, 20
Smith, Charlotte, 34
Smith, Goldwin, 166, 208
Spanish Armada, 152, 174
Spencer, Herbert, 212, 217, 234
Stanley, Arthur Penrhyn, 275
Stewart, Dugald, 37, 67, 83
Stocking, George, 214
Stopes, Whitely, 234
Streets, Heather, 220

Stubbs, William, 15, 238, 239, 250, 261
  The Constitutional History of England, 254,
    255–8, 343

Tagore, Debendranath, 265, 269, 270, 278
Tagore, Dwarkanath, 265
Tagore, Dwijendranath, 270
Thackeray, William, 143
Thomas, J. J.
  Froudacity, 200
Thompson, Augustus Rivers, 321
Thorburn, Septimus, 234
Tipu Sultan, 67
  defeat at Seringapatem, 65
Tod, James, 11, 59, 68–71, 75, 76
  Annals and Antiquities of Rajasthan, 68–70
Tractarians, 153, 240
Trevelyan, Charles, 123, 142
Trevelyan, G. O., 267
tribalism, 39, 244
Trollope, Anthony, 220
Tupper, Lewis, 234
Tylor, E. B., 234
  *Researches into the Early History of
    Mankind*, 216

Unionism, 44, 333, 334–41
Unionist, 19, 20, 24, 44, 178, 299, 334, 338
utilitarian, 11, 59, 80, 121
utilitarianism, 11, 86, 227

Vernacular Press Act of 1878, 237
Vernacular Press Censorship Law, 321

Walpole, Horace, 34
Waverley.Walter Scott, novels
Wedderburn, William, 293
Wellesley, Lord Richard, 63, 71, 73, 77
Wentworth, W. C., 146
West, Raymond, 234
Westgarth, William
  The Colony of Victoria, 195
Wilberforce, William, 102
Wilkins, Charles, 60
Wilks, Mark
  Historical Sketches of South India, 67
Wilson, James, 234

Young, Frederick
  Imperial Federation, 207

zamindars, 61, 86, 91, 97, 98, 222, 234, 235,
    269, 319

Lightning Source UK Ltd.
Milton Keynes UK
UKOW04f0637040314

227520UK00012B/210/P

9 781107 638273